Over the past **two years**,

65 **economies**
carried out

87 **reforms**
increasing women's
economic opportunities.

TABLE OF
CONTENTS

FOREWORD

No economy can grow to its full potential unless both women and men participate fully. As half the world's population, women have an equal role in driving economic growth.

Women, Business and the Law 2018 is the fifth edition in a series of biennial reports measuring the legal obstacles to women who engage in economic activity around the world. Since the World Bank started this study a decade ago, our understanding has increased about how laws influence women's decisions to start and run businesses or get jobs.

The analysis draws on newly-collected data across seven indicators: accessing institutions, using property, getting a job, providing incentives to work, going to court, building credit, and protecting women from violence. The study expands coverage to 189 economies around the world.

The data show the challenge many women face in the quest for economic opportunity. One hundred and four economies still prevent women from working in certain jobs, simply because they are women. In 59 economies there are no laws on sexual harassment in the workplace. And in 18 economies, husbands can legally prevent their wives from working.

Social media movements such as China's #我也是; Latin America's #YoTambien; the Middle East's #أنا_كمان; and the United States' #MeToo have highlighted the prevalence of sexual harassment and violence in the workplace. But in many places, women still have no legal recourse. And every day we learn about industries that pay women less than men for doing the same work.

What actions can be taken to increase economic opportunity for women? How can governments improve labor market participation by their female citizens? Hard data helps answer these questions.

By informing politicians about the legal obstacles to women's economic opportunities, *Women, Business and the Law* makes a contribution towards promoting gender equality. The study celebrates the progress that has been made while emphasizing the work that remains to ensure equality of opportunity.

Kristalina Georgieva
Chief Executive Officer
The World Bank
Washington, DC

KEY FINDINGS

Women, Business and the Law 2018 is the fifth in a series of biennial reports measuring gender differences in legal treatment. Since this research started, the realization of the importance of women's entrepreneurship and employment has increased significantly, as has our understanding of the relationship between legal gender equality and women's economic outcomes.

Globally, over
2.7 billion
women are legally restricted from having the same choice of jobs as men.

While understanding that women's access to employment and entrepreneurial activities is related to many factors, the data in this report illustrate how laws and regulations limit women's economic participation.

Consider the case of a girl who grows up aspiring to be a ship's captain. She excels at school in the hopes of getting her dream job. Maybe she is even hired to do it, but then she is fired simply because of her gender. What does this do to her aspirations and the aspirations of every girl who comes after?

Now consider the case of Svetlana Medvedeva, who studied navigation in college and graduated as a navigation officer in the Russian Federation. She applied to work as a ship's helmsman and was selected. Later she was told she could not have that job as Regulation No. 162 lists helmsman as one of the 456 jobs deemed too arduous, harmful or dangerous for women.[1]

Medvedeva took the company to court based on the Russian Constitution's equality provisions. Her case was dismissed because the court held that the purpose of the regulation was to protect women's reproductive health. She appealed and her appeal was dismissed. She further appealed to the court of cassation. That appeal was also dismissed. She then brought her case to the United Nations Committee on the Elimination of Discrimination against Women. The Committee found that she had been discriminated against because of her gender.[2]

After this decision, and five years after her case began, Medvedeva once again went before a Russian district court. In September 2017 the court found that she had indeed been discriminated against. However the court did not order the company to hire her and the ban on women ship navigators is still in place.[3]

Meanwhile other economies are making progress on the issue of gender legal parity. In 2016 the Constitutional Court of Colombia struck down as discriminatory the labor code's prohibitions on women's work in mining and in jobs deemed hazardous and arduous.[4] Bulgaria, Kiribati and Poland also eliminated all restrictions on women's employment.

From the outset, the purpose of the *Women, Business and the Law* report has been to inform research and policy discussions on how laws and regulations influence women's economic activity. This has largely occurred. From comprehending the importance of family law to women's economic decision-making to recognizing the effect of violence against women on their employment opportunities, *Women, Business and the Law* has contributed to a better understanding of why legal gender equality matters.

But not enough has been done to reach legal gender equality. Many laws prevent women from working or running a business. For example, 104 economies still have laws preventing women from working in specific jobs, 59 economies have no laws on sexual harassment in the workplace, and in 18 economies, husbands can legally prevent their wives from working. What effect do laws like these have on women's economic choices?

More research and evidence are needed to understand the effects of laws and regulations on women's entrepreneurship and employment so that policymakers can better understand which policies to promote. *Women, Business and the Law* builds on a growing body of research that stresses the importance of laws in shaping women's economic opportunities and improving gender equality. Research has called into question the notion that economic growth alone increases gender equality. Rather, continuous policy commitments to gender equality are required to achieve it.[5]

What is new in this edition?

To understand where laws facilitate or hinder gender equality and women's economic participation, *Women, Business and the Law 2018* is providing scores for the first time for each of its seven indicators: accessing institutions, using property, getting a job, providing incentives to work, going to court, building credit and protecting women from violence. The indicator scores are a number between 0 and 100, with 100 being the best. The scores are obtained by calculating the unweighted average of the scored questions within that indicator, and scaling the result to 100.

The indicator scores facilitate research and policy discussions on how varying legal environments influence women's

economic opportunities and outcomes. The scored questions are based on two criteria: their relevance to women's human rights as set out in the international women's rights framework, including the Convention on the Elimination of all Forms of Discrimination Against Women (CEDAW), and research demonstrating their importance for women's economic empowerment (table 1.1).

Women's international human rights, as set out in CEDAW, serve as the underlying justification for each scored question. For areas covering violence against women, reference to international treaty law has been supplemented by the UN Declaration on the Elimination of Violence against Women and the CEDAW Committee's General Recommendations. Questions on maternity leave use the International Labour Organization's Maternity Protection Convention of 2000 as a benchmark (figure 1.1).

Fifty questions are scored within the seven indicators (box 1.1). The scored questions fall into three categories: those with explicit gender-based differences affecting women's entrepreneurship or employment (such as gender-based job restrictions), those reflecting the absence of laws protecting women (such as the lack of legislation on sexual harassment), and those examining institutions or processes that are likely to help women (such as anti-discrimination commissions). Details on the methodology and scoring of each question are available in the Data Notes chapter.

This report covers data for 189 economies including 16 that were not covered in the previous report: Cabo Verde; the Central African Republic; the Comoros; Cyprus; Eritrea; The Gambia; Guinea-Bissau; Kiribati; Libya; the Marshall Islands; the Federated States of Micronesia; Palau; Samoa; San Marino; the Solomon Islands; and Vanuatu.

Women, Business and the Law 2018 also presents a case study on women's financial inclusion and the law examining how legal and regulatory environments

influence women's demand for financial services.

The *Women, Business and the Law* indicators complement other gender indexes that are constructed using outcome variables and, in some cases, qualitative assessments (figure 1.2). Although *Women, Business and the Law* focuses on key legal and regulatory areas that are directly controlled by policymakers, there are many other factors that influence women's economic opportunities—including educational levels and social and cultural norms—that are not captured.

Other indexes take varying approaches to developing gender indicators and present different views of women's societal position. *Women, Business and the Law* is one of the only global datasets that uses quantitative, objective data to measure legal gender gaps in policies. The "About *Women, Business and the Law*" chapter provides information on what is measured and what is not.

Women, Business and the Law scoring is correlated with the Global Gender Gap, Social Institutions and Gender, Gender Inequality and Gender-related Development indexes (figure 1.3). Showing that the policy variables measured by *Women, Business and the Law* are associated with outcomes tells us that the law influences what happens on the ground in areas such as empowerment, participation in the labor market and command over economic resources. As a result, one way to influence outcomes for women may be to reform laws and regulations that make it more difficult for women to participate in business and employment.

BOX 1.1 *WOMEN, BUSINESS AND THE LAW* SCORED QUESTIONS

Accessing institutions

1. Are married women required by law to obey their husbands?
2. Can a woman legally apply for a passport in the same way as a man?
3. Can a woman legally apply for a national ID card in the same way as a man?
4. Can a woman legally travel outside the country in the same way as a man?
5. Can a woman legally travel outside her home in the same way as a man?
6. Can a woman legally get a job or pursue a trade or profession in the same way as a man?
7. Can a woman legally sign a contract in the same way as a man?
8. Can a woman legally register a business in the same way as a man?
9. Can a woman legally open a bank account in the same way as a man?
10. Can a woman legally choose where to live in the same way as a man?
11. Can a woman legally be "head of household" or "head of family" in the same way as a man?

Using property

12. Who legally administers marital property?
13. Does the law provide for valuation of nonmonetary contributions?
14. Do men and women have equal ownership rights to immovable property?
15. Do sons and daughters have equal rights to inherit assets from their parents?
16. Do female and male surviving spouses have equal rights to inherit assets?

Getting a job

17. Is there paid leave available to women of at least 14 weeks?
18. Do women receive at least 2/3 of their wages for the first 14 weeks or the duration of the leave if it is shorter?
19. What is the percentage of maternity leave benefits paid by the government?
20. What is the difference between leave reserved for women and men relative to leave reserved for women, as a function of who pays?
21. Is there paid parental leave?
22. Does the law mandate equal remuneration for work of equal value?
23. Does the law mandate nondiscrimination based on gender in employment?
24. Is dismissal of pregnant workers prohibited?
25. Can parents work flexibly?
26. Can women work the same night hours as men?
27. Can women work in jobs deemed hazardous, arduous or morally inappropriate in the same way as men?
28. Are women able to work in the same industries as men?
29. Are women able to perform the same tasks at work as men?

30. Are the ages at which men and women can retire with full pension benefits equal?
31. Are the ages at which men and women can retire with partial pension benefits equal?
32. Are the mandatory retirement ages for men and women equal?

Providing incentives to work

33. Are mothers guaranteed an equivalent position after maternity leave?
34. Does the government support or provide childcare services?
35. Are payments for childcare tax deductible?
36. Is primary education free and compulsory?
37. Are there specific tax deductions or tax credits that are only applicable to men?

Going to court

38. Does a woman's testimony carry the same evidentiary weight in court as a man's?
39. Does the law establish an anti-discrimination commission?
40. Does the law mandate legal aid in civil and family matters?
41. Is there a small claims court or a fast-track procedure for small claims?

Building credit

42. Do retailers provide information to private credit bureaus or public credit registries?
43. Do utility companies provide information to private credit bureaus or public credit registries?
44. Does the law prohibit discrimination by creditors on the basis of sex or gender in access to credit?
45. Does the law prohibit discrimination by creditors on the basis of marital status in access to credit?

Protecting women from violence

46. Is there legislation specifically addressing domestic violence? If not, are there aggravated penalties for crimes committed against a spouse or family member?
47. Is there legislation on sexual harassment in employment?
48. Is there legislation on sexual harassment in education?
49. Are there criminal penalties for sexual harassment in employment?
50. Are there civil remedies for sexual harassment in employment?

TABLE 1.1 WOMEN, BUSINESS AND THE LAW INDICATORS AND RELATED RESEARCH

Indicator	Research
Accessing institutions	A 2000 reform of Ethiopia's Family Code eliminated a husband's ability to stop his wife from working, among other things. Although the reform has now been implemented throughout Ethiopia, it was first introduced in three regions and two cities. In these areas, women's labor force participation and work outside the home increased. Women were also more likely to work full-time and in higher-skilled jobs.[a] Freedom of movement is a significant indicator of empowerment. It has been linked with women's economic independence as well as their expanded voice and agency.[b]
Using property	The gender asset gap can undermine women's bargaining power and capacity to engage in economic activities.[c] Giving women greater access to assets through inheritance can change outcomes for children, particularly girls. In 1994, two states in India reformed the Hindu Succession Act to allow women and men the same ability to inherit joint family property. This altered control over assets within families and increased parental investments in daughters. Mothers who benefited from the reform spent twice as much on their daughters' education, and women were more likely to have bank accounts and sanitary latrines where the reform occurred. The reform has now taken place across India.[d]
Getting a job	Policies such as paid parental leave are associated with increases in women's employment; however, extended durations of parental leave lead to reductions in women's relative wages.[e] Meanwhile, restrictions on women's work limit their ability to get the jobs they want and maximize their earning potential. Russia had a high gender earnings differential during its transition to a market economy, largely because of legal restrictions on the jobs women could perform.[f] Differences in wages and job tenure can largely explain the pension gap between women and men.[g]
Providing incentives to work	Support for mothers—such as tax credits and the availability of childcare for young children—can increase women's participation in the labor force.[h] Evidence suggests that spending on early education and childcare can increase women's labor force participation and reduce gender gaps.[i]
Going to court	Gender inequality can adversely affect women's ability to use the legal system. Access to legal aid and other services can improve women's access to justice.[j] Evidence shows that access to civil legal aid can reduce the need for social welfare programs, the time children spend in foster care and instances of domestic violence.[k]
Building credit	Prior to the passage of the 1974 Equal Credit Opportunity Act in the United States, banks often had explicit policies treating women differently from men. When the Act prohibited sex-based classifications and income discounting, the change seems to have had a dramatic effect on banking policies toward women. For example, the legislation had a favorable impact on women's ability to obtain mortgage funds.[l]
Protecting women from violence	In economies where husbands can prohibit their wives from working or where there is a high prevalence of violence against women, women are less likely to have formal accounts, savings or credit.[m] Meanwhile, sexual harassment at work undermines authority, reinforces gender stereotypes, and reduces women to sexual objects. A study of women who experienced sexual harassment at work in a United States community found that sexual harassment increases financial stress and can significantly alter a woman's career trajectory.[n]

[a] Hallward-Driemeier and Gajigo 2013.
[b] Nagaraja 2013.
[c] Deere and León 2003.
[d] Deininger et al. 2014.
[e] Ruhm 1998.
[f] Ogloblin 1999.
[g] Johnson 1999.
[h] Averett, Peters and Waldman 2006.
[i] Olivetti and Petrongolo 2017.
[j] Australia Law Reform Commission 1994.
[k] Abel and Vignola 2010.
[l] Ladd 1982.
[m] Demirguc-Kunt, Klapper and Singer 2013.
[n] McLaughlin, Uggen and Blackstone 2017.

FIGURE 1.1

WOMEN, BUSINESS AND THE LAW INDICATORS AND WOMEN'S PRINCIPAL CORRESPONDING HUMAN RIGHTS

Accessing institutions

- Equality before the law and legal capacity identical to that of men (CEDAW, Art. 15(1)-(2))
- Equality with regard to the law relating to the movement of persons and freedom to choose one's residence and domicile (CEDAW, Art. 15(4))
- Equality in all matters relating to marriage and family relations (CEDAW, Art. 16), including the right to choose a profession and an occupation (CEDAW, Art. 16(1)(g))
- Appropriate measures to be adopted by States to modify the social and cultural patterns of conduct of men and women, with a view to achieving the elimination of [...] practices which are based on the idea of the inferiority or the superiority of either of the sexes or on stereotyped roles for men and women (CEDAW, Art. 5(a))

Using property

- Equal rights to conclude contracts and administer property (CEDAW, Art. 15(2))
- Equal rights in all matters relating to marriage and family relations (CEDAW, Art. 16(1)), including same rights for both spouses in respect of ownership, acquisition, management, administration, enjoyment and disposition of property (CEDAW, Art. 16(1)(h))

Getting a job

- Freedom from discrimination on grounds of marriage or maternity, prohibition of dismissal on the grounds of pregnancy, and paid maternity leave (CEDAW, Art. 11(2) and ILO Maternity Protection Convention N. 183, Arts. 8 and 9)
- Right to a period of maternity leave of not less than 14 weeks (ILO Maternity Protection Convention N. 183, Art. 4(1))
- Right to cash benefits, in accordance with national law, of not less than two-thirds of the woman's previous earnings (ILO Maternity Protection Convention N. 183, Art. 6(3))
- Cash benefits to be provided through compulsory social insurance or public funds, with exceptions (ILO Maternity Protection Convention N. 183, Art. 6(8))
- Freedom from discrimination in the field of employment (CEDAW, Art. 11); Right to work (CEDAW, Art. 11(1)(a)); Same employment opportunities, including the application of the same criteria for selection in matters of employment (CEDAW, Art. 11(1)(b)); Free choice of profession and employment (CEDAW, Art. 11(1)(c)); Equal remuneration and equal treatment for work of equal value (CEDAW, Art. 11(1)(d)); Equal social security, retirement, leave, and other paid benefits (CEDAW, Art. 11(1)(e))

Providing incentives to work

- Paid maternity leave or comparable social benefits without loss of former employment, seniority or social allowances (CEDAW, Art. 11(2)(b))
- Provision of supporting social services to enable parents to combine family obligations with work responsibilities and participation in public life, such as child-care facilities (CEDAW, Art. 11(2)(c))
- Freedom from discrimination and equality in economic life (CEDAW, Art. 13)
- Right to education (CEDAW, Art. 10)

Going to court

- Freedom from discrimination on the basis of sex (CEDAW, Art. 2)
- Legal protection of rights of women and effective protection of women against any act of discrimination through competent national tribunals (CEDAW, Art. 2(c))
- Exercise and enjoyment of all human rights and fundamental freedoms on basis of equality with men (CEDAW, Art. 3)
- Equality before the law and in all stages of procedure in courts and tribunals (CEDAW, Art. 15(1)-(2))
- The CEDAW Committee recommends States to ensure that women have recourse to affordable, accessible and timely remedies, with legal aid and assistance as necessary, to be determined in a fair hearing by a competent and independent court or tribunal (CEDAW GR N. 28 Par. 34)

Building credit

- Freedom from discrimination in economic life and access to bank loans, mortgages and other forms of financial credit on equal basis with men (CEDAW, Art. 13(b))
- Access to agricultural credit and loans for rural women (CEDAW, Art. 14(2)(g))

Protecting women from violence

- Violence against women includes sexual harassment. States should punish violence against women in accordance with national legislation (DEVAW, Arts. 2(b) and 4(c-d))
- The CEDAW Committee recommends States to include information on legislative and other measures against sexual harassment in their periodic reports (CEDAW GR N. 12 and 19 Par. 24(j) and (t))
- Violence against women encompasses physical, sexual and psychological violence occurring in the family. States should investigate and punish violence against women in accordance with national legislation (DEVAW, Arts. 2(a) and 4(c))

FIGURE 1.2   OTHER GLOBAL GENDER INDEXES

Global Gender Gap Index	Social Institutions and Gender Index	Gender Inequality Index	Gender-related Development Index
The World Economic Forum's Global Gender Gap Index quantifies the magnitude of gender disparities and tracks progress over time across 144 economies and four thematic areas: Economic Participation and Opportunity, Educational Attainment, Health and Survival and Political Empowerment. It uses mainly quantitative outcome variables, such as the ratio of female to male labor force participation.	The OECD's Social Institutions and Gender Index scores 160 economies on discrimination in social institutions. The composite measure is an unweighted average of five sub-indices: discriminatory family code, restricted physical integrity, son bias, restricted resources and assets and restricted civil liberties. The data are both quantitative and qualitative.	The UN's Gender Inequality Index provides a composite measure reflecting inequality of achievement between women and men in 159 economies. The index covers five indicators in three dimensions: reproductive health, empowerment (as measured by educational attainment and parliamentary representation) and the labor market. The indicators are based on quantitative outcome variables.	The UN's Gender-related Development Index examines gender differences in development outcomes in health, education and equitable command over economic resources. Covering 160 economies, the indicators are based on outcome variables and measure the gender gap by showing the female human development index as a percentage of the male.

Sources: World Economic Forum, OECD Development Center, and United Nations Development Program databases.

FIGURE 1.3   *WOMEN, BUSINESS AND THE LAW* SCORED INDICATORS ARE ASSOCIATED WITH OTHER GENDER INDEXES

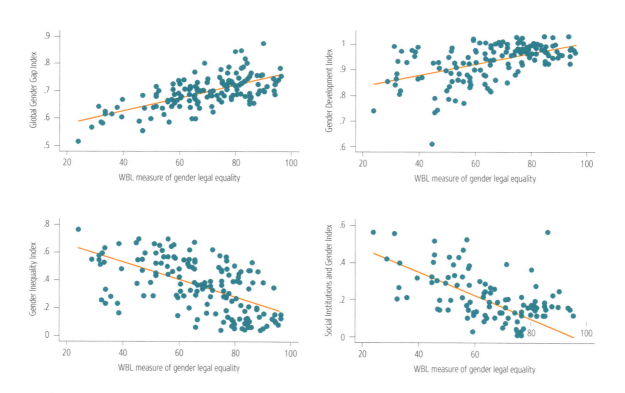

Sources: Women, Business and the Law, World Economic Forum, OECD Development Center, and the United Nations Development Program databases.
Note: The WBL measure of gender legal equality is calculated as the average of the seven scored WBL indicators. Higher values mean greater gender equality in the Global Gender Gap Index (2016) and the Gender Development Index (2015); higher values mean worse gender equality in the Gender Inequality Index (2015) and the Social Institutions and Gender Index (2014).

Why do legal gender differences matter for women's economic participation?

Gender gaps in entrepreneurship are associated with decreased income and aggregate productivity. Research estimates that gender gaps cause an average income loss of 15% in OECD economies, 40% of which is due to entrepreneurship gaps. Losses are estimated to be significantly higher in developing countries.[6] Additionally, legal gender differences are estimated to decrease female labor force participation and undermine GDP growth.[7] Research estimates that for some economies, a large fraction of country differences in output per capita can be attributed to gender inequality, and many countries can increase output per capita by discouraging gender barriers in the labor market.[8]

The evidence indicates that laws can influence women's economic participation. In the United States, for example, more women started getting patents in the 19th century after some states passed laws granting women property rights in their own name as well as granting the ability for women to act as sole traders and retain their own earnings.[9] This same set of legal changes led to families investing more in their daughters' secondary education.[10]

Equality of opportunity allows women to make the choices that are best for them, their families and their communities. However, equal opportunities in getting a job or starting a business do not exist where legal gender differences are prevalent. Legal restrictions constrain women's ability to make economic decisions and can have far-reaching consequences. For example, women may decide not to work or start businesses in economies where the law makes it more difficult for them to do so (figure 1.4).

Where are laws better or worse for women?

The seven indicator scores make it easier to identify economies in which women can participate in specific economic activity by region as well as to identify economies in which there is room for improvement. While no economy gets a perfect score in all 7 indicators, economies that score in the top 20 across each indicator include the United Kingdom, New Zealand and Spain.

OECD high-income economies tend to have the highest average scores across most indicators. Economies in the Middle East and North Africa tend to have the lowest average scores across most indicators (figure 1.5).

Over a third of the economies examined have at least one constraint on women's legal capacity as measured by accessing institutions. Similarly close to 40% of

---

FIGURE 1.4 **WITH LESS GENDER LEGAL EQUALITY IN AN ECONOMY, FEWER WOMEN WORK OR OWN BUSINESSES**

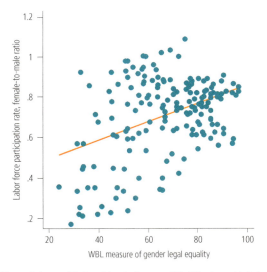
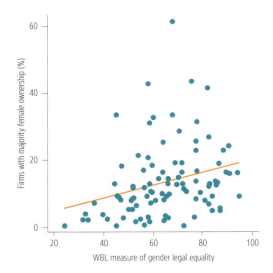

Sources: Women, Business and the Law, Enterprise Surveys and World Development Indicators databases.
Note: The WBL measure of gender legal equality is calculated as the average of the seven scored WBL indicators. The positive relationships between the WBL measure of gender legal equality and the ratio of female-to-male labor force participation rate (2016), and the WBL measure of gender legal equality and the percentage of firms with majority female ownership are statistically significant at least at the 5% level after controlling for the log of GNI per capita (2015), the ratio of female-to-male years (mean) of education (age 25+) (2015), the proportion of seats held by women in national parliaments (2016), and the rule of law (2016). Sources for the control variables include the World Development Indicators and Barro-Lee Educational Attainment databases. Regression analyses are based on 164 and 93 economies for which data are available, respectively. These statistical relationships should not be interpreted as causal.

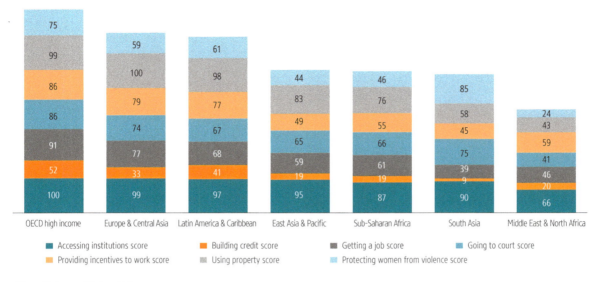

Source: *Women, Business and the Law* database.

economies have at least one constraint on women's property rights as measured by the using property indicator.

Twenty-one economies from across 5 regions receive a score of 0 in the protecting women from violence indicator. In the Middle East and North Africa, 35% of the economies score 0 in this indicator, as do 19% of economies in Sub-Saharan Africa. Economies from other regions which score 0 include Haiti, the Federated States of Micronesia, Myanmar, Russia and Uzbekistan.

While the global average in getting a job is 67, South Asian economies have an average score of 39, the lowest across all regions.

For the building credit indicator, there is much room for improvement globally; 42% of economies score 0 on this indicator. Four regions—East Asia and the Pacific, the Middle East and North Africa, South Asia and Sub-Saharan Africa—each have an average score of 20 or below. The average score for low income economies is 8 (figure 1.6).

Which economies improved the most over the past two years?

Women, Business and the Law captured 87 changes toward legal gender equality across 65 economies, among the scored questions, over the last two years.

Of the five economies implementing the most reforms, four are in Sub-Saharan Africa: the Democratic Republic of Congo, Kenya, Tanzania and Zambia. One, Iraq, is in the Middle East and North Africa. Each of these economies reformed in three or more *Women, Business and the Law* indicators.

FIGURE 1.6   HIGH-INCOME ECONOMIES PERFORM BEST ACROSS INDICATORS

Source: *Women, Business and the Law* database.

The Democratic Republic of Congo reformed its family code to allow married women to sign contracts, get jobs, open bank accounts and register businesses in the same way as married men. The economy also removed the obligation for a married woman to obey her husband and has allowed spouses to mutually choose the marital home. Additionally, the Democratic Republic of Congo lifted restrictions on women's ability to work at night in public or private industrial establishments. Further, the economy also now mandates nondiscrimination based on gender in various aspects of employment including hiring and promotions. Finally, the Democratic Republic of Congo now prohibits gender discrimination by creditors in financial transactions.

Kenya has enacted its first domestic violence law, which protects family members, spouses, former spouses and partners from physical, sexual, psychological and economic abuse. Kenya also now provides legal aid in civil matters and has improved access to credit information by distributing data from two utility companies that report positive and negative payment information.

Tanzania made primary education both free and compulsory and its new Legal Aid Act allows for legal aid in civil proceedings. Additionality, Tanzania improved access to credit information by distributing data from retailers.

Zambia's Gender Equity and Equality Act now prohibits gender discrimination in various aspects of employment and mandates equal remuneration for work of equal value. Zambia also established the Gender Equality Commission and prohibits discrimination based on gender and marital status in access to credit. Finally, Zambia established civil remedies for sexual harassment in employment.

Iraq enacted a new law that introduced electronic passports. The application process is now the same for men and women and no longer requires women to bring a guardian. Iraq also criminalized sexual harassment in employment. Iraq now guarantees workers returning from maternity leave the same position or a similar position with the same wage. Iraq also increased the length of paid maternity leave from 72 to 98 days. The country's new labor code now prohibits

discrimination based on gender in various aspects of employment including hiring and dismissal. However, the labor code also allows employers to terminate employees' contracts when they reach the retirement age, which is unequal for men and women.

While Sub-Saharan Africa had the most reforms, South Asia had the highest percentage of reforming economies. Half of the economies in South Asia had at least one reform followed by Sub-Saharan Africa (45%), Europe and Central Asia (44%), and East Asia and the Pacific (40%) (figure 1.7).

The lowest percentage of reforming economies are OECD high-income economies (16%). However OECD high-income economies also have the best average scores across indicators.

The indicator with the most reforms was getting a job (28 economies) followed by building credit (24 economies). The least movement occurred in using property with only Ecuador demonstrating positive reform (figure 1.8). However, reforms affecting property are the slowest to occur.

FIGURE 1.7   SOUTH ASIA HAS THE HIGHEST PERCENTAGE OF ECONOMIES THAT IMPROVED

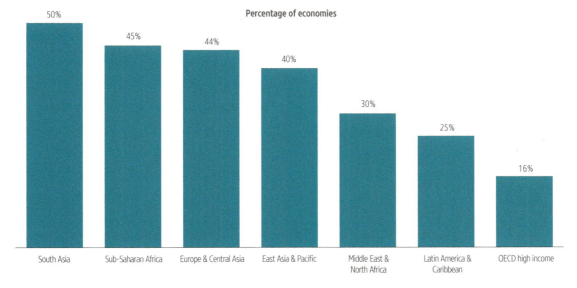

Source: *Women, Business and the Law* database.

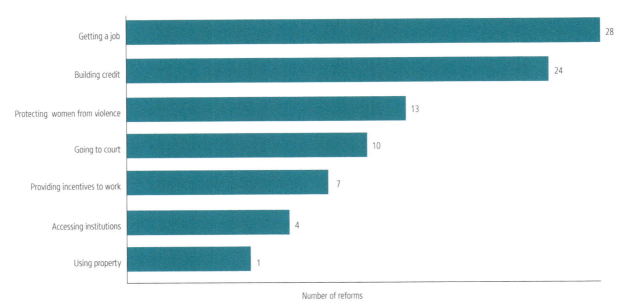

FIGURE 1.8 **THE MOST IMPROVEMENTS OCCURRED IN GETTING A JOB**

Getting a job — 28
Building credit — 24
Protecting women from violence — 13
Going to court — 10
Providing incentives to work — 7
Accessing institutions — 4
Using property — 1

Number of reforms

Source: Women, Business and the Law database.

The chapter on Reform Summaries provides a description of all reforms.

The following sections provide an overview of the main results by indicator.

Accessing institutions

The ability to make effective choices and transform them into economic outcomes is dependent on a supportive regulatory framework. *Women, Business and the Law's* accessing institutions indicator examines laws governing women's interactions with public authorities and the private sector to determine where women's agency and economic activities may be limited. There are several spheres in which women may face constraints on their legal capacity to act or ability to conduct transactions.

For example, limitations on married women's legal capacity, including the ability to work without their husbands'

permission, weakens decision-making ability. Additionally, when women cannot independently decide where they want to go, travel or live, they may face difficulty getting to work or conducting business transactions. Such restrictions may stem from women's role in traditional societies, which was often limited by a fathers' or husbands' guardianship.

Today, this trend has largely been reversed among former colonial powers. In 1938 and 1975 respectively, France and Spain recognized a married woman's ability to contract in her own name. Many of their former colonies, however, continue to use old legal codes and have not adopted similar reforms.

In economies such as Equatorial Guinea, for instance, the 1960 Spanish Civil Code is still in force. Equatorial Guinea is now the only economy examined where a woman needs her husband's permission to sign a contract. Similarly, Chad, Guinea-Bissau and Niger still rely on colonial versions of civil laws that do not allow

married women to open bank accounts without their husbands' permissions.

Constraints on women's agency and freedom of movement also persist (table 1.2). For example, in 18 economies women cannot get a job or pursue a trade or profession without permission. An exception to this is the Democratic Republic of Congo, which recently reformed a family code that was introduced by Belgium and adopted from the Code Napoléon. The reform allows married women to sign contracts, open bank accounts, register businesses, and get jobs without written permission from their husbands.

Reforms increasing women's access to institutions may contribute to women holding greater positions of authority. *Women, Business and the Law* analysis shows that women are more likely to hold leadership positions in public life when they have increased legal decision-making abilities (figure 1.9).

TABLE 1.2 — OVER ONE-THIRD OF ECONOMIES STILL RESTRICT WOMEN'S AGENCY AND FREEDOM OF MOVEMENT

Action that women cannot legally perform in the same way as men	Economies	Number of economies
Apply for a passport	Afghanistan; Algeria; Bahrain; Barbados; Belize; Benin; Botswana; Cameroon; Congo, Rep.; Cyprus; Dominica; Egypt, Arab Rep.; Fiji; Gabon; Grenada; Guyana; Haiti; Iran, Islamic Rep.; Jordan; Malawi; Mali; Myanmar; Nigeria; Oman; Pakistan; Philippines; Samoa; Saudi Arabia; Seychelles; Solomon Islands; St. Vincent and the Grenadines; Sudan; Trinidad and Tobago; Uganda; United Arab Emirates; Yemen, Rep.; Zambia	37
Choose where to live	Afghanistan; Bahrain; Benin; Brunei Darussalam; Burkina Faso; Cameroon; Central African Republic; Chad; Comoros; Congo, Rep.; Equatorial Guinea; Gabon; Guinea; Guinea-Bissau; Haiti; Iran, Islamic Rep.; Iraq; Jordan; Kuwait; Malaysia; Mali; Niger; Oman; Qatar; Saudi Arabia; Senegal; Sudan; Syrian Arab Republic; United Arab Emirates; West Bank and Gaza; Yemen, Rep.	31
Be head of household	Bahrain; Burundi; Cameroon; Central African Republic; Chad; Chile; Comoros; Congo, Dem. Rep.; Congo, Rep.; Djibouti; Gabon; Guinea; Guinea-Bissau; Indonesia; Iran, Islamic Rep.; Iraq; Jordan; Libya; Madagascar; Mali; Mauritania; Morocco; Niger; Oman; San Marino; Saudi Arabia; Senegal; Sudan; Tunisia; United Arab Emirates; Yemen, Rep.	31
Get a job without permission	Bahrain; Cameroon; Chad; Comoros; Gabon; Guinea; Guinea-Bissau; Iran, Islamic Rep.; Jordan; Kuwait; Mauritania; Niger; Qatar; Sudan; Syrian Arab Republic; United Arab Emirates; West Bank and Gaza; Yemen, Rep.	18
Travel outside the home	Afghanistan; Bahrain; Brunei Darussalam; Egypt, Arab Rep.; Iran, Islamic Rep.; Iraq; Jordan; Kuwait; Malaysia; Oman; Qatar; Saudi Arabia; Sudan; Syrian Arab Republic; United Arab Emirates; West Bank and Gaza; Yemen, Rep.	17
Apply for a national identity card	Afghanistan; Algeria; Benin; Cameroon; Congo, Rep.; Egypt, Arab Rep.; Mauritius; Namibia; Oman; Pakistan; Saudi Arabia	11
Travel outside the country	Iran, Islamic Rep.; Iraq; Qatar; Saudi Arabia; Sudan; Syrian Arab Republic	6
Register a business	Bhutan; Guinea-Bissau; Pakistan; Suriname	4
Open a bank account	Chad; Guinea-Bissau; Niger	3
Sign a contract	Equatorial Guinea	1

Source: Women, Business and the Law database.

FIGURE 1.9 — WOMEN ARE MORE LIKELY TO HOLD LEADERSHIP POSITIONS IN PUBLIC LIFE WHEN THEY HAVE GREATER DECISION-MAKING ABILITY

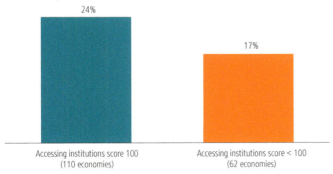

Proportion of seats held by women in national parliaments (%)

- 24% — Accessing institutions score 100 (110 economies)
- 17% — Accessing institutions score < 100 (62 economies)

Sources: Women, Business and the Law and World Development Indicators databases.
Note: The difference in the percentages illustrated is statistically significant at the 1% level after controlling for the log of GNI per capita (2015), the ratio of female-to-male (mean) years of education (age 25+) (2015), and the rule of law (2016). Sources for the control variables include the World Development Indicators and Barro-Lee Educational Attainment databases. Regression analysis is based on 172 economies for which data are available. This statistical relationship should not be interpreted as causal.

Using property

Strong property rights can allow women to leverage assets for economic gain. The using property indicator examines women's ability to acquire, access, manage and control property as a function of inheritance and marital property regimes. Access to property through these means can both increase women's financial security and provide them with the necessary collateral to start businesses.

Women, Business and the Law finds that women's property rights are positively associated with their leadership positions in the private sector. Women are less likely to have leadership positions in business in economies where their property rights are constrained (figure 1.10).

Systems of property ownership for spouses provide for the management of

FIGURE 1.10

WOMEN ARE LESS LIKELY TO HOLD LEADERSHIP POSITIONS IN BUSINESS WHEN THEY LACK PROPERTY RIGHTS

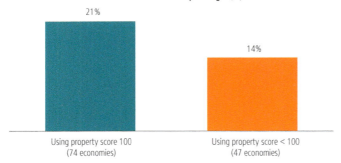

Firms with a female top manager (%)

Using property score 100
(74 economies)

Using property score < 100
(47 economies)

Sources: Women, Business and the Law and Enterprise Surveys databases.
Note: The difference in the percentages illustrated is statistically significant at the 10% level after controlling for the log of GNI per capita (2015), the ratio of female-to-male (mean) years of education (age 25+) (2015), the proportion of seats held by women in national parliaments (2016), and the rule of law (2016). Sources for the control variables include the World Development Indicators and Barro-Lee Educational Attainment databases. Regression analysis is based on 121 economies for which data are available. This statistical relationship should not be interpreted as causal.

of certain property regimes for women's property rights. For example, a comparative study of Ecuador, Ghana and the Indian state of Karnataka found that in separate property regimes, gender gaps in assets and wealth tend to be larger. In contrast, these asset and wealth gaps are smaller under community property regimes. The results show that in Ghana and Karnataka, women constitute just 38% and 20% of landowners, respectively. Both economies have a default separation of property regime. However, in Ecuador, where the default marital regime is community of property, women make up 51% of agricultural landowners.

Having strong property rights, including through marital property regimes, is a critical component of land ownership. Control of land or housing can provide direct economic benefits to women entrepreneurs (box 1.2).

Because women are more likely to perform unpaid activities that benefit the household such as child or elder care, they typically have fewer monetized contributions than men and therefore acquire fewer assets during marriage. Recognition of these nonmonetary contributions is important upon the dissolution of marriage as it can grant women access to a share of marital property. Though these contributions are

marital estates during and after marriage. In most economies this system is set by default. Called a marital property regime, it determines the allocation of assets between spouses and automatically applies to spouses that do not opt out.

Of the marital property regimes covered by *Women, Business and the Law*, the most common are separate property

and community property. While separate property regimes allow each spouse to retain ownership and control over their own property with full administrative rights, community property regimes treat the property of either spouse as joint property regardless of who paid for it.

Studies arising from the Gender Asset Gap Project emphasize the importance

BOX 1.2

JOINT TITLING AND LAND REGISTRATION HELP EMPOWER WOMEN

Strong property rights and titling schemes encourage asset-based lending, or loans secured by collateral. Having titled property is particularly important for women in low-income economies, where entrepreneurship offers a chance to overcome poverty. Titled property provides proof of ownership, which facilitates its use as collateral. Government policies promoting joint titling, in which more than one person has ownership rights, can expand the pool of property women can use as collateral for bank financing. For some women, this may mean the chance to access credit and start a business.

Women, Business and the Law finds that some economies legally establish joint titling for married couples through marital property regimes or land laws. For example, Lesotho's Land Act establishes that property titles are held jointly for spouses whose marital regime is community property. In the Philippines, every title certificate belonging to a married couple is in the name of both spouses, as mandated by Presidential Decree 1529. Vietnam's Land Law also establishes joint titling when land use rights and houses are joint property. Some other economies with joint titling include Albania; Brazil; Bulgaria; Burkina Faso; Kosovo; Lithuania; the former Yugoslav Republic of Macedonia; Namibia; Paraguay; Rwanda; Slovenia; South Africa and Spain.

Additionally, some economies have introduced innovative laws to further promote women's land registration. For example, Nepal's 2017 Finance Act has discounted fees to register property jointly by spouses or under a woman's name. Serbia applies similar discounts. Finally, rural women and women heads of household in Colombia have preferential access to rural land formalization programs through Decree No. 902.

Sources: De Soto 2001; Giovarelli and Girma 2013; Ali, Deininger and Goldstein 2014.

implicitly recognized in community property regimes, separate property regimes can penalize a spouse that does not earn an income during marriage. This income penalty can be mitigated in divorce by explicitly recognizing nonmonetary contributions to a household.

Of the 189 economies examined by *Women, Business and the Law*, 134 recognize nonmonetary contributions. These economies include all with default community property regimes and 28 of the 75 economies with separate property regimes.

Another reason for gaps between women's and men's ownership of assets may be inheritance rights. Often inheritance offers an opportunity for both men and women to own land or housing. For widows inheritance may be the only way to acquire ownership over assets and can be

a crucial component of economic security after the death of a spouse. However, in 36 of the 189 economies covered, widows are not granted the same inheritance rights as widowers. Further, 39 economies prevent daughters from inheriting the same proportion of assets as sons. Differences such as these can limit a woman's economic prospects during a vulnerable phase of life.

Getting a job

The getting a job indicator examines laws and regulations affecting the millions of women working in formal employment globally. Starting from when a woman applies for a job through to when she retires, this indicator explores the policies that affect a woman's ability to work including her job prospects, earning

potential, career growth and ability to balance work and family.

In the economies that score well under the getting a job indicator, more women tend to work relative to men. In these economies women also earn more money relative to men which demonstrates that labor market laws can both encourage women to enter the formal labor force and increase their earning potential (figure 1.11).

Job restrictions

Economies grow faster when more women work.[11] Although current good practice calls for gender equality in work opportunities, this has not always been the case historically. For example, the ILO's *Underground Work (Women) Convention* of 1935 and its 1919, 1934 and 1948 conventions on women's night

---

FIGURE 1.11   **GENDER EQUALITY IN LABOR LAW IS ASSOCIATED WITH MORE WOMEN WORKING AND EARNING MORE RELATIVE TO MEN**

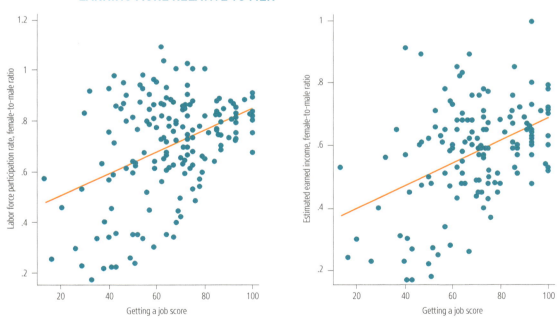

Sources: Women, Business and the Law and World Development Indicators databases; World Economic Forum *Global Gender Gap Report 2016* (Table C3, p.47).
Note: The positive relationships between the getting a job score and the ratio of female-to-male labor force participation rate (2016), and the getting a job score and the ratio of female-to-male estimated earned income (2016) are statistically significant at the 1% level after controlling for the log of GNI per capita (2015), the ratio of female-to-male years (mean) of education (age 25+) (2015), the proportion of seats held by women in national parliaments (2016), and the rule of law (2016). Sources for the control variables include the World Development Indicators and Barro-Lee Educational Attainment databases. Regression analyses are based on 164 and 138 economies for which data are available, respectively. These statistical relationships should not be interpreted as causal.

work called on states to prohibit women's employment in underground mines and night work in industrial undertakings. Similarly, in the years following the Industrial Revolution, several economies banned women from certain jobs to protect them from unsafe working conditions (box 1.3).

Though conditions have improved for both men and women over time, many gender-based restrictions remain. Industry restrictions, such as those on mining, are particularly common. Sixty-five economies restrict women from working in mining. Women also face job restrictions in industries such as manufacturing (47 economies), construction (37 economies), energy (29 economies), agriculture (27 economies), water (26 economies) and transportation (21 economies).

Additionally, in 29 of the 189 economies covered, women cannot work the same night hours as men. Night work restrictions exist in every region except in OECD high-income economies. The restrictions are most common in South Asia and the Middle East and North Africa, where women cannot work the same night hours as men in 63% and 55% of economies,

---

BOX 1.3   THE LASTING EFFECTS OF LEGACY LEGISLATION

Certain job restrictions are largely due to legacy legislation reflecting outdated safety standards. Restrictions on women's work in mining in many Commonwealth economies, for example, can be traced back to the United Kingdom's Mines and Collieries Act of 1842. Currently, almost half of Commonwealth economies place limits on the jobs women can do. In the Commonwealth of Independent States (CIS), most economies have a lengthy list of job restrictions for women, a remnant of a 1932 Soviet Union Law. Of the nine CIS economies covered, only Armenia does not have such restrictions. Similar trends exist in Francophone Africa, Lusophone Africa and the Spanish-speaking world.

Seventy-five percent of economies in Francophone Africa have regulations restricting women's employment, with many mirroring a 1954 ordinance from the former federation of French West Africa. Among these economies are Benin, Burkina Faso, Cameroon, the Central African Republic, Chad, the Democratic Republic of Congo, the Republic of Congo, Côte d'Ivoire, Gabon, Guinea, Madagascar, Mali, Mauritania, Niger and Senegal.

Portuguese and Spanish legacy legislation has also left a mark in many former colonies. Portugal first introduced a series of decrees restricting women's work in the 1890s. These decrees were not fully repealed until the early 2000s. Currently, almost every country in Lusophone Africa and Brazil has at least one restriction on women's work. Spain enacted a decree in 1957 prohibiting women from a variety of jobs, including in mining, certain construction jobs and electricity. This decree was repealed only in 1995. Currently, 12 economies in the Spanish-speaking world place legal restrictions on women's work: Argentina, Bolivia, Chile, Colombia, Costa Rica, Ecuador, Equatorial Guinea, Guatemala, Honduras, Nicaragua, Panama and Uruguay.

---

respectively. In total 104 economies continue to place restrictions on women's employment (figure 1.12). Research estimates that eliminating barriers that prevent women from working in certain sectors or occupations could increase

---

FIGURE 1.12   RESTRICTIONS ON WOMEN'S EMPLOYMENT EXIST IN ALL REGIONS

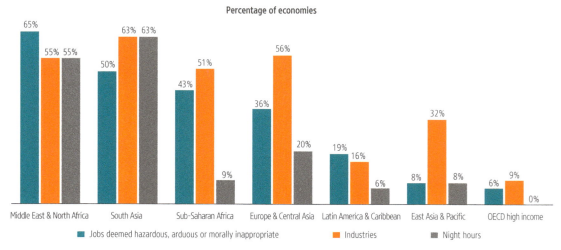

Percentage of economies

Region	Jobs deemed hazardous, arduous or morally inappropriate	Industries	Night hours
Middle East & North Africa	65%	55%	55%
South Asia	50%	63%	63%
Sub-Saharan Africa	43%	51%	9%
Europe & Central Asia	36%	56%	20%
Latin America & Caribbean	19%	16%	6%
East Asia & Pacific	8%	32%	8%
OECD high income	6%	9%	0%

Source: *Women, Business and the Law* database.

labor productivity by as much as 25% in some economies simply by increasing women's labor force participation.[12]

Workplace protections

Workplace protections, however, can facilitate women's ability to secure and sustain employment. For example legal protections such as gender-based nondiscrimination in employment can encourage the entry of women into the workforce. Similarly guaranteeing equal remuneration for work of equal value can ensure that women are not discriminated against when receiving wages and benefits.

Although almost 80% of the studied economies prohibit gender discrimination in employment, only 40% mandate equal remuneration for work of equal value. This standard originates from the ILO's Equal Remuneration Convention and provides a broader framework than equal pay for equal work as it allows a comparison between not only the same or similar jobs, but also between different jobs of equal value.

Most OECD high-income economies and economies in Europe and Central Asia mandate equal remuneration for work of equal value. Forty percent of the economies in Sub-Saharan Africa also do so, while only 25% or fewer of the economies in Latin America and the Caribbean, the Middle East and North Africa, East Asia and the Pacific and South Asia mandate equal remuneration.

Leave benefits

The regulatory environment also plays a significant role in shaping women's ability to both get jobs and remain in the labor force after starting a family. Maternity, paternity and parental leave schemes can help recognize and redistribute unpaid care work. Ensuring job-protected leave of adequate length and pay for both parents is critical for a variety of health, economic and social development outcomes. The International Labour Organization's (ILO) 2000 Maternity Protection Convention establishes a minimum of 98

days (14 weeks) of paid maternity leave. Wage replacement is set at a minimum of 67% (2/3) of earnings ideally provided through compulsory social insurance or public funds.

Globally the median length of paid maternity leave matches the ILO standard of 14 weeks with corresponding wage replacement varying from 25% to 100% of earnings. Only 7 economies have no paid leave available to mothers. These economies include the Marshall Islands, the Federated States of Micronesia, Palau, Papua New Guinea, Suriname, Tonga and the United States.

The cost of hiring women of childbearing age is higher for employers in economies in which laws mandate that employers pay for leave benefits and in which the length of leave available to mothers significantly exceeds the length of leave available to fathers. The median length of paid paternity leave is only 5 days in the 91 economies that mandate it meaning maternity leave is a full 93 days longer on average.

In India, for example, employers may view the recent increase of maternity leave from 84 to 182 days as a disincentive to hiring women because employers bear the full cost. Employers have no legal obligation to provide paid paternity leave. The disparity between the cost of hiring women compared to men may also lead employers to reduce women's salaries to compensate for paying women higher leave benefits.

However if the cost of maternity leave is paid for by the government, firms do not necessarily face higher costs for hiring women. Governments pay 100% of leave benefits for mothers in 96 economies. In 53 economies employers pay 100% of leave benefits. In 27 economies, governments pay 50% or more of such benefits.

Some economies are shifting away from maternity and paternity leave in favor of parental leave. For example, in 2015 the United Kingdom reformed its leave policies so that 37 weeks of paid maternity

leave may be taken as shared, paid parental leave. Of the 42 economies with paid parental leave, almost 90% provide it in addition to maternity leave. Paid parental leave is most commonly found in high and upper-middle-income economies.

Parental leave is normally available to both parents. However, women tend to use it more than men. Although longer and higher paid leave for mothers has significant benefits, too much time out of the labor force may negatively affect a woman's career progression and earnings.[13] The key to designing leave policies that do not exacerbate gender inequality may be in promoting fathers' uptake of leave (table 1.3).

A recent report examining more than 100 leading studies related to infant and child health and well-being, maternal health, gender equality and economic impact concluded that the optimal length of paid leave to ensure optimal infant and child health and well-being is one year split equally between parents.[14]

When maternity, paternity and parental leave end, working parents continue to have family responsibilities that may affect their jobs. Laws that promote flexible work arrangements can reduce work-family conflicts. Moreover the ability to work reduced hours, to work variable hours (flextime), to telework or to have working-time autonomy can benefit both businesses and employees by reducing operational costs and turnover expenses and by improving productivity and work-life balance.[15] Of the economies covered by *Women, Business and the Law*, just 33 economies explicitly grant parents the right to request or obtain flexible work arrangements by law.

Retirement

When it comes to leaving the workforce, statutory retirement ages set career expectations and durations for working men and women. Laws that establish earlier retirement ages for women can negatively affect their lifetime earnings,

TABLE 1.3   POLICIES TO PROMOTE FATHERS' UPTAKE OF PARENTAL LEAVE

Economy	Examples
Austria	Parents each receive an additional bonus cash payment if they share their leave equally or at least 60:40.
France	Parents receive higher payments if they both take some leave.
Italy	Parents receive an additional month of leave if the father takes at least 3 of the initial 10 months.
Germany	Parents receive pay for an additional 2 months of leave if they each take at least 2 of the initial 12 months.
Japan	Parents receive an additional 2 months of paid leave if they share the initial 12 months.
Korea, Rep.	The second parent to take parental leave (typically the father) receives 100% of his wages up to a ceiling for 3 months. The first parent receives 40%.
Norway	Seventy days of the total postnatal parental leave period are reserved for each parent.
Portugal	Parents who share the initial 120 days of parental leave receive an additional 30 days.
Romania	The parent who did not initially request parental leave (typically the father) is obliged to take 1 of the 24 months of leave.
Sweden	Ninety of the 480 days of paid parental leave are reserved for each parent.

Source: *Women, Business and the Law* database.

pension benefits and retirement savings as well as their career growth prospects. When women are required to retire at an earlier age than men, they end their working lives with fewer years of employment. Conversely, if women enjoy the same statutory retirement age as men, years of employment are equalized and labor force participation can be encouraged.

Gender-differentiated retirement ages exist in every region of the world with the highest percentages in economies in the Middle East and North Africa (58%) and Europe and Central Asia (40%). Retirement is mandatory in almost a quarter of economies with gender-differentiated retirement ages.

In 41 of the 189 economies measured, women can retire with full benefits 1 to 10 years earlier than men. Most economies with gender-differentiated retirement ages have a 5-year gap between women's and men's retirement ages. The largest gap is in China where women can retire at age 50, 10 years before men.

In 13 economies laws allow women to retire with partial benefits earlier than

men. These economies include Albania, Algeria, Bahrain, Brazil, Bulgaria, Costa Rica, the Islamic Republic of Iran, the Kyrgyz Republic, Pakistan, Panama, Switzerland, the United Arab Emirates and the Republic of Yemen. In economies with such differences, women may forgo promotions and raises through early retirement. Women also contribute less to their pensions and savings in these circumstances, which can lead to financial hardship in retirement.[16]

Providing incentives to work

Governments can also facilitate balancing work and family by supporting and incentivizing mothers' ability to return to the workforce after childbirth. Income tax regulations and support for age-appropriate childcare and education can affect a woman's decision to enter and remain in the workforce. The providing incentives to work indicator analyzes such benefits and the ways in which they can influence women's decisions to work.

The ease, cost and availability of care for young children can affect whether

a mother works outside the home. Because women are often the primary caregivers for children, public assistance for childcare can create opportunities for women to enter the workforce. For example one study found that among OECD economies the availability of public childcare for children below the age of 5 years is strongly correlated with employment rates of mothers with young children.[17]

Over two-thirds of the economies covered by *Women, Business and the Law* directly provide childcare services or subsidize private childcare services. In Finland, for instance, municipal early childhood education is available from when the maternity and parental allowance periods finish until the child goes to primary school. As an alternative parents can choose to use private day care centers whose fees will be covered by the Social Insurance Institution through the Private Daycare Allowance. In other economies such as Ghana, Brazil and Costa Rica, preschool is free and compulsory starting at age four. Policies such as these can make childcare more affordable and enable parents to work.

Personal income tax deductions for childcare fees can also reduce the burden of childcare costs for parents. Though less common than publicly provided or subsidized childcare, this type of tax deduction can influence a parent's decision to return to or enter the workforce.

In 33 of the economies covered childcare payments are tax deductible. All the economies that provide for tax deductible childcare payments are upper-middle and high-income, except Bhutan and El Salvador. Bhutan is also the only economy in South Asia to provide this incentive, and only one economy in the Middle East and North Africa region—Malta—provides the benefit.

Women, Business and the Law finds that the enrollment of children in preprimary education is higher in economies that provide deductions for childcare fees than in economies without such deductions (figure 1.13).

A woman's decision to participate in formal employment may be affected in economies where there are gender differences in personal income tax regulations. Some economies grant tax deductions or credits to male taxpayers by default, reducing their taxable income and increasing take home pay. In some cases, this may mean that women pay disproportionately higher taxes than men. Without access to the same deductions or credits, women end up paying more in taxes which reduces their take home pay and provides a disincentive to entering the formal labor market.

Of the 189 economies covered, 15— Benin, Brunei Darussalam, Burkina Faso, the Democratic Republic of Congo, the Republic of Congo, Guinea, Indonesia, Iraq, the Lao People's Democratic Republic, Libya, Malaysia, Morocco, the Philippines, Togo and Tunisia—grant tax deductions or credits to male taxpayers by default.

In Guinea for example, a male taxpayer is entitled to a deduction for each dependent child and each wife. Minor children of married taxpayers are considered dependents of the husband. The wife receives tax benefits only if the husband is absent or incapacitated. In Iraq women receive tax deductions only if they are unmarried, divorced or widowed. In Malaysia a male taxpayer receives tax deductions for his dependent wife.

In limited circumstances women may be able to receive the same deductions or credits that men receive, but not by default. For example in cases of joint filing in Togo, tax credits for dependents are provided to the male head of household. The wife can also receive this head of household tax credit, but only if specific criteria are met.

Similarly, in Tunisia the male head of household receives tax deductions for dependent parents and children. The wife can receive these same deductions if she is considered the head of household. However this happens only if the husband has no income or if the wife remarries and has custody of the children.

Going to court

By strengthening the rule of law and narrowing inequality, access to justice allows people to use the legal system to advocate for their interests and ensures enforcement of the law. The going to court indicator assesses women's access to justice by examining justice institutions and procedures enhancing access to the legal system.

Unequal treatment in court can undermine women's legal capacities. The provision of testimony plays a key role in the outcome of any case and is a witness's opportunity to present an accurate rendering of facts. Testimony can affect the distribution of resources among women and men particularly in cases where economic rights are at issue.

Women, Business and the Law examines where women's testimony does not carry the same evidentiary weight in court as men's. In 16 economies the law differentiates between the evidentiary value of women's and men's testimony. Twelve of these economies are in the Middle East and North Africa (Bahrain, the Islamic Republic of Iran, Iraq, Jordan, Kuwait, Libya, Oman, Qatar, Saudi Arabia, the Syrian Arab Republic, West Bank and Gaza and the Republic of Yemen), two are in Sub-Saharan Africa (Mauritania and Sudan), one is in East Asia and the Pacific (Brunei Darussalam) and one is in South Asia (Pakistan).

Institutions that are not courts can also play an important role in ensuring women's access to justice. Anti-discrimination commissions are independent from the justice system and responsible for protecting, monitoring and promoting fundamental rights. *Women, Business and the Law* examines anti-discrimination commissions that are mandated to receive complaints of gender discrimination by both public and private actors.

Commissions can advise governments on policy issues such as occupational segregation, the gender wage gap and

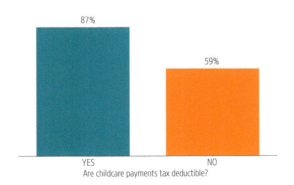

FIGURE 1.13 **ENROLLMENT IN PREPRIMARY SCHOOL IS HIGHER WHERE CHILDCARE FEES ARE TAX DEDUCTIBLE**

School enrollment, preprimary (% gross)

87%

59%

YES

NO

Are childcare payments tax deductible?

Sources: Women, Business and the Law and World Development Indicators databases.
Note: The difference in the percentages illustrated is statistically significant at the 10% level after controlling for the log of GNI per capita (2015), the proportion of seats held by women in national parliaments (2016), and the rule of law (2016). Source for the control variables is the World Development Indicators database. Regression analysis is based on 127 economies for which data are available. This statistical relationship should not be interpreted as causal.

women's labor force participation. For example New Zealand's Human Rights Commission examined equal employment opportunities in the female-dominated elderly care sector. Based on its recommendations regarding pay, working conditions and workforce training, the Employment Court found that a care workers' low pay was a breach of the Equal Pay Act.[18]

Of the 189 economies covered by *Women, Business and the Law*, 93 have established commissions that receive complaints from victims of gender discrimination (map 1.1). Europe and Central Asia has the highest percentage of economies with such institutions at 72%. In contrast, only 20% of the economies in the Middle East and North Africa have established them.

For women who cannot afford legal representation, the provision of legal aid can improve access to courts. A recent study in the United States shows that the funding of legal services can return as much as 11 times the amount invested. For example a woman who suffers domestic abuse and uses legal aid to get a restraining order loses fewer days of work. Similarly a mother who can secure spousal and child support with the assistance of civil legal aid may not require public benefits.[19] This was the case in Ecuador where three legal aid clinics were established to assist poor women and children. Because of the support provided by these clinics there was a 17% reduction in the probability that women would suffer domestic violence following a divorce. Inversely, the probability that female clients would receive child support increased by 10%.[20]

Women, Business and the Law data show that 120 economies mandate legal aid in civil or family matters. For example, in 2016 Ethiopia passed legislation mandating legal aid services for indigent women in civil actions. Tanzania's Legal Aid Act of 2017 also authorized legal aid in civil and criminal proceedings.

Legal formalities and the cost of litigation, both direct and indirect, can further discourage women and poor people from accessing justice. Relaxed rules of procedure could enhance courts' responsiveness to demands for the enforcement of social and economic rights.[21] One way to achieve this is through the establishment of small claims courts which hear civil cases involving relatively small amounts of money. Procedures in these courts are simplified with reduced cost and faster

MAP 1.1 DOES THE LAW ESTABLISH AN ANTI-DISCRIMINATION COMMISSION?

This map was produced by the Cartography Unit of the World Bank Group. The boundaries, colors, denominations and any other information shown on this map do not imply, on the part of the World Bank Group, any judgment on the legal status of any territory, or any endorsement or acceptance of such boundaries.

IBRD 43544 | MARCH 2018

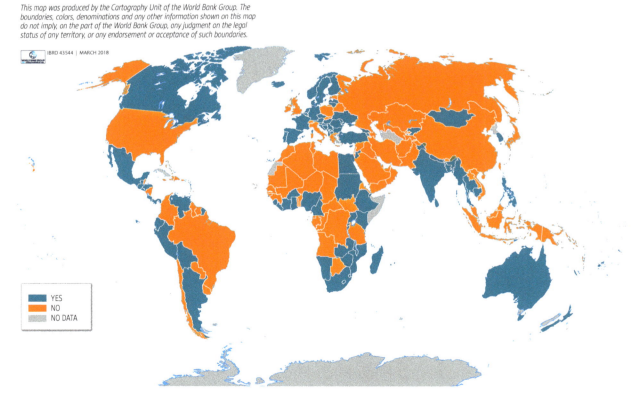

YES
NO
NO DATA

Source: Women, Business and the Law database.

judgment time. Small claims courts are ideal for small businesses, many of which are owned by women.

Women, Business and the Law finds that 131 economies worldwide have small claims courts. Among these are Côte d'Ivoire and Indonesia, which each introduced small claims courts in 2015. Other economies, however, have elected to abolish small claims courts. New codes of civil procedure in Ecuador and Hungary recently eliminated small claims in favor of resolution by arbitration or mediation.

Building credit

A strong institutional environment is key to expanding access to finance for women-owned businesses. If effective, it should recognize the constraints women face when accessing credit including the effects of discrimination and women's limited credit history compared to men's. The building credit indicator assesses women's access to finance and the strength of credit reporting systems. Establishing a good credit history may help women who lack access to property build reputation collateral for loans.

The ability to build such a history, however, could be affected by discriminatory lenders. Policy interventions can encourage women's entrepreneurship by prohibiting discrimination by creditors based on gender and marital status.

Legislation prohibiting gender-based discrimination in financial services exists in 72 of the 189 economies examined. Thirty-six of these economies also prohibit discrimination in financial services based on marital status. Such provisions can be found in a variety of legislation ranging from nondiscrimination and gender equality laws to credit acts and consumer protection ordinances.

In Latin America and the Caribbean such provisions are particularly common in consumer protection laws. For example Nicaragua's consumer protection law

puts a duty on providers to offer financial services without discrimination based on gender or marital status. In Europe and Central Asia gender equality acts often prohibit discrimination. For example Albania's Gender Equality Act prohibits discrimination in banking services, including loans, deposits and financing.

Women, Business and the Law data show that more women have formal accounts at financial institutions and debit cards in their own names in economies where the law prohibits discrimination based on gender in access to credit (figure 1.14).

Protecting women from violence

Protection against violence is also important to ensuring women's economic empowerment. Violence against women undermines economic empowerment by preventing employment and blocking access to financial resources. Women can

function more freely in societies and the business world when not faced with the threat of violence. The protecting women from violence indicator examines the existence and scope of legislation on violence against women including domestic violence and sexual harassment.

Domestic violence is gender-specific violence perpetrated by family members or intimate partners and can encompass different types of abuse. Worldwide nearly 1 in 3 women have experienced physical or sexual violence from an intimate partner. Intimate partners commit as many as 38% of all murders of women.[22] Domestic violence legislation is a key first step towards ensuring women's protection.

Of the 189 economies examined, 45 do not have laws on domestic violence. However, 9 of these 45 economies— Belgium, Canada, Chad, Djibouti, Estonia, Libya, Madagascar, Morocco and Tunisia—have aggravated penalties for specific types of abuse committed between spouses or family members

---

FIGURE 1.14   **MORE WOMEN HAVE ACCOUNTS AT FINANCIAL INSTITUTIONS AND DEBIT CARDS WHERE THE LAW PROHIBITS GENDER-BASED DISCRIMINATION IN ACCESS TO CREDIT**

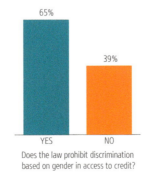

Account at a financial institution, female (% age 15+)

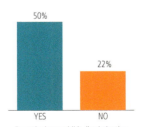

Debit card in own name, female (% age 15+)

Sources: Women, Business and the Law and Global Findex (2014) databases.
Note: The differences in the percentages illustrated are statistically significant at least at the 10% level after controlling for the log of GNI per capita (2015), the ratio of female-to-male (mean) years of education (age 25+) (2015), the proportion of seats held by women in national parliaments (2016), and the rule of law (2016). Sources for the control variables include the World Development Indicators and Barro-Lee Educational Attainment databases. Regression analyses are based on 133 economies for which data are available. These statistical relationships should not be interpreted as causal.

rather than domestic violence laws. This addresses the issue by intensifying penalties for intrahousehold violence.

Of the remaining 36 economies with no domestic violence laws or aggravated penalties for violence at home, 19 are in Sub-Saharan Africa and 10 are in the Middle East and North Africa. Economies in other regions are also missing such laws. These economies include Afghanistan, Armenia, Haiti, the Federated States of Micronesia, Myanmar, Russia and Uzbekistan.

Although women are statistically at greater risk of violence from an intimate partner, other forms of violence are also common. In the workplace and other arenas, for example, women may face sexual harassment. Sexual harassment involves the abuse of a position of hierarchy or a significant power disparity.

Traditionally sexual harassment has been linked to employment. However sexual harassment may occur in other spheres including education. Economies have begun addressing sexual harassment through various types of legislation including anti-discrimination statutes and criminal law.[23]

Women, Business and the Law finds that women are more likely to have majority ownership in firms in economies where workplace sexual harassment laws exist (figure 1.15).

Of the 189 economies covered by Women, Business and the Law, 130, including every economy in South Asia, have laws prohibiting sexual harassment in employment. However, 59 economies still do not have such laws.

In the Middle East and North Africa, for example, 70% of the examined economies do not have legislation protecting women from sexual harassment at work. In East Asia and the Pacific approximately half of the examined economies do not have such laws. In Latin American and the Caribbean approximately one-third of economies do not. In Europe and

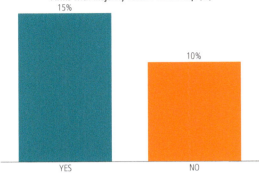

Firms with majority female ownership (%)

YES — 15%
NO — 10%

Is there legislation addressing sexual harassment in employment?

Sources: Women, Business and the Law and Enterprise Surveys databases.
Note: The difference in the percentages illustrated is significant at the 5% level after controlling for the log of GNI per capita (2015), the ratio of female-to-male (mean) years of education (ages 25+) (2015), the proportion of seats held by women in national parliaments (2016), and the rule of law (2016). Sources for the control variables include the World Development Indicators and Barro-Lee Educational Attainment databases. Regression analysis is based on 93 economies for which data are available. This statistical relationship should not be interpreted as causal.

Central Asia approximately a quarter of economies lack workplace harassment laws. Japan is the only OECD high-income economy that does not legally protect women from sexual harassment at work.

However, some economies have recently reformed in this area. One economy, Cameroon, adopted a new criminal code covering sexual harassment in employment and education.

Without such protections in place sexual harassment at work can undermine careers, the ability to work and the employment climate.

From inform to reform

By scoring these seven spheres of working women's lives, Women, Business and the Law hopes to highlight legislation affecting women's prospects as employees and entrepreneurs and to identify potential areas for reform. There is growing evidence linking women's legal rights and economic opportunities. Women, Business and the

Law 2018 provides a rich body of data across its seven indicators that can be used to generate policy action and to lay a roadmap for further research.

Notes

1   United Nations Committee on the Elimination of Discrimination Against Women (CEDAW Committee). 2016. "Communication No. 60/2013: Views Adopted by the Committee at its Sixty-Third Session (February 15-March 4, 2016)." CEDAW/C/63/D/60/2013, United Nations, New York.

2   Id.

3   Supreme Court of the Russian Federation, Decision No. 46-KG 17-24, July 24, 2017, http://www.supcourt.ru/stor_pdf .php?id=1566432.

4   Constitutional Court of the Republic of Colombia, Decision C-586/16, October 26, 2016, http://www .corteconstitucional.gov.co /RELATORIA/2016/C-586-16.htm.

5   Duflo 2012.

6   Cuberes and Teignier 2016.

7   Gonzales et al. 2015.

8   Cavalcanti and Tavares 2016.

9   Khan 1996.

10   Geddes, Lueck and Tennyson 2012.

11   Aguirre 2012.

12   World Bank 2011.

13   Kahn, Garcia-Manglano and Bianchi 2014.

14   Schulte et al. 2017.

15   Shepard, Clifton and Kruse 1996; Halpern 2005; Lister 2010.

16   Chłoń-Domińczak 2017.

17   OECD 2001.

18   APF and GANHRI 2017.

19   Buckwalter-Poza 2016.

20   Owen and Portillo 2003.

21   Gloppen and Kanyongolo 2007.

22   WHO 2013.

23   Numhauser-Henning 2012.

References

Abel, Laura K., and Susan Vignola. 2010. "Economic and Other Benefits Associated with the Provision of Civil Legal Aid." *Seattle Journal for Social Justice* 9 (1): 139–68.

Aguirre, DeAnne, Leila Hoteit, Christine Rupp and Karim Sabbagh. 2012. "Empowering the Third Billion: Women and the World of Work in 2012." Booz and Company.

Ali, Daniel Ayalew, Klaus Deininger and Markus Goldstein. 2014. "Environmental and Gender Impacts of Land Tenure Regularization in Africa: Pilot Evidence from Rwanda." *Journal of Development Economics* 110: 262–75.

APF (Asia Pacific Forum) and GANHRI (Global Alliance of National Human Rights Institutions). 2017. "Concept Note: The Role of National Human Rights Institutions in Promoting and Protecting Women's Economic Participation in the Changing World of Work." Sydney, Australia: APF and GANHRI.

Australia Law Reform Commission. 1994. "Equality before the Law: Justice for Women." Government of Australia: Report No. 69, Part 1.

Averett, Susan L., H. Elizabeth Peters and Donald M. Waldman. 2006. "Tax Credits, Labor Supply, and Child Care." *Review of Economics and Statistics* 79 (1): 125–35.

Buckwalter-Poza, Rebecca. 2016. *Making Justice Equal*. Center for American Progress.

Cavalcanti, Tiago V. de V., and José Tavares. 2016. "The Output Cost of Gender Discrimination: A Model-Based Macroeconomics Estimate." *Economic Journal* 126 (590): 109–34.

Chłoń-Domińczak, Agnieszka. 2017. "Gender Gap in Pensions: Looking Ahead." Study for the FEMM Committee, Directorate-General for Internal Policies, European Parliament, Brussels, Belgium.

Cuberes, David, and Mark Teignier. 2016. "Aggregate Effects of Gender Gaps in the Labor Market: A Quantitative Estimate." *Journal of Human Capital* 10 (1): 1-32.

De Soto, Hernando. 2001. "The Mystery of Capital." *Finance and Development* 38 (1).

Deere, Carmen Diana, and Magdalena León. 2003. "The Gender Asset Gap: Land in Latin America." *World Development* 31 (6): 925–47.

Deininger, Klaus, Hari Nagarajan, Fang Xia and Songqing Jin. 2014. "Inheritance Law Reform, Empowerment, and Human Capital Accumulation: Second-Generation Effects from India." Policy Research Working Paper 7086, World Bank Group, Washington, DC.

Demirgüç-Kunt, Asli, Leora Klapper and Dorothe Singer. 2013. "Financial Inclusion and Legal Discrimination against Women: Evidence from Developing Countries." Policy Research Working Paper 6416, World Bank, Washington, DC.

Duflo, Esther. 2012. "Women Empowerment and Economic Development." *Journal of Economic Literature* 50 (4): 1051–79.

Geddes, Rick, Dean Lueck and Sharon Tennyson. 2012. "Human Capital Accumulation and the Expansion of Women's Economic Rights." *Journal of Law and Economics* 55 (4): 839–67.

Giovarelli, Renée and Hirut Girma. 2013. "Gender Implications of Joint Land Titles in Ethiopia (Brief)." LANDESA.

Gloppen, Siri and Fidelis Edge Kanyongolo. 2007. "Courts and the Poor in Malawi: Economic Marginalization, Vulnerability, and the Law." *International Journal of Constitutional Law* 5 (2): 258–93.

Gonzales, Christian, Sonali Jain-Chandra, Kalpana Kochhar and Monique Newiak. 2015. "Fair Play: More Equal Laws Boost Female Labor Force Participation." IMF Staff Discussion Note SDN/15/02, International Monetary Fund, Washington, DC.

Hallward-Driemeier, Mary, and Ousman Gajigo. 2013. "Strengthening Economic Rights and Women's Occupational Choice: The Impact of Reforming Ethiopia's Family Law." Policy Research Working Paper 6695, World Bank, Washington, DC.

Halpern, D. F. 2005. "How Time-Flexible Work Policies Can Reduce Stress, Improve Health, and Save Money." *Stress and Health* 21: 157–68.

Johnson, Richard W. 1999. "The Gender Gap in Pension Wealth: Is Women's Progress in the Labor Market Equalizing Benefits?" The Retirement Project, Brief Series 1, Urban Institute, Washington, DC.

Kahn, Joan R., Javier García-Manglano and Suzanne M. Bianchi. 2014. "The Motherhood Penalty at Midlife: Long-Term Effects of Children on Women's Careers." *Journal of Marriage and the Family* 76 (1): 56–72.

Khan, B. Zorina. 1996. "Married Women's Property Laws and Female Commercial Activity: Evidence from United States Patent Records, 1790-1895." *Journal of Economic History* 56 (2): 356–88.

Ladd, Helen F. 1982. "Equal Credit Opportunity: Women and Mortgage Credit." *American Economic Review* 72 (2): 166–70.

Lister, Kate. 2010. "Workshifting Benefits: The Bottom Line." Telework Researchers Network.

McLaughlin, Heather, Christopher Uggen and Amy Blackstone. 2017. "The Economic and Career Effects of Sexual Harassment on Working Women." *Gender & Society* 31 (3): 333–58.

Nagaraja, B. 2013. "Empowerment of Women in India: A Critical Analysis." *Journal of Humanities and Social Science* 9 (2): 45–52.

Numhauser-Henning, Ann. 2012. "Harassment related to Sex and Sexual Harassment Law in 33 European Countries, Discrimination versus Dignity." Lund University Faculty of Law.

Organisation for Economic Co-operation and Development (OECD). 2001. "Balancing Work and Family Life: Helping Parents into Paid Employment." Chapter 4 in *OECD Employment Outlook 2001*. Paris: OECD.

Ogloblin, Constantin G. 1999. "The Gender Earnings Differential in the Russian Transition Economy." *Industrial and Labor Relations Review* 52 (4): 602–27.

Olivetti, Claudia, and Barbara Petrongolo. 2017. "The Economic Consequences of Family Policies: Lessons from a Century of Legislation in High-Income Countries." *Journal of Economic Perspectives* 31 (1): 205–30.

Owen, Bruce M., and Jorge E. Portillo. 2003. "Legal Reform, Externalities and Economic Development: Measuring the Impact of Legal Aid on Poor Women in Ecuador." John M. Olin Program in Law and Economics Working Paper No. 255, Public Law & Legal Theory Working Paper Series Research Paper No. 55, Stanford Law School, Stanford, CA.

Ruhm, Christopher J. 1998. "The Economic Consequences of Parental Leave Mandates: Lessons from Europe." *Quarterly Journal of Economics* 113 (1): 285–317.

Schulte, Brigid, Alieza Durana, Brian Stout and Jonathan Moyer. 2017. *Paid Family Leave: How Much Time Is Enough?* Washington, DC: New America.

Shepard, Edward M., III, Thomas J. Clifton and Douglas Kruse. 1996. "Flexible Work Hours and Productivity: Some Evidence from the Pharmaceutical Industry." *Industrial Relations: A Journal of Economy and Society* 35: 123–39.

WHO (World Health Organization). 2013. "Global and Regional Estimates of Violence Against Women Prevalence and Health Effects of Intimate Partner Violence and Non-Partner Sexual Violence." Geneva: WHO.

World Bank. 2011. *World Development Report 2012: Gender Equality and Development*.

ABOUT
WOMEN, BUSINESS AND THE LAW

Major differences in legal gender parity persist around the world. Many laws continue to prevent women from improving their own well-being and that of their families by working or running a business.

In its fifth edition, *Women, Business and the Law* expands to

189
economies.

How can governments improve women's access to entrepreneurial and employment activities? Answering this question requires understanding many factors—from access to education and health care, to social and cultural norms and many things beyond. One important factor is how laws, regulations and institutions differentiate between women and men in ways that affect women's incentives or capacity to work or set up and run a business.

Since its inception in 2009, *Women, Business and the Law* has collected data on laws and regulations constraining women's entrepreneurship and employment. The data set illuminates how government policies limit women's economic participation through unequal laws and a business environment that does not adequately support women's employment.

This edition of *Women, Business and the Law* introduces an innovation by scoring questions at the indicator level. The indicator-level scoring is meant to promote discussion and analysis on which laws

matter the most for women's entrepreneurship and employment, as well as encourage economies to follow good practices and to reform.

By gathering and analyzing quantitative data to compare gender legal differences across economies and over time, *Women, Business and the Law* offers objective benchmarks for assessing where reforms have occurred that are helpful in measuring global progress toward gender legal equality (box 2.1).

Women, Business and the Law 2018, the fifth in a series, provides data on legal and regulatory barriers to women's entrepreneurship and employment in 189 economies, up from 173 covered in the 2016 edition (table 2.1). This expansion enhances the global data on laws and regulations affecting women's prospects as entrepreneurs and employees while allowing broader comparison.

TABLE 2.1 **EXPANDED GEOGRAPHIC COVERAGE**

Region	Economies previously in the report	Economies added to the report	Total number of economies
East Asia & Pacific	Brunei Darussalam; Cambodia; China; Fiji; Hong Kong SAR, China; Indonesia; Lao PDR; Malaysia; Mongolia; Myanmar; Papua New Guinea; Philippines; Singapore; Taiwan, China; Thailand; Timor-Leste; Tonga; Vietnam	Kiribati; Marshall Islands; Micronesia, Fed. Sts.; Palau; Samoa; Solomon Islands; Vanuatu	25
Europe & Central Asia	Albania; Armenia; Azerbaijan; Belarus; Bosnia and Herzegovina; Bulgaria; Croatia; Georgia; Kazakhstan; Kosovo; Kyrgyz Republic; Latvia; Lithuania; Macedonia, FYR; Moldova; Montenegro; Romania; Russian Federation; Serbia; Tajikistan; Turkey; Ukraine; Uzbekistan	Cyprus; San Marino	25
OECD high income	Australia; Austria; Belgium; Canada; Chile; Czech Republic; Denmark; Estonia; Finland; France; Germany; Greece; Hungary; Iceland; Ireland; Israel; Italy; Japan; Korea, Rep.; Luxembourg; Netherlands; New Zealand; Norway; Poland; Portugal; Slovak Republic; Slovenia; Spain; Sweden; Switzerland; United Kingdom; United States		32
Latin America & Caribbean	Antigua and Barbuda; Argentina; Bahamas, The; Barbados; Belize; Bolivia; Brazil; Colombia; Costa Rica; Dominica; Dominican Republic; Ecuador; El Salvador; Grenada; Guatemala; Guyana; Haiti; Honduras; Jamaica; Mexico; Nicaragua; Panama; Paraguay; Peru; Puerto Rico (U.S.); St. Kitts and Nevis; St. Lucia; St. Vincent and the Grenadines; Suriname; Trinidad and Tobago; Uruguay; Venezuela, RB		32
Middle East & North Africa	Algeria; Bahrain; Djibouti; Egypt, Arab Rep.; Iran, Islamic Rep.; Iraq; Jordan; Kuwait; Lebanon; Malta; Morocco; Oman; Qatar; Saudi Arabia; Syrian Arab Republic; Tunisia; United Arab Emirates; West Bank and Gaza; Yemen, Rep.	Libya	20
South Asia	Afghanistan; Bangladesh; Bhutan; India; Maldives; Nepal; Pakistan; Sri Lanka		8
Sub-Saharan Africa	Angola; Benin; Botswana; Burkina Faso; Burundi; Cameroon; Chad; Congo, Dem. Rep.; Congo, Rep.; Côte d'Ivoire; Ethiopia; Equatorial Guinea; Gabon; Ghana; Guinea; Kenya; Lesotho; Liberia; Madagascar; Malawi; Mali; Mauritania; Mauritius; Mozambique; Namibia; Niger; Nigeria; Rwanda; São Tomé and Príncipe; Senegal; Seychelles; Sierra Leone; South Africa; South Sudan; Sudan; Swaziland; Tanzania; Togo; Uganda; Zambia; Zimbabwe	Cabo Verde; Central African Republic; Comoros; Eritrea; Gambia, The; Guinea-Bissau	47

What does *Women, Business and the Law* measure?

Women, Business and the Law 2018 provides quantitative measures of laws and regulations affecting women's economic opportunities in seven areas: accessing institutions, using property, getting a job, providing incentives to work, going to court, building credit and protecting women from violence.

- **Accessing institutions** explores women's ability to interact with public authorities and the private sector in the same ways as men, through examining constraints on women's legal capacity.

- **Using property** analyzes women's ability to access and use property based on their ability to own, manage, control and inherit it. It also examines whether legislation accounts for nonmonetary contributions, such as unpaid care for children or the elderly, in distributing assets upon the dissolution of marriage.

- **Getting a job** assesses restrictions on women's ability to work, such as prohibitions on working at night or in certain industries. It also covers laws on maternity, paternity and parental leave, retirement ages, equal remuneration for work of equal value, nondiscrimination at work and flexible work options.

- **Providing incentives to work** examines childcare and tax support, through assessing tax deductions and credits, childcare and primary education.

- **Going to court** explores women's ability to access justice by examining the evidentiary weight of women's testimony, the existence of justice institutions such as anti-discrimination commissions and small claims courts and mandates for legal aid.

- **Building credit** examines credit bureaus and registries that collect information from retailers and utility companies. It also covers nondiscrimination in access to credit based on gender and marital status.

- **Protecting women from violence** considers laws on domestic violence and sexual harassment in education and employment.

In addition, a case study is included examining how discriminatory laws can affect women's demand for financial services. For example, limited access to and control over property constrain women's ability to provide collateral for loans. Similarly, gender differences in getting identification can make it more difficult for women to open bank accounts, especially where there are stringent identification requirements.

What does *Women, Business and the Law* not measure?

Equal opportunities for women in business and the workplace depend on the interplay of economic, social and cultural factors. For example, unless women have opportunities to get an education or build their skills, equalizing laws affecting entrepreneurship and employment mean little. Other factors, such as infrastructure—for example, safe transportation—might also affect women's ability and desire to work in certain locations or at night. And social and cultural norms may prevent women from running businesses or working outside the home.

While recognizing that many issues affect women's economic opportunities, *Women, Business and the Law* focuses on the formal legal and regulatory environment determining whether women can open their own businesses or work. Not everything of importance is covered. Rather the report is concerned with the laws governing the formal economy. Although most women in developing economies start businesses or work in the informal economy, a goal of this project is to define some of the features of the legal framework that make it more difficult for women to transition from the informal to the formal economy.

While focusing on written legislation, the report recognizes the often-large gaps between the laws on the books and actual practice: women do not always have access to the equality that formal laws establish. One reason for this may be poor implementation of legislation due to weak enforcement or design or low capacity.

Identifying legal differences is one step toward better understanding where women's economic rights may be restricted in practice. Of the countries covered by the report, only the Islamic Republic of Iran, Palau, Sudan, Tonga and the United States are not parties to the United Nations Convention on the Elimination of All Forms of Discrimination against Women.[1] Thus, most women in the economies covered should have access to formal equality. But, as the report shows, that is not the case in many economies.

Methodological strengths and limitations

The *Women, Business and the Law* methodology was designed to be an easily replicable way to benchmark the legal and regulatory environment for women as entrepreneurs and employees. This approach has advantages and limitations (table 2.2).

A key consideration for the project is that the indicators are comparable across economies. The indicators are based on standardized assumptions. One example of a standardized assumption used for maternity leave is that the woman in question is having one child. While maternity leave rules often differ for twins, only data for individual births is captured by the question.

Another assumption is the location of the woman in question is in the largest business city of the economy. However,

TABLE 2.2 METHODOLOGICAL STRENGTHS AND LIMITATIONS

Feature	Strengths	Limitations
Use of standardized assumptions	Makes data comparable across economies and methodology transparent	Reduces scope of data; only regulatory reforms in the areas measured can be systematically tracked
Focus on largest business city	Makes data collection manageable (cost effective) and data comparable	Reduces representativeness of data for an economy if there are significant differences across locations
Focus on the most populous group	Makes data comparable across economies, especially where there are parallel legal systems prescribing different rights for different groups of women	Restrictions that apply only to minority populations may be missed
Focus on the formal sector	Keeps attention on formal sector—where regulations are relevant	Unable to reflect reality for women in the informal sector—which may be a significant number of women in many economies
Focus on the law	Makes indicators "actionable" because the law is what policymakers can change	Where systematic compliance with the law is lacking, regulatory changes alone will not achieve the desired results

legislation may differ within federal economies, where laws affecting women can vary by state. Even in nonfederal economies, women in rural areas and small towns may face more restrictive local legislation.

In addition, where several sets of personal law[2] prescribe different rights and obligations for different groups of women, the data focus on the most populous group, which may mean that restrictions that apply only to minority populations are missed. A detailed explanation of the report's methodology—including all the questions asked and assumptions made—is provided in the data notes.

Women, Business and the Law recognizes the limitations of standardized assumptions, but while such assumptions come at the expense of specificity, they also ensure data comparability.

The data set does not include qualitative assessments. Outcome variables, such as female labor force participation rates, also are not part of the data set, although they are used in the analysis for this report.

Rules and regulations are directly controlled by policy makers—and they are often where policy makers start when

they set out to change the incentives that govern women's economic lives. Women, Business and the Law not only shows where gender differences exist in the law, but it also points to specific laws that may lend themselves to reform. Its quantitative measures support

research on how specific regulations affect women's incentives to participate in economic activity. Moreover, the data set is updated every two years, making it possible to analyze variations over time.

How are the data collected?

The Women, Business and the Law data are based on domestic laws and regulations. The data cover small economies and some of the poorest economies, for which little or no data are available in other data sets. The new areas of coverage are based on consultations across the World Bank Group and with external experts, including international organizations, civil society organizations, academics and private sector actors.

The report's indicators were constructed based on responses from practitioners with expertise in family, labor and criminal law, including lawyers, judges, academics and members of civil society organizations working on gender

FIGURE 2.1 HOW WOMEN, BUSINESS AND THE LAW DATA ARE COLLECTED

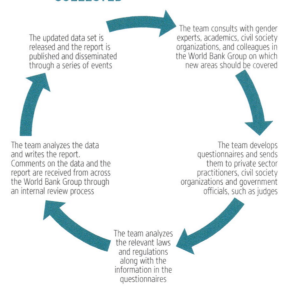

The updated data set is released and the report is published and disseminated through a series of events

The team consults with gender experts, academics, civil society organizations, and colleagues in the World Bank Group on which new areas should be covered

The team analyzes the data and writes the report. Comments on the data and the report are received from across the World Bank Group through an internal review process

The team develops questionnaires and sends them to private sector practitioners, civil society organizations and government officials, such as judges

The team analyzes the relevant laws and regulations along with the information in the questionnaires

issues. The data were collected through several rounds of interaction with these respondents—through responses to questionnaires, conference calls, written correspondence and visits by the team (figure 2.1). The data in this report are current as of June 1, 2017.

In addition to filling out written questionnaires, *Women, Business and the Law* respondents provide references to the relevant laws and regulations. The *Women, Business and the Law* team collects the relevant texts and checks the questionnaire responses for accuracy. All questionnaire responses are verified against codified sources of national law, including laws, statutes, rules, regulations and procedures, in areas such as labor, social security, civil procedure, tax, violence against women, marriage and family, inheritance and others. *Doing Business 2018* surveys were also used to develop some questions in the building credit indicator.

Women, Business and the Law requires each legal data point to have a citable legal source, and sources for every data point are posted on the project website (http://wbl.worldbank.org) to ensure that the data are transparent. More detailed data on each economy, including links to the legal sources, are also provided on the *Women, Business and the Law* website. Feedback is welcome and can be offered through the website.

What's next?

During the two-year period between the publication of this report and the *Women, Business and the Law 2020* report, the team will carry out a robust consultative process with a variety of stakeholders on the optimal design and construction of a gender equality index through which women's entrepreneurship and employment can be examined. The indicator-level scoring presented in this report is the first step in this process.

Notes

1 Palau and the United States have signed but not ratified the Convention.

2 Personal law refers to non-customary legal systems that stem from tradition or doctrinal texts, which are sometimes uncodified.

WOMEN'S FINANCIAL INCLUSION
AND THE LAW

In 2014 Madame Ngetsi wanted to formalize a small business that she was running in Kinshasa, the Democratic Republic of Congo. To do so, she would need to register her company and open a bank account. Along the way, she might need a loan to grow her business. But legally, Madame Ngetsi needed her husband's permission to do any of these activities under the family code that existed at the time.

Discriminatory laws can affect **women's demand** for financial services and impede their ability **to save, borrow, pay** or **insure themselves** against risk.

This is just one example of how women's decision making is limited by laws interfering with their economic activities. Such laws can affect women's ability to save, borrow, pay or insure themselves against risk.

Discriminatory laws can affect women's demand for financial services. For example, limited access to and control over property constrain women's ability to provide collateral for loans. Similarly, gender differences in getting identification can make it more difficult for women to open bank accounts, especially where there are stringent identification requirements to do so.

Financial inclusion involves access to and usage of various financial services, such as savings, payments, credit and insurance from formal service providers. Basic financial inclusion can entail a simple deposit account at a bank or a transaction on a mobile money service account. It can also encompass loans from formal financial institutions or insurance products that allow people to manage their financial risks.

The World Bank Group's 2014 Global Findex database revealed that although almost all OECD high-income economies have universal access to financial services, only slightly more than half of developing economies do. Globally 61% of adults have an account at a financial institution. However, 2 billion people remain unbanked, of which more than half are women. When it comes to women's financial inclusion, a large gender gap in access to and usage of financial services persists.[1]

Identification matters for financial inclusion

Know Your Customer (KYC) requirements oblige financial institutions to verify a customer's identity by checking and confirming identification. Such rules are an important part of anti-money laundering and countering the financing of terrorism regimes, and help preserve the integrity of financial markets. However, they can sometimes exclude segments of the population who are more likely to lack identification—such as low-income populations or women. A survey conducted by the Alliance for Financial Inclusion reports that 25% of the respondents perceived KYC requirements as a barrier to women.[2]

Gender inequality can play a role in making access to identification more burdensome for women, as some laws and regulations make it more difficult for women to obtain a national identity (ID) card or passport or register the birth of a child in the same way as men (box 3.1). *Women, Business and the Law* data show there are at least 48 legal differences for women compared with men when applying for an ID or passport in the economies examined.

Specifically, married women cannot get an ID card in the same way as married men in 11 economies (concentrated in South Asia, the Middle East and North Africa and Sub-Saharan Africa). In Pakistan, for example, a married woman must provide her marriage contract and her husband's ID card or an electronic confirmation by her husband when renewing her national ID card.

However, change is occurring. In 2016, Senegal reformed regulations imposing additional requirements on married women when applying for ID cards. The new regulations no longer require married women's ID cards to include their husband's name. Consequently, a wife no longer must provide supporting documentation to establish her husband's name, and procedures are now the same for men and women.

Tiered KYC requirements are a promising solution to help women with limited proof of identity and other necessary documentation, such as proof of address and source of income, open basic savings and payment accounts. Tiered KYC regimes use a risk-based approach where the requirements are less stringent for low-value or simplified bank accounts that can have a balance cap or carry transaction and access restrictions. A high level of due diligence is not necessarily appropriate and economic for these small accounts.[3] Instead, knowledge of the customer's identity (customer identification and verification) and the ability to track transactions are often sufficient.

Under this framework, more relaxed, small-value accounts are the ideal tool to allow access to financial services to new (low-income) customers. Several economies, including Ghana and Tanzania, have implemented a tier-based approach for KYC rules.

The use of innovative and secure means of identification, such as biometric IDs, yield specific benefits for women, allowing them to overcome distribution barriers for national IDs and facilitating the delivery of digital financial services. A biometric ID is an identity card containing

---

BOX 3.1   REGISTERING A BIRTH

Having a birth certificate—and the registration that precedes it—is foundational. Birth certificates are the first step toward a legal identity and are required to obtain passports, ID cards, marriage certificates and driver's licenses. Birth certificates may also be needed to obtain family allowances, social security and insurance, enroll children in school and access credit and pensions.

However, in some economies, mothers cannot register the birth of a child in the same way as fathers. In Greece, the father is legally obligated to register the child; the mother needs a special mandate by a notary attorney to do so. In Barbados, Fiji and Namibia, a mother can legally register the newborn only when the father is dead, absent or incapable. And in The Gambia, the father is legally required to register children born within a marriage, and the mother has this legal responsibility for children born outside marriage.

Most economies require a parent to show notification of a live birth, issued by the hospital, and some form of personal identification. Economies without robust civil identification systems often allow proof of identity through witnesses, such as village elders, teachers or religious leaders. In El Salvador and Senegal, for example, two witnesses with an identity document can attest for the registration when the parents lack documentation. By contrast, Morocco requires extensive documentation, including a copy of the mother's birth certificate, family book and records of the child's first vaccinations.

Unmarried parents must overcome significant hurdles where the system does not recognize children born outside marriage—as is the case in Bahrain and Nepal—or requires additional procedures for registering their birth, as in Iraq, Jordan and Morocco, where an unmarried parent must obtain a court order to register their child.

Birth registration and birth certificates should be free, to encourage parents to register their children and get a certificate. However, some economies, such as Lebanon, Pakistan and Tajikistan, charge for registering births.

Other economies do not charge for registering births, but do charge for the birth certificates, including Australia, Barbados, Côte d'Ivoire, Ecuador, Ethiopia, Malawi, the Philippines, Rwanda, Senegal and Togo.

Although many economies are moving toward eliminating costs for birth registration within the required timeframe (which can range from 10 days to 1 year), some still charge for late registration. For example, in Kenya, birth registration is free if done within 6 months, but a fee is charged after that. The aim is to encourage early registration. However, the fee can deter parents from registering births at all. Other economies that charge for birth registration after the required timeframe include Angola, El Salvador, Ghana, Jamaica, Lesotho, Sri Lanka, Tajikistan and Vietnam.

No additional documentation should be necessary to register a child after the required timeframe. But in Burkina Faso a judgment is needed to register a child after the time limit of 2 months and in Lebanon, after 1 year. Meanwhile, in 2013 Indonesia's Constitutional Court removed a requirement that the General Courts must provide a statement to get a birth certificate for a child over age 1.

Sources: Women, Business and the Law database; Sumner 2015.

biometric information, such as fingerprints and facial patterns, which can be easily and quickly verified online.

In India, until recently, banks had to perform KYC processes each time a financial interaction occurred, even if the same customer wanted to open two accounts at the same bank. Now, a photograph and fingerprint or signature are sufficient documentation to open a restricted bank account, if the holder applies within a year for Aadhar, a unique registration number issued by the national ID program. This number is replacing the myriad identification cards that were utilized earlier for different purposes. Banks and other institutions can easily access the Aadhar database for their KYC procedures.[4]

Laws restricting women's agency and mobility can hinder their financial inclusion

Laws can limit women's legal capacity through requiring permission—usually from a husband—to carry out everyday activities. This can constrain women's financial inclusion. *Women, Business and the Law* data show that in 31 economies, the husband is legally considered head of household, which can have implications ranging from government land allocation to who receives government benefits within a household.

At a more basic level, Chad, Guinea-Bissau and Niger are now the only economies where married women still need permission to open a bank account. In Equatorial Guinea, a wife still needs her husband's permission to sign a contract.

Legal restrictions can limit women's mobility and decision making. In 31 economies, married women cannot choose where to live in the same way as married men. In 18 economies, they cannot work outside the home in the same way as a married man. And in 17 economies, married women cannot travel outside the home in the same way as married men (Afghanistan, Bahrain, Brunei Darussalam, the Arab Republic of Egypt, the Islamic Republic of Iran, Iraq, Jordan, Kuwait, Malaysia, Oman, Qatar, Saudi Arabia, Sudan, Syria, the United Arab Emirates, West Bank and Gaza and the Republic of Yemen). Where this is the case, women may have difficulties traveling to banks or other service providers and may not be able to earn an independent income or live in a place that offers the opportunity to work or access services.

Laws restricting women's economic independence also restrict their access and usage of financial services. For example, where married women are prohibited from working, women are less likely to have accounts, formal credit or savings. Where women can be head of household or women are not required by law to obey their husbands, women are more likely to use formal financial products.[5]

Where married women cannot choose where to live in the same way as men, gender gaps in financial inclusion are higher for women's access to bank accounts and their capacity to borrow from a financial institution (figure 3.1).

FIGURE 3.1   **GENDER GAPS IN ACCOUNT OWNERSHIP AND CAPACITY TO BORROW FROM A FINANCIAL INSTITUTION ARE HIGHER WHERE WOMEN'S MOBILITY IS CONSTRAINED**

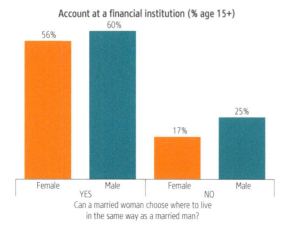

Account at a financial institution (% age 15+)

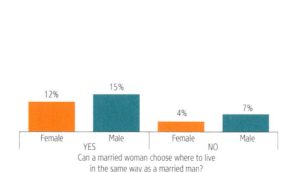

Borrowed from a financial institution (% age 15+)

Sources: *Women, Business and the Law* and Global Findex (2014) databases.
Note: The differences in the percentages illustrated for females (% age 15+) are statistically significant at the 1% level after accounting for the log of GNI per capita (2015), domestic credit to private sector (% of GDP), financial system deposits to GDP (%), and the rule of law (2016). Sources for the control variables include the World Development Indicators and the Gallup country databases. Regression analyses are based on 126 economies for which data are available. These statistical relationships should not be interpreted as causal.

Barriers to women's access and control over property can affect their financial inclusion

Evidence suggests that gender differences in asset ownership are an influential factor affecting women's ability to access credit. Limited access to assets is also a major reason why women are rejected for loans, as banks can be reluctant to lend to customers who lack traditional collateral.[6]

Family, inheritance and land laws are important in allocating assets between men and women. These laws come into play at different stages of a woman's lifecycle, determining what a daughter will inherit from her parents and what assets a woman can access during her marriage and as a divorcee or widow. Where these laws are favorable, women have greater economic independence.[7]

Most economies establish a default marital property regime determining the allocation of assets between spouses. Common options are full or partial community property regimes or separate property regimes. In full community property regimes, the property of either spouse acquired before and during marriage is treated as joint property regardless of who paid for it. In partial community property regimes assets acquired before marriage are regarded as the separate property of the acquiring spouse and assets acquired after marriage are regarded as the couple's joint property. In separate property regimes, each spouse retains ownership and control over property they paid for. *Women, Business and the Law* data shows that 6 economies have a default full community property regime; 77 economies have a default partial community property regime; and 75 have a default separate property regime.

A study on gender asset and wealth gaps in Ecuador, Ghana and the Indian state of Karnataka used household asset surveys to estimate married women's share of couples' wealth. It found that in Ecuador married women owned 44% of couples' wealth; in Ghana they owned 19%; and in Karnataka they owned 9%. The much larger share of couples' wealth held by married women in Ecuador was explained by the country's partial community property regime, where most assets are owned jointly by wives and husbands. Married women's smaller share of couples' wealth in Ghana and Karnataka was largely explained by their separation of property regimes, where assets are not jointly owned.[8]

Although separate property regimes are gender neutral, they can penalize women who do not build up an income during marriage. This effect can be mitigated in divorce by the legal recognition of nonmonetary contributions such as unpaid care. The recognition of nonmonetary contributions within separate property regimes may also make a difference to women's financial inclusion. Gender gaps in women having a debit card and using it are larger in separate property regimes that do not recognize nonmonetary contributions than in those that do (figure 3.2).

In Morocco and Tunisia, the default marital property regime is separation of property. Both economies have introduced an option of partial community property in reforms to the family law—Morocco in 2004 and Tunisia in 1998. However,

FIGURE 3.2   GAPS ARE SMALLER IN ACCESS TO AND USE OF DEBIT CARDS WHERE WOMEN'S NONMONETARY CONTRIBUTIONS ARE RECOGNIZED IN SEPARATE PROPERTY REGIMES

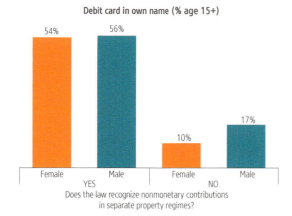

Debit card in own name (% age 15+)

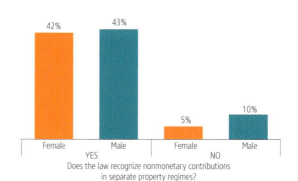

Debit card used in the past year (% age 15+)

Sources: Women, Business and the Law and Global Findex (2014) databases.

Note: The differences in the percentages illustrated for females (% age 15+) are statistically significant at least at the 5% level after accounting for the log of GNI per capita (2015), domestic credit to private sector (% of GDP), financial system deposits to GDP (%), and the rule of law (2016). Sources for the control variables include the World Development Indicators and the Gallup country databases. Regression analyses are based on 44 economies for which data are available. These statistical relationships should not be interpreted as causal.

uptake has been low partly due to lack of awareness, social norms and complex procedures.[9] The World Bank's *World Development Report 2015* highlights how changing a default option can change norms, such as those around employees' adoption of pension plans. Making enrollment in a pension plan the default option—so that employees must choose to opt out—is a way to ensure that most employees end up being covered.[10] Similarly, making a partial community property regime the default option could increase uptake.

Likewise, the recognition of women's unpaid work—through recognizing nonmonetary contributions—should be a default setting, whether through a joint property regime or by adding specific laws on nonmonetary contributions to separate property regimes.

Removing the husband's sole control over property is also critical. The reform of the family code in Ethiopia, which did away with the husband's sole control over marital property and the need for his permission to work outside the home, was linked to more women working in full-time jobs outside the home and in more productive sectors.[11]

Unequal inheritance rights are also a barrier to women's financial inclusion

Access to assets through inheritance is also important for women and girls. Widows may depend on inheritance for financial security, and daughters may become more economically independent and have greater educational opportunities if they are allowed equal inheritance rights with sons.

In 36 of the 189 economies covered by *Women, Business and the Law*, widows do not have the same inheritance rights as widowers. And 39 of the 189 economies measured prevent daughters from inheriting in the same way as sons.

Improving women's inheritance rights can lead to better outcomes. One study in India found improved inheritance rights led to a greater likelihood of women having bank accounts.[12] Women are also more likely to have housing finance where inheritance rights are equal for widows and daughters (figure 3.3). One possible explanation for this is women may have fewer assets to use as collateral where inheritance rights are unequal.

It is also important to look at how accounts transfer when the account holder dies. In Kenya, for example, it is difficult for widows to get access to their deceased husband's bank account. Safaricom's policy on M-Pesa and M-Shwari accounts provides that account balances stay in the deceased's account until they are claimed. But wives cannot automatically claim their husband's account money. The policy requires that when an M-Pesa subscriber dies with a will, the next of kin must present copies of the death certificate, ID and grant of probate to Safaricom. If an M-Pesa subscriber dies without a will, the next of kin must also

present letters of administration.[13] If no one claims the money within two years, it is transferred to the Unclaimed Financial Assets Authority, a government institution. In 2015, Safaricom handed over $4.8 million to the Unclaimed Financial Assets Authority.[14]

Allowing a husband to name his wife as a beneficiary at the time the account is established can sidestep these procedures and make a difference for widows.

Lack of credit histories can hinder women's access to finance

Access to formal credit relies heavily on asset-based lending, but where women have limited access to property they are less likely to use it as collateral. Information-sharing institutions, such as credit bureaus and registries, are important determinants of private credit development.[15] Where they collect the types

---

FIGURE 3.3   **GENDER GAPS ARE SMALLER IN HAVING A MORTGAGE WHERE INHERITANCE RIGHTS ARE EQUAL FOR WOMEN AND GIRLS**

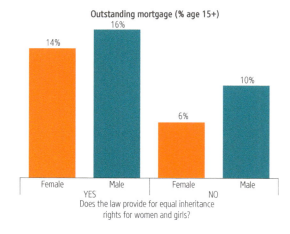

Outstanding mortgage (% age 15+)

Does the law provide for equal inheritance rights for women and girls?

YES — Female 14%, Male 16%
NO — Female 6%, Male 10%

Sources: Women, Business and the Law and Global Findex (2014) databases.
Note: The difference in the percentages illustrated for females (% age 15+) is statistically significant at the 10% level after accounting for the log of GNI per capita (2015), domestic credit to private sector (% of GDP), financial system deposits to GDP (%), and the rule of law (2016). Sources for the control variables include the World Development Indicators and the Gallup country databases. Regression analysis is based on 120 economies for which data are available. This statistical relationship should not be interpreted as causal.

of reputation collateral that women are more likely to have, such as a record of successful repayments to microfinance institutions or retailers, this may help women build their credit histories and ultimately access finance.

But in many developing economies, credit bureaus and registries are uncommon. Where they do exist, they may limit themselves to covering high loan amounts that preclude the vast number of female borrowers who have smaller loans. Among the 189 economies covered by *Women, Business and the Law*, 50 do not have a public credit registry or private credit bureau that covers more than 5% of the adult population.

Women, Business and the Law data show that microfinance repayment data are collected and distributed by credit bureaus and registries in 83 economies, with 75 of these sharing positive credit information such as on-time payments and the amounts of loans—allowing microfinance borrowers to leverage successful repayment histories to build reputation collateral (figure 3.4).

Bureaus and registries in 57 economies share retail payment data, with 43 sharing positive credit information. For utility repayment data, the total is 60 economies, of which 41 require the provision of positive credit information. In a minority of economies, 23 of the 189, all three institutions (microfinance institutions, retailers and utility companies) provide positive credit repayment data to credit agencies.

Women's leadership is limited in the banking sector and decision-making bodies

Recent studies show how female participation in the banking sector and decision-making bodies can have a positive impact on financial inclusion. For example, access to the internet and mobile phones and financial inclusion

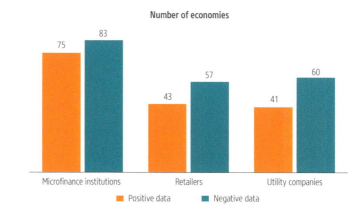

FIGURE 3.4 **ECONOMIES WHERE NON-BANK INSTITUTIONS REPORT POSITIVE AND NEGATIVE CREDIT INFORMATION**

Number of economies

	Microfinance institutions	Retailers	Utility companies
Positive data	75	43	41
Negative data	83	57	60

■ Positive data   ■ Negative data

Source: *Women, Business and the Law* database.

are especially linked to the presence of women in leadership roles.[16] Studies on female leadership in other decision-making bodies have shown impacts on issues affecting women. For example, female representation in national parliaments at levels of 25% and above makes it more likely for discriminatory property laws to be reformed in the next 5 years compared with 15 years before such levels of representation.[17]

When it comes to corporate boards, some research links gender diversity to better company performance, including in areas such as greater returns on sales and assets.[18] *Women, Business and the Law* data show that 11 economies have legal quotas for women on corporate boards (Belgium, France, Germany, Iceland, India, Israel, Italy, the Netherlands, Norway and Spain), with the most recent addition being the United Arab Emirates which introduced a quota of 20% for publicly listed companies in 2016.

A 2016 study across 26 OECD countries shows the evolution in the number of female board members of central banks.[19] As of January 2016, women represented only 14% of board members. Forty-two percent of the central banks covered had no women on their board. This

level has remained constant since 2003. Comparable findings emerge from a 2017 study analyzing central bank boards, with a broader sample of 112 countries from different income groups.[20] Women represent only 15% of the board members in these countries. Thirty percent have no female board members, and 48% have less than 10%. Another 2017 study shows that since 1950, only 56 women have chaired a central bank.[21] In 2015 only 16 women (8.7%) chaired a central bank, of a total of 184 worldwide.

Women are also underrepresented at senior levels in the financial sector overall. Recent data gathered from 50 of the largest banks, insurers, asset managers and professional services firms show that only 25% of top executives are female.[22]

The way forward

It is important to make the links between women's financial inclusion and the legal environment as early as possible. Consider the example of Madame Ngetsi in the Democratic Republic of Congo. The good news is she can now open a bank account, get a loan, sign a contract, register her business and register land without any need for her husband's permission, following reforms to the family code in 2016.

But there is still work to be done. Husbands still control marital property and they are still legally the head of household. Prevailing social norms did not allow for a complete overhaul of barriers to women's financial inclusion, but rather incremental steps. This is often the pattern of legal reform, even in high-income economies. Married women in France gained equal rights to work outside the home in 1965, become head of household in 1970, and administer property in 1985.

Legal reform is a crucial element that needs to be embedded in broader strategies to advance women's financial inclusion. According to surveyed members of the Alliance for Financial Inclusion, the main barriers identified for women are financial literacy (75%), collateral requirements (66%) and the sociocultural environment.[23] Regulatory requirements can prevent women from accessing financial services. Consequently, some economies, such as Paraguay, have chosen to include an assessment of the legal and regulatory framework in their national financial inclusion strategy.[24]

More research is needed on many related issues, such as how labor laws, the gender wage gap or childcare can affect women's access to and use of financial services. Digital financial services have the potential to close gender gaps but may still be hindered by the same basic constraints: women's lack of assets and legal autonomy can prevent women from reaping all the benefits that technology can offer. Understanding and tackling these legal constraints should be part of an overall strategy to accelerate women's financial inclusion. Data on gender-differentiated laws can help identify the gaps and monitor progress in closing these gaps over time.

Notes

1   Demirgüç-Kunt et al. 2015.

2   AFI 2017a.

3   Gelb 2016.

4   Anderson et al. 2016; Gelb 2016.

5   Demirgüç-Kunt, Klapper and Singer 2013.

6   Stupnytska et al. 2014.

7   Thomas, Contreras and Frankenberg 2002.

8   Deere et al. 2013.

9   World Bank 2015.

10   World Bank Group 2015.

11   Hallward-Driemeier and Gajigo 2013.

12   Deininger et al. 2014.

13   "M-PESA Next of Kin Claim," Safaricom, last accessed March 5, 2018, https://www.safaricom.co.ke/personal/m-pesa/m-pesa-legal/m-pesa-next-of-kin-claim.

14   "Ksh500m Unclaimed M-Pesa Deposits," Business Today, February 4, 2015, https://businesstoday.co.ke/ksh500m-unclaimed-m-pesa-deposits.

15   Djankov, McLiesh and Shleifer 2007.

16   Woetzel et al. 2015.

17   Hallward-Driemeier, Hasan and Bodgdana Rusu 2013.

18   Isidro and Sobral 2015.

19   Charlety, Romelli and Santacreu-Vasut 2017.

20   Romelli, Masciandaro and Profeta 2017.

21   Diouf and Pepin 2017.

22   Noonan et al. 2017.

23   AFI 2017b.

24   AFI 2015.

References

AFI (Alliance for Financial Inclusion). 2015. *National Financial Inclusion Strategies. Current State of Practice.* AFI, Kuala Lumpur.

———. 2017a. "Integrating Gender and Women's Financial Inclusion into National Strategies." Guideline Note 27, AFI, Kuala Lumpur.

———. 2017b. "Sex-Disaggregated Data Toolkit: How to Leverage Sex-Disaggregated Financial Inclusion Data to Accelerate Women's Financial Inclusion." Guideline Note 26, AFI, Kuala Lumpur.

Anderson, C. Leigh, Pierre Biscaye, Sarah Coney, Eugenia Ho, Brian Hutchinson, Mia Neidhardt and Travis Reynolds. 2016. *ITU-T Focus Group Digital Financial Services: Review of National Identity Programs.* Geneva: International Telecommunication Union.

Charlety, Patricia, Davide Romelli and Estefania Santacreu-Vasut. 2017. "Appointments to Central Bank Boards: Does Gender Matter?" *Economics Letters* 155: 59–61.

Deere, Carmen Diana, Abena D. Oduro, Hema Swaminathan and Cheryl Doss. 2013. "Property Rights and the Gender Distribution of Wealth in Ecuador, Ghana and India." *The Journal of Economic Inequality* 11 (2): 249-65.

Deininger, Klaus, Hari Nagarajan, Fang Xia and Songqing Jin. 2014. "Inheritance Law Reform, Empowerment, and Human Capital Accumulation: Second-Generation Effects from India." Policy Research Working Paper 7086, World Bank Group, Washington, DC.

Demirgüç-Kunt, Asli, Leora Klapper and Dorothe Singer. 2013. "Financial Inclusion and Legal Discrimination against Women: Evidence from Developing Countries." Policy Research Working Paper 6416, World Bank, Washington, DC.

Demirgüç-Kunt, Asli, Leora Klapper, Dorothe Singer and Peter Van Oudheusden. 2015. "The Global Findex Database 2014: Measuring Financial Inclusion around the World." Policy Research Working Paper 7255, World Bank, Washington, DC.

Diouf, Ibrahima, and Dominique Pepin. 2017. "Gender and Central Banking." *Economic Modelling* 61: 193–206.

Djankov, Simeon, Caralee McLiesh and Andrei Shleifer. 2007. "Private Credit in 129 Countries." Journal of Financial Economics 12 (2): 77-99.

Gelb, Alan. 2016. "Balancing Financial Integrity with Financial Inclusion: The Risk-Based Approach to 'Know Your Customer.'" Policy Paper 074, Center for Global Development, Washington, DC.

Hallward-Driemeier, Mary, and Ousman Gajigo. 2013. "Strengthening Economic Rights and Women's Occupational Choice: The Impact of Reforming Ethiopia's Family Law." Policy Research Working Paper 6695, World Bank, Washington, DC.

Hallward-Driemeier, Mary, Tazeen Hasan and Anca Bodgdana Rusu. 2013. "Women's Legal Rights over 50 Years: Progress, Stagnation or Regression?" Policy Research Working Paper 6616, World Bank, Washington, DC.

Isidro, H. & Sobral, M. 2015. "The Effects of Women on Corporate Boards on Firm Value, Financial Performance, and Ethical and Social Compliance." *Journal of Business Ethics* 132(1): 1–19.

Noonan, Laura, Alan Smith, David Blood and Martin Stabe. 2017. "Women Still Miss Out on Management in Finance: FT Research Reveals Failure to Close Gender Gap in Middle and Senior Roles." *Financial Times*, FT Series: Management's Missing Women.

Romelli, Davide, Donato Masciandaro and Paola Profeta. 2017. "Gender and Monetary Policymaking: Trends, Drivers and Effects." Conference on Gender and Macroeconomics, International Monetary Fund, Washington, DC.

Stupnytska, Anna, Kathryn Koch, Amy MacBeath, Sandra Lawson and Kathy Matsui. 2014. *Giving Credit Where It Is Due: How Closing the Credit Gap for Women-Owned SMEs Can Drive Global Growth*. Goldman Sachs.

Thomas, Duncan, Dante Contreras and Elizabeth Frankenberg. 2002. "Distribution of Power within the Household and Child Health." Unpublished.

Woetzel, Jonathan, Anu Madgavkar, Kweilin Ellingrud, Eric Labile, Sandrine Devillard, Eric Kutcher, James Manyika, Richard Dobbs and Mekala Krishnan. 2015. *The Power of Parity: How Advancing Women's Equality Can Add $12 Trillion to Global Growth*. McKinsey Global Institute.

World Bank. 2015. *Morocco—Mind the Gap: Empowering Women for a More Open, Inclusive and Prosperous Society*. World Bank, Washington, DC.

World Bank Group. 2015. *Women, Business and the Law 2016: Getting to Equal*. Washington, DC: World Bank Group.

SUMMARIES
OF *WOMEN, BUSINESS AND THE LAW* REFORMS

In the two-year period from May 1, 2015 through June 1, 2017, *Women, Business and the Law* recorded 87 regulatory reforms towards gender equality in employment and entrepreneurial activity in scored areas, with 65 economies implementing at least one reform moving towards gender equality.

+ Reform increasing gender parity

O Reform neutral to gender parity

✖ Reform decreasing gender parity

Afghanistan

+ Protecting women from violence
Afghanistan now prohibits sexual harassment in employment and education. It also established criminal penalties and civil remedies for sexual harassment in employment.

Albania

+ Getting a job
Albania introduced 3 days of paid paternity leave. The new labor code also mandates equal remuneration for men and women who do work of equal value.

+ Providing incentives to work
Albania's new labor code also guarantees that after maternity leave, employees can return to their job or to an equivalent job on terms that are no less favorable than before the leave.

Algeria

+ Protecting women from violence
Algeria criminalized domestic violence, including physical, psychological and economic violence.

Angola

✖ Getting a job
Angola increased the number of legal restrictions on women's work.

+ Building credit
Additionally, Angola now prohibits discrimination by creditors in financial transactions based on gender.

Azerbaijan

+ Getting a job
Azerbaijan is gradually increasing and equalizing the ages at which men and women can retire and receive pension benefits.

Bahrain

+ Protecting women from violence
Bahrain introduced its first domestic violence law, which protects spouses and family members and covers physical, sexual, psychological and economic violence.

Bangladesh

✖ Getting a job
Bangladesh now prohibits women from carrying, lifting or removing weighty goods and instruments. It also establishes different weight-lifting thresholds for men and women.

Bhutan

+ Providing incentives to work
Bhutan increased the maximum amount of educational expenses that can be deducted from income taxes.

+ Building credit
Bhutan improved access to credit information by distributing positive and negative payment data from utility companies.

Bolivia

+ Building credit
Bolivia enhanced access to credit information by starting to report data from utility companies.

Bosnia and Herzegovina

+ Getting a job
Bosnia and Herzegovina eliminated several restrictions on women's employment, including in jobs deemed arduous, jobs deemed hazardous and underwater work. It also eliminated the possibility for men and women to retire early and receive partial pension benefits, which was previously unequal.

+ Going to court
Bosnia and Herzegovina adopted the Law on Free Legal Aid in 2016 to provide legal assistance in civil procedures.

Botswana

+ Building credit

Botswana improved access to credit information by beginning to distribute data from utility companies, including positive and negative data.

Brunei Darussalam

+ Building credit

Brunei Darussalam improved access to credit information by distributing data from two utility companies.

Bulgaria

+ ✖ Getting a job

Bulgaria removed all restrictions on women's employment. It is also gradually increasing and equalizing the ages at which men and women can retire with full pension benefits.

However, the ages at which men and women can retire with partial pension benefits are now unequal.

Burundi

+ Protecting women from violence

Burundi introduced civil remedies for sexual harassment in employment.

Cameroon

+ Protecting women from violence

Cameroon adopted a new criminal code that covers sexual harassment in employment and education, and established criminal penalties for sexual harassment.

Chad

+ Protecting women from violence

Chad adopted a new criminal code that aggravates penalties for domestic violence and criminalizes sexual harassment in employment.

China

+ Getting a job

China introduced 3 days of paid paternity leave. It also now entitles all women—regardless of age—to 128 days of paid maternity leave. Previously, women younger than age 25 were entitled to 98 days of maternity leave, whereas women older than age 25 were entitled to 128 days.

+ Building credit

China improved access to credit information by reporting payment histories from utility companies, including positive and negative data.

Colombia

+ Getting a job

Colombia increased paid maternity leave from 98 to 126 days. It also removed restrictions on women's employment in mining and jobs deemed hazardous and arduous.

Congo, Dem. Rep.

+ Accessing institutions

The Democratic Republic of Congo reformed its family code to allow married women to sign a contract, get a job, open a bank account and register a business in the same way as married men. It also removed the obligation for a married woman to obey her husband and allows spouses to choose the marital home mutually.

+ Getting a job

The Democratic Republic of Congo lifted restrictions on women's ability to work at night in public or private industrial establishments. It also now mandates nondiscrimination based on gender in various aspects of employment, including hiring and promotions.

+ Building credit

The Democratic Republic of Congo now prohibits discrimination based on gender in access to credit.

Côte d'Ivoire

+ Providing incentives to work

Côte d'Ivoire made primary school compulsory for all children ages 6–16 years.

+ Going to court

Côte d'Ivoire also established a small claims procedure in 2015, and raised the maximum amount for small claims in 2017.

Dominican Republic

+ Getting a job

The Dominican Republic increased the length of paid maternity leave from 84 to 98 days.

Ecuador

+ Using property

Ecuador equalized men's and women's property rights by repealing the provision favoring husbands' decisions in cases of disagreement between spouses when administering assets during marriage.

✖ Going to court

A new code of civil procedure eliminated small claims procedures in Ecuador.

El Salvador

+ Getting a job

El Salvador increased the length of paid maternity leave from 84 to 112 days.

Ethiopia

+ Going to court

Ethiopia now requires the Attorney General to provide free legal aid services to women and others who lack the financial capacity to institute civil actions in federal court.

Fiji

✖ Building credit

The credit bureau in Fiji suspended operations and no longer reports data from utilities and retailers, therefore decreasing access to credit.

Guinea

✚ Building credit

Guinea prohibited discrimination based on gender and marital status when accessing goods and services, including financial services.

✚ Protecting women from violence

Guinea criminalized sexual harassment, including in the workplace.

Guyana

✚ Building credit

Guyana improved access to credit information by expanding the credit bureau's coverage so that it now covers more than 5% of the population. It reports data from utility companies and retailers.

Honduras

◯ Using property

Partial community is now the default marital property regime in Honduras. Both spouses must agree when administering property during marriage.

Hungary

✖ Going to court

Hungary eliminated small claims courts and procedures; ordinary procedures now apply in the lowest courts.

Iceland

✚ Building credit

Iceland enhanced access to credit information by starting to report data from utility companies. It also prohibited discrimination based on gender when accessing goods and services, including financial services.

India

✚ ✖ Getting a job

India increased the length of paid maternity leave from 84 to 182 days.

But as employers pay the full cost of maternity leave, the cost of hiring women of childbearing age has increased from the employer's perspective.

Indonesia

✚ Going to court

Indonesia established a small claims procedure in 2015.

Iran, Islamic Rep.

✚ Building credit

The Islamic Republic of Iran improved access to credit information by reporting data on credit payments from an automobile retailer.

Iraq

✚ Accessing institutions

Iraq enacted a new passport law in 2015 that introduces electronic passports. The application process is now the same for men and women and does not require women to bring a guardian.

✚ ✖ Getting a job

Iraq increased the length of paid maternity leave from 72 to 98 days. Further, its new labor code prohibits discrimination based on gender in various aspects of employment, including hiring and dismissal.

However, the new labor code allows employers to terminate employees' contracts when they reach the retirement age, which is unequal for men and women.

✚ Providing incentives to work

Iraq now guarantees workers returning from maternity leave the same position or a similar position with the same wage.

✚ Protecting women from violence

Iraq enacted a new labor code that specifically addresses and criminalizes sexual harassment in employment.

Ireland

✚ Getting a job

Ireland introduced 10 days of paid paternity leave.

Israel

✚ Getting a job

Israel increased the length of paid maternity leave from 98 to 105 days, and now allows the mother to transfer one week of maternity leave to the father.

Italy

✚ Getting a job

Italy increased paid paternity leave from 1 to 2 days.

Kenya

✚ Going to court

Kenya's new Legal Aid Act provides legal aid services in civil matters.

✚ Building credit

Kenya improved access to credit information by distributing data from two utility companies that report positive and negative payment information.

✚ Protecting women from violence

Kenya enacted its first domestic violence law, which protects family members, spouses and former spouses and partners (including non-cohabiting partners) from physical, sexual, psychological and economic abuse.

Kiribati

+ Getting a job

Kiribati's new labor code lifted all restrictions on women's employment, including restrictions on working at night and in mining.

+ Providing incentives to work

It also guarantees employees returning from maternity leave the same or an equivalent position.

Kosovo

+ Going to court

Kosovo established an anti-discrimination commission that allows women to submit complaints of discrimination to an Ombudsperson.

+ Building credit

Kosovo also enacted a new nondiscrimination law in 2015, which introduced marital status as a category protected from discrimination when accessing credit.

Latvia

+ Building credit

Latvia improved access to credit information by launching a private credit bureau. It reports payment data from utility companies and retailers.

Lesotho

+ Building credit

Lesotho expanded the credit bureau's coverage to include more than 5% of the population. The bureau reports data from both utility companies and retailers.

Liberia

+ Getting a job

Liberia increased the length of paid maternity leave from 90 to 98 days. Further, the new labor code mandates equal remuneration for work of equal value, as well as prohibits discrimination based on gender in various aspects of employment, including hiring, promotions and dismissal.

+ Providing incentives to work

Liberia's new labor code also guarantees employees returning from maternity leave an equivalent position.

Lithuania

+ Protecting women from violence

Lithuania prohibited sexual harassment in education and established civil remedies for sexual harassment in the workplace.

Luxembourg

+ Getting a job

Luxembourg increased the percentage of wages received during parental leave from 77% to 100%.

Macedonia, FYR

+ Building credit

The former Yugoslav Republic of Macedonia improved access to credit information by beginning to distribute data from retailers, including positive and negative data.

Malawi

+ Building credit

Malawi improved access to credit information by establishing a new credit bureau that reports data collected from utility companies.

Malaysia

+ Protecting women from violence

Malaysia now allows victims of sexual harassment to seek civil remedies.

Maldives

+ Building credit

Maldives prohibited discrimination based on gender and marital status when accessing financial services.

Marshall Islands

+ Going to court

Established in 2015, the Human Rights Committee of the Marshall Islands receives complaints of discrimination based on gender.

Mauritius

+ Getting a job

Mauritius increased the length of maternity leave from 84 to 98 days.

Moldova

+ Getting a job

Moldova introduced 10 days of paid paternity leave. It is also gradually increasing and equalizing the ages at which men and women can retire and receive full pension benefits.

Mongolia

+ Getting a job

Mongolia is gradually increasing and equalizing the ages at which men and women can retire and receive pension benefits.

Namibia

+ Building credit

Namibia enhanced access to credit information by starting to report data from utility companies.

New Zealand

+ Getting a job

New Zealand replaced maternity leave with parental leave and increased it from 112 to 126 days.

Nigeria

+ Building credit

Nigeria improved access to credit information by beginning to distribute data from utility companies, including positive and negative data.

Panama

+ Getting a job

Panama introduced 3 days of paid paternity leave.

Paraguay

+ Getting a job

Paraguay increased the length of paid maternity leave from 63 to 98 days and the percentage of wages received during maternity leave from 50% to 75%. It also increased the length of paid paternity leave from 2 to 10 days.

Peru

+ Getting a job

Peru increased the length of paid maternity leave from 90 to 98 days.

Poland

+ ✖ Getting a job

Poland replaced 42 days of paid maternity leave with paid parental leave. It also eliminated all restrictions on women's employment.

However, it reversed a 2012 law that was gradually increasing and equalizing the retirement ages for men and women. Now, the retirement age is set to be lowered back to 60 years for women and 65 for men.

Portugal

+ Getting a job

Portugal increased the length of paid paternity leave from 20 to 25 days.

Rwanda

+ Accessing institutions

Rwanda granted both spouses equal rights to choose the marital home. It also removed the provision designating the husband as "head of household."

+ Getting a job

Rwanda increased the percentage of wages received during maternity leave from 60% to 100%. Additionally, the employer and government now share the cost of maternity benefits, whereas previously the employer was solely responsible.

Senegal

+ Accessing institutions

Senegal enacted a new national identity card law in 2016, introducing biometric cards. The application process is now equal for men and women.

Seychelles

+ Getting a job

The Seychelles introduced 5 days of paid paternity leave.

Singapore

+ Getting a job

Singapore increased the length of paid paternity leave from 5 to 10 days.

Slovak Republic

+ Getting a job

The Slovak Republic increased the percentage of wages received during maternity leave from 65% to 75%.

Slovenia

+ Protecting women from violence

Slovenia prohibited sexual harassment in education.

South Africa

+ Getting a job

South Africa increased the percentage of wages received during maternity leave from 60% to 66%.

Spain

+ Getting a job

Spain increased the length of paid paternity leave from 15 to 30 days.

St. Vincent and the Grenadines

+ ✖ Getting a job

St. Vincent and the Grenadines increased the percentage of wages received during maternity leave from 75% to 87%.

But as employers pay for maternity leave, the cost of hiring women of childbearing age has increased from the employer's perspective.

Sweden

+ Getting a job

Sweden increased the allocation of parental leave for mothers and fathers from 60 to 90 days.

Taiwan, China

+ Providing incentives to work

Taiwan, China's legislation on early childhood education now applies to children ages two and older. Previously, children ages four and older were covered.

+ Building credit

Taiwan, China enhanced access to credit information by starting to report data from retailers, including positive and negative data.

Tajikistan

+ Getting a job

Tajikistan abolished the general restriction on women's ability to work at night.

Tanzania

+ Providing incentives to work
Tanzania made primary education free and compulsory.

+ Going to court
The Legal Aid Act of 2017 mandates legal aid for indigent persons in civil proceedings in Tanzania.

+ Building credit
Tanzania improved access to credit information by distributing data from retailers.

Timor-Leste

+ Getting a job
Timor-Leste introduced a social security system that provides maternity benefits.

Tunisia

+ Building credit
Tunisia strengthened credit reporting by distributing payment information from a telecommunications company.

Turkey

+ Getting a job
Turkey introduced part-time work options for parents until their child's compulsory schooling begins. It also prohibited discrimination based on gender in several aspects of employment, such as promotions.

+ Going to court
Turkey's 2016 law establishing the Human Rights and Equality Institution allows victims to submit complaints about gender discrimination.

Vietnam

+ Getting a job
Vietnam introduced 5 days of paid paternity leave provided by the government.

West Bank and Gaza

+ Getting a job
West Bank and Gaza introduced a social security system that provides maternity benefits and increased the length of paid maternity leave from 70 to 84 days.

+ Providing incentives to work
In 2017, West Bank and Gaza passed a new education law mandating the government to provide one year of free and compulsory public preschool.

Zambia

+ Getting a job
Zambia's Gender Equity and Equality Act now prohibits gender discrimination in various aspects of employment. It also mandates equal remuneration for work of equal value.

+ Going to court
The Gender Equity and Equality Act also established the Gender Equality Commission in Zambia.

+ Building credit
Zambia now prohibits discrimination based on gender and marital status in access to credit.

+ Protecting women from violence
Zambia established civil remedies for sexual harassment in employment.

DATA NOTES

Women, Business and the Law monitors laws and regulations affecting women's ability to be entrepreneurs and employees. Legislation in various areas of the law can directly and indirectly affect women's economic potential.

For the first time, ***Women, Business and the Law*** includes a scoring of **50** questions.

Accordingly, *Women, Business and the Law* captures laws that directly differentiate between men and women, as well as laws that indirectly have a greater impact on women's ability to earn an income, start a business or get a job. *Women, Business and the Law* worked with local experts in each of the 189 covered economies to determine the sources of gender differentiation in the law. The information that local experts provided was checked for accuracy through a rigorous review process. Each answer was cross-verified with primary legal sources, resulting in revision or expansion of the information collected. The data in this report are current as of June 1, 2017.

With regard to women's rights, different economies reflect different cultural norms and values in their legislation. Although progress has been made toward gender parity, restrictions that limit women's economic prospects remain. This report provides objective, easily comparable data to inform dialogue about women's economic rights and opportunities. The methodology was designed to benchmark the legal and regulatory environment for women as entrepreneurs and employees.

Women, Business and the Law provides comparable data across 189 economies, covering the following seven indicators:

- **Accessing institutions** explores women's ability to interact with public authorities and the private sector in the same ways as men, through examining constraints on women's legal capacity.

- **Using property** analyzes women's ability to access and use property based on their ability to own, manage, control and inherit it. It also examines whether legislation accounts for nonmonetary contributions, such as unpaid care for children or the elderly, in distributing assets upon the dissolution of marriage.

- **Getting a job** assesses restrictions on women's ability to work, such as prohibitions on working at night or in certain industries. It also covers laws on maternity, paternity and parental leave, retirement ages, equal remuneration for work of equal value, nondiscrimination at work and flexible work options.

- **Providing incentives to work** examines childcare and tax support, through assessing tax deductions and credits, childcare and primary education.

- **Going to court** explores women's ability to access justice through examining the evidentiary weight of women's testimony, the existence of justice institutions such as anti-discrimination commissions and small claims courts and mandates for legal aid.

- **Building credit** examines credit bureaus and registries that collect information from retailers and utility companies. It also covers nondiscrimination in access to credit based on gender and marital status.

- **Protecting women from violence** considers laws on domestic violence and sexual harassment in education and employment.

Economy characteristics and coverage

The economies covered in this report are listed in table 5.1. Box 5.1 explains the economy characteristics such as regions and income groups.

Women, Business and the Law uses formal laws as a starting point for analysis and the report's indicators were constructed using responses from expert country practitioners in family law, labor law and criminal law, including lawyers, judges, academics and members of civil society organizations working on gender issues. The data were collected through several rounds of interaction with these

| TABLE 5.1 | ECONOMIES COVERED BY *WOMEN, BUSINESS AND THE LAW* |

Region	Total number of economies	Economies covered
East Asia & Pacific	25	Brunei Darussalam; Cambodia; China; Fiji; Hong Kong SAR, China; Indonesia; Kiribati; Lao PDR; Malaysia; Marshall Islands; Micronesia, Fed. Sts.; Mongolia; Myanmar; Palau; Papua New Guinea; Philippines; Samoa; Singapore; Solomon Islands; Taiwan, China; Thailand; Timor-Leste; Tonga; Vanuatu; Vietnam
Europe & Central Asia	25	Albania; Armenia; Azerbaijan; Belarus; Bosnia and Herzegovina; Bulgaria; Croatia; Cyprus; Georgia; Kazakhstan; Kosovo; Kyrgyz Republic; Latvia; Lithuania; Macedonia, FYR; Moldova; Montenegro; Romania; Russian Federation; San Marino; Serbia; Tajikistan; Turkey; Ukraine; Uzbekistan
OECD high income	32	Australia; Austria; Belgium; Canada; Chile; Czech Republic; Denmark; Estonia; Finland; France; Germany; Greece; Hungary; Iceland; Ireland; Israel; Italy; Japan; Korea, Rep.; Luxembourg; Netherlands; New Zealand; Norway; Poland; Portugal; Slovak Republic; Slovenia; Spain; Sweden; Switzerland; United Kingdom; United States
Latin America & Caribbean	32	Antigua and Barbuda; Argentina; Bahamas, The; Barbados; Belize; Bolivia; Brazil; Colombia; Costa Rica; Dominica; Dominican Republic; Ecuador; El Salvador; Grenada; Guatemala; Guyana; Haiti; Honduras; Jamaica; Mexico; Nicaragua; Panama; Paraguay; Peru; Puerto Rico; St. Kitts and Nevis; St. Lucia; St. Vincent and the Grenadines; Suriname; Trinidad and Tobago; Uruguay; Venezuela, RB
Middle East & North Africa	20	Algeria; Bahrain; Djibouti; Egypt, Arab Rep.; Iran, Islamic Rep.; Iraq; Jordan; Kuwait; Lebanon; Libya; Malta; Morocco; Oman; Qatar; Saudi Arabia; Syrian Arab Republic; Tunisia; United Arab Emirates; West Bank and Gaza; Yemen, Rep.
South Asia	8	Afghanistan; Bangladesh; Bhutan; India; Maldives; Nepal; Pakistan; Sri Lanka
Sub-Saharan Africa	47	Angola; Benin; Botswana; Burkina Faso; Burundi; Cabo Verde; Cameroon; Central African Republic; Chad; Comoros; Congo, Dem. Rep.; Congo, Rep.; Côte d'Ivoire; Equatorial Guinea; Eritrea; Ethiopia; Gabon; Gambia, The; Ghana; Guinea; Guinea-Bissau; Kenya; Lesotho; Liberia; Madagascar; Malawi; Mali; Mauritania; Mauritius; Mozambique; Namibia; Niger; Nigeria; Rwanda; São Tomé and Príncipe; Senegal; Seychelles; Sierra Leone; South Africa; South Sudan; Sudan; Swaziland; Tanzania; Togo; Uganda; Zambia; Zimbabwe

respondents—through responses to standardized questionnaires, conference calls, written correspondence and visits by the team.

In addition to filling out written questionnaires, *Women, Business and the Law* respondents provided references to relevant laws and regulations. The *Women, Business and the Law* team collects the texts of relevant laws and regulations and checks questionnaire responses for accuracy. Questionnaire responses are verified against codified sources of national law, including constitutions, marriage and family codes, labor laws, passport procedures, inheritance statutes, tax regulations, gender equality laws, civil procedure rules, social security codes, criminal laws and laws on violence against women. Additionally, *Doing Business 2018* surveys were used to develop some of the questions for the building credit and providing incentives to work indicators.

Women, Business and the Law requires each legal data point to have a specific citable legal source; the legal source is provided for every data point on the project website (http://wbl.worldbank.org) to ensure transparency of the data. More detailed data on each economy, including links to the legal sources used, are also provided on the project website.

The report team welcomes feedback on the methodology and construction of this set of indicators. We look forward to improving its coverage and scope. Feedback is welcome on all aspects of the report and can be offered through the *Women, Business and the Law* website.

The *Women, Business and the Law* methodology has several useful characteristics:

- It is transparent and uses information derived directly from laws and regulations.

- Because standard assumptions are used when collecting the data, comparisons are valid across economies.

- The data identify potential obstacles to women in business and legislation that can be changed because of this new information.

Although *Women, Business and the Law* focuses on written legislation, there is often a large gap between laws on the books and actual practices. Women do not always have access to the equality they are legally entitled to. This project attempts to identify areas in which formal legal differentiation still exists and then clarify the impacts of these legal differences on women.

In *Women, Business and the Law 2018*, three new scored questions were added across two of the seven indicators. The new questions are footnoted throughout the text. Any methodological changes made are described in the summary of methodology changes section of the Data Notes. For more information about the full set of data collected this cycle, please visit our website at http://wbl.worldbank.org.

The sections below provide detailed explanations of the methodology used to answer the 50 scored questions asked across 189 economies for a total of 9,450 data points.

The project has data available for an additional 116 questions which are not scored, for a total of 21,924 data points. Unscored questions fall into three categories. First, some questions constitute component parts of scored questions. For example, to understand if there is paid leave available to women of at least 14 weeks, *Women, Business and the Law* must first understand if the law mandates maternity leave or parental leave. And then it must understand how many days such maternity leave or parental leave is paid for. Second, some questions do not directly relate to women's entrepreneurship or employment, although they are important for gender equality. For example, the series of questions on protection orders fall into this category. And third, some questions are important to understand the legal framework, but do not in and of themselves, denote a good practice. For example, questions on the nature of the marital property regimes. Detailed information on all unscored questions is available on the project website at http://wbl.worldbank.org.

The following section focuses on the 50 scored questions, which are grouped by indicator. Each question is followed by information on how the answers were standardized and made comparable across all economies, as well as on how the questions are scored. Assumptions, where used, are also listed. The indicator scores (a number between 0 and 100, 100 being the best) are obtained by calculating the unweighted average of the scored questions in that indicator, and scaling the result to 100.

Accessing institutions

Assumptions

It is assumed that the woman

- Resides in the main business city of the economy being examined.

- Has reached the legal age of majority and is capable of making decisions as an adult; if there is no legal age of majority, the woman is assumed to be 30 years old.

- Is sane, competent, in good health and has no criminal record.

- Is a lawful citizen of the economy examined.

- Where the question assumes the woman or man is married, the marriage is monogamous and registered with the authorities.

- Where the question assumes the woman or man is unmarried, she or he has never been married.

- Where the answer differs according to the legal system applicable to the woman in question (as may be the case in economies where there is legal plurality), the answer used will be the one that applies to the majority of the population.

Answers to the questions are based on codified law and not how that law is applied in practice. Therefore, customary law is not taken into account unless it has been codified. Questions on the status of customary law within the legal system refer to its existence and position within the hierarchy of legislation, but do not assess its content. Reciprocal restrictions that govern the conduct of both spouses are not covered; this indicator measures only restrictions that govern the conduct of the wife, not the husband.

This topic addresses whether a woman can engage in certain legal transactions in the same way as a man. Differences related to property transactions are taken into account only for the using property indicator. Accessing institutions does not count this type of difference.

1. Are married women required by law to obey their husbands?

   - The answer is "Yes" if
     - there is an explicit provision stating that a married woman must obey her husband; or
     - a provision states that disobedience toward her husband has legal ramifications for the wife, such as loss of maintenance.
   - The answer is "No" if there is no provision that a married woman must obey her husband.
   - Scoring: Yes = 0; No = 1.

2. Can a woman legally apply for a passport in the same way as a man?

   - The answer is "Yes" if, upon reaching the legal age of majority, all civil legal acts can be completed and there are no differences in the way a woman or man obtains a passport.
   - The answer is "No" if
     - an adult woman needs the permission or signature of her husband, father, other male relative or guardian to apply for a passport; or
     - the passport application of an adult woman requires a reference to her husband or father's name, any other male relative or guardian;
     - documentation is required from a woman that is not required from a man, e.g., a marriage certificate.
   - Scoring: Yes = 1; No = 0.

3. Can a woman legally apply for a national ID card in the same way as a man?

   - The answer is "Yes" if there are no inequalities in the process for obtaining a national identity card. If married men must provide a marriage certificate or birth certificate as proof of name, whereas married women must provide a marriage certificate, the answer is still "Yes."
   - The answer is "No" if
     - a married woman must provide a marriage certificate, but a married man need not; or
     - a woman requires additional signatures, such as those of her husband, father, other male relative or guardian, which are not required for a man; or
     - a married woman must indicate the name of her spouse, but a married man is not so required; or
     - a woman must indicate the name of her father, other male relative or guardian, but a man is not required to do so; or
     - the identity card of a married woman displays the name of her spouse, but the identity card of a married man does not;
     - identity cards are optional for women, but required for men.
   - The answer is "N/A" if there is no national identity card that is universally accepted based on an implemented national registration system that issues national ID cards.
   - Scoring Yes = 1; No = 0; N/A (no national ID) = not scored.

4. Can a woman legally travel outside the country in the same way as a man?

   - The answer is "Yes" if there are no restrictions on a woman traveling alone internationally.
   - The answer is "No" if permission, additional documentation or the presence of a guardian is required for a woman to leave the country; however, this permission must be different from what is required to get a passport, which is covered in a separate question.
   - The answer is also "No" if the law requires a married woman to accompany her husband out of the country if he so wishes.
   - Scoring: Yes = 1; No = 0.

5. Can a woman legally travel outside her home in the same way as a man?

   - The answer is "Yes" if there are no restrictions on a woman traveling alone domestically.
   - The answer is "No" if
     - permission, additional documentation or the presence of her husband or a guardian is required for a woman to travel domestically; or
     - a woman must justify her reasons to her husband, father or guardian for leaving the home;
     - leaving the home without a valid reason is considered disobedience with consequences under the law, for example, loss of her right to financial maintenance.
   - Scoring: Yes = 1; No = 0.

6. Can a woman legally get a job or pursue a trade or profession in the same way as a man?

- The answer is "Yes" if

  - no permission is needed for a woman to get a job or practice a trade or profession; or

  - there is no restriction in family or civil law on a woman's ability to work.

- The answer is "No" if

  - a husband can prevent his wife from getting or keeping a job or pursuing a trade or profession; or

  - permission or additional documentation is required, or if a husband or guardian can prevent a woman from getting or keeping job or pursuing a trade or profession; or

  - it is considered a form of disobedience with legal ramifications for a wife to engage in employment contrary to her husband's wishes or the interests of the family.

- Scoring: Yes = 1; No = 0.

7. Can a woman legally sign a contract in the same way as a man?

- The answer is "Yes" if full legal capacity is obtained upon the age of majority and there are no restrictions on a woman signing legally binding contracts.

- The answer is "No" if a woman has limited legal capacity to sign a binding contract or needs the signature, consent or permission of her husband to legally bind herself.

- This question does not concern restrictions on married women signing contracts specifically related to marital property governed by the default marital property regime; these are covered under the using property indicator.

- Scoring: Yes = 1; No = 0.

8. Can a woman legally register a business in the same way as a man?

- The answer is "Yes" if a woman obtains full legal capacity upon reaching the age of majority and there are no restrictions on a woman registering a business.

- The answer is "No" if

  - a woman has limited legal capacity to register a business; this includes situations where she needs her husband's or a guardian's permission, signature or consent to register a business; or

  - the registration process at any stage requires additional information or documentation for women not required of men.

- The answer is also "No" for member states of regional bodies, such as the Organization for the Harmonization of Corporate Law in Africa (OHADA) for which supranational law applies (e.g., OHADA Uniform Act on General Commercial Law) when domestic law contravenes these supranational rules and limits the legal capacity of women.

- Scoring: Yes = 1; No = 0.

9. Can a woman legally open a bank account in the same way as a man?

- The answer is "Yes" if

  - there are no restrictions on a woman opening a bank account;

  - the law explicitly states that a married woman may open a bank account, or that both spouses may open bank accounts in their own names.

- The answer is "No" if

  - specific provisions limit the ability of a woman to open a bank account, such as those stating that a married woman who is separately employed from her husband may open a bank

account in her own name (because that implies that a woman without a separate income stream may not); or

  - any other required permissions or additional documentation.

- Only provisions from the body of family law in the economy are systematically reviewed.

- Scoring: Yes = 1; No = 0.

10. Can a woman legally choose where to live in the same way as a man?

- The answer is "Yes" if there are no restrictions on a woman choosing where to live.

- The answer is "No" if there are explicit restrictions on a woman choosing where to live or if the husband chooses the family residence or marital home or has more weight in determining where the family will live.

- Scoring: Yes = 1; No = 0.

11. Can a woman legally be "head of household" or "head of family" in the same way as a man?

- The answer is "Yes" if the definition of head of household is codified and there are no explicit restrictions on a woman becoming "head of household" or "head of family."

- The answer is "No" if

  - there is an explicit restriction on a woman becoming "head of household" or "head of family," e.g., a provision stating that only men or husbands can be so designated or that men "lead" or "represent the family;"

  - a male is designated as the default family member who receives the family book or equivalent document that is necessary for access to services.

- The answer is "N/A" if the definition of head of household is not codified.

- This question does not assess gender inequalities in the tax code, which are captured by the providing incentives to work indicator.
- Scoring: Yes = 1; No = 0.

Using property

Assumptions

It is assumed that the woman

- Resides in the economy's main business city.
- Has reached the legal age of majority and is capable of making decisions as an adult; if there is no legal age of majority, the woman is assumed to be 30 years old.
- Is sane, competent, in good health and has no criminal record.
- Is a lawful citizen of the economy being examined.
- Where the question assumes that the woman or man is unmarried, she or he has never been married.
- Where the question assumes that the woman or man is married, the marriage is monogamous and registered with the authorities. De facto marriages or customary unions are not measured.
- Where the question assumes that the woman or man is married, the marital property regime under which she or he is married is assumed to be the default marital property regime, and it is also assumed that the marital property regime will not change during the course of the marriage. In economies where there is no default marital property regime, it is assumed that the couple is married under the most common regime for that jurisdiction.
- Where the answer differs according to the legal system that applies to the woman—as may occur in economies where legal plurality exists—the answer used will be the one that applies to the majority of the population.

The answers to these questions are based on the law as codified in the main business city and not the practice of that law. Therefore, customary law is not taken into account unless it has been codified. Unwritten, social or cultural norms are also not taken into account.

The questions for the using property indicator are designed to determine what management and control of property look like under the default marital property regime in each economy covered. For all questions relating to the ability of married women to carry out activities independently of their husbands, the key concern is reciprocity. Unequal treatment is counted only where a married man can carry out the activity and his wife is not able to do so equally.

The main areas of differentiation between women and men in exercising property rights lie in the rights granted under various marital property regimes. Some of these grant spouses equal treatment in property ownership. Other regimes grant husbands administrative control over jointly owned marital property. Still others grant husbands administrative control over their wives' property. The marital property regime also determines property ownership and administrative rights when a marriage is dissolved.

The default marital property regime is the set of rules that apply to the ownership and management of property within marriage and when the marriage ends, when there is no prenuptial agreement. *Women, Business and the Law* classifies default marital property regimes as follows:

Separation of property. All assets and income acquired by the spouses before they marry and during the marriage remain the separate property of the acquiring spouse. At the time of divorce or the death of one of the spouses, each spouse retains ownership of all assets and income brought to the marriage or acquired during the marriage by that person and any value that has accrued to that property.

Partial community property. Assets acquired before the marriage are regarded as the separate property of the acquiring spouse, and assets and income acquired after the marriage, with a few exceptions specified by law, are regarded as joint property of the couple. This regime also applies to cases where assets acquired before the marriage and assets acquired during the marriage are regarded as the separate property of the acquiring spouse, but the accrued value of the property acquired by any of the spouses is considered joint property. At the time of dissolution of the marriage by divorce or death, the joint property or its accrued value is divided equally between the spouses.

Full community property. All assets and income, whether brought into the marriage or acquired during the marriage—with a few exceptions specified by law—become the joint property of the couple. If the marriage is dissolved, all joint property is divided equally between the spouses.

Deferred full or partial community property. The rules of full or partial community of property apply at the time the marriage is dissolved; until then, separation of property applies.

Other. The default marital property regime does not fit any of the above four descriptions. This is also the case when the rules concerning the default marital property regime are not regulated by codified law, but are governed by unwritten customs.

There is no default marital property regime. The law requires the spouses to opt in to the marital property regime of their choice—with legal alternatives provided—before or at the time of the marriage. In economies where there is no default marital property regime, the most common regime is used when answering the subsequent questions.

12. Who legally administers marital property?

- For this question, marital property refers to all property owned by either spouse and both spouses during the marriage. The answer to this question assumes that the default marital property regime applies and is classified as follows:

- **Original owner.** Each spouse retains administrative power over the assets she or he brings into or acquires during the marriage and their accrued value. No consent is needed from the other spouse for transactions in separate property. This administrative scheme is usually found in separation of property regimes and can also be found in deferred full or partial community regimes. It does not cover special provisions concerning the marital home.

- **Separate with spousal consent.** Each spouse administers her or his separate property, but for major transactions, such as selling or pledging the property as collateral, spousal consent is needed. This administrative scheme is mostly found in separation of property regimes, but can also be found in deferred full or partial community and partial community regimes.

- **Both must agree.** Both spouses have equal rights in the administration and transaction of joint property; they perform all acts of administration together and, if one of the spouses has been delegated administrative rights by the other, spousal consent is implied. This administrative scheme is mostly seen in full and partial community property regimes.

- **Husband.** The husband has administrative rights over all property, including any separate property of the wife. This scheme is found only in partial community regimes.

- **Other.** This alternative applies wherever the administrative scheme does not fit into any of the previous categories. It includes, for example, cases in which in principle the law provides for both spouses to administer marital property, but if they disagree, the husband is given the power to ultimately decide or other members of the family have a say in how the property is administered. Where there is disagreement on how to administer marital property, a court may decide. This alternative also applies when the default marital property regime is based on unwritten custom.

- Scoring: "Husband" = 0; all other answers = 1.

13. Does the law provide for valuation of nonmonetary contributions?

- This question is designed to measure if, at the time a marriage is dissolved, the division of property benefits both spouses. The process of dividing property upon divorce is examined to identify whether caring for minor children, taking care of the family home or any other nonmonetized contribution from the stay-at-home spouse, usually the wife, is taken into consideration. It does not consider regular payment obligations in the form of maintenance or alimony.

- The answer is "Yes"

  - where an explicit legal recognition of such contributions is found and the law provides for equal or equitable division of the property or the transfer of a lump sum to the stay-at-home spouse based on the nonmonetary contributions; or

  - when the default marital property regime is full community, partial community or deferred full or partial community, because these regimes implicitly recognize nonmonetary contributions at the time of property division and benefit both spouses regardless of who purchased the property or holds title to it.

- The answer is "No" where

  - the default marital property regime is separation of property or other, and there is no explicit legal provision providing for equal or equitable division of property based on nonmonetary contributions.

- Scoring: Yes = 1; No = 0.

14. Do men and women have equal ownership rights to immovable property?

- The answer is "Yes" when

  - there is no specific legal restriction related to property applied to women or men based on gender; or

  - aspects related to property during marriage fall under a mix of custom, law and judicial precedent and no sources, including Convention on the Elimination of All Forms of Discrimination Against Women (CEDAW) reports, reveal the existence of inequality.

- The answer is "No" when

  - legal restrictions on property ownership are applied to women or men based on gender; or

  - there are gender differences in the legal treatment of spousal property (e.g., if husbands are granted administrative control over marital property).

- The answer is ".." where aspects related to property during marriage fall under unwritten custom or judicial discretion in the absence of a legal framework.

- Scoring: Yes = 1; No = 0; ".." = not scored.

15. Do sons and daughters have equal rights to inherit assets from their parents?

- This question examines whether there are gender-based differences in the rules of intestate succession for transfer of property from parents to children.

- The answer is "Yes" when the law recognizes children as heirs to property without any restrictions based on gender.

- The answer is also "Yes" when aspects related to inheritance fall under a mix of custom, law and judicial precedent and all sources, including CEDAW reports, do not reveal the existence of inequality.

- The answer is "No" when there are gender-based differences in the recognition of children as heirs to property.

- The answer is also "No" when aspects related to inheritance fall under custom and sources confirm that the customary system is influenced by unequal personal law.

- The answer is ".." where aspects related to inheritance fall under unwritten custom.

- Scoring: Yes = 1; No = 0; ".." = not scored.

16. Do female and male surviving spouses have equal rights to inherit assets?

- For this question, it is assumed that the deceased spouse left no children or any other heirs, other than the surviving spouse.

- This question examines whether both spouses have equal rank and rights to inherit assets when there is no will.

- The answer is "Yes" when surviving spouses of either gender have the same legal rights.

- The answer is also "Yes" when the aspects related to inheritance fall

under a mix of custom, law and judicial precedent and secondary sources, including CEDAW reports, do not reveal the existence of inequality.

- The answer is "No" where there are gender-based differences in inheritance.

- The answer is also "No" when aspects related to inheritance fall under custom and sources confirm that the customary system is influenced by unequal personal law.

- The answer is ".." where aspects related to inheritance fall under unwritten custom.

- Scoring: Yes = 1; No = 0; ".." = not scored.

Getting a job

Assumptions

It is assumed that the woman

- Resides in the economy's main business city.

- Has reached the legal age of majority and is capable of making decisions as an adult.

- Is a lawful citizen of the economy being examined.

- For purposes of determining parental benefits, is in a legally recognized marriage with the other parent of the child.

- For purposes of determining maternity or parental leave, that she gave birth to her first child without complications on June 1, 2017, at age 30, and her child is in good health.

- Is sane, competent, in good health and has no criminal record.

- Has been working long enough to accrue any maternity and parental benefits.

- Will be nursing until the child is 1 year old.

- Is working as a cashier in the food retail sector in a supermarket or grocery store that has 60 employees.

It is assumed that the man

- Resides in the economy's main business city.

- Has reached the legal age of majority and is capable of making decisions as an adult.

- Is a lawful citizen of the economy being examined.

- For purposes of determining parental benefits, is in a legally recognized marriage with the other parent of the child.

- For purposes of determining paternity leave or parental leave, has a first child who was born on June 1, 2017, without complications, was 30 years old when his child was born and the child is in good health.

- Is sane, competent, in good health and has no criminal record.

- Has been working long enough to accrue any paternity and parental benefits.

- Is working as a cashier in the food retail sector in a supermarket or grocery store that has 60 employees.

The topic contains questions on leave benefits for expectant and new parents, workplace protections for women and parents, restrictions on women's employment, and retirement ages. In general, the answers to the questions in the getting a job indicator are based on written law and not collective bargaining agreements; however, the latter are taken into account when two conditions are met:

- They cover more than 50% of the workforce in the food retail sector.

- They apply to individuals who were not party to the original collective bargaining agreement.

17. Is there paid leave available to women of at least 14 weeks?

- The answer is "Yes" if the law establishes at least 14 weeks of paid leave that is available to women for the birth of a child, either through maternity or parental leave.

- The answer is "No" if the law does not establish paid leave for expectant and new mothers, or if the length of paid leave is less than 14 weeks.

- Scoring: Yes = 1; No (because no paid leave) = 0; No (because paid leave < 14 weeks) = calculated as the distance to frontier where the frontier is 14 weeks.

18. Do women receive at least 2/3 of their wages for the first 14 weeks or the duration of the leave if it is shorter?

- The answer is "Yes" if

  - women receive at least 2/3 of their wages during the first 14 weeks of their leave (if their leave is longer than 14 weeks); or

  - women receive at least 2/3 of their wages during the duration of their leave (if their leave is shorter than 14 weeks).

- The answer is "No" if

  - the law does not establish any paid leave for expectant and new mothers;

  - women receive less than 2/3 of their wages during their leave (or the first 14 weeks of their leave if the total leave is longer than 14 weeks).

- Scoring: Yes = 1; No (because no paid leave) = 0; No (because women receive less than 2/3 of their wages) = calculated as the distance to frontier where the frontier is 2/3 (67%).

19. What is the percentage of maternity leave benefits paid by the government?

- This question examines the percentage of maternity leave benefits that are administered by the government. "Government" refers to social insurance or public funds.

- Where paid maternity leave does not exist but there is paid parental leave, the question examines the percentage of parental leave benefits paid by the government.

- Employer contributions to government funds (such as social security) that pay leave benefits are not considered employer payment of maternity benefits.

- The answer is 0% if the employer is solely liable for paying leave benefits.

- The answer is N/A if there is no paid leave available to expectant and new mothers.

- Scoring: proportion of maternity leave benefits paid by the government (i.e., if government pays all, answer is 100%, if employer pays all, answer is 0%). If N/A (there is no paid maternity leave) this question is not scored.

20. What is the difference between leave reserved for women and men relative to leave reserved for women, as a function of who pays?

- This question covers the difference between leave reserved for women and leave reserved for men relative to leave reserved to women as a function of who pays to recognize the possible burden of hiring women placed on employers.

- Leave reserved for women includes paid maternity leave and days of paid parental leave allotted to the mother. Leave reserved for men includes paid paternity leave and days of paid parental leave allotted to the father.

- Scoring: The question is calculated and scored as

  - ((paid maternity leave + any mother quota in parental leave) - (paid paternity leave + any father quota in parental leave)) / (paid maternity leave + any mother quota in parental leave) * percentage of leave paid by the government;

  - if the government pays 100%, the score is 1;

  - if there is no paid maternity leave this question is not scored.

21. Is there paid parental leave?

- The answer is "Yes" if the law explicitly mandates the right to some form of paid parental leave either shared between mother and father or as an individual entitlement.

- The answer is "No" if the law does not explicitly mandate the right to some form of paid parental leave either shared between mother and father or as an individual entitlement.

- Scoring: Yes = 1; No = 0.

22. Does the law mandate equal remuneration for work of equal value?

- This question captures whether employers are legally obliged to pay equal remuneration to male and female employees who perform work of equal value.

- "Remuneration" refers to the ordinary, basic or minimum wage or salary and any additional emoluments payable directly or indirectly, whether in cash or in kind, by the employer to the worker and arising from the worker's employment.

- "Work of equal value" refers not only to the same or similar jobs, but also to different jobs of the same value.

- Scoring: Yes = 1; No = 0.

23. Does the law mandate nondiscrimination based on gender in
employment?[1]

   - This question is designed to determine whether the law generally
   prevents or penalizes gender-based
   discrimination in employment.

   - Laws that mandate equal treatment or equality between women
   and men in employment are also
   counted for this question.

   - Where the law mandates nondiscrimination in multiple aspects
   of employment (such as in job
   advertisements, hiring and dismissal) on the basis of gender, the
   answer is "Yes."

   - Scoring: Yes = 1; No = 0.

24. Is dismissal of pregnant workers
prohibited?

   - This question is designed to determine whether pregnancy can serve
   as grounds for dismissal.

   - The answer is "Yes" if the law explicitly prohibits or penalizes the
   dismissal of pregnant women or if
   termination of contract based on
   pregnancy is considered a form of
   unlawful termination, unfair dismissal or wrongful discharge.

   - The answer is "No" if the law only
   prohibits the dismissal of pregnant workers during maternity
   leave or for a limited period of
   the pregnancy.

   - Scoring: Yes = 1; No = 0.

25. Can parents work flexibly?

   - The answer is "Yes" if the law
   explicitly permits flexible work arrangements for employees who
   have minor children, such as part-
   time work, reduced hours, flextime
   work and teleworking. This includes
   the right to request flexible work
   and the right to obtain flexible
   work. It does not include parental
   leave that can be taken flexibly.

   - The answer is "No" if only women
   are entitled to flexible work.

   - Scoring: Yes = 1; No = 0.

26. Can women work the same night
hours as men?

   - This question is designed to determine whether nonpregnant and
   nonnursing women are prohibited
   from working at night or cannot
   work the same night hours as men.
   Night-hour restrictions on women
   in specified industries are captured
   in later questions.

   - The answer is "Yes" if there are
   no restrictions on women working at night. If the law conditions
   women's ability to work at night on
   employer compliance with safety
   measures (such as providing transportation to and from work), the
   answer is also "Yes."

   - The answer is "No" if the law
   broadly prohibits women from
   working at night or limits the hours
   women can work.

   - The answer is also "No" if the
   law only allows women to work
   at night in certain circumstances,
   such as in cases of *force majeure*
   or if the woman works for her family's business.

   - If various sectors of the economy
   are regulated separately (i.e., no
   central labor law), it is assumed
   that the woman is employed as
   a cashier in a grocery store or
   supermarket.

   - Where the law indicates that a
   given ministry or minister may
   promulgate regulations restricting
   women's work at night, this is considered a restriction even if no such
   regulation has been issued.

   - Scoring: Yes = 1; No = 0.

27. Can women work in jobs deemed
hazardous, arduous or morally inappropriate in the same way as men?

   - The answer is "Yes" if there are
   no laws that prohibit women from
   working in a broad and subjective
   category of jobs deemed hazardous, arduous, or morally or socially
   inappropriate.

   - The answer is "No" if

      - the employer can determine
      whether particular jobs are too
      hazardous for women but not
      for men. In such cases, the law
      explicitly uses the term "hazard-
      ous" or its synonyms to describe
      a broad category of jobs that
      women—but not men—are
      prohibited from doing. Work of
      a hazardous nature includes, for
      example, jobs that could have a
      harmful effect on or increased
      risk to women's lives or health,
      given women's psycho-physical
      qualities, or jobs not deemed
      to have a harmful effect on or
      increased risk to men's life or
      health, given men's psycho-
      physical qualities;

      - the employer can determine
      whether particular jobs are
      morally inappropriate or so-
      cially harmful for women but
      not for men. In such cases,
      the law explicitly uses the term
      "morally inappropriate" or its
      synonyms to describe a broad
      category of jobs that women—
      but not men—are prohibited
      from doing. Work that is mor-
      ally inappropriate includes, for
      example, employment that is
      considered not in accordance
      with the "moral development"
      only of women;

      - the employer can determine
      whether particular jobs are too
      arduous for women but not for
      men. In such cases, the law ex-
      plicitly uses the term "arduous"
      or its synonyms to describe
      a broad category of jobs that
      women—but not men—are

prohibited from doing. Work of an arduous nature includes jobs that involve particularly hard manual labor or jobs that are considered to exceed women's capabilities;

- the law indicates that a given minister or ministry may promulgate regulations restricting women's work in hazardous, arduous, or morally or socially inappropriate jobs, even if no such regulation has been issued.

- Scoring: Yes = 1; No = 0.

28. Are women able to work in the same industries as men?

- The answer is "Yes" if there are no restrictions on women working in mining, construction, manufacturing, energy, water, agriculture and transportation sectors.

- The answer is "No" if there are full or partial restrictions on women working in mining, construction, manufacturing, energy, water, agriculture or transportation sectors.

- Scoring: Yes = 1; No = 0.

29. Are women able to perform the same tasks at work as men?

- The answer is "Yes" if

  - there are no restrictions on women working in metal work;

  - there are no restrictions on women engaging in jobs with a minimum weightlifting requirement, or if there are no differences between the amount of weight men and women can lift;

  - there are no other restrictions on women's employment (not including jobs in mining, construction, factories, agriculture, transport, energy, water sector, which are captured in separate questions).

- The answer is "No" if

- there are full or partial restrictions on women working in metal work;

- there are full or partial restrictions on women engaging in jobs that require lifting weights above a certain threshold;

- women cannot perform work requiring heavy lifting, for example, if the law prohibits women from working in jobs that involve the loading and unloading of goods;

- there are restrictions on women doing particular jobs—such as working with certain chemicals or substances—but not on men doing them; or

- women are prohibited from working in certain settings in which men are allowed to work.

- Scoring: Yes = 1; No = 0.

The following assumptions are specific to the following questions on retirement benefits:

- The individual was born in 1977.

- The individual has been continuously employed since age 25.

- The answers are rounded to the nearest year.

30. Are the ages at which men and women can retire with full pension benefits equal?

- The answer is "Yes" if the ages at which men and a women can retire with full pension benefits is the same.

- The answer is "No" if there is a difference in the age at which a man and a woman can retire with full pension benefits.

- The answer is "N/A" if there is no national law on pension benefits.

- Scoring: Yes = 1; No (because women retire earlier) = calculated as distance to frontier where the frontier is 10 years; N/A = not scored.

31. Are the ages at which men and women can retire with partial pension benefits equal?

- This question examines the relative ages at which men and women can retire with partial but not with full pension benefits, because he or she did not accumulate enough work experience or contributions, has not reached the age that would qualify him or her for a full pension or continues to work part-time upon reaching the retirement age.

- The answer is "Yes" if the ages at which men and women can receive partial pension benefits are the same.

- The answer is "No" if there is no difference in the age at which a man and a woman can receive partial pension benefits.

- The answer is "N/A" if

  - the law does not establish an age at which men and women can receive partial benefits; or

  - there is no national law on pension benefits.

- Scoring: Yes = 1; No (because women retire earlier) = calculated as distance to frontier where the frontier is 10 years; N/A = not scored.

32. Are the mandatory retirement ages for men and women equal?

- This question examines the relative ages at which men and women must cease employment or can be terminated by their employer. Even if the law allows employers and employees to contract for work beyond that age, retirement is still considered mandatory because the employer can legally oblige the employee to retire.

- The answer is "Yes" if the age at which a man or woman must retire is the same.

- The answer is "No" if the ages at which men or women must retire are different.

- The answer is "N/A" if there is no mandatory retirement age for men and women.

- Scoring: Yes = 1; No (because women retire earlier) = calculated as distance to frontier where the frontier is 6 years; N/A = not scored.

Providing incentives to work

Assumptions

It is assumed that both parents

- Have reached the legal age of majority and are capable of making decisions as adults. If there is no legal age of majority, parents are assumed to be 30 years old.

- Are in a legally recognized marriage.

- Are sane, competent, in good health, have no criminal record, and are lawful citizens.

- Reside in the economy's main business city.

- Are employed in a private sector company.

- Share one child.

33. Are mothers guaranteed an equivalent position after maternity leave?

- The question captures whether the employer has a legal obligation to reinstate an employee returning from maternity leave to an equivalent or better position than the employee had pre-leave.

- Where the maternity leave regime explicitly states that the employee may not be indefinitely replaced, the answer is assumed to be "Yes."

- Where the maternity leave regime explicitly establishes a suspension of the employee's contract, the answer is assumed to be "Yes."

- In economies that also have parental leave and the law guarantees return after the leave to the same or an equivalent position paid at the same rate but is silent on guaranteeing the same position after maternity leave, the answer is "Yes."

- In economies that only have parental leave and the law guarantees return after the leave to the same or an equivalent position paid at the same rate, the answer is "Yes."

- Scoring: Yes = 1; No = 0.

34. Does the government support or provide childcare services?

- This question captures public childcare services that are completely funded by the government or government-funded with co-pay by parents. It also covers public childcare centers that are available universally to all families regardless of their income level.

- Government support or nontax benefits include funding and/or nonmonetary support.

- The answer is "Yes" if

  - the government provides, establishes or mandates childcare services; or

  - childcare is available universally but there are priority criteria for admission when there is not enough space for all children; or

  - private, stand-alone childcare centers receive nontax benefits from the government in the form of financial or nonmonetary support, such as providing building and school equipment as well as start-up grants; or

  - private, stand-alone childcare centers receive nontax benefits only if they meet certain ordinary requirements, such as the number of children enrolled in the childcare center or the location of the childcare center.

- The answer is "No" if

  - government childcare service is provided to a group of people qualified by something other than income level; or

  - the service is 100% run by non-state institutions; or

  - private, stand-alone childcare centers do not receive any non-tax benefits; or

  - private childcare centers receive nontax benefits only if they meet certain extraordinary requirements, such as a budget deficit.

- Scoring: Yes = 1; No = 0.

35. Are payments for childcare tax deductible?

- The answer is "Yes" if childcare or education expenses are deductible in the personal income tax law; for this question, childcare expenses cover various options: kindergartens or crèches, day care centers, after-school centers, in-home care and child-minding arrangements.

- The answer is "No" if childcare or education payments are not deductible in the personal income tax law.

- The answer is "No" if childcare or education tax deductions are only applied to childcare allowances granted by the government (tax exemptions on government allowances).

- The answer is "No" if employees receive tax benefits on payments for the use of employer-provided childcare centers only.

- Scoring: Yes = 1; No = 0.

36. Is primary education free and compulsory?

- The answer is "Yes" if primary education is compulsory, fully publicly funded and provided by the government universally, regardless of the families' income level.

- The answer is "No" if either of the above elements are not met.

- Scoring: Yes = 1; No = 0.

37. Are there specific tax deductions or tax credits that are only applicable to men?

- This question is designed to determine whether the personal income tax law differentiates between men and women on deductions and credits and includes instances where tax-specific deductions and credits can only be granted to male heads of household.

- The answer is "Yes" if the personal income tax law grants tax deductions or credits that apply only to male taxpayers.

- The answer is "Yes" if the personal income tax law grants tax deductions or credits that can only be granted to the head of household and the tax law defines the head of household as the male by default.

- The answer is "No" if the personal income tax law does not differentiate between men and women in terms of tax benefits.

- The answer is ".." where there is no information available on tax deductions or tax credits.

- Scoring: Yes = 0; No = 1; ".." = not scored.

Going to court

Assumptions

It is assumed that the woman

- Resides in the economy's main business city.

- Has reached the legal age of majority and is capable of making decisions as an adult.

- Is sane, competent, in good health and has no criminal record.

- Where the answer differs according to the legal system that applies to the woman (e.g. where different laws govern different groups of people within an economy), the answer used is the one that applies to the majority of the population.

38. Does a woman's testimony carry the same evidentiary weight in court as a man's?

- This question covers the weight of women's evidentiary testimony in all court cases, and does not include differences in testimony when executing contracts (i.e., marriage).

- The answer is "Yes" if the law does not differentiate between the evidentiary value of women's and men's testimony.

- The answer is "No" if the law explicitly differentiates between the evidentiary value of women's and men's testimony.

- Scoring: Yes = 1; No = 0.

39. Does the law establish an anti-discrimination commission?[2]

- This question looks at institutions that have been established in addition to courts, but are state bodies with a constitutional and/or legislative mandate to protect and promote principles of equality. Although they are part of the state apparatus and funded by the state, they operate and function independently from the government.

- Commissions are specialized, independent bodies tasked with receiving complaints of gender discrimination. The bodies considered may take such forms as women's commissions, ombudspersons or national human rights institutions.

- The answer is "Yes" if the commission is mandated to receive complaints of gender discrimination by public and private actors.

- The answer is "No" if there is no such commission, or if the body in question does not receive complaints of gender discrimination by public and private actors.

- Scoring: Yes = 1; No = 0.

40. Does the law mandate legal aid in civil and family matters?[3]

- The answer is "Yes" if the constitution or another law establishes the right to legal aid or assistance in most civil and/or family matters.

- The answer is "No" if the constitution or another law provides for legal aid and assistance, but civil and/or family matters are not eligible.

- The answer is "No" if the constitution or another law establishes only the right to counsel or the mandatory presence of an attorney in civil matters.

- Scoring: Yes = 1; No = 0.

41. Is there a small claims court or a fast-track procedure for small claims?

- Small claims courts hear civil cases between private litigants involving relatively small amounts of money. Although the names of such courts vary by jurisdiction, common features include relaxed rules of civil procedure, the appearance of adversaries without legal representation, the use of plain language and informal evidentiary rules. Fast-track procedural rules for small claims operate similarly; however, cases are tried in courts of more general jurisdiction.

- The answer is "Yes" if

  - there is a small claims court or a fast-track procedure for civil claims of small value and a maximum value for cases that may be heard; and

- the small claims court or fast-track procedure has jurisdiction to hear at least general civil cases.

- The answer is "No" if
  - there is a small claims court or fast-track procedure, but it is competent only to hear commercial claims, not all civil claims; or
  - few types of civil disputes are within the jurisdiction of the small claims court (e.g., rent disputes only).

- Scoring: Yes = 1; No = 0.

Building credit

The background information for the questions on credit registries and bureaus comes from the depth of credit information index that is part of the *Doing Business 2018* getting credit indicator. That index covers rules affecting the scope, accessibility and quality of credit information available through private credit bureaus and public credit registries. Credit bureaus and registries are only considered if their coverage extends to at least 5% of the adult population within an economy.

42. Do retailers provide information to private credit bureaus or public credit registries?

- For the answer to this question to be "Yes," it is sufficient that any private credit bureau or public credit registry in the economy in question collects information from any retailer.

- The answer is "No" if retailers do not provide information to credit bureaus or registries.

- The answer is "N/A" if there is no credit bureau or registry in the economy or if their coverage extends to less than 5% of the adult population.

- Scoring: Yes = 1; No = 0; N/A = 0.

43. Do utility companies provide information to private credit bureaus or public credit registries?

- For the answer to this question to be "Yes," it is sufficient that any private credit bureau or public credit registry in the economy in question collects information from a utility company.

- The answer is "No" if utility companies do not provide information to credit bureaus or registries.

- The answer is "N/A" if there is no credit bureau or registry in the economy or if their coverage extends to less than 5% of the adult population.

- Scoring: Yes =1; No = 0; N/A = 0.

44. Does the law prohibit discrimination by creditors on the basis of sex or gender in access to credit?

- The answer is "Yes" if
  - the law prohibits discrimination on the basis of sex or gender, or provides for equal access for both sexes when conducting financial transactions, such as applying for credit or loans; or
  - the law prohibits discrimination on the basis of sex or gender when conducting entrepreneurial activities or receiving financial assistance; or
  - the law prohibits discrimination on the basis of sex or gender or prescribes equality of the sexes when accessing goods and services, and the definition of services in law, regulation or legal interpretation covers financial services.

- The answer is "No" if the law does not prohibit such discrimination.

- Scoring: Yes = 1; No = 0.

45. Does the law prohibit discrimination by creditors on the basis of marital status in access to credit?

- The answer is "Yes" if
  - the law specifically prohibits discrimination on the basis of marital status or provides for equal access irrespective of marital status when conducting financial transactions, such as applying for credit or loans; or
  - the law prohibits discrimination on the basis of marital status when conducting entrepreneurial activities or receiving financial assistance; or
  - the law prohibits discrimination on the basis of marital status when accessing goods and services, and the definition of services in law, regulation or legal interpretation covers financial services.

- The answer is "No" if the law does not prohibit such discrimination.

- Scoring: Yes = 1; No = 0.

Protecting women from violence

Assumptions

It is assumed that the woman

- Resides in the main business city of the economy being examined.

- Is a lawful citizen of the economy where she resides.

The answers to the questions in this topic are based on statutory or codified law for civil law systems, and on case law, i.e., law established by judicial decision in cases as binding precedent for common law systems. Therefore, customary law is not taken into account, unless it has been codified or upheld by case law, and the answers are based solely on the letter of the law and not the implementation or practice thereof.

46. Is there legislation specifically addressing domestic violence? If not, are there aggravated penalties for crimes committed against a spouse or family member?

- The answer is "Yes" if

  - there is legislation addressing domestic violence, i.e., violence between spouses, within the family or members of the same household or in interpersonal relationships, including intimate partner violence that includes criminal sanctions or provides for protection orders for domestic violence; or

  - the legislation addresses "harassment" that clearly affects physical and/or mental health, such that damage is implied, as within the scope of domestic violence.

- The answer is "No, but aggravated penalties exist" if there is no domestic violence legislation but penalties in the criminal code are increased for offenses committed by a spouse, family member or intimate partner.

- The answer is "No" if

  - there is no legislation addressing domestic violence or the law only refers to or prohibits domestic violence but does not provide for sanctions or protection orders; or

  - the law enables women to obtain a protection order only if the husband has been convicted of the offense or she has ceased to reside in the common home; or

  - the law protects only a specific category of women (e.g., pregnant), a specific member of the family (e.g., children), but not all family members, or defines the offense in connection with

specific motives (e.g., violence against a person while performing a professional or civil duty); and

  - there are no aggravated penalties for crimes committed against a spouse, family member or intimate partner.

- Scoring: Yes = 1; No, but aggravated penalties exist = 0.5; No = 0.

47. Is there legislation on sexual harassment in employment?

- The question covers provisions on sexual harassment in the workplace or in employment, whether or not sanctions apply.

- The answer is "Yes" if

  - there is a law or provision that specifically protects against sexual harassment in employment, including unwelcome sexual advances, requests for sexual favors, verbal or physical conduct or gestures of a sexual nature, annoyance if understood to include harassment with sexual content, or any other behavior of a sexual nature that might reasonably be expected or be perceived to cause offense or humiliation to another in connection with employment, including provisions on inducing indecent or lewd behavior coupled with financial or official dependence or authority, abuse of position or authority, or language that can be clearly interpreted to mean such dependence or abuse; or sexual harassment is considered a form of discrimination in employment and the law protects against discrimination.

- The answer is "No" if

  - there is no legislation specifically addressing sexual harassment in employment; or

  - the behavior or gesture of a sexual nature addressed in the

law includes the use of force or violence or the threat of force or violence, which is understood to constitute a crime, e.g., sexual assault or abuse; or

  - the conduct covered by legislation is not directed at a specific individual; or

  - the law only allows an employee to terminate employment based on sexual harassment but provides for no other protection or form of redress; however, a provision allowing the employer to terminate an employee's contract for committing sexual harassment will be considered; or

  - the law or provision covers only public or only private sector employees, but not both; or

  - the law or provision protects only a specific category of women or those in a specific area or sector of employment, e.g., protection from sexual harassment in political functions, or applicable only to government or state-owned enterprises; or

  - the law accounts only for sexual acts, including intercourse or copulation, as clearly involving contact of or with genital organs; or

  - the law or provision states only that the employer has a duty to prevent sexual harassment, but no provisions exist to prohibit or provide sanctions or other form of redress for sexual harassment; or

  - the law addresses harassment in general but makes no reference to acts of a sexual nature or contact.

- Scoring: Yes = 1; No = 0.

48. Is there legislation on sexual harassment in education?

- The question covers provisions addressing sexual harassment in education, education facilities, schools or where the offender is in the role of educator, professor or in charge of the education of the victim, whether or not there are sanctions associated with the provision.

- The answer is "Yes" if the law specifically covers sexual harassment in education or contains language that can clearly be interpreted as sexual harassment in education.

- The answer is "No" if

  - the law does not specifically cover sexual harassment in education; or

  - the law covers only education within the scope of work, such as vocational training in the workplace, but not education generally; or

  - the law covers sexual harassment only in public or only in private education, but not in both; or

  - the law or provision only covers students up to a certain age (e.g., 18 years).

- Scoring: Yes = 1; No = 0.

49. Are there criminal penalties for sexual harassment in employment?

- The answer is "Yes" if

  - the law establishes criminal sanctions, such as fines and imprisonment, for sexual harassment in employment.

- The answer is "No" if

  - There are no criminal sanctions for sexual harassment in employment; or

  - the law on sexual harassment in employment refers to penalties for more serious offenses in the criminal code, such as for sexual assault; or

  - the law only prohibits sexual harassment in employment and sets forth that the employer

should apply discretionary sanctions.

- Scoring: Yes = 1; No = 0.

50. Are there civil remedies for sexual harassment in employment?

- The answer is "Yes" if

  - the law provides for civil remedies or compensation for victims of sexual harassment in employment or the workplace, such as recovery of monetary damages for loss of employment opportunities and wages, expenses and compensation for emotional damages; or

  - the provision on sexual harassment in employment or the workplace in the criminal code provides for reparation of damages for offenses covered by the code.

- The answer is "No" if the law does not provide for civil remedies or compensation for victims of sexual harassment in employment or the workplace.

- Scoring: Yes = 1; No = 0.

Summary of methodology changes

There were some changes in the methodology between *Women, Business and the Law 2016* and *Women, Business and the Law 2018*. For that reason, the data for previous cycles—which can be found on the *Women, Business and the Law* website—were recomputed to match the new methodology. Four of the topics had changes in methodology, as described below:

Accessing institutions. The methodology for the questions on whether a woman can legally be designated "head of household" in the same way as a man will no longer reflect inequalities in the tax code, as these are captured by the providing incentives to work indicator.

Getting a job. It is now assumed that a woman or man earns the minimum wage rather than the average value added per worker for calculating maternity, paternity and parental benefits. Answers to the questions on parental benefits now reflect the applicable leave policies in force as of June 1, 2017. The length of paternity leave is now counted in work days when it is less than 30 days. The question on flexible work no longer requires easier access to flexible work to be provided to parents than to non-parents. The question on whether women can work the same night hours as men now captures laws that restrict women from working at night in the food retail sector in addition to broad restrictions on women's night work. The questions on the ages at which men and women can retire with partial benefits are now answered as "N/A" where the law does not establish an age at which partial benefits can be collected. It is also no longer assumed that a woman has raised one child for purposes of calculating the age at which she can retire and receive pension benefits.

Providing incentives to work. The definition of childcare has been revised to cover services provided to children between the ages of 1 and 5. Previously, childcare covered services provided to children age 6 and below. The question on whether childcare expenses are tax deductible now covers education expenses in addition to childcare expenses (where there is an explicit reference to childcare).

Going to court. Explicit restrictions on women's testimony relative to men's across all civil and criminal cases are taken into account, except when differences exist in the execution of marriage contracts.

Notes

1   This is a new question.

2   This is a new question.

3   This is a new question.

ECONOMY
TABLES

	AFGHANISTAN	ALBANIA
REGION	South Asia	Europe & Central Asia
INCOME GROUP	Low income	Upper middle income
FEMALE POPULATION	16,782,979	1,451,769
FEMALE LABOR FORCE (% OF TOTAL LABOR FORCE)	17%	42%

ACCESSING INSTITUTIONS
Score: 55 / **Score: 100**

	AFGHANISTAN	ALBANIA
1. Are wives required to obey their husbands?	Yes	No
Can a woman legally do the following in the same way as a man:		
2. Apply for a passport?	No	Yes
3. Apply for a national ID card?	No	Yes
4. Travel outside the country?	Yes	Yes
5. Travel outside her home?	No	Yes
6. Get a job?	Yes	Yes
7. Sign a contract?	Yes	Yes
8. Register a business?	Yes	Yes
9. Open a bank account?	Yes	Yes
10. Choose where to live?	No	Yes
11. Be "head of household"?	N/A	N/A

USING PROPERTY
Score: 40 / **Score: 100**

	AFGHANISTAN	ALBANIA
12. Who legally administers marital property?	Original owner	Both must agree
13. Does the law provide for valuation of nonmonetary contributions?	No	Yes
14. Do men and women have equal ownership rights to immovable property?	Yes	Yes
15. Do sons and daughters have equal inheritance rights?	No	Yes
16. Do female and male surviving spouses have equal inheritance rights?	No	Yes

GETTING A JOB
Score: 29 / **Score: 79**

	AFGHANISTAN	ALBANIA
17. Is there paid leave available to women of at least 14 weeks?	No	Yes
18. Do women receive at least 2/3 of their wages for the first 14 weeks or the duration of the leave if it is shorter?	Yes	Yes
19. What is the percentage of maternity leave benefits paid by the government?	0%	100%
20. What is the difference between leave reserved for women and men relative to leave reserved for women, as a function of who pays?	0.11	1
21. Is there paid parental leave?	No	No
22. Does the law mandate equal remuneration for work of equal value?	No	Yes
23. Does the law mandate nondiscrimination based on gender in employment?	No	Yes
24. Is dismissal of pregnant workers prohibited?	No	Yes
25. Can parents work flexibly?	No	No
26. Can women work the same night hours as men?	No	Yes
27. Can women work in jobs deemed hazardous, arduous or morally inappropriate in the same way as men?	No	Yes
28. Are women able to work in the same industries as men?	No	Yes
29. Are women able to perform the same tasks at work as men?	Yes	No
30. Are the ages at which men and women can retire with full pension benefits equal?	N/A	No
31. Are the ages at which men and women can retire with partial pension benefits equal?	N/A	No
32. Are the mandatory retirement ages for men and women equal?	Yes	N/A

PROVIDING INCENTIVES TO WORK
Score: 60 / **Score: 80**

	AFGHANISTAN	ALBANIA
33. Are mothers guaranteed an equivalent position after maternity leave?	No	Yes
34. Does the government support or provide childcare services?	Yes	Yes
35. Are payments for childcare tax deductible?	No	No
36. Is primary education free and compulsory?	Yes	Yes
37. Are there tax deductions or credits specific to men?	No	No

GOING TO COURT
Score: 50 / **Score: 75**

	AFGHANISTAN	ALBANIA
38. Does a woman's testimony carry the same evidentiary weight in court as a man's?	Yes	Yes
39. Does the law establish an anti-discrimination commission?	No	Yes
40. Does the law mandate legal aid in civil/family matters?	Yes	Yes
41. Is there a small claims court/fast-track procedure?	No	No

BUILDING CREDIT
Score: 0 / **Score: 50**

	AFGHANISTAN	ALBANIA
42. Do retailers provide information to credit agencies?	N/A	No
43. Do utility companies provide information to credit agencies?	N/A	No
44. Is discrimination based on gender prohibited in access to credit?	No	Yes
45. Is discrimination based on marital status prohibited in access to credit?	No	Yes

PROTECTING WOMEN FROM VIOLENCE
Score: 80 / **Score: 80**

	AFGHANISTAN	ALBANIA
46. Is there legislation specifically addressing domestic violence? If not, are there aggravated penalties for crimes committed against a spouse or family member?	No	Yes
47. Is there legislation on sexual harassment in employment?	Yes	Yes
48. Is there legislation on sexual harassment in education?	Yes	Yes
49. Are there criminal penalties for sexual harassment in employment?	Yes	No
50. Are there civil remedies for sexual harassment in employment?	Yes	Yes

Note: See the data notes for more details on the scoring of each indicator.

	ALGERIA	ANGOLA
REGION	Middle East & North Africa	Sub-Saharan Africa
INCOME GROUP	Upper middle income	Lower middle income
FEMALE POPULATION	20,179,815	14,512,041
FEMALE LABOR FORCE (% OF TOTAL LABOR FORCE)	18%	50%

ACCESSING INSTITUTIONS

	Score: 82	Score: 100
1. Are wives required to obey their husbands?	No	No
Can a woman legally do the following in the same way as a man:		
2. Apply for a passport?	No	Yes
3. Apply for a national ID card?	No	Yes
4. Travel outside the country?	Yes	Yes
5. Travel outside her home?	Yes	Yes
6. Get a job?	Yes	Yes
7. Sign a contract?	Yes	Yes
8. Register a business?	Yes	Yes
9. Open a bank account?	Yes	Yes
10. Choose where to live?	Yes	Yes
11. Be "head of household"?	N/A	N/A

USING PROPERTY

	Score: 40	Score: 100
12. Who legally administers marital property?	Original owner	Both must agree
13. Does the law provide for valuation of nonmonetary contributions?	No	Yes
14. Do men and women have equal ownership rights to immovable property?	Yes	Yes
15. Do sons and daughters have equal inheritance rights?	No	Yes
16. Do female and male surviving spouses have equal inheritance rights?	No	Yes

GETTING A JOB

	Score: 51	Score: 71
17. Is there paid leave available to women of at least 14 weeks?	Yes	No
18. Do women receive at least 2/3 of their wages for the first 14 weeks or the duration of the leave if it is shorter?	Yes	Yes
19. What is the percentage of maternity leave benefits paid by the government?	100%	100%
20. What is the difference between leave reserved for women and men relative to leave reserved for women, as a function of who pays?	1	1
21. Is there paid parental leave?	No	No
22. Does the law mandate equal remuneration for work of equal value?	Yes	Yes
23. Does the law mandate nondiscrimination based on gender in employment?	No	Yes
24. Is dismissal of pregnant workers prohibited?	No	Yes
25. Can parents work flexibly?	No	Yes
26. Can women work the same night hours as men?	No	Yes
27. Can women work in jobs deemed hazardous, arduous or morally inappropriate in the same way as men?	No	No
28. Are women able to work in the same industries as men?	Yes	No
29. Are women able to perform the same tasks at work as men?	Yes	No
30. Are the ages at which men and women can retire with full pension benefits equal?	No	Yes
31. Are the ages at which men and women can retire with partial pension benefits equal?	No	N/A
32. Are the mandatory retirement ages for men and women equal?	No	N/A

PROVIDING INCENTIVES TO WORK

	Score: 80	Score: 60
33. Are mothers guaranteed an equivalent position after maternity leave?	Yes	No
34. Does the government support or provide childcare services?	Yes	Yes
35. Are payments for childcare tax deductible?	No	No
36. Is primary education free and compulsory?	Yes	Yes
37. Are there tax deductions or credits specific to men?	No	No

GOING TO COURT

	Score: 50	Score: 25
38. Does a woman's testimony carry the same evidentiary weight in court as a man's?	Yes	Yes
39. Does the law establish an anti-discrimination commission?	No	No
40. Does the law mandate legal aid in civil/family matters?	Yes	No
41. Is there a small claims court/fast-track procedure?	No	No

BUILDING CREDIT

	Score: 0	Score: 25
42. Do retailers provide information to credit agencies?	N/A	N/A
43. Do utility companies provide information to credit agencies?	N/A	N/A
44. Is discrimination based on gender prohibited in access to credit?	No	Yes
45. Is discrimination based on marital status prohibited in access to credit?	No	No

PROTECTING WOMEN FROM VIOLENCE

	Score: 60	Score: 20
46. Is there legislation specifically addressing domestic violence? If not, are there aggravated penalties for crimes committed against a spouse or family member?	Yes	Yes
47. Is there legislation on sexual harassment in employment?	Yes	No
48. Is there legislation on sexual harassment in education?	No	No
49. Are there criminal penalties for sexual harassment in employment?	Yes	No
50. Are there civil remedies for sexual harassment in employment?	No	No

Note: See the data notes for more details on the scoring of each indicator.

	ANTIGUA AND BARBUDA	ARGENTINA
REGION	Latin America & Caribbean	Latin America & Caribbean
INCOME GROUP	High income	Upper middle income
FEMALE POPULATION	52,690	22,389,459
FEMALE LABOR FORCE (% OF TOTAL LABOR FORCE)	..	41%

ACCESSING INSTITUTIONS

	Score: 100	Score: 100
1. Are wives required to obey their husbands?	No	No
Can a woman legally do the following in the same way as a man:		
2. Apply for a passport?	Yes	Yes
3. Apply for a national ID card?	N/A	Yes
4. Travel outside the country?	Yes	Yes
5. Travel outside her home?	Yes	Yes
6. Get a job?	Yes	Yes
7. Sign a contract?	Yes	Yes
8. Register a business?	Yes	Yes
9. Open a bank account?	Yes	Yes
10. Choose where to live?	Yes	Yes
11. Be "head of household"?	N/A	N/A

USING PROPERTY

	Score: 80	Score: 100
12. Who legally administers marital property?	Original owner	Separate with spousal consent
13. Does the law provide for valuation of nonmonetary contributions?	No	Yes
14. Do men and women have equal ownership rights to immovable property?	Yes	Yes
15. Do sons and daughters have equal inheritance rights?	Yes	Yes
16. Do female and male surviving spouses have equal inheritance rights?	Yes	Yes

GETTING A JOB

	Score: 70	Score: 63
17. Is there paid leave available to women of at least 14 weeks?	No	No
18. Do women receive at least 2/3 of their wages for the first 14 weeks or the duration of the leave if it is shorter?	Yes	Yes
19. What is the percentage of maternity leave benefits paid by the government?	77%	100%
20. What is the difference between leave reserved for women and men relative to leave reserved for women, as a function of who pays?	0.77	1
21. Is there paid parental leave?	No	No
22. Does the law mandate equal remuneration for work of equal value?	No	Yes
23. Does the law mandate nondiscrimination based on gender in employment?	Yes	Yes
24. Is dismissal of pregnant workers prohibited?	No	Yes
25. Can parents work flexibly?	No	No
26. Can women work the same night hours as men?	Yes	Yes
27. Can women work in jobs deemed hazardous, arduous or morally inappropriate in the same way as men?	Yes	No
28. Are women able to work in the same industries as men?	Yes	No
29. Are women able to perform the same tasks at work as men?	Yes	No
30. Are the ages at which men and women can retire with full pension benefits equal?	Yes	No
31. Are the ages at which men and women can retire with partial pension benefits equal?	Yes	N/A
32. Are the mandatory retirement ages for men and women equal?	N/A	Yes

PROVIDING INCENTIVES TO WORK

	Score: 40	Score: 100
33. Are mothers guaranteed an equivalent position after maternity leave?	No	Yes
34. Does the government support or provide childcare services?	No	Yes
35. Are payments for childcare tax deductible?	No	Yes
36. Is primary education free and compulsory?	Yes	Yes
37. Are there tax deductions or credits specific to men?	No	No

GOING TO COURT

	Score: 50	Score: 75
38. Does a woman's testimony carry the same evidentiary weight in court as a man's?	Yes	Yes
39. Does the law establish an anti-discrimination commission?	No	Yes
40. Does the law mandate legal aid in civil/family matters?	No	No
41. Is there a small claims court/fast-track procedure?	Yes	Yes

BUILDING CREDIT

	Score: 0	Score: 50
42. Do retailers provide information to credit agencies?	N/A	Yes
43. Do utility companies provide information to credit agencies?	N/A	Yes
44. Is discrimination based on gender prohibited in access to credit?	No	No
45. Is discrimination based on marital status prohibited in access to credit?	No	No

PROTECTING WOMEN FROM VIOLENCE

	Score: 20	Score: 40
46. Is there legislation specifically addressing domestic violence? If not, are there aggravated penalties for crimes committed against a spouse or family member?	Yes	Yes
47. Is there legislation on sexual harassment in employment?	No	Yes
48. Is there legislation on sexual harassment in education?	No	No
49. Are there criminal penalties for sexual harassment in employment?	No	No
50. Are there civil remedies for sexual harassment in employment?	No	No

Note: See the data notes for more details on the scoring of each indicator.

	ARMENIA	AUSTRALIA
REGION	Europe & Central Asia	High income: OECD
INCOME GROUP	Lower middle income	High income
FEMALE POPULATION	1,580,790	12,074,743
FEMALE LABOR FORCE (% OF TOTAL LABOR FORCE)	47%	46%

ACCESSING INSTITUTIONS

	Score: 100	Score: 100
1. Are wives required to obey their husbands?	No	No
Can a woman legally do the following in the same way as a man:		
2. Apply for a passport?	Yes	Yes
3. Apply for a national ID card?	Yes	N/A
4. Travel outside the country?	Yes	Yes
5. Travel outside her home?	Yes	Yes
6. Get a job?	Yes	Yes
7. Sign a contract?	Yes	Yes
8. Register a business?	Yes	Yes
9. Open a bank account?	Yes	Yes
10. Choose where to live?	Yes	Yes
11. Be "head of household"?	N/A	N/A

USING PROPERTY

	Score: 100	Score: 100
12. Who legally administers marital property?	Both must agree	Original owner
13. Does the law provide for valuation of nonmonetary contributions?	Yes	Yes
14. Do men and women have equal ownership rights to immovable property?	Yes	Yes
15. Do sons and daughters have equal inheritance rights?	Yes	Yes
16. Do female and male surviving spouses have equal inheritance rights?	Yes	Yes

GETTING A JOB

	Score: 86	Score: 100
17. Is there paid leave available to women of at least 14 weeks?	Yes	Yes
18. Do women receive at least 2/3 of their wages for the first 14 weeks or the duration of the leave if it is shorter?	Yes	Yes
19. What is the percentage of maternity leave benefits paid by the government?	100%	100%
20. What is the difference between leave reserved for women and men relative to leave reserved for women, as a function of who pays?	1	1
21. Is there paid parental leave?	No	Yes
22. Does the law mandate equal remuneration for work of equal value?	No	Yes
23. Does the law mandate nondiscrimination based on gender in employment?	Yes	Yes
24. Is dismissal of pregnant workers prohibited?	Yes	Yes
25. Can parents work flexibly?	Yes	Yes
26. Can women work the same night hours as men?	Yes	Yes
27. Can women work in jobs deemed hazardous, arduous or morally inappropriate in the same way as men?	Yes	Yes
28. Are women able to work in the same industries as men?	Yes	Yes
29. Are women able to perform the same tasks at work as men?	Yes	Yes
30. Are the ages at which men and women can retire with full pension benefits equal?	Yes	Yes
31. Are the ages at which men and women can retire with partial pension benefits equal?	N/A	N/A
32. Are the mandatory retirement ages for men and women equal?	N/A	N/A

PROVIDING INCENTIVES TO WORK

	Score: 80	Score: 80
33. Are mothers guaranteed an equivalent position after maternity leave?	Yes	Yes
34. Does the government support or provide childcare services?	Yes	Yes
35. Are payments for childcare tax deductible?	No	No
36. Is primary education free and compulsory?	Yes	Yes
37. Are there tax deductions or credits specific to men?	No	No

GOING TO COURT

	Score: 50	Score: 100
38. Does a woman's testimony carry the same evidentiary weight in court as a man's?	Yes	Yes
39. Does the law establish an anti-discrimination commission?	Yes	Yes
40. Does the law mandate legal aid in civil/family matters?	No	Yes
41. Is there a small claims court/fast-track procedure?	No	Yes

BUILDING CREDIT

	Score: 25	Score: 100
42. Do retailers provide information to credit agencies?	No	Yes
43. Do utility companies provide information to credit agencies?	Yes	Yes
44. Is discrimination based on gender prohibited in access to credit?	No	Yes
45. Is discrimination based on marital status prohibited in access to credit?	No	Yes

PROTECTING WOMEN FROM VIOLENCE

	Score: 20	Score: 80
46. Is there legislation specifically addressing domestic violence? If not, are there aggravated penalties for crimes committed against a spouse or family member?	No	Yes
47. Is there legislation on sexual harassment in employment?	Yes	Yes
48. Is there legislation on sexual harassment in education?	No	Yes
49. Are there criminal penalties for sexual harassment in employment?	No	No
50. Are there civil remedies for sexual harassment in employment?	No	Yes

Note: See the data notes for more details on the scoring of each indicator.

	AUSTRIA	AZERBAIJAN
REGION	High income: OECD	Europe & Central Asia
INCOME GROUP	High income	Upper middle income
FEMALE POPULATION	4,447,318	4,901,191
FEMALE LABOR FORCE (% OF TOTAL LABOR FORCE)	47%	49%

ACCESSING INSTITUTIONS

	Score: 100	Score: 100
1. Are wives required to obey their husbands?	No	No
Can a woman legally do the following in the same way as a man:		
2. Apply for a passport?	Yes	Yes
3. Apply for a national ID card?	Yes	Yes
4. Travel outside the country?	Yes	Yes
5. Travel outside her home?	Yes	Yes
6. Get a job?	Yes	Yes
7. Sign a contract?	Yes	Yes
8. Register a business?	Yes	Yes
9. Open a bank account?	Yes	Yes
10. Choose where to live?	Yes	Yes
11. Be "head of household"?	N/A	N/A

USING PROPERTY

	Score: 100	Score: 100
12. Who legally administers marital property?	Original owner	Both must agree
13. Does the law provide for valuation of nonmonetary contributions?	Yes	Yes
14. Do men and women have equal ownership rights to immovable property?	Yes	Yes
15. Do sons and daughters have equal inheritance rights?	Yes	Yes
16. Do female and male surviving spouses have equal inheritance rights?	Yes	Yes

GETTING A JOB

	Score: 100	Score: 57
17. Is there paid leave available to women of at least 14 weeks?	Yes	Yes
18. Do women receive at least 2/3 of their wages for the first 14 weeks or the duration of the leave if it is shorter?	Yes	Yes
19. What is the percentage of maternity leave benefits paid by the government?	100%	100%
20. What is the difference between leave reserved for women and men relative to leave reserved for women, as a function of who pays?	1	1
21. Is there paid parental leave?	Yes	Yes
22. Does the law mandate equal remuneration for work of equal value?	Yes	No
23. Does the law mandate nondiscrimination based on gender in employment?	Yes	Yes
24. Is dismissal of pregnant workers prohibited?	Yes	Yes
25. Can parents work flexibly?	Yes	No
26. Can women work the same night hours as men?	Yes	No
27. Can women work in jobs deemed hazardous, arduous or morally inappropriate in the same way as men?	Yes	No
28. Are women able to work in the same industries as men?	Yes	No
29. Are women able to perform the same tasks at work as men?	Yes	No
30. Are the ages at which men and women can retire with full pension benefits equal?	Yes	Yes
31. Are the ages at which men and women can retire with partial pension benefits equal?	N/A	N/A
32. Are the mandatory retirement ages for men and women equal?	N/A	N/A

PROVIDING INCENTIVES TO WORK

	Score: 80	Score: 80
33. Are mothers guaranteed an equivalent position after maternity leave?	No	Yes
34. Does the government support or provide childcare services?	Yes	Yes
35. Are payments for childcare tax deductible?	Yes	No
36. Is primary education free and compulsory?	Yes	Yes
37. Are there tax deductions or credits specific to men?	No	No

GOING TO COURT

	Score: 100	Score: 25
38. Does a woman's testimony carry the same evidentiary weight in court as a man's?	Yes	Yes
39. Does the law establish an anti-discrimination commission?	Yes	No
40. Does the law mandate legal aid in civil/family matters?	Yes	No
41. Is there a small claims court/fast-track procedure?	Yes	No

BUILDING CREDIT

	Score: 100	Score: 25
42. Do retailers provide information to credit agencies?	Yes	No
43. Do utility companies provide information to credit agencies?	Yes	No
44. Is discrimination based on gender prohibited in access to credit?	Yes	Yes
45. Is discrimination based on marital status prohibited in access to credit?	Yes	No

PROTECTING WOMEN FROM VIOLENCE

	Score: 60	Score: 60
46. Is there legislation specifically addressing domestic violence? If not, are there aggravated penalties for crimes committed against a spouse or family member?	Yes	Yes
47. Is there legislation on sexual harassment in employment?	Yes	Yes
48. Is there legislation on sexual harassment in education?	No	No
49. Are there criminal penalties for sexual harassment in employment?	No	No
50. Are there civil remedies for sexual harassment in employment?	Yes	Yes

Note: See the data notes for more details on the scoring of each indicator.

	BAHAMAS, THE	BAHRAIN
REGION	Latin America & Caribbean	Middle East & North Africa
INCOME GROUP	High income	High income
FEMALE POPULATION	199,663	542,483
FEMALE LABOR FORCE (% OF TOTAL LABOR FORCE)	47%	21%

ACCESSING INSTITUTIONS

	Score: 100	Score: 45
1. Are wives required to obey their husbands?	No	Yes
Can a woman legally do the following in the same way as a man:		
2. Apply for a passport?	Yes	No
3. Apply for a national ID card?	N/A	Yes
4. Travel outside the country?	Yes	Yes
5. Travel outside her home?	Yes	No
6. Get a job?	Yes	No
7. Sign a contract?	Yes	Yes
8. Register a business?	Yes	Yes
9. Open a bank account?	Yes	Yes
10. Choose where to live?	Yes	No
11. Be "head of household"?	N/A	No

USING PROPERTY

	Score: 100	Score: 40
12. Who legally administers marital property?	Original owner	Original owner
13. Does the law provide for valuation of nonmonetary contributions?	Yes	No
14. Do men and women have equal ownership rights to immovable property?	Yes	Yes
15. Do sons and daughters have equal inheritance rights?	Yes	No
16. Do female and male surviving spouses have equal inheritance rights?	Yes	No

GETTING A JOB

	Score: 75	Score: 41
17. Is there paid leave available to women of at least 14 weeks?	No	No
18. Do women receive at least 2/3 of their wages for the first 14 weeks or the duration of the leave if it is shorter?	Yes	Yes
19. What is the percentage of maternity leave benefits paid by the government?	67%	0%
20. What is the difference between leave reserved for women and men relative to leave reserved for women, as a function of who pays?	0.67	0.02
21. Is there paid parental leave?	No	No
22. Does the law mandate equal remuneration for work of equal value?	No	No
23. Does the law mandate nondiscrimination based on gender in employment?	Yes	Yes
24. Is dismissal of pregnant workers prohibited?	Yes	Yes
25. Can parents work flexibly?	No	No
26. Can women work the same night hours as men?	Yes	Yes
27. Can women work in jobs deemed hazardous, arduous or morally inappropriate in the same way as men?	Yes	No
28. Are women able to work in the same industries as men?	Yes	No
29. Are women able to perform the same tasks at work as men?	Yes	No
30. Are the ages at which men and women can retire with full pension benefits equal?	Yes	No
31. Are the ages at which men and women can retire with partial pension benefits equal?	Yes	No
32. Are the mandatory retirement ages for men and women equal?	N/A	Yes

PROVIDING INCENTIVES TO WORK

	Score: 80	Score: 40
33. Are mothers guaranteed an equivalent position after maternity leave?	Yes	No
34. Does the government support or provide childcare services?	Yes	No
35. Are payments for childcare tax deductible?	No	No
36. Is primary education free and compulsory?	Yes	Yes
37. Are there tax deductions or credits specific to men?	No	No

GOING TO COURT

	Score: 50	Score: 25
38. Does a woman's testimony carry the same evidentiary weight in court as a man's?	Yes	No
39. Does the law establish an anti-discrimination commission?	No	No
40. Does the law mandate legal aid in civil/family matters?	No	No
41. Is there a small claims court/fast-track procedure?	Yes	Yes

BUILDING CREDIT

	Score: 0	Score: 25
42. Do retailers provide information to credit agencies?	N/A	Yes
43. Do utility companies provide information to credit agencies?	N/A	No
44. Is discrimination based on gender prohibited in access to credit?	No	No
45. Is discrimination based on marital status prohibited in access to credit?	No	No

PROTECTING WOMEN FROM VIOLENCE

	Score: 60	Score: 20
46. Is there legislation specifically addressing domestic violence? If not, are there aggravated penalties for crimes committed against a spouse or family member?	Yes	Yes
47. Is there legislation on sexual harassment in employment?	Yes	No
48. Is there legislation on sexual harassment in education?	No	No
49. Are there criminal penalties for sexual harassment in employment?	Yes	No
50. Are there civil remedies for sexual harassment in employment?	No	No

Note: See the data notes for more details on the scoring of each indicator.

	BANGLADESH	BARBADOS
REGION	South Asia	Latin America & Caribbean
INCOME GROUP	Lower middle income	High income
FEMALE POPULATION	80,706,124	148,498
FEMALE LABOR FORCE (% OF TOTAL LABOR FORCE)	29%	50%

ACCESSING INSTITUTIONS

	Score: 100	Score: 91
1. Are wives required to obey their husbands?	No	No
Can a woman legally do the following in the same way as a man:		
2. Apply for a passport?	Yes	No
3. Apply for a national ID card?	Yes	Yes
4. Travel outside the country?	Yes	Yes
5. Travel outside her home?	Yes	Yes
6. Get a job?	Yes	Yes
7. Sign a contract?	Yes	Yes
8. Register a business?	Yes	Yes
9. Open a bank account?	Yes	Yes
10. Choose where to live?	Yes	Yes
11. Be "head of household"?	N/A	N/A

USING PROPERTY

	Score: 40	Score: 100
12. Who legally administers marital property?	Original Owner	Original owner
13. Does the law provide for valuation of nonmonetary contributions?	No	Yes
14. Do men and women have equal ownership rights to immovable property?	Yes	Yes
15. Do sons and daughters have equal inheritance rights?	No	Yes
16. Do female and male surviving spouses have equal inheritance rights?	No	Yes

GETTING A JOB

	Score: 29	Score: 66
17. Is there paid leave available to women of at least 14 weeks?	Yes	No
18. Do women receive at least 2/3 of their wages for the first 14 weeks or the duration of the leave if it is shorter?	Yes	Yes
19. What is the percentage of maternity leave benefits paid by the government?	0%	100%
20. What is the difference between leave reserved for women and men relative to leave reserved for women, as a function of who pays?	0	1
21. Is there paid parental leave?	No	No
22. Does the law mandate equal remuneration for work of equal value?	No	No
23. Does the law mandate nondiscrimination based on gender in employment?	No	No
24. Is dismissal of pregnant workers prohibited?	No	Yes
25. Can parents work flexibly?	No	No
26. Can women work the same night hours as men?	Yes	Yes
27. Can women work in jobs deemed hazardous, arduous or morally inappropriate in the same way as men?	No	Yes
28. Are women able to work in the same industries as men?	No	Yes
29. Are women able to perform the same tasks at work as men?	No	No
30. Are the ages at which men and women can retire with full pension benefits equal?	N/A	Yes
31. Are the ages at which men and women can retire with partial pension benefits equal?	N/A	Yes
32. Are the mandatory retirement ages for men and women equal?	Yes	N/A

PROVIDING INCENTIVES TO WORK

	Score: 40	Score: 80
33. Are mothers guaranteed an equivalent position after maternity leave?	No	Yes
34. Does the government support or provide childcare services?	No	Yes
35. Are payments for childcare tax deductible?	No	No
36. Is primary education free and compulsory?	Yes	Yes
37. Are there tax deductions or credits specific to men?	No	No

GOING TO COURT

	Score: 100	Score: 75
38. Does a woman's testimony carry the same evidentiary weight in court as a man's?	Yes	Yes
39. Does the law establish an anti-discrimination commission?	Yes	No
40. Does the law mandate legal aid in civil/family matters?	Yes	Yes
41. Is there a small claims court/fast-track procedure?	Yes	Yes

BUILDING CREDIT

	Score: 0	Score: 0
42. Do retailers provide information to credit agencies?	N/A	N/A
43. Do utility companies provide information to credit agencies?	N/A	N/A
44. Is discrimination based on gender prohibited in access to credit?	No	No
45. Is discrimination based on marital status prohibited in access to credit?	No	No

PROTECTING WOMEN FROM VIOLENCE

	Score: 60	Score: 20
46. Is there legislation specifically addressing domestic violence? If not, are there aggravated penalties for crimes committed against a spouse or family member?	Yes	Yes
47. Is there legislation on sexual harassment in employment?	Yes	No
48. Is there legislation on sexual harassment in education?	Yes	No
49. Are there criminal penalties for sexual harassment in employment?	No	No
50. Are there civil remedies for sexual harassment in employment?	No	No

Note: See the data notes for more details on the scoring of each indicator.

	BELARUS	BELGIUM
REGION	Europe & Central Asia	High income: OECD
INCOME GROUP	Upper middle income	High income
FEMALE POPULATION	5,088,808	5,756,184
FEMALE LABOR FORCE (% OF TOTAL LABOR FORCE)	50%	46%

ACCESSING INSTITUTIONS

	Score: 100	Score: 100
1. Are wives required to obey their husbands?	No	No
Can a woman legally do the following in the same way as a man:		
2. Apply for a passport?	Yes	Yes
3. Apply for a national ID card?	N/A	Yes
4. Travel outside the country?	Yes	Yes
5. Travel outside her home?	Yes	Yes
6. Get a job?	Yes	Yes
7. Sign a contract?	Yes	Yes
8. Register a business?	Yes	Yes
9. Open a bank account?	Yes	Yes
10. Choose where to live?	Yes	Yes
11. Be *head of household*?	N/A	N/A

USING PROPERTY

	Score: 100	Score: 100
12. Who legally administers marital property?	Both must agree	Both must agree
13. Does the law provide for valuation of nonmonetary contributions?	Yes	Yes
14. Do men and women have equal ownership rights to immovable property?	Yes	Yes
15. Do sons and daughters have equal inheritance rights?	Yes	Yes
16. Do female and male surviving spouses have equal inheritance rights?	Yes	Yes

GETTING A JOB

	Score: 68	Score: 93
17. Is there paid leave available to women of at least 14 weeks?	Yes	Yes
18. Do women receive at least 2/3 of their wages for the first 14 weeks or the duration of the leave if it is shorter?	Yes	Yes
19. What is the percentage of maternity leave benefits paid by the government?	100%	100%
20. What is the difference between leave reserved for women and men relative to leave reserved for women, as a function of who pays?	1	1
21. Is there paid parental leave?	Yes	Yes
22. Does the law mandate equal remuneration for work of equal value?	Yes	Yes
23. Does the law mandate nondiscrimination based on gender in employment?	Yes	Yes
24. Is dismissal of pregnant workers prohibited?	Yes	Yes
25. Can parents work flexibly?	No	No
26. Can women work the same night hours as men?	Yes	Yes
27. Can women work in jobs deemed hazardous, arduous or morally inappropriate in the same way as men?	No	Yes
28. Are women able to work in the same industries as men?	No	Yes
29. Are women able to perform the same tasks at work as men?	No	Yes
30. Are the ages at which men and women can retire with full pension benefits equal?	No	Yes
31. Are the ages at which men and women can retire with partial pension benefits equal?	N/A	Yes
32. Are the mandatory retirement ages for men and women equal?	N/A	N/A

PROVIDING INCENTIVES TO WORK

	Score: 80	Score: 100
33. Are mothers guaranteed an equivalent position after maternity leave?	Yes	Yes
34. Does the government support or provide childcare services?	Yes	Yes
35. Are payments for childcare tax deductible?	No	Yes
36. Is primary education free and compulsory?	Yes	Yes
37. Are there tax deductions or credits specific to men?	No	No

GOING TO COURT

	Score: 50	Score: 100
38. Does a woman's testimony carry the same evidentiary weight in court as a man's?	Yes	Yes
39. Does the law establish an anti-discrimination commission?	No	Yes
40. Does the law mandate legal aid in civil/family matters?	Yes	Yes
41. Is there a small claims court/fast-track procedure?	No	Yes

BUILDING CREDIT

	Score: 0	Score: 50
42. Do retailers provide information to credit agencies?	No	Yes
43. Do utility companies provide information to credit agencies?	No	No
44. Is discrimination based on gender prohibited in access to credit?	No	Yes
45. Is discrimination based on marital status prohibited in access to credit?	No	No

PROTECTING WOMEN FROM VIOLENCE

	Score: 20	Score: 50
46. Is there legislation specifically addressing domestic violence? If not, are there aggravated penalties for crimes committed against a spouse or family member?	Yes	No, but aggravated penalties exist
47. Is there legislation on sexual harassment in employment?	No	Yes
48. Is there legislation on sexual harassment in education?	No	No
49. Are there criminal penalties for sexual harassment in employment?	No	No
50. Are there civil remedies for sexual harassment in employment?	No	Yes

Note: See the data notes for more details on the scoring of each indicator.

	BELIZE	BENIN
REGION	Latin America & Caribbean	Sub-Saharan Africa
INCOME GROUP	Upper middle income	Low income
FEMALE POPULATION	184,144	5,448,067
FEMALE LABOR FORCE (% OF TOTAL LABOR FORCE)	40%	49%

ACCESSING INSTITUTIONS

	Score: 90	Score: 73
1. Are wives required to obey their husbands?	No	No
Can a woman legally do the following in the same way as a man:		
2. Apply for a passport?	No	No
3. Apply for a national ID card?	N/A	No
4. Travel outside the country?	Yes	Yes
5. Travel outside her home?	Yes	Yes
6. Get a job?	Yes	Yes
7. Sign a contract?	Yes	Yes
8. Register a business?	Yes	Yes
9. Open a bank account?	Yes	Yes
10. Choose where to live?	Yes	No
11. Be "head of household"?	N/A	N/A

USING PROPERTY

	Score: 100	Score: 80
12. Who legally administers marital property?	Original owner	Original owner
13. Does the law provide for valuation of nonmonetary contributions?	Yes	No
14. Do men and women have equal ownership rights to immovable property?	Yes	Yes
15. Do sons and daughters have equal inheritance rights?	Yes	Yes
16. Do female and male surviving spouses have equal inheritance rights?	Yes	Yes

GETTING A JOB

	Score: 64	Score: 60
17. Is there paid leave available to women of at least 14 weeks?	Yes	Yes
18. Do women receive at least 2/3 of their wages for the first 14 weeks or the duration of the leave if it is shorter?	Yes	Yes
19. What is the percentage of maternity leave benefits paid by the government?	100%	50%
20. What is the difference between leave reserved for women and men relative to leave reserved for women, as a function of who pays?	1	0.52
21. Is there paid parental leave?	No	No
22. Does the law mandate equal remuneration for work of equal value?	No	Yes
23. Does the law mandate nondiscrimination based on gender in employment?	No	Yes
24. Is dismissal of pregnant workers prohibited?	Yes	Yes
25. Can parents work flexibly?	No	No
26. Can women work the same night hours as men?	Yes	Yes
27. Can women work in jobs deemed hazardous, arduous or morally inappropriate in the same way as men?	Yes	No
28. Are women able to work in the same industries as men?	No	No
29. Are women able to perform the same tasks at work as men?	Yes	No
30. Are the ages at which men and women can retire with full pension benefits equal?	Yes	Yes
31. Are the ages at which men and women can retire with partial pension benefits equal?	N/A	Yes
32. Are the mandatory retirement ages for men and women equal?	N/A	N/A

PROVIDING INCENTIVES TO WORK

	Score: 40	Score: 60
33. Are mothers guaranteed an equivalent position after maternity leave?	No	Yes
34. Does the government support or provide childcare services?	No	Yes
35. Are payments for childcare tax deductible?	No	No
36. Is primary education free and compulsory?	Yes	Yes
37. Are there tax deductions or credits specific to men?	No	Yes

GOING TO COURT

	Score: 50	Score: 25
38. Does a woman's testimony carry the same evidentiary weight in court as a man's?	Yes	Yes
39. Does the law establish an anti-discrimination commission?	No	No
40. Does the law mandate legal aid in civil/family matters?	No	No
41. Is there a small claims court/fast-track procedure?	Yes	No

BUILDING CREDIT

	Score: 0	Score: 0
42. Do retailers provide information to credit agencies?	N/A	N/A
43. Do utility companies provide information to credit agencies?	N/A	N/A
44. Is discrimination based on gender prohibited in access to credit?	No	No
45. Is discrimination based on marital status prohibited in access to credit?	No	No

PROTECTING WOMEN FROM VIOLENCE

	Score: 80	Score: 80
46. Is there legislation specifically addressing domestic violence? If not, are there aggravated penalties for crimes committed against a spouse or family member?	Yes	Yes
47. Is there legislation on sexual harassment in employment?	Yes	Yes
48. Is there legislation on sexual harassment in education?	Yes	Yes
49. Are there criminal penalties for sexual harassment in employment?	No	Yes
50. Are there civil remedies for sexual harassment in employment?	Yes	No

Note: See the data notes for more details on the scoring of each indicator.

	BHUTAN	BOLIVIA
REGION	South Asia	Latin America & Caribbean
INCOME GROUP	Lower middle income	Lower middle income
FEMALE POPULATION	369,452	5,436,260
FEMALE LABOR FORCE (% OF TOTAL LABOR FORCE)	40%	41%

ACCESSING INSTITUTIONS

	Score: 91	Score: 100
1. Are wives required to obey their husbands?	No	No
Can a woman legally do the following in the same way as a man:		
2. Apply for a passport?	Yes	Yes
3. Apply for a national ID card?	Yes	Yes
4. Travel outside the country?	Yes	Yes
5. Travel outside her home?	Yes	Yes
6. Get a job?	Yes	Yes
7. Sign a contract?	Yes	Yes
8. Register a business?	No	Yes
9. Open a bank account?	Yes	Yes
10. Choose where to live?	Yes	Yes
11. Be "head of household"?	N/A	N/A

USING PROPERTY

	Score: 80	Score: 100
12. Who legally administers marital property?	Other	Both must agree
13. Does the law provide for valuation of nonmonetary contributions?	No	Yes
14. Do men and women have equal ownership rights to immovable property?	Yes	Yes
15. Do sons and daughters have equal inheritance rights?	Yes	Yes
16. Do female and male surviving spouses have equal inheritance rights?	Yes	Yes

GETTING A JOB

	Score: 59	Score: 60
17. Is there paid leave available to women of at least 14 weeks?	No	No
18. Do women receive at least 2/3 of their wages for the first 14 weeks or the duration of the leave if it is shorter?	Yes	Yes
19. What is the percentage of maternity leave benefits paid by the government?	0%	100%
20. What is the difference between leave reserved for women and men relative to leave reserved for women, as a function of who pays?	0.09	1
21. Is there paid parental leave?	No	No
22. Does the law mandate equal remuneration for work of equal value?	Yes	Yes
23. Does the law mandate nondiscrimination based on gender in employment?	Yes	No
24. Is dismissal of pregnant workers prohibited?	Yes	Yes
25. Can parents work flexibly?	No	No
26. Can women work the same night hours as men?	Yes	No
27. Can women work in jobs deemed hazardous, arduous or morally inappropriate in the same way as men?	Yes	No
28. Are women able to work in the same industries as men?	Yes	Yes
29. Are women able to perform the same tasks at work as men?	No	Yes
30. Are the ages at which men and women can retire with full pension benefits equal?	N/A	No
31. Are the ages at which men and women can retire with partial pension benefits equal?	N/A	N/A
32. Are the mandatory retirement ages for men and women equal?	N/A	N/A

PROVIDING INCENTIVES TO WORK

	Score: 60	Score: 80
33. Are mothers guaranteed an equivalent position after maternity leave?	Yes	Yes
34. Does the government support or provide childcare services?	No	Yes
35. Are payments for childcare tax deductible?	Yes	No
36. Is primary education free and compulsory?	No	Yes
37. Are there tax deductions or credits specific to men?	No	No

GOING TO COURT

	Score: 25	Score: 50
38. Does a woman's testimony carry the same evidentiary weight in court as a man's?	Yes	Yes
39. Does the law establish an anti-discrimination commission?	No	Yes
40. Does the law mandate legal aid in civil/family matters?	No	No
41. Is there a small claims court/fast-track procedure?	No	No

BUILDING CREDIT

	Score: 25	Score: 100
42. Do retailers provide information to credit agencies?	No	Yes
43. Do utility companies provide information to credit agencies?	Yes	Yes
44. Is discrimination based on gender prohibited in access to credit?	No	Yes
45. Is discrimination based on marital status prohibited in access to credit?	No	Yes

PROTECTING WOMEN FROM VIOLENCE

	Score: 80	Score: 80
46. Is there legislation specifically addressing domestic violence? If not, are there aggravated penalties for crimes committed against a spouse or family member?	Yes	Yes
47. Is there legislation on sexual harassment in employment?	Yes	Yes
48. Is there legislation on sexual harassment in education?	No	Yes
49. Are there criminal penalties for sexual harassment in employment?	Yes	Yes
50. Are there civil remedies for sexual harassment in employment?	Yes	No

Note: See the data notes for more details on the scoring of each indicator.

	BOSNIA AND HERZEGOVINA	BOTSWANA
REGION	Europe & Central Asia	Sub-Saharan Africa
INCOME GROUP	Upper middle income	Upper middle income
FEMALE POPULATION	1,766,644	1,125,991
FEMALE LABOR FORCE (% OF TOTAL LABOR FORCE)	39%	47%

ACCESSING INSTITUTIONS

	Score: 100	Score: 91
1. Are wives required to obey their husbands?	No	No
Can a woman legally do the following in the same way as a man:		
2. Apply for a passport?	Yes	No
3. Apply for a national ID card?	Yes	Yes
4. Travel outside the country?	Yes	Yes
5. Travel outside her home?	Yes	Yes
6. Get a job?	Yes	Yes
7. Sign a contract?	Yes	Yes
8. Register a business?	Yes	Yes
9. Open a bank account?	Yes	Yes
10. Choose where to live?	Yes	Yes
11. Be "head of household"?	N/A	N/A

USING PROPERTY

	Score: 100	Score: 60
12. Who legally administers marital property?	Both must agree	Original Owner
13. Does the law provide for valuation of nonmonetary contributions?	Yes	No
14. Do men and women have equal ownership rights to immovable property?	Yes	Yes
15. Do sons and daughters have equal inheritance rights?	Yes	No
16. Do female and male surviving spouses have equal inheritance rights?	Yes	Yes

GETTING A JOB

	Score: 79	Score: 47
17. Is there paid leave available to women of at least 14 weeks?	Yes	No
18. Do women receive at least 2/3 of their wages for the first 14 weeks or the duration of the leave if it is shorter?	No	No
19. What is the percentage of maternity leave benefits paid by the government?	100%	0%
20. What is the difference between leave reserved for women and men relative to leave reserved for women, as a function of who pays?	1	0
21. Is there paid parental leave?	No	No
22. Does the law mandate equal remuneration for work of equal value?	Yes	No
23. Does the law mandate nondiscrimination based on gender in employment?	Yes	No
24. Is dismissal of pregnant workers prohibited?	Yes	No
25. Can parents work flexibly?	Yes	No
26. Can women work the same night hours as men?	No	Yes
27. Can women work in jobs deemed hazardous, arduous or morally inappropriate in the same way as men?	Yes	Yes
28. Are women able to work in the same industries as men?	No	Yes
29. Are women able to perform the same tasks at work as men?	Yes	Yes
30. Are the ages at which men and women can retire with full pension benefits equal?	Yes	Yes
31. Are the ages at which men and women can retire with partial pension benefits equal?	N/A	N/A
32. Are the mandatory retirement ages for men and women equal?	Yes	N/A

PROVIDING INCENTIVES TO WORK

	Score: 80	Score: 20
33. Are mothers guaranteed an equivalent position after maternity leave?	Yes	No
34. Does the government support or provide childcare services?	Yes	No
35. Are payments for childcare tax deductible?	No	No
36. Is primary education free and compulsory?	Yes	No
37. Are there tax deductions or credits specific to men?	No	No

GOING TO COURT

	Score: 100	Score: 75
38. Does a woman's testimony carry the same evidentiary weight in court as a man's?	Yes	Yes
39. Does the law establish an anti-discrimination commission?	Yes	No
40. Does the law mandate legal aid in civil/family matters?	Yes	Yes
41. Is there a small claims court/fast-track procedure?	Yes	Yes

BUILDING CREDIT

	Score: 100	Score: 50
42. Do retailers provide information to credit agencies?	Yes	Yes
43. Do utility companies provide information to credit agencies?	Yes	Yes
44. Is discrimination based on gender prohibited in access to credit?	Yes	No
45. Is discrimination based on marital status prohibited in access to credit?	Yes	No

PROTECTING WOMEN FROM VIOLENCE

	Score: 100	Score: 20
46. Is there legislation specifically addressing domestic violence? If not, are there aggravated penalties for crimes committed against a spouse or family member?	Yes	Yes
47. Is there legislation on sexual harassment in employment?	Yes	No
48. Is there legislation on sexual harassment in education?	Yes	No
49. Are there criminal penalties for sexual harassment in employment?	Yes	No
50. Are there civil remedies for sexual harassment in employment?	Yes	No

Note: See the data notes for more details on the scoring of each indicator.

	BRAZIL	BRUNEI DARUSSALAM
REGION	Latin America & Caribbean	East Asia & Pacific
INCOME GROUP	Upper middle income	High income
FEMALE POPULATION	105,581,634	205,281
FEMALE LABOR FORCE (% OF TOTAL LABOR FORCE)	43%	43%

ACCESSING INSTITUTIONS

	Score: 100	Score: 73
1. Are wives required to obey their husbands?	No	Yes
Can a woman legally do the following in the same way as a man:		
2. Apply for a passport?	Yes	Yes
3. Apply for a national ID card?	Yes	Yes
4. Travel outside the country?	Yes	Yes
5. Travel outside her home?	Yes	No
6. Get a job?	Yes	Yes
7. Sign a contract?	Yes	Yes
8. Register a business?	Yes	Yes
9. Open a bank account?	Yes	Yes
10. Choose where to live?	Yes	No
11. Be *head of household*?	N/A	N/A

USING PROPERTY

	Score: 100	Score: 60
12. Who legally administers marital property?	Both must agree	Original owner
13. Does the law provide for valuation of nonmonetary contributions?	Yes	Yes
14. Do men and women have equal ownership rights to immovable property?	Yes	Yes
15. Do sons and daughters have equal inheritance rights?	Yes	No
16. Do female and male surviving spouses have equal inheritance rights?	Yes	No

GETTING A JOB

	Score: 64	Score: 55
17. Is there paid leave available to women of at least 14 weeks?	Yes	No
18. Do women receive at least 2/3 of their wages for the first 14 weeks or the duration of the leave if it is shorter?	Yes	Yes
19. What is the percentage of maternity leave benefits paid by the government?	100%	40%
20. What is the difference between leave reserved for women and men relative to leave reserved for women, as a function of who pays?	1	0.4
21. Is there paid parental leave?	No	No
22. Does the law mandate equal remuneration for work of equal value?	No	No
23. Does the law mandate nondiscrimination based on gender in employment?	Yes	No
24. Is dismissal of pregnant workers prohibited?	Yes	No
25. Can parents work flexibly?	No	No
26. Can women work the same night hours as men?	Yes	Yes
27. Can women work in jobs deemed hazardous, arduous or morally inappropriate in the same way as men?	Yes	Yes
28. Are women able to work in the same industries as men?	Yes	Yes
29. Are women able to perform the same tasks at work as men?	No	Yes
30. Are the ages at which men and women can retire with full pension benefits equal?	No	Yes
31. Are the ages at which men and women can retire with partial pension benefits equal?	No	N/A
32. Are the mandatory retirement ages for men and women equal?	No	N/A

PROVIDING INCENTIVES TO WORK

	Score: 100	Score: 20
33. Are mothers guaranteed an equivalent position after maternity leave?	Yes	No
34. Does the government support or provide childcare services?	Yes	No
35. Are payments for childcare tax deductible?	Yes	No
36. Is primary education free and compulsory?	Yes	Yes
37. Are there tax deductions or credits specific to men?	No	Yes

GOING TO COURT

	Score: 75	Score: 25
38. Does a woman's testimony carry the same evidentiary weight in court as a man's?	Yes	No
39. Does the law establish an anti-discrimination commission?	No	No
40. Does the law mandate legal aid in civil/family matters?	Yes	No
41. Is there a small claims court/fast-track procedure?	Yes	Yes

BUILDING CREDIT

	Score: 50	Score: 25
42. Do retailers provide information to credit agencies?	Yes	No
43. Do utility companies provide information to credit agencies?	Yes	Yes
44. Is discrimination based on gender prohibited in access to credit?	No	No
45. Is discrimination based on marital status prohibited in access to credit?	No	No

PROTECTING WOMEN FROM VIOLENCE

	Score: 80	Score: 20
46. Is there legislation specifically addressing domestic violence? If not, are there aggravated penalties for crimes committed against a spouse or family member?	Yes	Yes
47. Is there legislation on sexual harassment in employment?	Yes	No
48. Is there legislation on sexual harassment in education?	No	No
49. Are there criminal penalties for sexual harassment in employment?	Yes	No
50. Are there civil remedies for sexual harassment in employment?	Yes	No

Note: See the data notes for more details on the scoring of each indicator.

	BULGARIA	BURKINA FASO
REGION	Europe & Central Asia	Sub-Saharan Africa
INCOME GROUP	Upper middle income	Low income
FEMALE POPULATION	3,666,246	9,389,543
FEMALE LABOR FORCE (% OF TOTAL LABOR FORCE)	46%	45%

ACCESSING INSTITUTIONS

	Score: 100	Score: 91
1. Are wives required to obey their husbands?	No	No
Can a woman legally do the following in the same way as a man:		
2. Apply for a passport?	Yes	Yes
3. Apply for a national ID card?	Yes	Yes
4. Travel outside the country?	Yes	Yes
5. Travel outside her home?	Yes	Yes
6. Get a job?	Yes	Yes
7. Sign a contract?	Yes	Yes
8. Register a business?	Yes	Yes
9. Open a bank account?	Yes	Yes
10. Choose where to live?	Yes	No
11. Be "head of household"?	N/A	N/A

USING PROPERTY

	Score: 100	Score: 100
12. Who legally administers marital property?	Both must agree	Both must agree
13. Does the law provide for valuation of nonmonetary contributions?	Yes	Yes
14. Do men and women have equal ownership rights to immovable property?	Yes	Yes
15. Do sons and daughters have equal inheritance rights?	Yes	Yes
16. Do female and male surviving spouses have equal inheritance rights?	Yes	Yes

GETTING A JOB

	Score: 91	Score: 57
17. Is there paid leave available to women of at least 14 weeks?	Yes	Yes
18. Do women receive at least 2/3 of their wages for the first 14 weeks or the duration of the leave if it is shorter?	Yes	Yes
19. What is the percentage of maternity leave benefits paid by the government?	100%	100%
20. What is the difference between leave reserved for women and men relative to leave reserved for women, as a function of who pays?	1	1
21. Is there paid parental leave?	Yes	No
22. Does the law mandate equal remuneration for work of equal value?	Yes	No
23. Does the law mandate nondiscrimination based on gender in employment?	Yes	Yes
24. Is dismissal of pregnant workers prohibited?	Yes	Yes
25. Can parents work flexibly?	No	No
26. Can women work the same night hours as men?	Yes	Yes
27. Can women work in jobs deemed hazardous, arduous or morally inappropriate in the same way as men?	Yes	No
28. Are women able to work in the same industries as men?	Yes	No
29. Are women able to perform the same tasks at work as men?	Yes	No
30. Are the ages at which men and women can retire with full pension benefits equal?	Yes	Yes
31. Are the ages at which men and women can retire with partial pension benefits equal?	No	N/A
32. Are the mandatory retirement ages for men and women equal?	N/A	N/A

PROVIDING INCENTIVES TO WORK

	Score: 80	Score: 60
33. Are mothers guaranteed an equivalent position after maternity leave?	Yes	Yes
34. Does the government support or provide childcare services?	Yes	Yes
35. Are payments for childcare tax deductible?	No	No
36. Is primary education free and compulsory?	Yes	Yes
37. Are there tax deductions or credits specific to men?	No	Yes

GOING TO COURT

	Score: 75	Score: 100
38. Does a woman's testimony carry the same evidentiary weight in court as a man's?	Yes	Yes
39. Does the law establish an anti-discrimination commission?	Yes	Yes
40. Does the law mandate legal aid in civil/family matters?	Yes	Yes
41. Is there a small claims court/fast-track procedure?	No	Yes

BUILDING CREDIT

	Score: 50	Score: 0
42. Do retailers provide information to credit agencies?	No	N/A
43. Do utility companies provide information to credit agencies?	No	N/A
44. Is discrimination based on gender prohibited in access to credit?	Yes	No
45. Is discrimination based on marital status prohibited in access to credit?	Yes	No

PROTECTING WOMEN FROM VIOLENCE

	Score: 80	Score: 40
46. Is there legislation specifically addressing domestic violence? If not, are there aggravated penalties for crimes committed against a spouse or family member?	Yes	No
47. Is there legislation on sexual harassment in employment?	Yes	Yes
48. Is there legislation on sexual harassment in education?	Yes	No
49. Are there criminal penalties for sexual harassment in employment?	No	Yes
50. Are there civil remedies for sexual harassment in employment?	Yes	No

Note: See the data notes for more details on the scoring of each indicator.

	BURUNDI	CABO VERDE
REGION	Sub-Saharan Africa	Sub-Saharan Africa
INCOME GROUP	Low income	Lower middle income
FEMALE POPULATION	5,322,148	273,205
FEMALE LABOR FORCE (% OF TOTAL LABOR FORCE)	52%	41%
ACCESSING INSTITUTIONS	Score: 91	Score: 100
1. Are wives required to obey their husbands?	No	No
Can a woman legally do the following in the same way as a man:		
2. Apply for a passport?	Yes	Yes
3. Apply for a national ID card?	Yes	Yes
4. Travel outside the country?	Yes	Yes
5. Travel outside her home?	Yes	Yes
6. Get a job?	Yes	Yes
7. Sign a contract?	Yes	Yes
8. Register a business?	Yes	Yes
9. Open a bank account?	Yes	Yes
10. Choose where to live?	Yes	Yes
11. Be "head of household"?	No	N/A
USING PROPERTY	Score: 100	Score: 100
12. Who legally administers marital property?	Both must agree	Both must agree
13. Does the law provide for valuation of nonmonetary contributions?	Yes	Yes
14. Do men and women have equal ownership rights to immovable property?	Yes	Yes
15. Do sons and daughters have equal inheritance rights?	..	Yes
16. Do female and male surviving spouses have equal inheritance rights?	..	Yes
GETTING A JOB	Score: 73	Score: 71
17. Is there paid leave available to women of at least 14 weeks?	No	No
18. Do women receive at least 2/3 of their wages for the first 14 weeks or the duration of the leave if it is shorter?	Yes	Yes
19. What is the percentage of maternity leave benefits paid by the government?	50%	90%
20. What is the difference between leave reserved for women and men relative to leave reserved for women, as a function of who pays?	0.52	0.9
21. Is there paid parental leave?	No	No
22. Does the law mandate equal remuneration for work of equal value?	No	No
23. Does the law mandate nondiscrimination based on gender in employment?	Yes	Yes
24. Is dismissal of pregnant workers prohibited?	Yes	Yes
25. Can parents work flexibly?	No	No
26. Can women work the same night hours as men?	Yes	Yes
27. Can women work in jobs deemed hazardous, arduous or morally inappropriate in the same way as men?	Yes	Yes
28. Are women able to work in the same industries as men?	Yes	Yes
29. Are women able to perform the same tasks at work as men?	Yes	Yes
30. Are the ages at which men and women can retire with full pension benefits equal?	Yes	No
31. Are the ages at which men and women can retire with partial pension benefits equal?	N/A	N/A
32. Are the mandatory retirement ages for men and women equal?	Yes	N/A
PROVIDING INCENTIVES TO WORK	Score: 40	Score: 60
33. Are mothers guaranteed an equivalent position after maternity leave?	No	No
34. Does the government support or provide childcare services?	Yes	Yes
35. Are payments for childcare tax deductible?	No	No
36. Is primary education free and compulsory?	No	Yes
37. Are there tax deductions or credits specific to men?	No	No
GOING TO COURT	Score: 75	Score: 50
38. Does a woman's testimony carry the same evidentiary weight in court as a man's?	Yes	Yes
39. Does the law establish an anti-discrimination commission?	Yes	No
40. Does the law mandate legal aid in civil/family matters?	No	No
41. Is there a small claims court/fast-track procedure?	Yes	Yes
BUILDING CREDIT	Score: 0	Score: 50
42. Do retailers provide information to credit agencies?	N/A	No
43. Do utility companies provide information to credit agencies?	N/A	No
44. Is discrimination based on gender prohibited in access to credit?	No	Yes
45. Is discrimination based on marital status prohibited in access to credit?	No	Yes
PROTECTING WOMEN FROM VIOLENCE	Score: 80	Score: 60
46. Is there legislation specifically addressing domestic violence? If not, are there aggravated penalties for crimes committed against a spouse or family member?	Yes	Yes
47. Is there legislation on sexual harassment in employment?	Yes	Yes
48. Is there legislation on sexual harassment in education?	No	No
49. Are there criminal penalties for sexual harassment in employment?	Yes	Yes
50. Are there civil remedies for sexual harassment in employment?	Yes	No

Note: See the data notes for more details on the scoring of each indicator.

	CAMBODIA	CAMEROON
REGION	East Asia & Pacific	Sub-Saharan Africa
INCOME GROUP	Lower middle income	Lower middle income
FEMALE POPULATION	8,072,646	11,718,078
FEMALE LABOR FORCE (% OF TOTAL LABOR FORCE)	50%	47%

ACCESSING INSTITUTIONS

	Score: 100	Score: 55
1. Are wives required to obey their husbands?	No	No
Can a woman legally do the following in the same way as a man:		
2. Apply for a passport?	Yes	No
3. Apply for a national ID card?	Yes	No
4. Travel outside the country?	Yes	Yes
5. Travel outside her home?	Yes	Yes
6. Get a job?	Yes	No
7. Sign a contract?	Yes	Yes
8. Register a business?	Yes	Yes
9. Open a bank account?	Yes	Yes
10. Choose where to live?	Yes	No
11. Be "head of household"?	N/A	No

USING PROPERTY

	Score: 100	Score: 60
12. Who legally administers marital property?	Both must agree	Husband
13. Does the law provide for valuation of nonmonetary contributions?	Yes	Yes
14. Do men and women have equal ownership rights to immovable property?	Yes	No
15. Do sons and daughters have equal inheritance rights?	Yes	Yes
16. Do female and male surviving spouses have equal inheritance rights?	Yes	Yes

GETTING A JOB

	Score: 62	Score: 53
17. Is there paid leave available to women of at least 14 weeks?	No	Yes
18. Do women receive at least 2/3 of their wages for the first 14 weeks or the duration of the leave if it is shorter?	No	Yes
19. What is the percentage of maternity leave benefits paid by the government?	0%	100%
20. What is the difference between leave reserved for women and men relative to leave reserved for women, as a function of who pays?	0	1
21. Is there paid parental leave?	No	No
22. Does the law mandate equal remuneration for work of equal value?	No	No
23. Does the law mandate nondiscrimination based on gender in employment?	Yes	No
24. Is dismissal of pregnant workers prohibited?	Yes	Yes
25. Can parents work flexibly?	No	No
26. Can women work the same night hours as men?	Yes	Yes
27. Can women work in jobs deemed hazardous, arduous or morally inappropriate in the same way as men?	Yes	No
28. Are women able to work in the same industries as men?	Yes	No
29. Are women able to perform the same tasks at work as men?	Yes	No
30. Are the ages at which men and women can retire with full pension benefits equal?	Yes	Yes
31. Are the ages at which men and women can retire with partial pension benefits equal?	N/A	Yes
32. Are the mandatory retirement ages for men and women equal?	N/A	N/A

PROVIDING INCENTIVES TO WORK

	Score: 80	Score: 80
33. Are mothers guaranteed an equivalent position after maternity leave?	Yes	Yes
34. Does the government support or provide childcare services?	Yes	Yes
35. Are payments for childcare tax deductible?	No	No
36. Is primary education free and compulsory?	Yes	Yes
37. Are there tax deductions or credits specific to men?	No	No

GOING TO COURT

	Score: 75	Score: 100
38. Does a woman's testimony carry the same evidentiary weight in court as a man's?	Yes	Yes
39. Does the law establish an anti-discrimination commission?	Yes	Yes
40. Does the law mandate legal aid in civil/family matters?	Yes	Yes
41. Is there a small claims court/fast-track procedure?	No	Yes

BUILDING CREDIT

	Score: 50	Score: 0
42. Do retailers provide information to credit agencies?	No	No
43. Do utility companies provide information to credit agencies?	No	No
44. Is discrimination based on gender prohibited in access to credit?	Yes	No
45. Is discrimination based on marital status prohibited in access to credit?	Yes	No

PROTECTING WOMEN FROM VIOLENCE

	Score: 60	Score: 60
46. Is there legislation specifically addressing domestic violence? If not, are there aggravated penalties for crimes committed against a spouse or family member?	Yes	No
47. Is there legislation on sexual harassment in employment?	Yes	Yes
48. Is there legislation on sexual harassment in education?	No	Yes
49. Are there criminal penalties for sexual harassment in employment?	Yes	Yes
50. Are there civil remedies for sexual harassment in employment?	No	No

Note: See the data notes for more details on the scoring of each indicator.

	CANADA	CENTRAL AFRICAN REPUBLIC
REGION	High income: OECD	Sub-Saharan Africa
INCOME GROUP	High income	Low income
FEMALE POPULATION	18,286,037	2,329,740
FEMALE LABOR FORCE (% OF TOTAL LABOR FORCE)	47%	45%

ACCESSING INSTITUTIONS

	Score: 100	Score: 82
1. Are wives required to obey their husbands?	No	No
Can a woman legally do the following in the same way as a man:		
2. Apply for a passport?	Yes	Yes
3. Apply for a national ID card?	N/A	Yes
4. Travel outside the country?	Yes	Yes
5. Travel outside her home?	Yes	Yes
6. Get a job?	Yes	Yes
7. Sign a contract?	Yes	Yes
8. Register a business?	Yes	Yes
9. Open a bank account?	Yes	Yes
10. Choose where to live?	Yes	No
11. Be "head of household"?	N/A	No

USING PROPERTY

	Score: 100	Score: 100
12. Who legally administers marital property?	Original owner	Both must agree
13. Does the law provide for valuation of nonmonetary contributions?	Yes	Yes
14. Do men and women have equal ownership rights to immovable property?	Yes	Yes
15. Do sons and daughters have equal inheritance rights?	Yes	Yes
16. Do female and male surviving spouses have equal inheritance rights?	Yes	Yes

GETTING A JOB

	Score: 92	Score: 45
17. Is there paid leave available to women of at least 14 weeks?	Yes	Yes
18. Do women receive at least 2/3 of their wages for the first 14 weeks or the duration of the leave if it is shorter?	No	No
19. What is the percentage of maternity leave benefits paid by the government?	100%	100%
20. What is the difference between leave reserved for women and men relative to leave reserved for women, as a function of who pays?	1	1
21. Is there paid parental leave?	Yes	No
22. Does the law mandate equal remuneration for work of equal value?	Yes	No
23. Does the law mandate nondiscrimination based on gender in employment?	Yes	No
24. Is dismissal of pregnant workers prohibited?	Yes	No
25. Can parents work flexibly?	No	No
26. Can women work the same night hours as men?	Yes	Yes
27. Can women work in jobs deemed hazardous, arduous or morally inappropriate in the same way as men?	Yes	No
28. Are women able to work in the same industries as men?	Yes	No
29. Are women able to perform the same tasks at work as men?	Yes	No
30. Are the ages at which men and women can retire with full pension benefits equal?	Yes	Yes
31. Are the ages at which men and women can retire with partial pension benefits equal?	Yes	N/A
32. Are the mandatory retirement ages for men and women equal?	N/A	Yes

PROVIDING INCENTIVES TO WORK

	Score: 100	Score: 60
33. Are mothers guaranteed an equivalent position after maternity leave?	Yes	Yes
34. Does the government support or provide childcare services?	Yes	No
35. Are payments for childcare tax deductible?	Yes	No
36. Is primary education free and compulsory?	Yes	Yes
37. Are there tax deductions or credits specific to men?	No	No

GOING TO COURT

	Score: 100	Score: 25
38. Does a woman's testimony carry the same evidentiary weight in court as a man's?	Yes	Yes
39. Does the law establish an anti-discrimination commission?	Yes	No
40. Does the law mandate legal aid in civil/family matters?	Yes	No
41. Is there a small claims court/fast-track procedure?	Yes	No

BUILDING CREDIT

	Score: 100	Score: 0
42. Do retailers provide information to credit agencies?	Yes	N/A
43. Do utility companies provide information to credit agencies?	Yes	N/A
44. Is discrimination based on gender prohibited in access to credit?	Yes	No
45. Is discrimination based on marital status prohibited in access to credit?	Yes	No

PROTECTING WOMEN FROM VIOLENCE

	Score: 70	Score: 60
46. Is there legislation specifically addressing domestic violence? If not, are there aggravated penalties for crimes committed against a spouse or family member?	No, but aggravated penalties exist	Yes
47. Is there legislation on sexual harassment in employment?	Yes	Yes
48. Is there legislation on sexual harassment in education?	No	No
49. Are there criminal penalties for sexual harassment in employment?	Yes	Yes
50. Are there civil remedies for sexual harassment in employment?	Yes	No

Note: See the data notes for more details on the scoring of each indicator.

	CHAD	CHILE
REGION	Sub-Saharan Africa	High income: OECD
INCOME GROUP	Low income	High income
FEMALE POPULATION	7,215,991	9,072,243
FEMALE LABOR FORCE (% OF TOTAL LABOR FORCE)	46%	41%

ACCESSING INSTITUTIONS

	Score: 64	Score: 91
1. Are wives required to obey their husbands?	No	No
Can a woman legally do the following in the same way as a man:		
2. Apply for a passport?	Yes	Yes
3. Apply for a national ID card?	Yes	Yes
4. Travel outside the country?	Yes	Yes
5. Travel outside her home?	Yes	Yes
6. Get a job?	No	Yes
7. Sign a contract?	Yes	Yes
8. Register a business?	Yes	Yes
9. Open a bank account?	No	Yes
10. Choose where to live?	No	Yes
11. Be "head of household"?	No	No

USING PROPERTY

	Score: 60	Score: 60
12. Who legally administers marital property?	Husband	Husband
13. Does the law provide for valuation of nonmonetary contributions?	Yes	Yes
14. Do men and women have equal ownership rights to immovable property?	No	No
15. Do sons and daughters have equal inheritance rights?	Yes	Yes
16. Do female and male surviving spouses have equal inheritance rights?	Yes	Yes

GETTING A JOB

	Score: 65	Score: 75
17. Is there paid leave available to women of at least 14 weeks?	Yes	Yes
18. Do women receive at least 2/3 of their wages for the first 14 weeks or the duration of the leave if it is shorter?	No	Yes
19. What is the percentage of maternity leave benefits paid by the government?	100%	100%
20. What is the difference between leave reserved for women and men relative to leave reserved for women, as a function of who pays?	1	1
21. Is there paid parental leave?	No	Yes
22. Does the law mandate equal remuneration for work of equal value?	Yes	No
23. Does the law mandate nondiscrimination based on gender in employment?	Yes	Yes
24. Is dismissal of pregnant workers prohibited?	Yes	Yes
25. Can parents work flexibly?	No	No
26. Can women work the same night hours as men?	Yes	Yes
27. Can women work in jobs deemed hazardous, arduous or morally inappropriate in the same way as men?	No	Yes
28. Are women able to work in the same industries as men?	No	Yes
29. Are women able to perform the same tasks at work as men?	No	No
30. Are the ages at which men and women can retire with full pension benefits equal?	Yes	No
31. Are the ages at which men and women can retire with partial pension benefits equal?	Yes	N/A
32. Are the mandatory retirement ages for men and women equal?	N/A	N/A

PROVIDING INCENTIVES TO WORK

	Score: 80	Score: 100
33. Are mothers guaranteed an equivalent position after maternity leave?	Yes	Yes
34. Does the government support or provide childcare services?	Yes	Yes
35. Are payments for childcare tax deductible?	No	Yes
36. Is primary education free and compulsory?	Yes	Yes
37. Are there tax deductions or credits specific to men?	No	No

GOING TO COURT

	Score: 75	Score: 75
38. Does a woman's testimony carry the same evidentiary weight in court as a man's?	Yes	Yes
39. Does the law establish an anti-discrimination commission?	No	No
40. Does the law mandate legal aid in civil/family matters?	Yes	Yes
41. Is there a small claims court/fast-track procedure?	Yes	Yes

BUILDING CREDIT

	Score: 0	Score: 25
42. Do retailers provide information to credit agencies?	N/A	Yes
43. Do utility companies provide information to credit agencies?	N/A	No
44. Is discrimination based on gender prohibited in access to credit?	No	No
45. Is discrimination based on marital status prohibited in access to credit?	No	No

PROTECTING WOMEN FROM VIOLENCE

	Score: 50	Score: 40
46. Is there legislation specifically addressing domestic violence? If not, are there aggravated penalties for crimes committed against a spouse or family member?	No, but aggravated penalties exist	Yes
47. Is there legislation on sexual harassment in employment?	Yes	Yes
48. Is there legislation on sexual harassment in education?	No	No
49. Are there criminal penalties for sexual harassment in employment?	Yes	No
50. Are there civil remedies for sexual harassment in employment?	No	No

Note: See the data notes for more details on the scoring of each indicator.

	CHINA	COLOMBIA
REGION	East Asia & Pacific	Latin America & Caribbean
INCOME GROUP	Upper middle income	Upper middle income
FEMALE POPULATION	668,260,013	24,708,199
FEMALE LABOR FORCE (% OF TOTAL LABOR FORCE)	44%	43%

ACCESSING INSTITUTIONS

	Score: 100	Score: 100
1. Are wives required to obey their husbands?	No	No
Can a woman legally do the following in the same way as a man:		
2. Apply for a passport?	Yes	Yes
3. Apply for a national ID card?	Yes	Yes
4. Travel outside the country?	Yes	Yes
5. Travel outside her home?	Yes	Yes
6. Get a job?	Yes	Yes
7. Sign a contract?	Yes	Yes
8. Register a business?	Yes	Yes
9. Open a bank account?	Yes	Yes
10. Choose where to live?	Yes	Yes
11. Be "head of household"?	N/A	N/A

USING PROPERTY

	Score: 100	Score: 100
12. Who legally administers marital property?	Both must agree	Original owner
13. Does the law provide for valuation of nonmonetary contributions?	Yes	Yes
14. Do men and women have equal ownership rights to immovable property?	Yes	Yes
15. Do sons and daughters have equal inheritance rights?	Yes	Yes
16. Do female and male surviving spouses have equal inheritance rights?	Yes	Yes

GETTING A JOB

	Score: 50	Score: 68
17. Is there paid leave available to women of at least 14 weeks?	Yes	Yes
18. Do women receive at least 2/3 of their wages for the first 14 weeks or the duration of the leave if it is shorter?	Yes	Yes
19. What is the percentage of maternity leave benefits paid by the government?	100%	100%
20. What is the difference between leave reserved for women and men relative to leave reserved for women, as a function of who pays?	1	1
21. Is there paid parental leave?	No	No
22. Does the law mandate equal remuneration for work of equal value?	No	No
23. Does the law mandate nondiscrimination based on gender in employment?	Yes	Yes
24. Is dismissal of pregnant workers prohibited?	Yes	Yes
25. Can parents work flexibly?	No	No
26. Can women work the same night hours as men?	Yes	Yes
27. Can women work in jobs deemed hazardous, arduous or morally inappropriate in the same way as men?	No	Yes
28. Are women able to work in the same industries as men?	No	Yes
29. Are women able to perform the same tasks at work as men?	No	No
30. Are the ages at which men and women can retire with full pension benefits equal?	No	No
31. Are the ages at which men and women can retire with partial pension benefits equal?	N/A	N/A
32. Are the mandatory retirement ages for men and women equal?	N/A	N/A

PROVIDING INCENTIVES TO WORK

	Score: 60	Score: 80
33. Are mothers guaranteed an equivalent position after maternity leave?	No	Yes
34. Does the government support or provide childcare services?	Yes	Yes
35. Are payments for childcare tax deductible?	No	No
36. Is primary education free and compulsory?	Yes	Yes
37. Are there tax deductions or credits specific to men?	No	No

GOING TO COURT

	Score: 75	Score: 50
38. Does a woman's testimony carry the same evidentiary weight in court as a man's?	Yes	Yes
39. Does the law establish an anti-discrimination commission?	No	No
40. Does the law mandate legal aid in civil/family matters?	Yes	No
41. Is there a small claims court/fast-track procedure?	Yes	Yes

BUILDING CREDIT

	Score: 25	Score: 50
42. Do retailers provide information to credit agencies?	No	Yes
43. Do utility companies provide information to credit agencies?	Yes	Yes
44. Is discrimination based on gender prohibited in access to credit?	No	No
45. Is discrimination based on marital status prohibited in access to credit?	No	No

PROTECTING WOMEN FROM VIOLENCE

	Score: 80	Score: 80
46. Is there legislation specifically addressing domestic violence? If not, are there aggravated penalties for crimes committed against a spouse or family member?	Yes	Yes
47. Is there legislation on sexual harassment in employment?	Yes	Yes
48. Is there legislation on sexual harassment in education?	No	No
49. Are there criminal penalties for sexual harassment in employment?	Yes	Yes
50. Are there civil remedies for sexual harassment in employment?	Yes	Yes

Note: See the data notes for more details on the scoring of each indicator.

	COMOROS	CONGO, DEM. REP.
REGION	Sub-Saharan Africa	Sub-Saharan Africa
INCOME GROUP	Low income	Low income
FEMALE POPULATION	394,276	39,460,508
FEMALE LABOR FORCE (% OF TOTAL LABOR FORCE)	42%	50%

ACCESSING INSTITUTIONS

	Score: 73	Score: 90
1. Are wives required to obey their husbands?	No	No
Can a woman legally do the following in the same way as a man:		
2. Apply for a passport?	Yes	Yes
3. Apply for a national ID card?	Yes	N/A
4. Travel outside the country?	Yes	Yes
5. Travel outside her home?	Yes	Yes
6. Get a job?	No	Yes
7. Sign a contract?	Yes	Yes
8. Register a business?	Yes	Yes
9. Open a bank account?	Yes	Yes
10. Choose where to live?	No	Yes
11. Be "head of household"?	No	No

USING PROPERTY

	Score: 40	Score: 60
12. Who legally administers marital property?	Original owner	Husband
13. Does the law provide for valuation of nonmonetary contributions?	No	Yes
14. Do men and women have equal ownership rights to immovable property?	Yes	No
15. Do sons and daughters have equal inheritance rights?	No	Yes
16. Do female and male surviving spouses have equal inheritance rights?	No	Yes

GETTING A JOB

	Score: 69	Score: 54
17. Is there paid leave available to women of at least 14 weeks?	Yes	Yes
18. Do women receive at least 2/3 of their wages for the first 14 weeks or the duration of the leave if it is shorter?	Yes	Yes
19. What is the percentage of maternity leave benefits paid by the government?	0%	0%
20. What is the difference between leave reserved for women and men relative to leave reserved for women, as a function of who pays?	0	0.02
21. Is there paid parental leave?	No	No
22. Does the law mandate equal remuneration for work of equal value?	Yes	No
23. Does the law mandate nondiscrimination based on gender in employment?	Yes	Yes
24. Is dismissal of pregnant workers prohibited?	Yes	Yes
25. Can parents work flexibly?	No	No
26. Can women work the same night hours as men?	Yes	Yes
27. Can women work in jobs deemed hazardous, arduous or morally inappropriate in the same way as men?	Yes	No
28. Are women able to work in the same industries as men?	Yes	Yes
29. Are women able to perform the same tasks at work as men?	Yes	Yes
30. Are the ages at which men and women can retire with full pension benefits equal?	N/A	No
31. Are the ages at which men and women can retire with partial pension benefits equal?	N/A	N/A
32. Are the mandatory retirement ages for men and women equal?	N/A	N/A

PROVIDING INCENTIVES TO WORK

	Score: 60	Score: 40
33. Are mothers guaranteed an equivalent position after maternity leave?	Yes	No
34. Does the government support or provide childcare services?	No	Yes
35. Are payments for childcare tax deductible?	No	No
36. Is primary education free and compulsory?	Yes	Yes
37. Are there tax deductions or credits specific to men?	No	Yes

GOING TO COURT

	Score: 50	Score: 50
38. Does a woman's testimony carry the same evidentiary weight in court as a man's?	Yes	Yes
39. Does the law establish an anti-discrimination commission?	Yes	No
40. Does the law mandate legal aid in civil/family matters?	No	No
41. Is there a small claims court/fast-track procedure?	No	Yes

BUILDING CREDIT

	Score: 0	Score: 25
42. Do retailers provide information to credit agencies?	No	N/A
43. Do utility companies provide information to credit agencies?	No	N/A
44. Is discrimination based on gender prohibited in access to credit?	No	Yes
45. Is discrimination based on marital status prohibited in access to credit?	No	No

PROTECTING WOMEN FROM VIOLENCE

	Score: 60	Score: 40
46. Is there legislation specifically addressing domestic violence? If not, are there aggravated penalties for crimes committed against a spouse or family member?	Yes	No
47. Is there legislation on sexual harassment in employment?	Yes	Yes
48. Is there legislation on sexual harassment in education?	No	No
49. Are there criminal penalties for sexual harassment in employment?	No	Yes
50. Are there civil remedies for sexual harassment in employment?	Yes	No

Note: See the data notes for more details on the scoring of each indicator.

	CONGO, REP.	COSTA RICA
REGION	Sub-Saharan Africa	Latin America & Caribbean
INCOME GROUP	Lower middle income	Upper middle income
FEMALE POPULATION	2,561,678	2,427,479
FEMALE LABOR FORCE (% OF TOTAL LABOR FORCE)	49%	38%

ACCESSING INSTITUTIONS

	Score: 64	Score: 100
1. Are wives required to obey their husbands?	No	No
Can a woman legally do the following in the same way as a man:		
2. Apply for a passport?	No	Yes
3. Apply for a national ID card?	No	Yes
4. Travel outside the country?	Yes	Yes
5. Travel outside her home?	Yes	Yes
6. Get a job?	Yes	Yes
7. Sign a contract?	Yes	Yes
8. Register a business?	Yes	Yes
9. Open a bank account?	Yes	Yes
10. Choose where to live?	No	Yes
11. Be "head of household"?	No	N/A

USING PROPERTY

	Score: 60	Score: 100
12. Who legally administers marital property?	Husband	Original owner
13. Does the law provide for valuation of nonmonetary contributions?	Yes	Yes
14. Do men and women have equal ownership rights to immovable property?	No	Yes
15. Do sons and daughters have equal inheritance rights?	Yes	Yes
16. Do female and male surviving spouses have equal inheritance rights?	Yes	Yes

GETTING A JOB

	Score: 40	Score: 59
17. Is there paid leave available to women of at least 14 weeks?	Yes	Yes
18. Do women receive at least 2/3 of their wages for the first 14 weeks or the duration of the leave if it is shorter?	Yes	Yes
19. What is the percentage of maternity leave benefits paid by the government?	50%	50%
20. What is the difference between leave reserved for women and men relative to leave reserved for women, as a function of who pays?	0.5	0.5
21. Is there paid parental leave?	No	No
22. Does the law mandate equal remuneration for work of equal value?	No	No
23. Does the law mandate nondiscrimination based on gender in employment?	No	Yes
24. Is dismissal of pregnant workers prohibited?	No	Yes
25. Can parents work flexibly?	No	No
26. Can women work the same night hours as men?	Yes	No
27. Can women work in jobs deemed hazardous, arduous or morally inappropriate in the same way as men?	No	No
28. Are women able to work in the same industries as men?	No	Yes
29. Are women able to perform the same tasks at work as men?	No	Yes
30. Are the ages at which men and women can retire with full pension benefits equal?	Yes	Yes
31. Are the ages at which men and women can retire with partial pension benefits equal?	N/A	No
32. Are the mandatory retirement ages for men and women equal?	Yes	N/A

PROVIDING INCENTIVES TO WORK

	Score: 40	Score: 60
33. Are mothers guaranteed an equivalent position after maternity leave?	Yes	No
34. Does the government support or provide childcare services?	No	Yes
35. Are payments for childcare tax deductible?	No	No
36. Is primary education free and compulsory?	Yes	Yes
37. Are there tax deductions or credits specific to men?	Yes	No

GOING TO COURT

	Score: 25	Score: 100
38. Does a woman's testimony carry the same evidentiary weight in court as a man's?	Yes	Yes
39. Does the law establish an anti-discrimination commission?	No	Yes
40. Does the law mandate legal aid in civil/family matters?	No	Yes
41. Is there a small claims court/fast-track procedure?	No	Yes

BUILDING CREDIT

	Score: 0	Score: 25
42. Do retailers provide information to credit agencies?	No	No
43. Do utility companies provide information to credit agencies?	No	Yes
44. Is discrimination based on gender prohibited in access to credit?	No	No
45. Is discrimination based on marital status prohibited in access to credit?	No	No

PROTECTING WOMEN FROM VIOLENCE

	Score: 0	Score: 100
46. Is there legislation specifically addressing domestic violence? If not, are there aggravated penalties for crimes committed against a spouse or family member?	No	Yes
47. Is there legislation on sexual harassment in employment?	No	Yes
48. Is there legislation on sexual harassment in education?	No	Yes
49. Are there criminal penalties for sexual harassment in employment?	No	Yes
50. Are there civil remedies for sexual harassment in employment?	No	Yes

Note: See the data notes for more details on the scoring of each indicator.

	CÔTE D'IVOIRE	CROATIA
REGION	Sub-Saharan Africa	Europe & Central Asia
INCOME GROUP	Lower middle income	Upper middle income
FEMALE POPULATION	11,652,737	2,158,502
FEMALE LABOR FORCE (% OF TOTAL LABOR FORCE)	41%	46%

ACCESSING INSTITUTIONS

	Score: 100	Score: 100
1. Are wives required to obey their husbands?	No	No
Can a woman legally do the following in the same way as a man:		
2. Apply for a passport?	Yes	Yes
3. Apply for a national ID card?	Yes	Yes
4. Travel outside the country?	Yes	Yes
5. Travel outside her home?	Yes	Yes
6. Get a job?	Yes	Yes
7. Sign a contract?	Yes	Yes
8. Register a business?	Yes	Yes
9. Open a bank account?	Yes	Yes
10. Choose where to live?	Yes	Yes
11. Be "head of household"?	N/A	N/A

USING PROPERTY

	Score: 60	Score: 100
12. Who legally administers marital property?	Husband	Both must agree
13. Does the law provide for valuation of nonmonetary contributions?	Yes	Yes
14. Do men and women have equal ownership rights to immovable property?	No	Yes
15. Do sons and daughters have equal inheritance rights?	Yes	Yes
16. Do female and male surviving spouses have equal inheritance rights?	Yes	Yes

GETTING A JOB

	Score: 80	Score: 93
17. Is there paid leave available to women of at least 14 weeks?	Yes	Yes
18. Do women receive at least 2/3 of their wages for the first 14 weeks or the duration of the leave if it is shorter?	Yes	Yes
19. What is the percentage of maternity leave benefits paid by the government?	100%	100%
20. What is the difference between leave reserved for women and men relative to leave reserved for women, as a function of who pays?	1	1
21. Is there paid parental leave?	No	Yes
22. Does the law mandate equal remuneration for work of equal value?	Yes	Yes
23. Does the law mandate nondiscrimination based on gender in employment?	Yes	Yes
24. Is dismissal of pregnant workers prohibited?	Yes	Yes
25. Can parents work flexibly?	No	No
26. Can women work the same night hours as men?	Yes	Yes
27. Can women work in jobs deemed hazardous, arduous or morally inappropriate in the same way as men?	No	Yes
28. Are women able to work in the same industries as men?	Yes	Yes
29. Are women able to perform the same tasks at work as men?	Yes	Yes
30. Are the ages at which men and women can retire with full pension benefits equal?	Yes	Yes
31. Are the ages at which men and women can retire with partial pension benefits equal?	Yes	N/A
32. Are the mandatory retirement ages for men and women equal?	N/A	N/A

PROVIDING INCENTIVES TO WORK

	Score: 80	Score: 80
33. Are mothers guaranteed an equivalent position after maternity leave?	Yes	Yes
34. Does the government support or provide childcare services?	Yes	Yes
35. Are payments for childcare tax deductible?	No	No
36. Is primary education free and compulsory?	Yes	Yes
37. Are there tax deductions or credits specific to men?	No	No

GOING TO COURT

	Score: 100	Score: 100
38. Does a woman's testimony carry the same evidentiary weight in court as a man's?	Yes	Yes
39. Does the law establish an anti-discrimination commission?	Yes	Yes
40. Does the law mandate legal aid in civil/family matters?	Yes	Yes
41. Is there a small claims court/fast-track procedure?	Yes	Yes

BUILDING CREDIT

	Score: 0	Score: 50
42. Do retailers provide information to credit agencies?	N/A	No
43. Do utility companies provide information to credit agencies?	N/A	No
44. Is discrimination based on gender prohibited in access to credit?	No	Yes
45. Is discrimination based on marital status prohibited in access to credit?	No	Yes

PROTECTING WOMEN FROM VIOLENCE

	Score: 40	Score: 100
46. Is there legislation specifically addressing domestic violence? If not, are there aggravated penalties for crimes committed against a spouse or family member?	No	Yes
47. Is there legislation on sexual harassment in employment?	Yes	Yes
48. Is there legislation on sexual harassment in education?	No	Yes
49. Are there criminal penalties for sexual harassment in employment?	Yes	Yes
50. Are there civil remedies for sexual harassment in employment?	No	Yes

Note: See the data notes for more details on the scoring of each indicator.

	CYPRUS	CZECH REPUBLIC
REGION	Europe & Central Asia	High income: OECD
INCOME GROUP	High income	High income
FEMALE POPULATION	573,265	5,371,530
FEMALE LABOR FORCE (% OF TOTAL LABOR FORCE)	46%	44%

ACCESSING INSTITUTIONS

	Score: 91	Score: 100
1. Are wives required to obey their husbands?	No	No
Can a woman legally do the following in the same way as a man:		
2. Apply for a passport?	No	Yes
3. Apply for a national ID card?	Yes	Yes
4. Travel outside the country?	Yes	Yes
5. Travel outside her home?	Yes	Yes
6. Get a job?	Yes	Yes
7. Sign a contract?	Yes	Yes
8. Register a business?	Yes	Yes
9. Open a bank account?	Yes	Yes
10. Choose where to live?	Yes	Yes
11. Be "head of household"?	N/A	N/A

USING PROPERTY

	Score: 100	Score: 100
12. Who legally administers marital property?	Original owner	Both must agree
13. Does the law provide for valuation of nonmonetary contributions?	Yes	Yes
14. Do men and women have equal ownership rights to immovable property?	Yes	Yes
15. Do sons and daughters have equal inheritance rights?	Yes	Yes
16. Do female and male surviving spouses have equal inheritance rights?	Yes	Yes

GETTING A JOB

	Score: 80	Score: 93
17. Is there paid leave available to women of at least 14 weeks?	Yes	Yes
18. Do women receive at least 2/3 of their wages for the first 14 weeks or the duration of the leave if it is shorter?	Yes	Yes
19. What is the percentage of maternity leave benefits paid by the government?	100%	100%
20. What is the difference between leave reserved for women and men relative to leave reserved for women, as a function of who pays?	1	1
21. Is there paid parental leave?	No	Yes
22. Does the law mandate equal remuneration for work of equal value?	Yes	Yes
23. Does the law mandate nondiscrimination based on gender in employment?	Yes	Yes
24. Is dismissal of pregnant workers prohibited?	Yes	Yes
25. Can parents work flexibly?	No	Yes
26. Can women work the same night hours as men?	Yes	Yes
27. Can women work in jobs deemed hazardous, arduous or morally inappropriate in the same way as men?	Yes	Yes
28. Are women able to work in the same industries as men?	No	Yes
29. Are women able to perform the same tasks at work as men?	Yes	No
30. Are the ages at which men and women can retire with full pension benefits equal?	Yes	Yes
31. Are the ages at which men and women can retire with partial pension benefits equal?	Yes	Yes
32. Are the mandatory retirement ages for men and women equal?	N/A	N/A

PROVIDING INCENTIVES TO WORK

	Score: 80	Score: 100
33. Are mothers guaranteed an equivalent position after maternity leave?	Yes	Yes
34. Does the government support or provide childcare services?	Yes	Yes
35. Are payments for childcare tax deductible?	No	Yes
36. Is primary education free and compulsory?	Yes	Yes
37. Are there tax deductions or credits specific to men?	No	No

GOING TO COURT

	Score: 100	Score: 75
38. Does a woman's testimony carry the same evidentiary weight in court as a man's?	Yes	Yes
39. Does the law establish an anti-discrimination commission?	Yes	Yes
40. Does the law mandate legal aid in civil/family matters?	Yes	Yes
41. Is there a small claims court/fast-track procedure?	Yes	No

BUILDING CREDIT

	Score: 25	Score: 25
42. Do retailers provide information to credit agencies?	No	No
43. Do utility companies provide information to credit agencies?	No	No
44. Is discrimination based on gender prohibited in access to credit?	Yes	Yes
45. Is discrimination based on marital status prohibited in access to credit?	No	No

PROTECTING WOMEN FROM VIOLENCE

	Score: 80	Score: 80
46. Is there legislation specifically addressing domestic violence? If not, are there aggravated penalties for crimes committed against a spouse or family member?	Yes	Yes
47. Is there legislation on sexual harassment in employment?	Yes	Yes
48. Is there legislation on sexual harassment in education?	No	Yes
49. Are there criminal penalties for sexual harassment in employment?	Yes	No
50. Are there civil remedies for sexual harassment in employment?	Yes	Yes

Note: See the data notes for more details on the scoring of each indicator.

	DENMARK	DJIBOUTI
REGION	High income: OECD	Middle East & North Africa
INCOME GROUP	High income	Lower middle income
FEMALE POPULATION	2,886,115	469,198
FEMALE LABOR FORCE (% OF TOTAL LABOR FORCE)	47%	42%

ACCESSING INSTITUTIONS

	Score: 100	Score: 82
1. Are wives required to obey their husbands?	No	Yes
Can a woman legally do the following in the same way as a man:		
2. Apply for a passport?	Yes	Yes
3. Apply for a national ID card?	N/A	Yes
4. Travel outside the country?	Yes	Yes
5. Travel outside her home?	Yes	Yes
6. Get a job?	Yes	Yes
7. Sign a contract?	Yes	Yes
8. Register a business?	Yes	Yes
9. Open a bank account?	Yes	Yes
10. Choose where to live?	Yes	Yes
11. Be "head of household"?	N/A	No

USING PROPERTY

	Score: 100	Score: 40
12. Who legally administers marital property?	Original owner	Original owner
13. Does the law provide for valuation of nonmonetary contributions?	Yes	No
14. Do men and women have equal ownership rights to immovable property?	Yes	Yes
15. Do sons and daughters have equal inheritance rights?	Yes	No
16. Do female and male surviving spouses have equal inheritance rights?	Yes	No

GETTING A JOB

	Score: 91	Score: 75
17. Is there paid leave available to women of at least 14 weeks?	Yes	Yes
18. Do women receive at least 2/3 of their wages for the first 14 weeks or the duration of the leave if it is shorter?	No	Yes
19. What is the percentage of maternity leave benefits paid by the government?	100%	50%
20. What is the difference between leave reserved for women and men relative to leave reserved for women, as a function of who pays?	1	0.52
21. Is there paid parental leave?	Yes	No
22. Does the law mandate equal remuneration for work of equal value?	Yes	Yes
23. Does the law mandate nondiscrimination based on gender in employment?	Yes	Yes
24. Is dismissal of pregnant workers prohibited?	Yes	Yes
25. Can parents work flexibly?	No	No
26. Can women work the same night hours as men?	Yes	Yes
27. Can women work in jobs deemed hazardous, arduous or morally inappropriate in the same way as men?	Yes	Yes
28. Are women able to work in the same industries as men?	Yes	Yes
29. Are women able to perform the same tasks at work as men?	Yes	Yes
30. Are the ages at which men and women can retire with full pension benefits equal?	Yes	No
31. Are the ages at which men and women can retire with partial pension benefits equal?	N/A	N/A
32. Are the mandatory retirement ages for men and women equal?	N/A	N/A

PROVIDING INCENTIVES TO WORK

	Score: 80	Score: 80
33. Are mothers guaranteed an equivalent position after maternity leave?	Yes	Yes
34. Does the government support or provide childcare services?	Yes	Yes
35. Are payments for childcare tax deductible?	No	No
36. Is primary education free and compulsory?	Yes	Yes
37. Are there tax deductions or credits specific to men?	No	No

GOING TO COURT

	Score: 100	Score: 75
38. Does a woman's testimony carry the same evidentiary weight in court as a man's?	Yes	Yes
39. Does the law establish an anti-discrimination commission?	Yes	Yes
40. Does the law mandate legal aid in civil/family matters?	Yes	Yes
41. Is there a small claims court/fast-track procedure?	Yes	No

BUILDING CREDIT

	Score: 75	Score: 50
42. Do retailers provide information to credit agencies?	Yes	N/A
43. Do utility companies provide information to credit agencies?	Yes	N/A
44. Is discrimination based on gender prohibited in access to credit?	Yes	Yes
45. Is discrimination based on marital status prohibited in access to credit?	No	Yes

PROTECTING WOMEN FROM VIOLENCE

	Score: 80	Score: 10
46. Is there legislation specifically addressing domestic violence? If not, are there aggravated penalties for crimes committed against a spouse or family member?	Yes	No, but aggravated penalties exist
47. Is there legislation on sexual harassment in employment?	Yes	No
48. Is there legislation on sexual harassment in education?	No	No
49. Are there criminal penalties for sexual harassment in employment?	Yes	No
50. Are there civil remedies for sexual harassment in employment?	Yes	No

Note: See the data notes for more details on the scoring of each indicator.

	DOMINICA	DOMINICAN REPUBLIC
REGION	Latin America & Caribbean	Latin America & Caribbean
INCOME GROUP	Upper middle income	Upper middle income
FEMALE POPULATION	..	5,344,459
FEMALE LABOR FORCE (% OF TOTAL LABOR FORCE)	..	41%

ACCESSING INSTITUTIONS

	Score: 90	Score: 100
1. Are wives required to obey their husbands?	No	No
Can a woman legally do the following in the same way as a man:		
2. Apply for a passport?	No	Yes
3. Apply for a national ID card?	N/A	Yes
4. Travel outside the country?	Yes	Yes
5. Travel outside her home?	Yes	Yes
6. Get a job?	Yes	Yes
7. Sign a contract?	Yes	Yes
8. Register a business?	Yes	Yes
9. Open a bank account?	Yes	Yes
10. Choose where to live?	Yes	Yes
11. Be "head of household"?	N/A	N/A

USING PROPERTY

	Score: 100	Score: 100
12. Who legally administers marital property?	Original owner	Both must agree
13. Does the law provide for valuation of nonmonetary contributions?	Yes	Yes
14. Do men and women have equal ownership rights to immovable property?	Yes	Yes
15. Do sons and daughters have equal inheritance rights?	Yes	Yes
16. Do female and male surviving spouses have equal inheritance rights?	Yes	Yes

GETTING A JOB

	Score: 46	Score: 73
17. Is there paid leave available to women of at least 14 weeks?	No	Yes
18. Do women receive at least 2/3 of their wages for the first 14 weeks or the duration of the leave if it is shorter?	Yes	Yes
19. What is the percentage of maternity leave benefits paid by the government?	80%	50%
20. What is the difference between leave reserved for women and men relative to leave reserved for women, as a function of who pays?	0.8	0.51
21. Is there paid parental leave?	No	No
22. Does the law mandate equal remuneration for work of equal value?	No	No
23. Does the law mandate nondiscrimination based on gender in employment?	No	Yes
24. Is dismissal of pregnant workers prohibited?	No	Yes
25. Can parents work flexibly?	No	No
26. Can women work the same night hours as men?	Yes	Yes
27. Can women work in jobs deemed hazardous, arduous or morally inappropriate in the same way as men?	Yes	Yes
28. Are women able to work in the same industries as men?	No	Yes
29. Are women able to perform the same tasks at work as men?	No	Yes
30. Are the ages at which men and women can retire with full pension benefits equal?	Yes	Yes
31. Are the ages at which men and women can retire with partial pension benefits equal?	N/A	Yes
32. Are the mandatory retirement ages for men and women equal?	N/A	N/A

PROVIDING INCENTIVES TO WORK

	Score: 80	Score: 100
33. Are mothers guaranteed an equivalent position after maternity leave?	Yes	Yes
34. Does the government support or provide childcare services?	Yes	Yes
35. Are payments for childcare tax deductible?	No	Yes
36. Is primary education free and compulsory?	Yes	Yes
37. Are there tax deductions or credits specific to men?	No	No

GOING TO COURT

	Score: 50	Score: 50
38. Does a woman's testimony carry the same evidentiary weight in court as a man's?	Yes	Yes
39. Does the law establish an anti-discrimination commission?	No	No
40. Does the law mandate legal aid in civil/family matters?	No	No
41. Is there a small claims court/fast-track procedure?	Yes	Yes

BUILDING CREDIT

	Score: 0	Score: 75
42. Do retailers provide information to credit agencies?	N/A	Yes
43. Do utility companies provide information to credit agencies?	N/A	Yes
44. Is discrimination based on gender prohibited in access to credit?	No	Yes
45. Is discrimination based on marital status prohibited in access to credit?	No	No

PROTECTING WOMEN FROM VIOLENCE

	Score: 20	Score: 100
46. Is there legislation specifically addressing domestic violence? If not, are there aggravated penalties for crimes committed against a spouse or family member?	Yes	Yes
47. Is there legislation on sexual harassment in employment?	No	Yes
48. Is there legislation on sexual harassment in education?	No	Yes
49. Are there criminal penalties for sexual harassment in employment?	No	Yes
50. Are there civil remedies for sexual harassment in employment?	No	Yes

Note: See the data notes for more details on the scoring of each indicator.

	ECUADOR	EGYPT, ARAB REP.
REGION	Latin America & Caribbean	Middle East & North Africa
INCOME GROUP	Upper middle income	Lower middle income
FEMALE POPULATION	8,194,817	47,330,802
FEMALE LABOR FORCE (% OF TOTAL LABOR FORCE)	41%	23%
ACCESSING INSTITUTIONS	Score: 100	Score: 64
1. Are wives required to obey their husbands?	No	Yes
Can a woman legally do the following in the same way as a man:		
2. Apply for a passport?	Yes	No
3. Apply for a national ID card?	Yes	No
4. Travel outside the country?	Yes	Yes
5. Travel outside her home?	Yes	No
6. Get a job?	Yes	Yes
7. Sign a contract?	Yes	Yes
8. Register a business?	Yes	Yes
9. Open a bank account?	Yes	Yes
10. Choose where to live?	Yes	Yes
11. Be "head of household"?	N/A	N/A
USING PROPERTY	Score: 100	Score: 40
12. Who legally administers marital property?	Both must agree	Original owner
13. Does the law provide for valuation of nonmonetary contributions?	Yes	No
14. Do men and women have equal ownership rights to immovable property?	Yes	Yes
15. Do sons and daughters have equal inheritance rights?	Yes	No
16. Do female and male surviving spouses have equal inheritance rights?	Yes	No
GETTING A JOB	Score: 74	Score: 59
17. Is there paid leave available to women of at least 14 weeks?	No	No
18. Do women receive at least 2/3 of their wages for the first 14 weeks or the duration of the leave if it is shorter?	Yes	Yes
19. What is the percentage of maternity leave benefits paid by the government?	75%	75%
20. What is the difference between leave reserved for women and men relative to leave reserved for women, as a function of who pays?	0.78	0.75
21. Is there paid parental leave?	No	No
22. Does the law mandate equal remuneration for work of equal value?	Yes	No
23. Does the law mandate nondiscrimination based on gender in employment?	Yes	Yes
24. Is dismissal of pregnant workers prohibited?	Yes	Yes
25. Can parents work flexibly?	No	No
26. Can women work the same night hours as men?	Yes	Yes
27. Can women work in jobs deemed hazardous, arduous or morally inappropriate in the same way as men?	Yes	No
28. Are women able to work in the same industries as men?	Yes	No
29. Are women able to perform the same tasks at work as men?	No	No
30. Are the ages at which men and women can retire with full pension benefits equal?	Yes	Yes
31. Are the ages at which men and women can retire with partial pension benefits equal?	N/A	Yes
32. Are the mandatory retirement ages for men and women equal?	N/A	Yes
PROVIDING INCENTIVES TO WORK	Score: 80	Score: 60
33. Are mothers guaranteed an equivalent position after maternity leave?	No	No
34. Does the government support or provide childcare services?	Yes	Yes
35. Are payments for childcare tax deductible?	Yes	No
36. Is primary education free and compulsory?	Yes	Yes
37. Are there tax deductions or credits specific to men?	No	No
GOING TO COURT	Score: 50	Score: 75
38. Does a woman's testimony carry the same evidentiary weight in court as a man's?	Yes	Yes
39. Does the law establish an anti-discrimination commission?	Yes	Yes
40. Does the law mandate legal aid in civil/family matters?	No	No
41. Is there a small claims court/fast-track procedure?	No	Yes
BUILDING CREDIT	Score: 50	Score: 25
42. Do retailers provide information to credit agencies?	Yes	Yes
43. Do utility companies provide information to credit agencies?	Yes	No
44. Is discrimination based on gender prohibited in access to credit?	No	No
45. Is discrimination based on marital status prohibited in access to credit?	No	No
PROTECTING WOMEN FROM VIOLENCE	Score: 100	Score: 60
46. Is there legislation specifically addressing domestic violence? If not, are there aggravated penalties for crimes committed against a spouse or family member?	Yes	No
47. Is there legislation on sexual harassment in employment?	Yes	Yes
48. Is there legislation on sexual harassment in education?	Yes	Yes
49. Are there criminal penalties for sexual harassment in employment?	Yes	Yes
50. Are there civil remedies for sexual harassment in employment?	Yes	No

Note: See the data notes for more details on the scoring of each indicator.

	EL SALVADOR	EQUATORIAL GUINEA
REGION	Latin America & Caribbean	Sub-Saharan Africa
INCOME GROUP	Lower middle income	Upper middle income
FEMALE POPULATION	3,370,548	595,644
FEMALE LABOR FORCE (% OF TOTAL LABOR FORCE)	42%	39%

ACCESSING INSTITUTIONS
	Score: 100	Score: 73
1. Are wives required to obey their husbands?	No	Yes
Can a woman legally do the following in the same way as a man:		
2. Apply for a passport?	Yes	Yes
3. Apply for a national ID card?	Yes	Yes
4. Travel outside the country?	Yes	Yes
5. Travel outside her home?	Yes	Yes
6. Get a job?	Yes	Yes
7. Sign a contract?	Yes	No
8. Register a business?	Yes	Yes
9. Open a bank account?	Yes	Yes
10. Choose where to live?	Yes	No
11. Be "head of household"?	N/A	N/A

USING PROPERTY
	Score: 100	Score: 60
12. Who legally administers marital property?	Original owner	Husband
13. Does the law provide for valuation of nonmonetary contributions?	Yes	Yes
14. Do men and women have equal ownership rights to immovable property?	Yes	No
15. Do sons and daughters have equal inheritance rights?	Yes	Yes
16. Do female and male surviving spouses have equal inheritance rights?	Yes	Yes

GETTING A JOB
	Score: 75	Score: 78
17. Is there paid leave available to women of at least 14 weeks?	Yes	No
18. Do women receive at least 2/3 of their wages for the first 14 weeks or the duration of the leave if it is shorter?	Yes	Yes
19. What is the percentage of maternity leave benefits paid by the government?	100%	100%
20. What is the difference between leave reserved for women and men relative to leave reserved for women, as a function of who pays?	1	1
21. Is there paid parental leave?	No	No
22. Does the law mandate equal remuneration for work of equal value?	No	Yes
23. Does the law mandate nondiscrimination based on gender in employment?	Yes	Yes
24. Is dismissal of pregnant workers prohibited?	Yes	Yes
25. Can parents work flexibly?	No	No
26. Can women work the same night hours as men?	Yes	Yes
27. Can women work in jobs deemed hazardous, arduous or morally inappropriate in the same way as men?	Yes	Yes
28. Are women able to work in the same industries as men?	Yes	Yes
29. Are women able to perform the same tasks at work as men?	Yes	No
30. Are the ages at which men and women can retire with full pension benefits equal?	No	Yes
31. Are the ages at which men and women can retire with partial pension benefits equal?	N/A	N/A
32. Are the mandatory retirement ages for men and women equal?	N/A	N/A

PROVIDING INCENTIVES TO WORK
	Score: 100	Score: 80
33. Are mothers guaranteed an equivalent position after maternity leave?	Yes	Yes
34. Does the government support or provide childcare services?	Yes	Yes
35. Are payments for childcare tax deductible?	Yes	No
36. Is primary education free and compulsory?	Yes	Yes
37. Are there tax deductions or credits specific to men?	No	No

GOING TO COURT
	Score: 100	Score: 25
38. Does a woman's testimony carry the same evidentiary weight in court as a man's?	Yes	Yes
39. Does the law establish an anti-discrimination commission?	Yes	No
40. Does the law mandate legal aid in civil/family matters?	Yes	No
41. Is there a small claims court/fast-track procedure?	Yes	No

BUILDING CREDIT
	Score: 75	Score: 0
42. Do retailers provide information to credit agencies?	Yes	No
43. Do utility companies provide information to credit agencies?	Yes	No
44. Is discrimination based on gender prohibited in access to credit?	Yes	No
45. Is discrimination based on marital status prohibited in access to credit?	No	No

PROTECTING WOMEN FROM VIOLENCE
	Score: 80	Score: 0
46. Is there legislation specifically addressing domestic violence? If not, are there aggravated penalties for crimes committed against a spouse or family member?	Yes	No
47. Is there legislation on sexual harassment in employment?	Yes	No
48. Is there legislation on sexual harassment in education?	Yes	No
49. Are there criminal penalties for sexual harassment in employment?	Yes	No
50. Are there civil remedies for sexual harassment in employment?	No	No

Note: See the data notes for more details on the scoring of each indicator.

	ERITREA	ESTONIA
REGION	Sub-Saharan Africa	High income: OECD
INCOME GROUP	Low income	High income
FEMALE POPULATION	3,073,210	699,671
FEMALE LABOR FORCE (% OF TOTAL LABOR FORCE)	..	49%

ACCESSING INSTITUTIONS

	Score: 100	Score: 100
1. Are wives required to obey their husbands?	No	No

Can a woman legally do the following in the same way as a man:

2. Apply for a passport?	Yes	Yes
3. Apply for a national ID card?	Yes	Yes
4. Travel outside the country?	Yes	Yes
5. Travel outside her home?	Yes	Yes
6. Get a job?	Yes	Yes
7. Sign a contract?	Yes	Yes
8. Register a business?	Yes	Yes
9. Open a bank account?	Yes	Yes
10. Choose where to live?	Yes	Yes
11. Be "head of household"?	N/A	N/A

USING PROPERTY

	Score: 100	Score: 100
12. Who legally administers marital property?	Both must agree	Both must agree
13. Does the law provide for valuation of nonmonetary contributions?	Yes	Yes
14. Do men and women have equal ownership rights to immovable property?	Yes	Yes
15. Do sons and daughters have equal inheritance rights?	Yes	Yes
16. Do female and male surviving spouses have equal inheritance rights?	Yes	Yes

GETTING A JOB

	Score: 59	Score: 93
17. Is there paid leave available to women of at least 14 weeks?	No	Yes
18. Do women receive at least 2/3 of their wages for the first 14 weeks or the duration of the leave if it is shorter?	Yes	Yes
19. What is the percentage of maternity leave benefits paid by the government?	0%	100%
20. What is the difference between leave reserved for women and men relative to leave reserved for women, as a function of who pays?	0	1
21. Is there paid parental leave?	No	Yes
22. Does the law mandate equal remuneration for work of equal value?	No	Yes
23. Does the law mandate nondiscrimination based on gender in employment?	Yes	Yes
24. Is dismissal of pregnant workers prohibited?	Yes	Yes
25. Can parents work flexibly?	No	No
26. Can women work the same night hours as men?	Yes	Yes
27. Can women work in jobs deemed hazardous, arduous or morally inappropriate in the same way as men?	Yes	Yes
28. Are women able to work in the same industries as men?	Yes	Yes
29. Are women able to perform the same tasks at work as men?	Yes	Yes
30. Are the ages at which men and women can retire with full pension benefits equal?	N/A	Yes
31. Are the ages at which men and women can retire with partial pension benefits equal?	N/A	Yes
32. Are the mandatory retirement ages for men and women equal?	N/A	N/A

PROVIDING INCENTIVES TO WORK

	Score: 60	Score: 80
33. Are mothers guaranteed an equivalent position after maternity leave?	Yes	Yes
34. Does the government support or provide childcare services?	No	Yes
35. Are payments for childcare tax deductible?	No	No
36. Is primary education free and compulsory?	Yes	Yes
37. Are there tax deductions or credits specific to men?	No	No

GOING TO COURT

	Score: 25	Score: 75
38. Does a woman's testimony carry the same evidentiary weight in court as a man's?	Yes	Yes
39. Does the law establish an anti-discrimination commission?	No	No
40. Does the law mandate legal aid in civil/family matters?	No	Yes
41. Is there a small claims court/fast-track procedure?	No	Yes

BUILDING CREDIT

	Score: 0	Score: 75
42. Do retailers provide information to credit agencies?	N/A	Yes
43. Do utility companies provide information to credit agencies?	N/A	Yes
44. Is discrimination based on gender prohibited in access to credit?	No	Yes
45. Is discrimination based on marital status prohibited in access to credit?	No	No

PROTECTING WOMEN FROM VIOLENCE

	Score: 60	Score: 70
46. Is there legislation specifically addressing domestic violence? If not, are there aggravated penalties for crimes committed against a spouse or family member?	No	No, but aggravated penalties exist
47. Is there legislation on sexual harassment in employment?	Yes	Yes
48. Is there legislation on sexual harassment in education?	Yes	Yes
49. Are there criminal penalties for sexual harassment in employment?	Yes	No
50. Are there civil remedies for sexual harassment in employment?	No	Yes

Note: See the data notes for more details on the scoring of each indicator.

	ETHIOPIA	FIJI
REGION	Sub-Saharan Africa	East Asia & Pacific
INCOME GROUP	Low income	Upper middle income
FEMALE POPULATION	51,291,704	442,142
FEMALE LABOR FORCE (% OF TOTAL LABOR FORCE)	47%	35%

ACCESSING INSTITUTIONS

	Score: 100	Score: 90
1. Are wives required to obey their husbands?	No	No
Can a woman legally do the following in the same way as a man:		
2. Apply for a passport?	Yes	No
3. Apply for a national ID card?	N/A	N/A
4. Travel outside the country?	Yes	Yes
5. Travel outside her home?	Yes	Yes
6. Get a job?	Yes	Yes
7. Sign a contract?	Yes	Yes
8. Register a business?	Yes	Yes
9. Open a bank account?	Yes	Yes
10. Choose where to live?	Yes	Yes
11. Be "head of household"?	N/A	N/A

USING PROPERTY

	Score: 100	Score: 100
12. Who legally administers marital property?	Both must agree	Original owner
13. Does the law provide for valuation of nonmonetary contributions?	Yes	Yes
14. Do men and women have equal ownership rights to immovable property?	Yes	Yes
15. Do sons and daughters have equal inheritance rights?	Yes	Yes
16. Do female and male surviving spouses have equal inheritance rights?	Yes	Yes

GETTING A JOB

	Score: 46	Score: 56
17. Is there paid leave available to women of at least 14 weeks?	No	No
18. Do women receive at least 2/3 of their wages for the first 14 weeks or the duration of the leave if it is shorter?	Yes	Yes
19. What is the percentage of maternity leave benefits paid by the government?	0%	0%
20. What is the difference between leave reserved for women and men relative to leave reserved for women, as a function of who pays?	0	0
21. Is there paid parental leave?	No	No
22. Does the law mandate equal remuneration for work of equal value?	No	No
23. Does the law mandate nondiscrimination based on gender in employment?	Yes	Yes
24. Is dismissal of pregnant workers prohibited?	Yes	Yes
25. Can parents work flexibly?	No	No
26. Can women work the same night hours as men?	Yes	Yes
27. Can women work in jobs deemed hazardous, arduous or morally inappropriate in the same way as men?	No	Yes
28. Are women able to work in the same industries as men?	No	No
29. Are women able to perform the same tasks at work as men?	No	Yes
30. Are the ages at which men and women can retire with full pension benefits equal?	Yes	Yes
31. Are the ages at which men and women can retire with partial pension benefits equal?	Yes	N/A
32. Are the mandatory retirement ages for men and women equal?	N/A	N/A

PROVIDING INCENTIVES TO WORK

	Score: 20	Score: 60
33. Are mothers guaranteed an equivalent position after maternity leave?	No	Yes
34. Does the government support or provide childcare services?	No	Yes
35. Are payments for childcare tax deductible?	No	No
36. Is primary education free and compulsory?	No	No
37. Are there tax deductions or credits specific to men?	No	No

GOING TO COURT

	Score: 100	Score: 100
38. Does a woman's testimony carry the same evidentiary weight in court as a man's?	Yes	Yes
39. Does the law establish an anti-discrimination commission?	Yes	Yes
40. Does the law mandate legal aid in civil/family matters?	Yes	Yes
41. Is there a small claims court/fast-track procedure?	Yes	Yes

BUILDING CREDIT

	Score: 0	Score: 0
42. Do retailers provide information to credit agencies?	N/A	N/A
43. Do utility companies provide information to credit agencies?	N/A	N/A
44. Is discrimination based on gender prohibited in access to credit?	No	No
45. Is discrimination based on marital status prohibited in access to credit?	No	No

PROTECTING WOMEN FROM VIOLENCE

	Score: 80	Score: 80
46. Is there legislation specifically addressing domestic violence? If not, are there aggravated penalties for crimes committed against a spouse or family member?	Yes	Yes
47. Is there legislation on sexual harassment in employment?	Yes	Yes
48. Is there legislation on sexual harassment in education?	Yes	Yes
49. Are there criminal penalties for sexual harassment in employment?	Yes	No
50. Are there civil remedies for sexual harassment in employment?	No	Yes

Note: See the data notes for more details on the scoring of each indicator.

	FINLAND	FRANCE
REGION	High income: OECD	High income: OECD
INCOME GROUP	High income	High income
FEMALE POPULATION	2,788,613	34,331,313
FEMALE LABOR FORCE (% OF TOTAL LABOR FORCE)	48%	47%

ACCESSING INSTITUTIONS

	Score: 100	Score: 100
1. Are wives required to obey their husbands?	No	No
Can a woman legally do the following in the same way as a man:		
2. Apply for a passport?	Yes	Yes
3. Apply for a national ID card?	Yes	Yes
4. Travel outside the country?	Yes	Yes
5. Travel outside her home?	Yes	Yes
6. Get a job?	Yes	Yes
7. Sign a contract?	Yes	Yes
8. Register a business?	Yes	Yes
9. Open a bank account?	Yes	Yes
10. Choose where to live?	Yes	Yes
11. Be "head of household"?	N/A	N/A

USING PROPERTY

	Score: 100	Score: 100
12. Who legally administers marital property?	Original owner	Both must agree
13. Does the law provide for valuation of nonmonetary contributions?	Yes	Yes
14. Do men and women have equal ownership rights to immovable property?	Yes	Yes
15. Do sons and daughters have equal inheritance rights?	Yes	Yes
16. Do female and male surviving spouses have equal inheritance rights?	Yes	Yes

GETTING A JOB

	Score: 97	Score: 88
17. Is there paid leave available to women of at least 14 weeks?	Yes	Yes
18. Do women receive at least 2/3 of their wages for the first 14 weeks or the duration of the leave if it is shorter?	Yes	Yes
19. What is the percentage of maternity leave benefits paid by the government?	70%	100%
20. What is the difference between leave reserved for women and men relative to leave reserved for women, as a function of who pays?	0.86	1
21. Is there paid parental leave?	Yes	Yes
22. Does the law mandate equal remuneration for work of equal value?	Yes	Yes
23. Does the law mandate nondiscrimination based on gender in employment?	Yes	Yes
24. Is dismissal of pregnant workers prohibited?	Yes	Yes
25. Can parents work flexibly?	Yes	No
26. Can women work the same night hours as men?	Yes	Yes
27. Can women work in jobs deemed hazardous, arduous or morally inappropriate in the same way as men?	Yes	Yes
28. Are women able to work in the same industries as men?	Yes	Yes
29. Are women able to perform the same tasks at work as men?	Yes	No
30. Are the ages at which men and women can retire with full pension benefits equal?	Yes	Yes
31. Are the ages at which men and women can retire with partial pension benefits equal?	Yes	Yes
32. Are the mandatory retirement ages for men and women equal?	N/A	Yes

PROVIDING INCENTIVES TO WORK

	Score: 80	Score: 100
33. Are mothers guaranteed an equivalent position after maternity leave?	Yes	Yes
34. Does the government support or provide childcare services?	Yes	Yes
35. Are payments for childcare tax deductible?	No	Yes
36. Is primary education free and compulsory?	Yes	Yes
37. Are there tax deductions or credits specific to men?	No	No

GOING TO COURT

	Score: 75	Score: 100
38. Does a woman's testimony carry the same evidentiary weight in court as a man's?	Yes	Yes
39. Does the law establish an anti-discrimination commission?	Yes	Yes
40. Does the law mandate legal aid in civil/family matters?	Yes	Yes
41. Is there a small claims court/fast-track procedure?	No	Yes

BUILDING CREDIT

	Score: 25	Score: 50
42. Do retailers provide information to credit agencies?	No	No
43. Do utility companies provide information to credit agencies?	No	No
44. Is discrimination based on gender prohibited in access to credit?	Yes	Yes
45. Is discrimination based on marital status prohibited in access to credit?	No	Yes

PROTECTING WOMEN FROM VIOLENCE

	Score: 100	Score: 60
46. Is there legislation specifically addressing domestic violence? If not, are there aggravated penalties for crimes committed against a spouse or family member?	Yes	Yes
47. Is there legislation on sexual harassment in employment?	Yes	Yes
48. Is there legislation on sexual harassment in education?	Yes	No
49. Are there criminal penalties for sexual harassment in employment?	Yes	Yes
50. Are there civil remedies for sexual harassment in employment?	Yes	No

Note: See the data notes for more details on the scoring of each indicator.

	GABON	GAMBIA, THE
REGION	Sub-Saharan Africa	Sub-Saharan Africa
INCOME GROUP	Upper middle income	Low income
FEMALE POPULATION	978,377	1,029,463
FEMALE LABOR FORCE (% OF TOTAL LABOR FORCE)	40%	44%

ACCESSING INSTITUTIONS

	Score: 55	Score: 100
1. Are wives required to obey their husbands?	Yes	No
Can a woman legally do the following in the same way as a man:		
2. Apply for a passport?	No	Yes
3. Apply for a national ID card?	Yes	Yes
4. Travel outside the country?	Yes	Yes
5. Travel outside her home?	Yes	Yes
6. Get a job?	No	Yes
7. Sign a contract?	Yes	Yes
8. Register a business?	Yes	Yes
9. Open a bank account?	Yes	Yes
10. Choose where to live?	No	Yes
11. Be "head of household"?	No	N/A

USING PROPERTY

	Score: 60	Score: 60
12. Who legally administers marital property?	Husband	Original owner
13. Does the law provide for valuation of nonmonetary contributions?	Yes	Yes
14. Do men and women have equal ownership rights to immovable property?	No	Yes
15. Do sons and daughters have equal inheritance rights?	Yes	No
16. Do female and male surviving spouses have equal inheritance rights?	Yes	No

GETTING A JOB

	Score: 73	Score: 67
17. Is there paid leave available to women of at least 14 weeks?	Yes	Yes
18. Do women receive at least 2/3 of their wages for the first 14 weeks or the duration of the leave if it is shorter?	Yes	Yes
19. What is the percentage of maternity leave benefits paid by the government?	100%	0%
20. What is the difference between leave reserved for women and men relative to leave reserved for women, as a function of who pays?	1	0.06
21. Is there paid parental leave?	No	No
22. Does the law mandate equal remuneration for work of equal value?	No	No
23. Does the law mandate nondiscrimination based on gender in employment?	Yes	Yes
24. Is dismissal of pregnant workers prohibited?	Yes	Yes
25. Can parents work flexibly?	No	No
26. Can women work the same night hours as men?	Yes	Yes
27. Can women work in jobs deemed hazardous, arduous or morally inappropriate in the same way as men?	Yes	Yes
28. Are women able to work in the same industries as men?	No	Yes
29. Are women able to perform the same tasks at work as men?	Yes	Yes
30. Are the ages at which men and women can retire with full pension benefits equal?	Yes	Yes
31. Are the ages at which men and women can retire with partial pension benefits equal?	N/A	Yes
32. Are the mandatory retirement ages for men and women equal?	Yes	N/A

PROVIDING INCENTIVES TO WORK

	Score: 80	Score: 60
33. Are mothers guaranteed an equivalent position after maternity leave?	Yes	Yes
34. Does the government support or provide childcare services?	Yes	No
35. Are payments for childcare tax deductible?	No	No
36. Is primary education free and compulsory?	Yes	Yes
37. Are there tax deductions or credits specific to men?	No	No

GOING TO COURT

	Score: 50	Score: 75
38. Does a woman's testimony carry the same evidentiary weight in court as a man's?	Yes	Yes
39. Does the law establish an anti-discrimination commission?	No	No
40. Does the law mandate legal aid in civil/family matters?	Yes	Yes
41. Is there a small claims court/fast-track procedure?	No	Yes

BUILDING CREDIT

	Score: 0	Score: 0
42. Do retailers provide information to credit agencies?	No	N/A
43. Do utility companies provide information to credit agencies?	No	N/A
44. Is discrimination based on gender prohibited in access to credit?	No	No
45. Is discrimination based on marital status prohibited in access to credit?	No	No

PROTECTING WOMEN FROM VIOLENCE

	Score: 0	Score: 40
46. Is there legislation specifically addressing domestic violence? If not, are there aggravated penalties for crimes committed against a spouse or family member?	No	Yes
47. Is there legislation on sexual harassment in employment?	No	No
48. Is there legislation on sexual harassment in education?	No	Yes
49. Are there criminal penalties for sexual harassment in employment?	No	No
50. Are there civil remedies for sexual harassment in employment?	No	No

Note: See the data notes for more details on the scoring of each indicator.

	GEORGIA	GERMANY
REGION	Europe & Central Asia	High income: OECD
INCOME GROUP	Lower middle income	High income
FEMALE POPULATION	1,943,709	42,021,652
FEMALE LABOR FORCE (% OF TOTAL LABOR FORCE)	46%	46%

ACCESSING INSTITUTIONS

	Score: 100	Score: 100
1. Are wives required to obey their husbands?	No	No
Can a woman legally do the following in the same way as a man:		
2. Apply for a passport?	Yes	Yes
3. Apply for a national ID card?	Yes	Yes
4. Travel outside the country?	Yes	Yes
5. Travel outside her home?	Yes	Yes
6. Get a job?	Yes	Yes
7. Sign a contract?	Yes	Yes
8. Register a business?	Yes	Yes
9. Open a bank account?	Yes	Yes
10. Choose where to live?	Yes	Yes
11. Be "head of household"?	N/A	N/A

USING PROPERTY

	Score: 100	Score: 100
12. Who legally administers marital property?	Both must agree	Separate with spousal consent
13. Does the law provide for valuation of nonmonetary contributions?	Yes	Yes
14. Do men and women have equal ownership rights to immovable property?	Yes	Yes
15. Do sons and daughters have equal inheritance rights?	Yes	Yes
16. Do female and male surviving spouses have equal inheritance rights?	Yes	Yes

GETTING A JOB

	Score: 75	Score: 85
17. Is there paid leave available to women of at least 14 weeks?	Yes	Yes
18. Do women receive at least 2/3 of their wages for the first 14 weeks or the duration of the leave if it is shorter?	Yes	Yes
19. What is the percentage of maternity leave benefits paid by the government?	100%	25%
20. What is the difference between leave reserved for women and men relative to leave reserved for women, as a function of who pays?	1	0.53
21. Is there paid parental leave?	No	Yes
22. Does the law mandate equal remuneration for work of equal value?	No	No
23. Does the law mandate nondiscrimination based on gender in employment?	Yes	Yes
24. Is dismissal of pregnant workers prohibited?	Yes	Yes
25. Can parents work flexibly?	No	Yes
26. Can women work the same night hours as men?	Yes	Yes
27. Can women work in jobs deemed hazardous, arduous or morally inappropriate in the same way as men?	Yes	Yes
28. Are women able to work in the same industries as men?	Yes	Yes
29. Are women able to perform the same tasks at work as men?	Yes	Yes
30. Are the ages at which men and women can retire with full pension benefits equal?	No	Yes
31. Are the ages at which men and women can retire with partial pension benefits equal?	N/A	Yes
32. Are the mandatory retirement ages for men and women equal?	N/A	N/A

PROVIDING INCENTIVES TO WORK

	Score: 60	Score: 80
33. Are mothers guaranteed an equivalent position after maternity leave?	No	No
34. Does the government support or provide childcare services?	Yes	Yes
35. Are payments for childcare tax deductible?	No	Yes
36. Is primary education free and compulsory?	Yes	Yes
37. Are there tax deductions or credits specific to men?	No	No

GOING TO COURT

	Score: 100	Score: 100
38. Does a woman's testimony carry the same evidentiary weight in court as a man's?	Yes	Yes
39. Does the law establish an anti-discrimination commission?	Yes	Yes
40. Does the law mandate legal aid in civil/family matters?	Yes	Yes
41. Is there a small claims court/fast-track procedure?	Yes	Yes

BUILDING CREDIT

	Score: 25	Score: 75
42. Do retailers provide information to credit agencies?	No	Yes
43. Do utility companies provide information to credit agencies?	Yes	Yes
44. Is discrimination based on gender prohibited in access to credit?	No	Yes
45. Is discrimination based on marital status prohibited in access to credit?	No	No

PROTECTING WOMEN FROM VIOLENCE

	Score: 40	Score: 60
46. Is there legislation specifically addressing domestic violence? If not, are there aggravated penalties for crimes committed against a spouse or family member?	Yes	Yes
47. Is there legislation on sexual harassment in employment?	Yes	Yes
48. Is there legislation on sexual harassment in education?	No	No
49. Are there criminal penalties for sexual harassment in employment?	No	No
50. Are there civil remedies for sexual harassment in employment?	No	Yes

Note: See the data notes for more details on the scoring of each indicator.

	GHANA	GREECE
REGION	Sub-Saharan Africa	High income: OECD
INCOME GROUP	Lower middle income	High income
FEMALE POPULATION	14,162,745	5,506,477
FEMALE LABOR FORCE (% OF TOTAL LABOR FORCE)	50%	44%

ACCESSING INSTITUTIONS

	Score: 100	Score: 100
1. Are wives required to obey their husbands?	No	No
Can a woman legally do the following in the same way as a man:		
2. Apply for a passport?	Yes	Yes
3. Apply for a national ID card?	Yes	Yes
4. Travel outside the country?	Yes	Yes
5. Travel outside her home?	Yes	Yes
6. Get a job?	Yes	Yes
7. Sign a contract?	Yes	Yes
8. Register a business?	Yes	Yes
9. Open a bank account?	Yes	Yes
10. Choose where to live?	Yes	Yes
11. Be "head of household"?	Yes	N/A

USING PROPERTY

	Score: 80	Score: 100
12. Who legally administers marital property?	Original owner	Original owner
13. Does the law provide for valuation of nonmonetary contributions?	No	Yes
14. Do men and women have equal ownership rights to immovable property?	Yes	Yes
15. Do sons and daughters have equal inheritance rights?	Yes	Yes
16. Do female and male surviving spouses have equal inheritance rights?	Yes	Yes

GETTING A JOB

	Score: 59	Score: 93
17. Is there paid leave available to women of at least 14 weeks?	No	Yes
18. Do women receive at least 2/3 of their wages for the first 14 weeks or the duration of the leave if it is shorter?	Yes	Yes
19. What is the percentage of maternity leave benefits paid by the government?	0%	100%
20. What is the difference between leave reserved for women and men relative to leave reserved for women, as a function of who pays?	0	1
21. Is there paid parental leave?	No	No
22. Does the law mandate equal remuneration for work of equal value?	No	Yes
23. Does the law mandate nondiscrimination based on gender in employment?	Yes	Yes
24. Is dismissal of pregnant workers prohibited?	Yes	Yes
25. Can parents work flexibly?	No	Yes
26. Can women work the same night hours as men?	Yes	Yes
27. Can women work in jobs deemed hazardous, arduous or morally inappropriate in the same way as men?	Yes	Yes
28. Are women able to work in the same industries as men?	No	Yes
29. Are women able to perform the same tasks at work as men?	Yes	Yes
30. Are the ages at which men and women can retire with full pension benefits equal?	Yes	Yes
31. Are the ages at which men and women can retire with partial pension benefits equal?	Yes	Yes
32. Are the mandatory retirement ages for men and women equal?	N/A	N/A

PROVIDING INCENTIVES TO WORK

	Score: 60	Score: 80
33. Are mothers guaranteed an equivalent position after maternity leave?	No	Yes
34. Does the government support or provide childcare services?	Yes	Yes
35. Are payments for childcare tax deductible?	No	No
36. Is primary education free and compulsory?	Yes	Yes
37. Are there tax deductions or credits specific to men?	No	No

GOING TO COURT

	Score: 75	Score: 75
38. Does a woman's testimony carry the same evidentiary weight in court as a man's?	Yes	Yes
39. Does the law establish an anti-discrimination commission?	Yes	No
40. Does the law mandate legal aid in civil/family matters?	Yes	Yes
41. Is there a small claims court/fast-track procedure?	No	Yes

BUILDING CREDIT

	Score: 0	Score: 25
42. Do retailers provide information to credit agencies?	No	No
43. Do utility companies provide information to credit agencies?	No	No
44. Is discrimination based on gender prohibited in access to credit?	No	Yes
45. Is discrimination based on marital status prohibited in access to credit?	No	No

PROTECTING WOMEN FROM VIOLENCE

	Score: 60	Score: 80
46. Is there legislation specifically addressing domestic violence? If not, are there aggravated penalties for crimes committed against a spouse or family member?	Yes	Yes
47. Is there legislation on sexual harassment in employment?	Yes	Yes
48. Is there legislation on sexual harassment in education?	No	No
49. Are there criminal penalties for sexual harassment in employment?	No	Yes
50. Are there civil remedies for sexual harassment in employment?	Yes	Yes

Note: See the data notes for more details on the scoring of each indicator.

	GRENADA	GUATEMALA
REGION	Latin America & Caribbean	Latin America & Caribbean
INCOME GROUP	Upper middle income	Lower middle income
FEMALE POPULATION	53,452	8,470,056
FEMALE LABOR FORCE (% OF TOTAL LABOR FORCE)	..	34%
ACCESSING INSTITUTIONS	Score: 90	Score: 100
1. Are wives required to obey their husbands?	No	No
Can a woman legally do the following in the same way as a man:		
2. Apply for a passport?	No	Yes
3. Apply for a national ID card?	N/A	Yes
4. Travel outside the country?	Yes	Yes
5. Travel outside her home?	Yes	Yes
6. Get a job?	Yes	Yes
7. Sign a contract?	Yes	Yes
8. Register a business?	Yes	Yes
9. Open a bank account?	Yes	Yes
10. Choose where to live?	Yes	Yes
11. Be "head of household"?	N/A	N/A
USING PROPERTY	Score: 80	Score: 100
12. Who legally administers marital property?	Original owner	Both must agree
13. Does the law provide for valuation of nonmonetary contributions?	No	Yes
14. Do men and women have equal ownership rights to immovable property?	Yes	Yes
15. Do sons and daughters have equal inheritance rights?	Yes	Yes
16. Do female and male surviving spouses have equal inheritance rights?	Yes	Yes
GETTING A JOB	Score: 81	Score: 70
17. Is there paid leave available to women of at least 14 weeks?	No	No
18. Do women receive at least 2/3 of their wages for the first 14 weeks or the duration of the leave if it is shorter?	Yes	Yes
19. What is the percentage of maternity leave benefits paid by the government?	74%	100%
20. What is the difference between leave reserved for women and men relative to leave reserved for women, as a function of who pays?	0.74	1
21. Is there paid parental leave?	No	No
22. Does the law mandate equal remuneration for work of equal value?	Yes	No
23. Does the law mandate nondiscrimination based on gender in employment?	Yes	Yes
24. Is dismissal of pregnant workers prohibited?	Yes	Yes
25. Can parents work flexibly?	No	No
26. Can women work the same night hours as men?	Yes	Yes
27. Can women work in jobs deemed hazardous, arduous or morally inappropriate in the same way as men?	Yes	No
28. Are women able to work in the same industries as men?	Yes	Yes
29. Are women able to perform the same tasks at work as men?	Yes	Yes
30. Are the ages at which men and women can retire with full pension benefits equal?	Yes	Yes
31. Are the ages at which men and women can retire with partial pension benefits equal?	N/A	N/A
32. Are the mandatory retirement ages for men and women equal?	N/A	N/A
PROVIDING INCENTIVES TO WORK	Score: 60	Score: 80
33. Are mothers guaranteed an equivalent position after maternity leave?	No	Yes
34. Does the government support or provide childcare services?	Yes	Yes
35. Are payments for childcare tax deductible?	No	No
36. Is primary education free and compulsory?	Yes	Yes
37. Are there tax deductions or credits specific to men?	No	No
GOING TO COURT	Score: 75	Score: 100
38. Does a woman's testimony carry the same evidentiary weight in court as a man's?	Yes	Yes
39. Does the law establish an anti-discrimination commission?	Yes	Yes
40. Does the law mandate legal aid in civil/family matters?	No	Yes
41. Is there a small claims court/fast-track procedure?	Yes	Yes
BUILDING CREDIT	Score: 0	Score: 50
42. Do retailers provide information to credit agencies?	N/A	Yes
43. Do utility companies provide information to credit agencies?	N/A	Yes
44. Is discrimination based on gender prohibited in access to credit?	No	No
45. Is discrimination based on marital status prohibited in access to credit?	No	No
PROTECTING WOMEN FROM VIOLENCE	Score: 20	Score: 20
46. Is there legislation specifically addressing domestic violence? If not, are there aggravated penalties for crimes committed against a spouse or family member?	Yes	Yes
47. Is there legislation on sexual harassment in employment?	No	No
48. Is there legislation on sexual harassment in education?	No	No
49. Are there criminal penalties for sexual harassment in employment?	No	No
50. Are there civil remedies for sexual harassment in employment?	No	No

Note: See the data notes for more details on the scoring of each indicator.

	GUINEA	GUINEA-BISSAU
REGION	Sub-Saharan Africa	Sub-Saharan Africa
INCOME GROUP	Low income	Low income
FEMALE POPULATION	6,178,592	914,413
FEMALE LABOR FORCE (% OF TOTAL LABOR FORCE)	49%	47%

ACCESSING INSTITUTIONS

	Score: 73	Score: 55
1. Are wives required to obey their husbands?	No	No
Can a woman legally do the following in the same way as a man:		
2. Apply for a passport?	Yes	Yes
3. Apply for a national ID card?	Yes	Yes
4. Travel outside the country?	Yes	Yes
5. Travel outside her home?	Yes	Yes
6. Get a job?	No	No
7. Sign a contract?	Yes	Yes
8. Register a business?	Yes	No
9. Open a bank account?	Yes	No
10. Choose where to live?	No	No
11. Be "head of household"?	No	No

USING PROPERTY

	Score: 60	Score: 60
12. Who legally administers marital property?	Original owner	Husband
13. Does the law provide for valuation of nonmonetary contributions?	No	Yes
14. Do men and women have equal ownership rights to immovable property?	Yes	No
15. Do sons and daughters have equal inheritance rights?	Yes	Yes
16. Do female and male surviving spouses have equal inheritance rights?	No	Yes

GETTING A JOB

	Score: 64	Score: 43
17. Is there paid leave available to women of at least 14 weeks?	Yes	No
18. Do women receive at least 2/3 of their wages for the first 14 weeks or the duration of the leave if it is shorter?	Yes	Yes
19. What is the percentage of maternity leave benefits paid by the government?	50%	100%
20. What is the difference between leave reserved for women and men relative to leave reserved for women, as a function of who pays?	0.5	1
21. Is there paid parental leave?	No	No
22. Does the law mandate equal remuneration for work of equal value?	Yes	No
23. Does the law mandate nondiscrimination based on gender in employment?	Yes	Yes
24. Is dismissal of pregnant workers prohibited?	Yes	No
25. Can parents work flexibly?	No	No
26. Can women work the same night hours as men?	Yes	No
27. Can women work in jobs deemed hazardous, arduous or morally inappropriate in the same way as men?	Yes	No
28. Are women able to work in the same industries as men?	No	No
29. Are women able to perform the same tasks at work as men?	No	Yes
30. Are the ages at which men and women can retire with full pension benefits equal?	Yes	N/A
31. Are the ages at which men and women can retire with partial pension benefits equal?	N/A	N/A
32. Are the mandatory retirement ages for men and women equal?	N/A	N/A

PROVIDING INCENTIVES TO WORK

	Score: 20	Score: 0
33. Are mothers guaranteed an equivalent position after maternity leave?	Yes	No
34. Does the government support or provide childcare services?	No	No
35. Are payments for childcare tax deductible?	No	No
36. Is primary education free and compulsory?	No	No
37. Are there tax deductions or credits specific to men?	Yes	...

GOING TO COURT

	Score: 50	Score: 75
38. Does a woman's testimony carry the same evidentiary weight in court as a man's?	Yes	Yes
39. Does the law establish an anti-discrimination commission?	No	No
40. Does the law mandate legal aid in civil/family matters?	Yes	Yes
41. Is there a small claims court/fast-track procedure?	No	Yes

BUILDING CREDIT

	Score: 50	Score: 0
42. Do retailers provide information to credit agencies?	N/A	N/A
43. Do utility companies provide information to credit agencies?	N/A	N/A
44. Is discrimination based on gender prohibited in access to credit?	Yes	No
45. Is discrimination based on marital status prohibited in access to credit?	Yes	No

PROTECTING WOMEN FROM VIOLENCE

	Score: 40	Score: 20
46. Is there legislation specifically addressing domestic violence? If not, are there aggravated penalties for crimes committed against a spouse or family member?	No	Yes
47. Is there legislation on sexual harassment in employment?	Yes	No
48. Is there legislation on sexual harassment in education?	No	No
49. Are there criminal penalties for sexual harassment in employment?	Yes	No
50. Are there civil remedies for sexual harassment in employment?	No	No

Note: See the data notes for more details on the scoring of each indicator.

	GUYANA	HAITI
REGION	Latin America & Caribbean	Latin America & Caribbean
INCOME GROUP	Upper middle income	Low income
FEMALE POPULATION	384,262	5,482,774
FEMALE LABOR FORCE (% OF TOTAL LABOR FORCE)	35%	48%

ACCESSING INSTITUTIONS

	Score: 91	Score: 82
1. Are wives required to obey their husbands?	No	No
Can a woman legally do the following in the same way as a man:		
2. Apply for a passport?	No	No
3. Apply for a national ID card?	Yes	Yes
4. Travel outside the country?	Yes	Yes
5. Travel outside her home?	Yes	Yes
6. Get a job?	Yes	Yes
7. Sign a contract?	Yes	Yes
8. Register a business?	Yes	Yes
9. Open a bank account?	Yes	Yes
10. Choose where to live?	Yes	No
11. Be "head of household"?	N/A	N/A

USING PROPERTY

	Score: 100	Score: 80
12. Who legally administers marital property?	Original owner	Other
13. Does the law provide for valuation of nonmonetary contributions?	Yes	Yes
14. Do men and women have equal ownership rights to immovable property?	Yes	No
15. Do sons and daughters have equal inheritance rights?	Yes	Yes
16. Do female and male surviving spouses have equal inheritance rights?	Yes	Yes

GETTING A JOB

	Score: 78	Score: 63
17. Is there paid leave available to women of at least 14 weeks?	No	No
18. Do women receive at least 2/3 of their wages for the first 14 weeks or the duration of the leave if it is shorter?	Yes	Yes
19. What is the percentage of maternity leave benefits paid by the government?	100%	0%
20. What is the difference between leave reserved for women and men relative to leave reserved for women, as a function of who pays?	1	0
21. Is there paid parental leave?	No	No
22. Does the law mandate equal remuneration for work of equal value?	Yes	No
23. Does the law mandate nondiscrimination based on gender in employment?	Yes	Yes
24. Is dismissal of pregnant workers prohibited?	Yes	Yes
25. Can parents work flexibly?	No	No
26. Can women work the same night hours as men?	Yes	Yes
27. Can women work in jobs deemed hazardous, arduous or morally inappropriate in the same way as men?	Yes	Yes
28. Are women able to work in the same industries as men?	Yes	Yes
29. Are women able to perform the same tasks at work as men?	No	Yes
30. Are the ages at which men and women can retire with full pension benefits equal?	Yes	Yes
31. Are the ages at which men and women can retire with partial pension benefits equal?	N/A	Yes
32. Are the mandatory retirement ages for men and women equal?	N/A	N/A

PROVIDING INCENTIVES TO WORK

	Score: 60	Score: 60
33. Are mothers guaranteed an equivalent position after maternity leave?	No	Yes
34. Does the government support or provide childcare services?	Yes	No
35. Are payments for childcare tax deductible?	No	No
36. Is primary education free and compulsory?	Yes	Yes
37. Are there tax deductions or credits specific to men?	No	No

GOING TO COURT

	Score: 50	Score: 50
38. Does a woman's testimony carry the same evidentiary weight in court as a man's?	Yes	Yes
39. Does the law establish an anti-discrimination commission?	No	No
40. Does the law mandate legal aid in civil/family matters?	No	No
41. Is there a small claims court/fast-track procedure?	Yes	Yes

BUILDING CREDIT

	Score: 100	Score: 0
42. Do retailers provide information to credit agencies?	Yes	N/A
43. Do utility companies provide information to credit agencies?	Yes	N/A
44. Is discrimination based on gender prohibited in access to credit?	Yes	No
45. Is discrimination based on marital status prohibited in access to credit?	Yes	No

PROTECTING WOMEN FROM VIOLENCE

	Score: 80	Score: 0
46. Is there legislation specifically addressing domestic violence? If not, are there aggravated penalties for crimes committed against a spouse or family member?	Yes	No
47. Is there legislation on sexual harassment in employment?	Yes	No
48. Is there legislation on sexual harassment in education?	No	No
49. Are there criminal penalties for sexual harassment in employment?	Yes	No
50. Are there civil remedies for sexual harassment in employment?	Yes	No

Note: See the data notes for more details on the scoring of each indicator.

	HONDURAS	HONG KONG SAR, CHINA
REGION	Latin America & Caribbean	East Asia & Pacific
INCOME GROUP	Lower middle income	High income
FEMALE POPULATION	4,558,443	3,896,413
FEMALE LABOR FORCE (% OF TOTAL LABOR FORCE)	38%	49%

ACCESSING INSTITUTIONS

	Score: 100	Score: 100
1. Are wives required to obey their husbands?	No	No
Can a woman legally do the following in the same way as a man:		
2. Apply for a passport?	Yes	Yes
3. Apply for a national ID card?	Yes	Yes
4. Travel outside the country?	Yes	Yes
5. Travel outside her home?	Yes	Yes
6. Get a job?	Yes	Yes
7. Sign a contract?	Yes	Yes
8. Register a business?	Yes	Yes
9. Open a bank account?	Yes	Yes
10. Choose where to live?	Yes	Yes
11. Be "head of household"?	N/A	N/A

USING PROPERTY

	Score: 100	Score: 100
12. Who legally administers marital property?	Both must agree	Original owner
13. Does the law provide for valuation of nonmonetary contributions?	Yes	Yes
14. Do men and women have equal ownership rights to immovable property?	Yes	Yes
15. Do sons and daughters have equal inheritance rights?	Yes	Yes
16. Do female and male surviving spouses have equal inheritance rights?	Yes	Yes

GETTING A JOB

	Score: 62	Score: 65
17. Is there paid leave available to women of at least 14 weeks?	No	No
18. Do women receive at least 2/3 of their wages for the first 14 weeks or the duration of the leave if it is shorter?	Yes	Yes
19. What is the percentage of maternity leave benefits paid by the government?	67%	0%
20. What is the difference between leave reserved for women and men relative to leave reserved for women, as a function of who pays?	0.67	0.04
21. Is there paid parental leave?	No	No
22. Does the law mandate equal remuneration for work of equal value?	No	No
23. Does the law mandate nondiscrimination based on gender in employment?	Yes	Yes
24. Is dismissal of pregnant workers prohibited?	Yes	Yes
25. Can parents work flexibly?	No	No
26. Can women work the same night hours as men?	Yes	Yes
27. Can women work in jobs deemed hazardous, arduous or morally inappropriate in the same way as men?	No	Yes
28. Are women able to work in the same industries as men?	Yes	Yes
29. Are women able to perform the same tasks at work as men?	Yes	Yes
30. Are the ages at which men and women can retire with full pension benefits equal?	No	Yes
31. Are the ages at which men and women can retire with partial pension benefits equal?	N/A	Yes
32. Are the mandatory retirement ages for men and women equal?	N/A	N/A

PROVIDING INCENTIVES TO WORK

	Score: 80	Score: 40
33. Are mothers guaranteed an equivalent position after maternity leave?	Yes	No
34. Does the government support or provide childcare services?	Yes	No
35. Are payments for childcare tax deductible?	No	No
36. Is primary education free and compulsory?	Yes	Yes
37. Are there tax deductions or credits specific to men?	No	No

GOING TO COURT

	Score: 100	Score: 100
38. Does a woman's testimony carry the same evidentiary weight in court as a man's?	Yes	Yes
39. Does the law establish an anti-discrimination commission?	Yes	Yes
40. Does the law mandate legal aid in civil/family matters?	Yes	Yes
41. Is there a small claims court/fast-track procedure?	Yes	Yes

BUILDING CREDIT

	Score: 75	Score: 50
42. Do retailers provide information to credit agencies?	Yes	No
43. Do utility companies provide information to credit agencies?	Yes	No
44. Is discrimination based on gender prohibited in access to credit?	Yes	Yes
45. Is discrimination based on marital status prohibited in access to credit?	No	Yes

PROTECTING WOMEN FROM VIOLENCE

	Score: 100	Score: 80
46. Is there legislation specifically addressing domestic violence? If not, are there aggravated penalties for crimes committed against a spouse or family member?	Yes	Yes
47. Is there legislation on sexual harassment in employment?	Yes	Yes
48. Is there legislation on sexual harassment in education?	Yes	Yes
49. Are there criminal penalties for sexual harassment in employment?	Yes	No
50. Are there civil remedies for sexual harassment in employment?	Yes	Yes

Note: See the data notes for more details on the scoring of each indicator.

	HUNGARY	ICELAND
REGION	High income: OECD	High income: OECD
INCOME GROUP	High income	High income
FEMALE POPULATION	5,142,381	166,842
FEMALE LABOR FORCE (% OF TOTAL LABOR FORCE)	46%	47%

ACCESSING INSTITUTIONS

	Score: 100	Score: 100
1. Are wives required to obey their husbands?	No	No
Can a woman legally do the following in the same way as a man:		
2. Apply for a passport?	Yes	Yes
3. Apply for a national ID card?	Yes	Yes
4. Travel outside the country?	Yes	Yes
5. Travel outside her home?	Yes	Yes
6. Get a job?	Yes	Yes
7. Sign a contract?	Yes	Yes
8. Register a business?	Yes	Yes
9. Open a bank account?	Yes	Yes
10. Choose where to live?	Yes	Yes
11. Be "head of household"?	N/A	N/A

USING PROPERTY

	Score: 100	Score: 100
12. Who legally administers marital property?	Both must agree	Original owner
13. Does the law provide for valuation of nonmonetary contributions?	Yes	Yes
14. Do men and women have equal ownership rights to immovable property?	Yes	Yes
15. Do sons and daughters have equal inheritance rights?	Yes	Yes
16. Do female and male surviving spouses have equal inheritance rights?	Yes	Yes

GETTING A JOB

	Score: 87	Score: 100
17. Is there paid leave available to women of at least 14 weeks?	Yes	Yes
18. Do women receive at least 2/3 of their wages for the first 14 weeks or the duration of the leave if it is shorter?	Yes	Yes
19. What is the percentage of maternity leave benefits paid by the government?	100%	100%
20. What is the difference between leave reserved for women and men relative to leave reserved for women, as a function of who pays?	1	1
21. Is there paid parental leave?	Yes	Yes
22. Does the law mandate equal remuneration for work of equal value?	No	Yes
23. Does the law mandate nondiscrimination based on gender in employment?	Yes	Yes
24. Is dismissal of pregnant workers prohibited?	Yes	Yes
25. Can parents work flexibly?	No	Yes
26. Can women work the same night hours as men?	Yes	Yes
27. Can women work in jobs deemed hazardous, arduous or morally inappropriate in the same way as men?	Yes	Yes
28. Are women able to work in the same industries as men?	Yes	Yes
29. Are women able to perform the same tasks at work as men?	Yes	Yes
30. Are the ages at which men and women can retire with full pension benefits equal?	Yes	Yes
31. Are the ages at which men and women can retire with partial pension benefits equal?	Yes	Yes
32. Are the mandatory retirement ages for men and women equal?	N/A	N/A

PROVIDING INCENTIVES TO WORK

	Score: 80	Score: 80
33. Are mothers guaranteed an equivalent position after maternity leave?	Yes	Yes
34. Does the government support or provide childcare services?	Yes	Yes
35. Are payments for childcare tax deductible?	No	No
36. Is primary education free and compulsory?	Yes	Yes
37. Are there tax deductions or credits specific to men?	No	No

GOING TO COURT

	Score: 75	Score: 75
38. Does a woman's testimony carry the same evidentiary weight in court as a man's?	Yes	Yes
39. Does the law establish an anti-discrimination commission?	Yes	Yes
40. Does the law mandate legal aid in civil/family matters?	Yes	Yes
41. Is there a small claims court/fast-track procedure?	No	No

BUILDING CREDIT

	Score: 50	Score: 75
42. Do retailers provide information to credit agencies?	No	Yes
43. Do utility companies provide information to credit agencies?	No	Yes
44. Is discrimination based on gender prohibited in access to credit?	Yes	Yes
45. Is discrimination based on marital status prohibited in access to credit?	Yes	No

PROTECTING WOMEN FROM VIOLENCE

	Score: 60	Score: 100
46. Is there legislation specifically addressing domestic violence? If not, are there aggravated penalties for crimes committed against a spouse or family member?	Yes	Yes
47. Is there legislation on sexual harassment in employment?	Yes	Yes
48. Is there legislation on sexual harassment in education?	Yes	Yes
49. Are there criminal penalties for sexual harassment in employment?	No	Yes
50. Are there civil remedies for sexual harassment in employment?	No	Yes

Note: See the data notes for more details on the scoring of each indicator.

	INDIA	INDONESIA
REGION	South Asia	East Asia & Pacific
INCOME GROUP	Lower middle income	Lower middle income
FEMALE POPULATION	637,908,142	129,677,167
FEMALE LABOR FORCE (% OF TOTAL LABOR FORCE)	25%	38%

ACCESSING INSTITUTIONS

	Score: 100	Score: 91
1. Are wives required to obey their husbands?	No	No
Can a woman legally do the following in the same way as a man:		
2. Apply for a passport?	Yes	Yes
3. Apply for a national ID card?	N/A	Yes
4. Travel outside the country?	Yes	Yes
5. Travel outside her home?	Yes	Yes
6. Get a job?	Yes	Yes
7. Sign a contract?	Yes	Yes
8. Register a business?	Yes	Yes
9. Open a bank account?	Yes	Yes
10. Choose where to live?	Yes	Yes
11. Be "head of household"?	N/A	No

USING PROPERTY

	Score: 80	Score: 60
12. Who legally administers marital property?	Original owner	Both must agree
13. Does the law provide for valuation of nonmonetary contributions?	No	Yes
14. Do men and women have equal ownership rights to immovable property?	Yes	Yes
15. Do sons and daughters have equal inheritance rights?	Yes	No
16. Do female and male surviving spouses have equal inheritance rights?	Yes	No

GETTING A JOB

	Score: 40	Score: 64
17. Is there paid leave available to women of at least 14 weeks?	Yes	No
18. Do women receive at least 2/3 of their wages for the first 14 weeks or the duration of the leave if it is shorter?	Yes	Yes
19. What is the percentage of maternity leave benefits paid by the government?	0%	0%
20. What is the difference between leave reserved for women and men relative to leave reserved for women, as a function of who pays?	0	0.02
21. Is there paid parental leave?	No	No
22. Does the law mandate equal remuneration for work of equal value?	No	No
23. Does the law mandate nondiscrimination based on gender in employment?	Yes	Yes
24. Is dismissal of pregnant workers prohibited?	Yes	Yes
25. Can parents work flexibly?	No	No
26. Can women work the same night hours as men?	No	Yes
27. Can women work in jobs deemed hazardous, arduous or morally inappropriate in the same way as men?	No	Yes
28. Are women able to work in the same industries as men?	No	Yes
29. Are women able to perform the same tasks at work as men?	No	Yes
30. Are the ages at which men and women can retire with full pension benefits equal?	Yes	Yes
31. Are the ages at which men and women can retire with partial pension benefits equal?	Yes	N/A
32. Are the mandatory retirement ages for men and women equal?	N/A	N/A

PROVIDING INCENTIVES TO WORK

	Score: 40	Score: 20
33. Are mothers guaranteed an equivalent position after maternity leave?	No	No
34. Does the government support or provide childcare services?	No	No
35. Are payments for childcare tax deductible?	No	No
36. Is primary education free and compulsory?	Yes	Yes
37. Are there tax deductions or credits specific to men?	No	Yes

GOING TO COURT

	Score: 100	Score: 75
38. Does a woman's testimony carry the same evidentiary weight in court as a man's?	Yes	Yes
39. Does the law establish an anti-discrimination commission?	Yes	No
40. Does the law mandate legal aid in civil/family matters?	Yes	Yes
41. Is there a small claims court/fast-track procedure?	Yes	Yes

BUILDING CREDIT

	Score: 0	Score: 0
42. Do retailers provide information to credit agencies?	No	No
43. Do utility companies provide information to credit agencies?	No	No
44. Is discrimination based on gender prohibited in access to credit?	No	No
45. Is discrimination based on marital status prohibited in access to credit?	No	No

PROTECTING WOMEN FROM VIOLENCE

	Score: 100	Score: 20
46. Is there legislation specifically addressing domestic violence? If not, are there aggravated penalties for crimes committed against a spouse or family member?	Yes	Yes
47. Is there legislation on sexual harassment in employment?	Yes	No
48. Is there legislation on sexual harassment in education?	Yes	No
49. Are there criminal penalties for sexual harassment in employment?	Yes	No
50. Are there civil remedies for sexual harassment in employment?	Yes	No

Note: See the data notes for more details on the scoring of each indicator.

	IRAN, ISLAMIC REP.	IRAQ
REGION	Middle East & North Africa	Middle East & North Africa
INCOME GROUP	Upper middle income	Upper middle income
FEMALE POPULATION	39,869,885	18,367,257
FEMALE LABOR FORCE (% OF TOTAL LABOR FORCE)	19%	20%

ACCESSING INSTITUTIONS

	Score: 36	Score: 55
1. Are wives required to obey their husbands?	Yes	Yes
Can a woman legally do the following in the same way as a man:		
2. Apply for a passport?	No	Yes
3. Apply for a national ID card?	Yes	Yes
4. Travel outside the country?	No	No
5. Travel outside her home?	No	No
6. Get a job?	No	Yes
7. Sign a contract?	Yes	Yes
8. Register a business?	Yes	Yes
9. Open a bank account?	Yes	Yes
10. Choose where to live?	No	No
11. Be "head of household"?	No	No

USING PROPERTY

	Score: 40	Score: 40
12. Who legally administers marital property?	Original owner	Original owner
13. Does the law provide for valuation of nonmonetary contributions?	No	No
14. Do men and women have equal ownership rights to immovable property?	Yes	Yes
15. Do sons and daughters have equal inheritance rights?	No	No
16. Do female and male surviving spouses have equal inheritance rights?	No	No

GETTING A JOB

	Score: 43	Score: 38
17. Is there paid leave available to women of at least 14 weeks?	Yes	Yes
18. Do women receive at least 2/3 of their wages for the first 14 weeks or the duration of the leave if it is shorter?	Yes	Yes
19. What is the percentage of maternity leave benefits paid by the government?	100%	0%
20. What is the difference between leave reserved for women and men relative to leave reserved for women, as a function of who pays?	1	0
21. Is there paid parental leave?	No	No
22. Does the law mandate equal remuneration for work of equal value?	No	No
23. Does the law mandate nondiscrimination based on gender in employment?	No	Yes
24. Is dismissal of pregnant workers prohibited?	No	No
25. Can parents work flexibly?	No	No
26. Can women work the same night hours as men?	Yes	No
27. Can women work in jobs deemed hazardous, arduous or morally inappropriate in the same way as men?	No	No
28. Are women able to work in the same industries as men?	Yes	Yes
29. Are women able to perform the same tasks at work as men?	No	Yes
30. Are the ages at which men and women can retire with full pension benefits equal?	No	No
31. Are the ages at which men and women can retire with partial pension benefits equal?	No	N/A
32. Are the mandatory retirement ages for men and women equal?	N/A	No

PROVIDING INCENTIVES TO WORK

	Score: 80	Score: 60
33. Are mothers guaranteed an equivalent position after maternity leave?	Yes	Yes
34. Does the government support or provide childcare services?	Yes	Yes
35. Are payments for childcare tax deductible?	No	No
36. Is primary education free and compulsory?	Yes	Yes
37. Are there tax deductions or credits specific to men?	No	Yes

GOING TO COURT

	Score: 0	Score: 0
38. Does a woman's testimony carry the same evidentiary weight in court as a man's?	No	No
39. Does the law establish an anti-discrimination commission?	No	No
40. Does the law mandate legal aid in civil/family matters?	No	No
41. Is there a small claims court/fast-track procedure?	No	No

BUILDING CREDIT

	Score: 25	Score: 0
42. Do retailers provide information to credit agencies?	Yes	N/A
43. Do utility companies provide information to credit agencies?	No	N/A
44. Is discrimination based on gender prohibited in access to credit?	No	No
45. Is discrimination based on marital status prohibited in access to credit?	No	No

PROTECTING WOMEN FROM VIOLENCE

	Score: 0	Score: 40
46. Is there legislation specifically addressing domestic violence? If not, are there aggravated penalties for crimes committed against a spouse or family member?	No	No
47. Is there legislation on sexual harassment in employment?	No	Yes
48. Is there legislation on sexual harassment in education?	No	No
49. Are there criminal penalties for sexual harassment in employment?	No	Yes
50. Are there civil remedies for sexual harassment in employment?	No	No

Note: See the data notes for more details on the scoring of each indicator.

	IRELAND	ISRAEL
REGION	High income: OECD	High income: OECD
INCOME GROUP	High income	High income
FEMALE POPULATION	2,390,143	4,305,618
FEMALE LABOR FORCE (% OF TOTAL LABOR FORCE)	45%	47%

ACCESSING INSTITUTIONS

	Score: 100	Score: 100
1. Are wives required to obey their husbands?	No	No
Can a woman legally do the following in the same way as a man:		
2. Apply for a passport?	Yes	Yes
3. Apply for a national ID card?	N/A	Yes
4. Travel outside the country?	Yes	Yes
5. Travel outside her home?	Yes	Yes
6. Get a job?	Yes	Yes
7. Sign a contract?	Yes	Yes
8. Register a business?	Yes	Yes
9. Open a bank account?	Yes	Yes
10. Choose where to live?	Yes	Yes
11. Be "head of household"?	N/A	N/A

USING PROPERTY

	Score: 100	Score: 100
12. Who legally administers marital property?	Original owner	Original owner
13. Does the law provide for valuation of nonmonetary contributions?	Yes	Yes
14. Do men and women have equal ownership rights to immovable property?	Yes	Yes
15. Do sons and daughters have equal inheritance rights?	Yes	Yes
16. Do female and male surviving spouses have equal inheritance rights?	Yes	Yes

GETTING A JOB

	Score: 85	Score: 72
17. Is there paid leave available to women of at least 14 weeks?	Yes	Yes
18. Do women receive at least 2/3 of their wages for the first 14 weeks or the duration of the leave if it is shorter?	No	Yes
19. What is the percentage of maternity leave benefits paid by the government?	100%	100%
20. What is the difference between leave reserved for women and men relative to leave reserved for women, as a function of who pays?	1	1
21. Is there paid parental leave?	No	No
22. Does the law mandate equal remuneration for work of equal value?	Yes	Yes
23. Does the law mandate nondiscrimination based on gender in employment?	Yes	Yes
24. Is dismissal of pregnant workers prohibited?	Yes	Yes
25. Can parents work flexibly?	No	No
26. Can women work the same night hours as men?	Yes	Yes
27. Can women work in jobs deemed hazardous, arduous or morally inappropriate in the same way as men?	Yes	No
28. Are women able to work in the same industries as men?	Yes	Yes
29. Are women able to perform the same tasks at work as men?	Yes	No
30. Are the ages at which men and women can retire with full pension benefits equal?	Yes	No
31. Are the ages at which men and women can retire with partial pension benefits equal?	N/A	Yes
32. Are the mandatory retirement ages for men and women equal?	N/A	Yes

PROVIDING INCENTIVES TO WORK

	Score: 80	Score: 60
33. Are mothers guaranteed an equivalent position after maternity leave?	Yes	No
34. Does the government support or provide childcare services?	Yes	Yes
35. Are payments for childcare tax deductible?	No	No
36. Is primary education free and compulsory?	Yes	Yes
37. Are there tax deductions or credits specific to men?	No	No

GOING TO COURT

	Score: 75	Score: 75
38. Does a woman's testimony carry the same evidentiary weight in court as a man's?	Yes	Yes
39. Does the law establish an anti-discrimination commission?	No	No
40. Does the law mandate legal aid in civil/family matters?	Yes	Yes
41. Is there a small claims court/fast-track procedure?	Yes	Yes

BUILDING CREDIT

	Score: 50	Score: 25
42. Do retailers provide information to credit agencies?	No	No
43. Do utility companies provide information to credit agencies?	No	Yes
44. Is discrimination based on gender prohibited in access to credit?	Yes	No
45. Is discrimination based on marital status prohibited in access to credit?	Yes	No

PROTECTING WOMEN FROM VIOLENCE

	Score: 100	Score: 100
46. Is there legislation specifically addressing domestic violence? If not, are there aggravated penalties for crimes committed against a spouse or family member?	Yes	Yes
47. Is there legislation on sexual harassment in employment?	Yes	Yes
48. Is there legislation on sexual harassment in education?	Yes	Yes
49. Are there criminal penalties for sexual harassment in employment?	Yes	Yes
50. Are there civil remedies for sexual harassment in employment?	Yes	Yes

Note: See the data notes for more details on the scoring of each indicator.

	ITALY	JAMAICA
REGION	High income: OECD	Latin America & Caribbean
INCOME GROUP	High income	Upper middle income
FEMALE POPULATION	31,130,010	1,446,431
FEMALE LABOR FORCE (% OF TOTAL LABOR FORCE)	42%	43%

ACCESSING INSTITUTIONS

	Score: 100	**Score: 100**
1. Are wives required to obey their husbands?	No	No
Can a woman legally do the following in the same way as a man:		
2. Apply for a passport?	Yes	Yes
3. Apply for a national ID card?	Yes	N/A
4. Travel outside the country?	Yes	Yes
5. Travel outside her home?	Yes	Yes
6. Get a job?	Yes	Yes
7. Sign a contract?	Yes	Yes
8. Register a business?	Yes	Yes
9. Open a bank account?	Yes	Yes
10. Choose where to live?	Yes	Yes
11. Be "head of household"?	N/A	N/A

USING PROPERTY

	Score: 100	**Score: 100**
12. Who legally administers marital property?	Both must agree	Original owner
13. Does the law provide for valuation of nonmonetary contributions?	Yes	Yes
14. Do men and women have equal ownership rights to immovable property?	Yes	Yes
15. Do sons and daughters have equal inheritance rights?	Yes	Yes
16. Do female and male surviving spouses have equal inheritance rights?	Yes	Yes

GETTING A JOB

	Score: 100	**Score: 47**
17. Is there paid leave available to women of at least 14 weeks?	Yes	No
18. Do women receive at least 2/3 of their wages for the first 14 weeks or the duration of the leave if it is shorter?	Yes	Yes
19. What is the percentage of maternity leave benefits paid by the government?	100%	0%
20. What is the difference between leave reserved for women and men relative to leave reserved for women, as a function of who pays?	1	0
21. Is there paid parental leave?	Yes	No
22. Does the law mandate equal remuneration for work of equal value?	Yes	No
23. Does the law mandate nondiscrimination based on gender in employment?	Yes	No
24. Is dismissal of pregnant workers prohibited?	Yes	Yes
25. Can parents work flexibly?	Yes	No
26. Can women work the same night hours as men?	Yes	Yes
27. Can women work in jobs deemed hazardous, arduous or morally inappropriate in the same way as men?	Yes	Yes
28. Are women able to work in the same industries as men?	Yes	No
29. Are women able to perform the same tasks at work as men?	Yes	Yes
30. Are the ages at which men and women can retire with full pension benefits equal?	Yes	Yes
31. Are the ages at which men and women can retire with partial pension benefits equal?	N/A	N/A
32. Are the mandatory retirement ages for men and women equal?	N/A	N/A

PROVIDING INCENTIVES TO WORK

	Score: 100	**Score: 80**
33. Are mothers guaranteed an equivalent position after maternity leave?	Yes	Yes
34. Does the government support or provide childcare services?	Yes	Yes
35. Are payments for childcare tax deductible?	Yes	No
36. Is primary education free and compulsory?	Yes	Yes
37. Are there tax deductions or credits specific to men?	No	No

GOING TO COURT

	Score: 75	**Score: 75**
38. Does a woman's testimony carry the same evidentiary weight in court as a man's?	Yes	Yes
39. Does the law establish an anti-discrimination commission?	No	No
40. Does the law mandate legal aid in civil/family matters?	Yes	Yes
41. Is there a small claims court/fast-track procedure?	Yes	Yes

BUILDING CREDIT

	Score: 25	**Score: 0**
42. Do retailers provide information to credit agencies?	No	No
43. Do utility companies provide information to credit agencies?	No	No
44. Is discrimination based on gender prohibited in access to credit?	Yes	No
45. Is discrimination based on marital status prohibited in access to credit?	No	No

PROTECTING WOMEN FROM VIOLENCE

	Score: 60	**Score: 20**
46. Is there legislation specifically addressing domestic violence? If not, are there aggravated penalties for crimes committed against a spouse or family member?	Yes	Yes
47. Is there legislation on sexual harassment in employment?	Yes	No
48. Is there legislation on sexual harassment in education?	No	No
49. Are there criminal penalties for sexual harassment in employment?	No	No
50. Are there civil remedies for sexual harassment in employment?	Yes	No

Note: See the data notes for more details on the scoring of each indicator.

	JAPAN	JORDAN
REGION	High income: OECD	Middle East & North Africa
INCOME GROUP	High income	Lower middle income
FEMALE POPULATION	65,250,540	4,616,022
FEMALE LABOR FORCE (% OF TOTAL LABOR FORCE)	43%	18%

ACCESSING INSTITUTIONS

	Score: 100	Score: 45
1. Are wives required to obey their husbands?	No	Yes
Can a woman legally do the following in the same way as a man:		
2. Apply for a passport?	Yes	No
3. Apply for a national ID card?	N/A	Yes
4. Travel outside the country?	Yes	Yes
5. Travel outside her home?	Yes	No
6. Get a job?	Yes	No
7. Sign a contract?	Yes	Yes
8. Register a business?	Yes	Yes
9. Open a bank account?	Yes	Yes
10. Choose where to live?	Yes	No
11. Be "head of household"?	Yes	No

USING PROPERTY

	Score: 100	Score: 40
12. Who legally administers marital property?	Original owner	Original owner
13. Does the law provide for valuation of nonmonetary contributions?	Yes	No
14. Do men and women have equal ownership rights to immovable property?	Yes	Yes
15. Do sons and daughters have equal inheritance rights?	Yes	No
16. Do female and male surviving spouses have equal inheritance rights?	Yes	No

GETTING A JOB

	Score: 87	Score: 41
17. Is there paid leave available to women of at least 14 weeks?	Yes	No
18. Do women receive at least 2/3 of their wages for the first 14 weeks or the duration of the leave if it is shorter?	Yes	Yes
19. What is the percentage of maternity leave benefits paid by the government?	100%	100%
20. What is the difference between leave reserved for women and men relative to leave reserved for women, as a function of who pays?	1	1
21. Is there paid parental leave?	Yes	No
22. Does the law mandate equal remuneration for work of equal value?	No	No
23. Does the law mandate nondiscrimination based on gender in employment?	Yes	No
24. Is dismissal of pregnant workers prohibited?	Yes	No
25. Can parents work flexibly?	Yes	No
26. Can women work the same night hours as men?	Yes	No
27. Can women work in jobs deemed hazardous, arduous or morally inappropriate in the same way as men?	Yes	Yes
28. Are women able to work in the same industries as men?	No	No
29. Are women able to perform the same tasks at work as men?	Yes	No
30. Are the ages at which men and women can retire with full pension benefits equal?	Yes	No
31. Are the ages at which men and women can retire with partial pension benefits equal?	Yes	Yes
32. Are the mandatory retirement ages for men and women equal?	N/A	N/A

PROVIDING INCENTIVES TO WORK

	Score: 60	Score: 80
33. Are mothers guaranteed an equivalent position after maternity leave?	No	Yes
34. Does the government support or provide childcare services?	Yes	Yes
35. Are payments for childcare tax deductible?	No	No
36. Is primary education free and compulsory?	Yes	Yes
37. Are there tax deductions or credits specific to men?	No	No

GOING TO COURT

	Score: 75	Score: 50
38. Does a woman's testimony carry the same evidentiary weight in court as a man's?	Yes	No
39. Does the law establish an anti-discrimination commission?	No	Yes
40. Does the law mandate legal aid in civil/family matters?	Yes	No
41. Is there a small claims court/fast-track procedure?	Yes	Yes

BUILDING CREDIT

	Score: 25	Score: 0
42. Do retailers provide information to credit agencies?	Yes	No
43. Do utility companies provide information to credit agencies?	No	No
44. Is discrimination based on gender prohibited in access to credit?	No	No
45. Is discrimination based on marital status prohibited in access to credit?	No	No

PROTECTING WOMEN FROM VIOLENCE

	Score: 20	Score: 20
46. Is there legislation specifically addressing domestic violence? If not, are there aggravated penalties for crimes committed against a spouse or family member?	Yes	Yes
47. Is there legislation on sexual harassment in employment?	No	No
48. Is there legislation on sexual harassment in education?	No	No
49. Are there criminal penalties for sexual harassment in employment?	No	No
50. Are there civil remedies for sexual harassment in employment?	No	No

Note: See the data notes for more details on the scoring of each indicator.

	KAZAKHSTAN	KENYA
REGION	Europe & Central Asia	Sub-Saharan Africa
INCOME GROUP	Upper middle income	Lower middle income
FEMALE POPULATION	9,200,746	24,243,511
FEMALE LABOR FORCE (% OF TOTAL LABOR FORCE)	49%	49%

ACCESSING INSTITUTIONS

	Score: 100	Score: 100
1. Are wives required to obey their husbands?	No	No

Can a woman legally do the following in the same way as a man:

2. Apply for a passport?	Yes	Yes
3. Apply for a national ID card?	Yes	Yes
4. Travel outside the country?	Yes	Yes
5. Travel outside her home?	Yes	Yes
6. Get a job?	Yes	Yes
7. Sign a contract?	Yes	Yes
8. Register a business?	Yes	Yes
9. Open a bank account?	Yes	Yes
10. Choose where to live?	Yes	Yes
11. Be "head of household"?	N/A	N/A

USING PROPERTY

	Score: 100	Score: 80
12. Who legally administers marital property?	Both must agree	Both must agree
13. Does the law provide for valuation of nonmonetary contributions?	Yes	Yes
14. Do men and women have equal ownership rights to immovable property?	Yes	Yes
15. Do sons and daughters have equal inheritance rights?	Yes	Yes
16. Do female and male surviving spouses have equal inheritance rights?	Yes	No

GETTING A JOB

	Score: 71	Score: 74
17. Is there paid leave available to women of at least 14 weeks?	Yes	No
18. Do women receive at least 2/3 of their wages for the first 14 weeks or the duration of the leave if it is shorter?	Yes	Yes
19. What is the percentage of maternity leave benefits paid by the government?	100%	0%
20. What is the difference between leave reserved for women and men relative to leave reserved for women, as a function of who pays?	1	0.11
21. Is there paid parental leave?	Yes	No
22. Does the law mandate equal remuneration for work of equal value?	No	Yes
23. Does the law mandate nondiscrimination based on gender in employment?	Yes	Yes
24. Is dismissal of pregnant workers prohibited?	Yes	Yes
25. Can parents work flexibly?	Yes	No
26. Can women work the same night hours as men?	Yes	Yes
27. Can women work in jobs deemed hazardous, arduous or morally inappropriate in the same way as men?	No	Yes
28. Are women able to work in the same industries as men?	No	Yes
29. Are women able to perform the same tasks at work as men?	No	Yes
30. Are the ages at which men and women can retire with full pension benefits equal?	Yes	Yes
31. Are the ages at which men and women can retire with partial pension benefits equal?	N/A	Yes
32. Are the mandatory retirement ages for men and women equal?	N/A	N/A

PROVIDING INCENTIVES TO WORK

	Score: 80	Score: 80
33. Are mothers guaranteed an equivalent position after maternity leave?	Yes	Yes
34. Does the government support or provide childcare services?	Yes	Yes
35. Are payments for childcare tax deductible?	No	No
36. Is primary education free and compulsory?	Yes	Yes
37. Are there tax deductions or credits specific to men?	No	No

GOING TO COURT

	Score: 75	Score: 100
38. Does a woman's testimony carry the same evidentiary weight in court as a man's?	Yes	Yes
39. Does the law establish an anti-discrimination commission?	No	Yes
40. Does the law mandate legal aid in civil/family matters?	Yes	Yes
41. Is there a small claims court/fast-track procedure?	Yes	Yes

BUILDING CREDIT

	Score: 0	Score: 25
42. Do retailers provide information to credit agencies?	No	No
43. Do utility companies provide information to credit agencies?	No	Yes
44. Is discrimination based on gender prohibited in access to credit?	No	No
45. Is discrimination based on marital status prohibited in access to credit?	No	No

PROTECTING WOMEN FROM VIOLENCE

	Score: 20	Score: 80
46. Is there legislation specifically addressing domestic violence? If not, are there aggravated penalties for crimes committed against a spouse or family member?	Yes	Yes
47. Is there legislation on sexual harassment in employment?	No	Yes
48. Is there legislation on sexual harassment in education?	No	Yes
49. Are there criminal penalties for sexual harassment in employment?	No	Yes
50. Are there civil remedies for sexual harassment in employment?	No	No

Note: See the data notes for more details on the scoring of each indicator.

	KIRIBATI	KOREA, REP.
REGION	East Asia & Pacific	High income: OECD
INCOME GROUP	Lower middle income	High income
FEMALE POPULATION	57,987	25,779,815
FEMALE LABOR FORCE (% OF TOTAL LABOR FORCE)	..	42%

ACCESSING INSTITUTIONS

	Score: 100	Score: 100
1. Are wives required to obey their husbands?	No	No
Can a woman legally do the following in the same way as a man:		
2. Apply for a passport?	Yes	Yes
3. Apply for a national ID card?	N/A	Yes
4. Travel outside the country?	Yes	Yes
5. Travel outside her home?	Yes	Yes
6. Get a job?	Yes	Yes
7. Sign a contract?	Yes	Yes
8. Register a business?	Yes	Yes
9. Open a bank account?	Yes	Yes
10. Choose where to live?	Yes	Yes
11. Be "head of household"?	N/A	N/A

USING PROPERTY

	Score: 75	Score: 100
12. Who legally administers marital property?	Other	Original Owner
13. Does the law provide for valuation of nonmonetary contributions?	No	Yes
14. Do men and women have equal ownership rights to immovable property?	..	Yes
15. Do sons and daughters have equal inheritance rights?	Yes	Yes
16. Do female and male surviving spouses have equal inheritance rights?	Yes	Yes

GETTING A JOB

	Score: 68	Score: 71
17. Is there paid leave available to women of at least 14 weeks?	No	Yes
18. Do women receive at least 2/3 of their wages for the first 14 weeks or the duration of the leave if it is shorter?	No	Yes
19. What is the percentage of maternity leave benefits paid by the government?	0%	33%
20. What is the difference between leave reserved for women and men relative to leave reserved for women, as a function of who pays?	0	0.35
21. Is there paid parental leave?	No	Yes
22. Does the law mandate equal remuneration for work of equal value?	Yes	No
23. Does the law mandate nondiscrimination based on gender in employment?	Yes	Yes
24. Is dismissal of pregnant workers prohibited?	Yes	Yes
25. Can parents work flexibly?	No	Yes
26. Can women work the same night hours as men?	Yes	Yes
27. Can women work in jobs deemed hazardous, arduous or morally inappropriate in the same way as men?	Yes	No
28. Are women able to work in the same industries as men?	Yes	No
29. Are women able to perform the same tasks at work as men?	Yes	Yes
30. Are the ages at which men and women can retire with full pension benefits equal?	Yes	Yes
31. Are the ages at which men and women can retire with partial pension benefits equal?	Yes	Yes
32. Are the mandatory retirement ages for men and women equal?	N/A	N/A

PROVIDING INCENTIVES TO WORK

	Score: 60	Score: 100
33. Are mothers guaranteed an equivalent position after maternity leave?	Yes	Yes
34. Does the government support or provide childcare services?	No	Yes
35. Are payments for childcare tax deductible?	No	Yes
36. Is primary education free and compulsory?	Yes	Yes
37. Are there tax deductions or credits specific to men?	No	No

GOING TO COURT

	Score: 50	Score: 100
38. Does a woman's testimony carry the same evidentiary weight in court as a man's?	Yes	Yes
39. Does the law establish an anti-discrimination commission?	No	Yes
40. Does the law mandate legal aid in civil/family matters?	No	Yes
41. Is there a small claims court/fast-track procedure?	Yes	Yes

BUILDING CREDIT

	Score: 0	Score: 25
42. Do retailers provide information to credit agencies?	N/A	Yes
43. Do utility companies provide information to credit agencies?	N/A	No
44. Is discrimination based on gender prohibited in access to credit?	No	No
45. Is discrimination based on marital status prohibited in access to credit?	No	No

PROTECTING WOMEN FROM VIOLENCE

	Score: 20	Score: 100
46. Is there legislation specifically addressing domestic violence? If not, are there aggravated penalties for crimes committed against a spouse or family member?	Yes	Yes
47. Is there legislation on sexual harassment in employment?	No	Yes
48. Is there legislation on sexual harassment in education?	No	Yes
49. Are there criminal penalties for sexual harassment in employment?	No	Yes
50. Are there civil remedies for sexual harassment in employment?	No	Yes

Note: See the data notes for more details on the scoring of each indicator.

	KOSOVO	KUWAIT
REGION	Europe & Central Asia	Middle East & North Africa
INCOME GROUP	Lower middle income	High income
FEMALE POPULATION	871,078	1,775,530
FEMALE LABOR FORCE (% OF TOTAL LABOR FORCE)	..	28%

ACCESSING INSTITUTIONS

	Score: 100	Score: 73
1. Are wives required to obey their husbands?	No	No
Can a woman legally do the following in the same way as a man:		
2. Apply for a passport?	Yes	Yes
3. Apply for a national ID card?	Yes	Yes
4. Travel outside the country?	Yes	Yes
5. Travel outside her home?	Yes	No
6. Get a job?	Yes	No
7. Sign a contract?	Yes	Yes
8. Register a business?	Yes	Yes
9. Open a bank account?	Yes	Yes
10. Choose where to live?	Yes	No
11. Be "head of household"?	N/A	N/A

USING PROPERTY

	Score: 100	Score: 40
12. Who legally administers marital property?	Both must agree	Original owner
13. Does the law provide for valuation of nonmonetary contributions?	Yes	No
14. Do men and women have equal ownership rights to immovable property?	Yes	Yes
15. Do sons and daughters have equal inheritance rights?	Yes	No
16. Do female and male surviving spouses have equal inheritance rights?	Yes	No

GETTING A JOB

	Score: 77	Score: 13
17. Is there paid leave available to women of at least 14 weeks?	Yes	No
18. Do women receive at least 2/3 of their wages for the first 14 weeks or the duration of the leave if it is shorter?	Yes	Yes
19. What is the percentage of maternity leave benefits paid by the government?	24%	0%
20. What is the difference between leave reserved for women and men relative to leave reserved for women, as a function of who pays?	0.25	0
21. Is there paid parental leave?	No	No
22. Does the law mandate equal remuneration for work of equal value?	Yes	No
23. Does the law mandate nondiscrimination based on gender in employment?	Yes	No
24. Is dismissal of pregnant workers prohibited?	Yes	No
25. Can parents work flexibly?	No	No
26. Can women work the same night hours as men?	Yes	No
27. Can women work in jobs deemed hazardous, arduous or morally inappropriate in the same way as men?	Yes	No
28. Are women able to work in the same industries as men?	Yes	No
29. Are women able to perform the same tasks at work as men?	Yes	No
30. Are the ages at which men and women can retire with full pension benefits equal?	Yes	N/A
31. Are the ages at which men and women can retire with partial pension benefits equal?	Yes	N/A
32. Are the mandatory retirement ages for men and women equal?	N/A	N/A

PROVIDING INCENTIVES TO WORK

	Score: 80	Score: 60
33. Are mothers guaranteed an equivalent position after maternity leave?	Yes	No
34. Does the government support or provide childcare services?	Yes	Yes
35. Are payments for childcare tax deductible?	No	No
36. Is primary education free and compulsory?	Yes	Yes
37. Are there tax deductions or credits specific to men?	No	No

GOING TO COURT

	Score: 100	Score: 25
38. Does a woman's testimony carry the same evidentiary weight in court as a man's?	Yes	No
39. Does the law establish an anti-discrimination commission?	Yes	No
40. Does the law mandate legal aid in civil/family matters?	Yes	No
41. Is there a small claims court/fast-track procedure?	Yes	Yes

BUILDING CREDIT

	Score: 50	Score: 25
42. Do retailers provide information to credit agencies?	No	Yes
43. Do utility companies provide information to credit agencies?	No	No
44. Is discrimination based on gender prohibited in access to credit?	Yes	No
45. Is discrimination based on marital status prohibited in access to credit?	Yes	No

PROTECTING WOMEN FROM VIOLENCE

	Score: 100	Score: 0
46. Is there legislation specifically addressing domestic violence? If not, are there aggravated penalties for crimes committed against a spouse or family member?	Yes	No
47. Is there legislation on sexual harassment in employment?	Yes	No
48. Is there legislation on sexual harassment in education?	Yes	No
49. Are there criminal penalties for sexual harassment in employment?	Yes	No
50. Are there civil remedies for sexual harassment in employment?	Yes	No

Note: See the data notes for more details on the scoring of each indicator.

	KYRGYZ REPUBLIC	LAO PDR
REGION	Europe & Central Asia	East Asia & Pacific
INCOME GROUP	Lower middle income	Lower middle income
FEMALE POPULATION	3,071,083	3,392,922
FEMALE LABOR FORCE (% OF TOTAL LABOR FORCE)	40%	50%

ACCESSING INSTITUTIONS

	Score: 100	Score: 100
1. Are wives required to obey their husbands?	No	No
Can a woman legally do the following in the same way as a man:		
2. Apply for a passport?	Yes	Yes
3. Apply for a national ID card?	Yes	Yes
4. Travel outside the country?	Yes	Yes
5. Travel outside her home?	Yes	Yes
6. Get a job?	Yes	Yes
7. Sign a contract?	Yes	Yes
8. Register a business?	Yes	Yes
9. Open a bank account?	Yes	Yes
10. Choose where to live?	Yes	Yes
11. Be "head of household"?	N/A	N/A

USING PROPERTY

	Score: 100	Score: 100
12. Who legally administers marital property?	Both must agree	Both must agree
13. Does the law provide for valuation of nonmonetary contributions?	Yes	Yes
14. Do men and women have equal ownership rights to immovable property?	Yes	Yes
15. Do sons and daughters have equal inheritance rights?	Yes	Yes
16. Do female and male surviving spouses have equal inheritance rights?	Yes	Yes

GETTING A JOB

	Score: 59	Score: 75
17. Is there paid leave available to women of at least 14 weeks?	Yes	Yes
18. Do women receive at least 2/3 of their wages for the first 14 weeks or the duration of the leave if it is shorter?	Yes	Yes
19. What is the percentage of maternity leave benefits paid by the government?	92%	100%
20. What is the difference between leave reserved for women and men relative to leave reserved for women, as a function of who pays?	0.92	1
21. Is there paid parental leave?	No	No
22. Does the law mandate equal remuneration for work of equal value?	No	No
23. Does the law mandate nondiscrimination based on gender in employment?	Yes	Yes
24. Is dismissal of pregnant workers prohibited?	Yes	Yes
25. Can parents work flexibly?	Yes	No
26. Can women work the same night hours as men?	Yes	Yes
27. Can women work in jobs deemed hazardous, arduous or morally inappropriate in the same way as men?	No	Yes
28. Are women able to work in the same industries as men?	No	Yes
29. Are women able to perform the same tasks at work as men?	No	Yes
30. Are the ages at which men and women can retire with full pension benefits equal?	No	No
31. Are the ages at which men and women can retire with partial pension benefits equal?	No	N/A
32. Are the mandatory retirement ages for men and women equal?	N/A	N/A

PROVIDING INCENTIVES TO WORK

	Score: 80	Score: 20
33. Are mothers guaranteed an equivalent position after maternity leave?	Yes	No
34. Does the government support or provide childcare services?	Yes	No
35. Are payments for childcare tax deductible?	No	No
36. Is primary education free and compulsory?	Yes	Yes
37. Are there tax deductions or credits specific to men?	No	Yes

GOING TO COURT

	Score: 75	Score: 25
38. Does a woman's testimony carry the same evidentiary weight in court as a man's?	Yes	Yes
39. Does the law establish an anti-discrimination commission?	Yes	No
40. Does the law mandate legal aid in civil/family matters?	Yes	No
41. Is there a small claims court/fast-track procedure?	No	No

BUILDING CREDIT

	Score: 25	Score: 25
42. Do retailers provide information to credit agencies?	No	No
43. Do utility companies provide information to credit agencies?	No	No
44. Is discrimination based on gender prohibited in access to credit?	Yes	Yes
45. Is discrimination based on marital status prohibited in access to credit?	No	No

PROTECTING WOMEN FROM VIOLENCE

	Score: 60	Score: 60
46. Is there legislation specifically addressing domestic violence? If not, are there aggravated penalties for crimes committed against a spouse or family member?	Yes	Yes
47. Is there legislation on sexual harassment in employment?	Yes	Yes
48. Is there legislation on sexual harassment in education?	No	No
49. Are there criminal penalties for sexual harassment in employment?	No	No
50. Are there civil remedies for sexual harassment in employment?	Yes	Yes

Note: See the data notes for more details on the scoring of each indicator.

	LATVIA	LEBANON
REGION	Europe & Central Asia	Middle East & North Africa
INCOME GROUP	High income: OECD	Upper middle income
FEMALE POPULATION	1,060,201	2,992,712
FEMALE LABOR FORCE (% OF TOTAL LABOR FORCE)	50%	24%

ACCESSING INSTITUTIONS

	Score: 100	Score: 100
1. Are wives required to obey their husbands?	No	No
Can a woman legally do the following in the same way as a man:		
2. Apply for a passport?	Yes	Yes
3. Apply for a national ID card?	Yes	Yes
4. Travel outside the country?	Yes	Yes
5. Travel outside her home?	Yes	Yes
6. Get a job?	Yes	Yes
7. Sign a contract?	Yes	Yes
8. Register a business?	Yes	Yes
9. Open a bank account?	Yes	Yes
10. Choose where to live?	Yes	Yes
11. Be "head of household"?	N/A	N/A

USING PROPERTY

	Score: 100	Score: 40
12. Who legally administers marital property?	Both must agree	Original owner
13. Does the law provide for valuation of nonmonetary contributions?	Yes	No
14. Do men and women have equal ownership rights to immovable property?	Yes	Yes
15. Do sons and daughters have equal inheritance rights?	Yes	No
16. Do female and male surviving spouses have equal inheritance rights?	Yes	No

GETTING A JOB

	Score: 100	Score: 54
17. Is there paid leave available to women of at least 14 weeks?	Yes	No
18. Do women receive at least 2/3 of their wages for the first 14 weeks or the duration of the leave if it is shorter?	Yes	Yes
19. What is the percentage of maternity leave benefits paid by the government?	100%	0%
20. What is the difference between leave reserved for women and men relative to leave reserved for women, as a function of who pays?	1	0
21. Is there paid parental leave?	Yes	No
22. Does the law mandate equal remuneration for work of equal value?	Yes	No
23. Does the law mandate nondiscrimination based on gender in employment?	Yes	Yes
24. Is dismissal of pregnant workers prohibited?	Yes	Yes
25. Can parents work flexibly?	Yes	No
26. Can women work the same night hours as men?	Yes	Yes
27. Can women work in jobs deemed hazardous, arduous or morally inappropriate in the same way as men?	Yes	Yes
28. Are women able to work in the same industries as men?	Yes	No
29. Are women able to perform the same tasks at work as men?	Yes	No
30. Are the ages at which men and women can retire with full pension benefits equal?	Yes	Yes
31. Are the ages at which men and women can retire with partial pension benefits equal?	Yes	Yes
32. Are the mandatory retirement ages for men and women equal?	N/A	Yes

PROVIDING INCENTIVES TO WORK

	Score: 80	Score: 60
33. Are mothers guaranteed an equivalent position after maternity leave?	Yes	No
34. Does the government support or provide childcare services?	Yes	Yes
35. Are payments for childcare tax deductible?	No	No
36. Is primary education free and compulsory?	Yes	Yes
37. Are there tax deductions or credits specific to men?	No	No

GOING TO COURT

	Score: 100	Score: 75
38. Does a woman's testimony carry the same evidentiary weight in court as a man's?	Yes	Yes
39. Does the law establish an anti-discrimination commission?	Yes	No
40. Does the law mandate legal aid in civil/family matters?	Yes	Yes
41. Is there a small claims court/fast-track procedure?	Yes	Yes

BUILDING CREDIT

	Score: 75	Score: 0
42. Do retailers provide information to credit agencies?	Yes	No
43. Do utility companies provide information to credit agencies?	Yes	No
44. Is discrimination based on gender prohibited in access to credit?	Yes	No
45. Is discrimination based on marital status prohibited in access to credit?	No	No

PROTECTING WOMEN FROM VIOLENCE

	Score: 60	Score: 20
46. Is there legislation specifically addressing domestic violence? If not, are there aggravated penalties for crimes committed against a spouse or family member?	Yes	Yes
47. Is there legislation on sexual harassment in employment?	Yes	No
48. Is there legislation on sexual harassment in education?	No	No
49. Are there criminal penalties for sexual harassment in employment?	No	No
50. Are there civil remedies for sexual harassment in employment?	Yes	No

Note: See the data notes for more details on the scoring of each indicator.

	LESOTHO	LIBERIA
REGION	Sub-Saharan Africa	Sub-Saharan Africa
INCOME GROUP	Lower middle income	Low income
FEMALE POPULATION	1,111,505	2,287,478
FEMALE LABOR FORCE (% OF TOTAL LABOR FORCE)	47%	48%

ACCESSING INSTITUTIONS

	Score: 100	Score: 100
1. Are wives required to obey their husbands?	No	No
Can a woman legally do the following in the same way as a man:		
2. Apply for a passport?	Yes	Yes
3. Apply for a national ID card?	Yes	Yes
4. Travel outside the country?	Yes	Yes
5. Travel outside her home?	Yes	Yes
6. Get a job?	Yes	Yes
7. Sign a contract?	Yes	Yes
8. Register a business?	Yes	Yes
9. Open a bank account?	Yes	Yes
10. Choose where to live?	Yes	Yes
11. Be "head of household"?	N/A	N/A

USING PROPERTY

	Score: 80	Score: 80
12. Who legally administers marital property?	Both must agree	Original owner
13. Does the law provide for valuation of nonmonetary contributions?	Yes	No
14. Do men and women have equal ownership rights to immovable property?	Yes	Yes
15. Do sons and daughters have equal inheritance rights?	No	Yes
16. Do female and male surviving spouses have equal inheritance rights?	Yes	Yes

GETTING A JOB

	Score: 56	Score: 73
17. Is there paid leave available to women of at least 14 weeks?	No	Yes
18. Do women receive at least 2/3 of their wages for the first 14 weeks or the duration of the leave if it is shorter?	Yes	Yes
19. What is the percentage of maternity leave benefits paid by the government?	0%	0%
20. What is the difference between leave reserved for women and men relative to leave reserved for women, as a function of who pays?	0	0
21. Is there paid parental leave?	No	No
22. Does the law mandate equal remuneration for work of equal value?	Yes	Yes
23. Does the law mandate nondiscrimination based on gender in employment?	Yes	Yes
24. Is dismissal of pregnant workers prohibited?	Yes	Yes
25. Can parents work flexibly?	No	No
26. Can women work the same night hours as men?	Yes	Yes
27. Can women work in jobs deemed hazardous, arduous or morally inappropriate in the same way as men?	Yes	Yes
28. Are women able to work in the same industries as men?	No	Yes
29. Are women able to perform the same tasks at work as men?	No	Yes
30. Are the ages at which men and women can retire with full pension benefits equal?	Yes	Yes
31. Are the ages at which men and women can retire with partial pension benefits equal?	N/A	Yes
32. Are the mandatory retirement ages for men and women equal?	N/A	N/A

PROVIDING INCENTIVES TO WORK

	Score: 40	Score: 80
33. Are mothers guaranteed an equivalent position after maternity leave?	No	Yes
34. Does the government support or provide childcare services?	No	Yes
35. Are payments for childcare tax deductible?	No	No
36. Is primary education free and compulsory?	Yes	Yes
37. Are there tax deductions or credits specific to men?	No	No

GOING TO COURT

	Score: 100	Score: 75
38. Does a woman's testimony carry the same evidentiary weight in court as a man's?	Yes	Yes
39. Does the law establish an anti-discrimination commission?	Yes	Yes
40. Does the law mandate legal aid in civil/family matters?	Yes	No
41. Is there a small claims court/fast-track procedure?	Yes	Yes

BUILDING CREDIT

	Score: 50	Score: 0
42. Do retailers provide information to credit agencies?	Yes	N/A
43. Do utility companies provide information to credit agencies?	Yes	N/A
44. Is discrimination based on gender prohibited in access to credit?	No	No
45. Is discrimination based on marital status prohibited in access to credit?	No	No

PROTECTING WOMEN FROM VIOLENCE

	Score: 20	Score: 0
46. Is there legislation specifically addressing domestic violence? If not, are there aggravated penalties for crimes committed against a spouse or family member?	No	No
47. Is there legislation on sexual harassment in employment?	Yes	No
48. Is there legislation on sexual harassment in education?	No	No
49. Are there criminal penalties for sexual harassment in employment?	No	No
50. Are there civil remedies for sexual harassment in employment?	No	No

Note: See the data notes for more details on the scoring of each indicator.

	LIBYA	LITHUANIA
REGION	Middle East & North Africa	Europe & Central Asia
INCOME GROUP	Upper middle income	High income
FEMALE POPULATION	3,134,355	1,550,375
FEMALE LABOR FORCE (% OF TOTAL LABOR FORCE)	25%	51%

ACCESSING INSTITUTIONS

	Score: 91	Score: 100
1. Are wives required to obey their husbands?	No	No
Can a woman legally do the following in the same way as a man:		
2. Apply for a passport?	Yes	Yes
3. Apply for a national ID card?	Yes	Yes
4. Travel outside the country?	Yes	Yes
5. Travel outside her home?	Yes	Yes
6. Get a job?	Yes	Yes
7. Sign a contract?	Yes	Yes
8. Register a business?	Yes	Yes
9. Open a bank account?	Yes	Yes
10. Choose where to live?	Yes	Yes
11. Be "head of household"?	No	N/A

USING PROPERTY

	Score: 40	Score: 100
12. Who legally administers marital property?	Original owner	Both must agree
13. Does the law provide for valuation of nonmonetary contributions?	No	Yes
14. Do men and women have equal ownership rights to immovable property?	Yes	Yes
15. Do sons and daughters have equal inheritance rights?	No	Yes
16. Do female and male surviving spouses have equal inheritance rights?	No	Yes

GETTING A JOB

	Score: 64	Score: 100
17. Is there paid leave available to women of at least 14 weeks?	Yes	Yes
18. Do women receive at least 2/3 of their wages for the first 14 weeks or the duration of the leave if it is shorter?	Yes	Yes
19. What is the percentage of maternity leave benefits paid by the government?	0%	100%
20. What is the difference between leave reserved for women and men relative to leave reserved for women, as a function of who pays?	0	1
21. Is there paid parental leave?	No	Yes
22. Does the law mandate equal remuneration for work of equal value?	Yes	Yes
23. Does the law mandate nondiscrimination based on gender in employment?	Yes	Yes
24. Is dismissal of pregnant workers prohibited?	Yes	Yes
25. Can parents work flexibly?	No	Yes
26. Can women work the same night hours as men?	Yes	Yes
27. Can women work in jobs deemed hazardous, arduous or morally inappropriate in the same way as men?	Yes	Yes
28. Are women able to work in the same industries as men?	Yes	Yes
29. Are women able to perform the same tasks at work as men?	Yes	Yes
30. Are the ages at which men and women can retire with full pension benefits equal?	No	Yes
31. Are the ages at which men and women can retire with partial pension benefits equal?	N/A	Yes
32. Are the mandatory retirement ages for men and women equal?	No	N/A

PROVIDING INCENTIVES TO WORK

	Score: 40	Score: 80
33. Are mothers guaranteed an equivalent position after maternity leave?	No	Yes
34. Does the government support or provide childcare services?	Yes	Yes
35. Are payments for childcare tax deductible?	No	No
36. Is primary education free and compulsory?	Yes	Yes
37. Are there tax deductions or credits specific to men?	Yes	No

GOING TO COURT

	Score: 25	Score: 100
38. Does a woman's testimony carry the same evidentiary weight in court as a man's?	No	Yes
39. Does the law establish an anti-discrimination commission?	No	Yes
40. Does the law mandate legal aid in civil/family matters?	No	Yes
41. Is there a small claims court/fast-track procedure?	Yes	Yes

BUILDING CREDIT

	Score: 0	Score: 75
42. Do retailers provide information to credit agencies?	N/A	Yes
43. Do utility companies provide information to credit agencies?	N/A	Yes
44. Is discrimination based on gender prohibited in access to credit?	No	Yes
45. Is discrimination based on marital status prohibited in access to credit?	No	No

PROTECTING WOMEN FROM VIOLENCE

	Score: 10	Score: 100
46. Is there legislation specifically addressing domestic violence? If not, are there aggravated penalties for crimes committed against a spouse or family member?	No, but aggravated penalties exist	Yes
47. Is there legislation on sexual harassment in employment?	No	Yes
48. Is there legislation on sexual harassment in education?	No	Yes
49. Are there criminal penalties for sexual harassment in employment?	No	Yes
50. Are there civil remedies for sexual harassment in employment?	No	Yes

Note: See the data notes for more details on the scoring of each indicator.

	LUXEMBOURG	MACEDONIA, FYR
REGION	High income: OECD	Europe & Central Asia
INCOME GROUP	High income	Upper middle income
FEMALE POPULATION	290,127	1,045,328
FEMALE LABOR FORCE (% OF TOTAL LABOR FORCE)	45%	39%

ACCESSING INSTITUTIONS

	Score: 100	Score: 100
1. Are wives required to obey their husbands?	No	No
Can a woman legally do the following in the same way as a man:		
2. Apply for a passport?	Yes	Yes
3. Apply for a national ID card?	Yes	Yes
4. Travel outside the country?	Yes	Yes
5. Travel outside her home?	Yes	Yes
6. Get a job?	Yes	Yes
7. Sign a contract?	Yes	Yes
8. Register a business?	Yes	Yes
9. Open a bank account?	Yes	Yes
10. Choose where to live?	Yes	Yes
11. Be "head of household"?	N/A	N/A

USING PROPERTY

	Score: 100	Score: 100
12. Who legally administers marital property?	Both must agree	Both must agree
13. Does the law provide for valuation of nonmonetary contributions?	Yes	Yes
14. Do men and women have equal ownership rights to immovable property?	Yes	Yes
15. Do sons and daughters have equal inheritance rights?	Yes	Yes
16. Do female and male surviving spouses have equal inheritance rights?	Yes	Yes

GETTING A JOB

	Score: 93	Score: 72
17. Is there paid leave available to women of at least 14 weeks?	Yes	Yes
18. Do women receive at least 2/3 of their wages for the first 14 weeks or the duration of the leave if it is shorter?	Yes	Yes
19. What is the percentage of maternity leave benefits paid by the government?	100%	100%
20. What is the difference between leave reserved for women and men relative to leave reserved for women, as a function of who pays?	1	1
21. Is there paid parental leave?	Yes	No
22. Does the law mandate equal remuneration for work of equal value?	Yes	No
23. Does the law mandate nondiscrimination based on gender in employment?	Yes	Yes
24. Is dismissal of pregnant workers prohibited?	Yes	Yes
25. Can parents work flexibly?	No	No
26. Can women work the same night hours as men?	Yes	Yes
27. Can women work in jobs deemed hazardous, arduous or morally inappropriate in the same way as men?	Yes	Yes
28. Are women able to work in the same industries as men?	Yes	No
29. Are women able to perform the same tasks at work as men?	Yes	Yes
30. Are the ages at which men and women can retire with full pension benefits equal?	Yes	No
31. Are the ages at which men and women can retire with partial pension benefits equal?	N/A	N/A
32. Are the mandatory retirement ages for men and women equal?	Yes	Yes

PROVIDING INCENTIVES TO WORK

	Score: 100	Score: 80
33. Are mothers guaranteed an equivalent position after maternity leave?	Yes	Yes
34. Does the government support or provide childcare services?	Yes	Yes
35. Are payments for childcare tax deductible?	Yes	No
36. Is primary education free and compulsory?	Yes	Yes
37. Are there tax deductions or credits specific to men?	No	No

GOING TO COURT

	Score: 75	Score: 100
38. Does a woman's testimony carry the same evidentiary weight in court as a man's?	Yes	Yes
39. Does the law establish an anti-discrimination commission?	No	Yes
40. Does the law mandate legal aid in civil/family matters?	Yes	Yes
41. Is there a small claims court/fast-track procedure?	Yes	Yes

BUILDING CREDIT

	Score: 25	Score: 100
42. Do retailers provide information to credit agencies?	N/A	Yes
43. Do utility companies provide information to credit agencies?	N/A	Yes
44. Is discrimination based on gender prohibited in access to credit?	Yes	Yes
45. Is discrimination based on marital status prohibited in access to credit?	No	Yes

PROTECTING WOMEN FROM VIOLENCE

	Score: 60	Score: 80
46. Is there legislation specifically addressing domestic violence? If not, are there aggravated penalties for crimes committed against a spouse or family member?	Yes	Yes
47. Is there legislation on sexual harassment in employment?	Yes	Yes
48. Is there legislation on sexual harassment in education?	No	Yes
49. Are there criminal penalties for sexual harassment in employment?	No	No
50. Are there civil remedies for sexual harassment in employment?	Yes	Yes

Note: See the data notes for more details on the scoring of each indicator.

	MADAGASCAR	MALAWI
REGION	Sub-Saharan Africa	Sub-Saharan Africa
INCOME GROUP	Low income	Low income
FEMALE POPULATION	12,481,298	9,056,940
FEMALE LABOR FORCE (% OF TOTAL LABOR FORCE)	49%	48%

ACCESSING INSTITUTIONS

	Score: 91	Score: 90
1. Are wives required to obey their husbands?	No	No
Can a woman legally do the following in the same way as a man:		
2. Apply for a passport?	Yes	No
3. Apply for a national ID card?	Yes	N/A
4. Travel outside the country?	Yes	Yes
5. Travel outside her home?	Yes	Yes
6. Get a job?	Yes	Yes
7. Sign a contract?	Yes	Yes
8. Register a business?	Yes	Yes
9. Open a bank account?	Yes	Yes
10. Choose where to live?	Yes	Yes
11. Be "head of household"?	No	N/A

USING PROPERTY

	Score: 100	Score: 100
12. Who legally administers marital property?	Both must agree	Original owner
13. Does the law provide for valuation of nonmonetary contributions?	Yes	Yes
14. Do men and women have equal ownership rights to immovable property?	Yes	Yes
15. Do sons and daughters have equal inheritance rights?	Yes	Yes
16. Do female and male surviving spouses have equal inheritance rights?	Yes	Yes

GETTING A JOB

	Score: 53	Score: 68
17. Is there paid leave available to women of at least 14 weeks?	Yes	No
18. Do women receive at least 2/3 of their wages for the first 14 weeks or the duration of the leave if it is shorter?	Yes	Yes
19. What is the percentage of maternity leave benefits paid by the government?	50%	0%
20. What is the difference between leave reserved for women and men relative to leave reserved for women, as a function of who pays?	0.5	0
21. Is there paid parental leave?	No	No
22. Does the law mandate equal remuneration for work of equal value?	No	Yes
23. Does the law mandate nondiscrimination based on gender in employment?	Yes	Yes
24. Is dismissal of pregnant workers prohibited?	Yes	Yes
25. Can parents work flexibly?	No	No
26. Can women work the same night hours as men?	Yes	Yes
27. Can women work in jobs deemed hazardous, arduous or morally inappropriate in the same way as men?	No	Yes
28. Are women able to work in the same industries as men?	No	Yes
29. Are women able to perform the same tasks at work as men?	No	Yes
30. Are the ages at which men and women can retire with full pension benefits equal?	Yes	Yes
31. Are the ages at which men and women can retire with partial pension benefits equal?	Yes	N/A
32. Are the mandatory retirement ages for men and women equal?	N/A	N/A

PROVIDING INCENTIVES TO WORK

	Score: 40	Score: 60
33. Are mothers guaranteed an equivalent position after maternity leave?	No	Yes
34. Does the government support or provide childcare services?	No	No
35. Are payments for childcare tax deductible?	No	No
36. Is primary education free and compulsory?	Yes	Yes
37. Are there tax deductions or credits specific to men?	No	No

GOING TO COURT

	Score: 50	Score: 100
38. Does a woman's testimony carry the same evidentiary weight in court as a man's?	Yes	Yes
39. Does the law establish an anti-discrimination commission?	Yes	Yes
40. Does the law mandate legal aid in civil/family matters?	No	Yes
41. Is there a small claims court/fast-track procedure?	No	Yes

BUILDING CREDIT

	Score: 0	Score: 25
42. Do retailers provide information to credit agencies?	No	No
43. Do utility companies provide information to credit agencies?	No	Yes
44. Is discrimination based on gender prohibited in access to credit?	No	No
45. Is discrimination based on marital status prohibited in access to credit?	No	No

PROTECTING WOMEN FROM VIOLENCE

	Score: 70	Score: 60
46. Is there legislation specifically addressing domestic violence? If not, are there aggravated penalties for crimes committed against a spouse or family member?	No, but aggravated penalties exist	Yes
47. Is there legislation on sexual harassment in employment?	Yes	Yes
48. Is there legislation on sexual harassment in education?	No	No
49. Are there criminal penalties for sexual harassment in employment?	Yes	Yes
50. Are there civil remedies for sexual harassment in employment?	Yes	No

Note: See the data notes for more details on the scoring of each indicator.

	MALAYSIA	MALDIVES
REGION	East Asia & Pacific	South Asia
INCOME GROUP	Upper middle income	Upper middle income
FEMALE POPULATION	14,679,700	208,132
FEMALE LABOR FORCE (% OF TOTAL LABOR FORCE)	38%	27%

ACCESSING INSTITUTIONS

	Score: 73	Score: 100
1. Are wives required to obey their husbands?	Yes	No
Can a woman legally do the following in the same way as a man:		
2. Apply for a passport?	Yes	Yes
3. Apply for a national ID card?	Yes	Yes
4. Travel outside the country?	Yes	Yes
5. Travel outside her home?	No	Yes
6. Get a job?	Yes	Yes
7. Sign a contract?	Yes	Yes
8. Register a business?	Yes	Yes
9. Open a bank account?	Yes	Yes
10. Choose where to live?	No	Yes
11. Be "head of household"?	N/A	N/A

USING PROPERTY

	Score: 60	Score: 40
12. Who legally administers marital property?	Original owner	Original owner
13. Does the law provide for valuation of nonmonetary contributions?	Yes	No
14. Do men and women have equal ownership rights to immovable property?	Yes	Yes
15. Do sons and daughters have equal inheritance rights?	No	No
16. Do female and male surviving spouses have equal inheritance rights?	No	No

GETTING A JOB

	Score: 37	Score: 62
17. Is there paid leave available to women of at least 14 weeks?	No	No
18. Do women receive at least 2/3 of their wages for the first 14 weeks or the duration of the leave if it is shorter?	Yes	Yes
19. What is the percentage of maternity leave benefits paid by the government?	0%	0%
20. What is the difference between leave reserved for women and men relative to leave reserved for women, as a function of who pays?	0	0.05
21. Is there paid parental leave?	No	No
22. Does the law mandate equal remuneration for work of equal value?	No	No
23. Does the law mandate nondiscrimination based on gender in employment?	No	Yes
24. Is dismissal of pregnant workers prohibited?	No	Yes
25. Can parents work flexibly?	No	No
26. Can women work the same night hours as men?	Yes	Yes
27. Can women work in jobs deemed hazardous, arduous or morally inappropriate in the same way as men?	Yes	Yes
28. Are women able to work in the same industries as men?	No	Yes
29. Are women able to perform the same tasks at work as men?	No	Yes
30. Are the ages at which men and women can retire with full pension benefits equal?	Yes	Yes
31. Are the ages at which men and women can retire with partial pension benefits equal?	Yes	N/A
32. Are the mandatory retirement ages for men and women equal?	N/A	N/A

PROVIDING INCENTIVES TO WORK

	Score: 60	Score: 60
33. Are mothers guaranteed an equivalent position after maternity leave?	No	Yes
34. Does the government support or provide childcare services?	Yes	No
35. Are payments for childcare tax deductible?	Yes	No
36. Is primary education free and compulsory?	Yes	Yes
37. Are there tax deductions or credits specific to men?	Yes	No

GOING TO COURT

	Score: 75	Score: 75
38. Does a woman's testimony carry the same evidentiary weight in court as a man's?	Yes	Yes
39. Does the law establish an anti-discrimination commission?	No	Yes
40. Does the law mandate legal aid in civil/family matters?	Yes	No
41. Is there a small claims court/fast-track procedure?	Yes	Yes

BUILDING CREDIT

	Score: 50	Score: 50
42. Do retailers provide information to credit agencies?	Yes	No
43. Do utility companies provide information to credit agencies?	Yes	No
44. Is discrimination based on gender prohibited in access to credit?	No	Yes
45. Is discrimination based on marital status prohibited in access to credit?	No	Yes

PROTECTING WOMEN FROM VIOLENCE

	Score: 60	Score: 80
46. Is there legislation specifically addressing domestic violence? If not, are there aggravated penalties for crimes committed against a spouse or family member?	Yes	Yes
47. Is there legislation on sexual harassment in employment?	Yes	Yes
48. Is there legislation on sexual harassment in education?	No	Yes
49. Are there criminal penalties for sexual harassment in employment?	No	No
50. Are there civil remedies for sexual harassment in employment?	Yes	Yes

Note: See the data notes for more details on the scoring of each indicator.

	MALI	MALTA
REGION	Sub-Saharan Africa	Middle East & North Africa
INCOME GROUP	Low income	High income
FEMALE POPULATION	8,907,055	219,260
FEMALE LABOR FORCE (% OF TOTAL LABOR FORCE)	43%	39%

ACCESSING INSTITUTIONS

	Score: 64	Score: 100
1. Are wives required to obey their husbands?	Yes	No
Can a woman legally do the following in the same way as a man:		
2. Apply for a passport?	No	Yes
3. Apply for a national ID card?	Yes	Yes
4. Travel outside the country?	Yes	Yes
5. Travel outside her home?	Yes	Yes
6. Get a job?	Yes	Yes
7. Sign a contract?	Yes	Yes
8. Register a business?	Yes	Yes
9. Open a bank account?	Yes	Yes
10. Choose where to live?	No	Yes
11. Be "head of household"?	No	Yes

USING PROPERTY

	Score: 80	Score: 100
12. Who legally administers marital property?	Original owner	Both must agree
13. Does the law provide for valuation of nonmonetary contributions?	No	Yes
14. Do men and women have equal ownership rights to immovable property?	Yes	Yes
15. Do sons and daughters have equal inheritance rights?	Yes	Yes
16. Do female and male surviving spouses have equal inheritance rights?	Yes	Yes

GETTING A JOB

	Score: 47	Score: 72
17. Is there paid leave available to women of at least 14 weeks?	Yes	Yes
18. Do women receive at least 2/3 of their wages for the first 14 weeks or the duration of the leave if it is shorter?	Yes	Yes
19. What is the percentage of maternity leave benefits paid by the government?	100%	22%
20. What is the difference between leave reserved for women and men relative to leave reserved for women, as a function of who pays?	1	0.23
21. Is there paid parental leave?	No	No
22. Does the law mandate equal remuneration for work of equal value?	No	Yes
23. Does the law mandate nondiscrimination based on gender in employment?	No	Yes
24. Is dismissal of pregnant workers prohibited?	No	Yes
25. Can parents work flexibly?	No	No
26. Can women work the same night hours as men?	Yes	Yes
27. Can women work in jobs deemed hazardous, arduous or morally inappropriate in the same way as men?	No	Yes
28. Are women able to work in the same industries as men?	No	Yes
29. Are women able to perform the same tasks at work as men?	No	No
30. Are the ages at which men and women can retire with full pension benefits equal?	Yes	Yes
31. Are the ages at which men and women can retire with partial pension benefits equal?	Yes	Yes
32. Are the mandatory retirement ages for men and women equal?	N/A	Yes

PROVIDING INCENTIVES TO WORK

	Score: 80	Score: 100
33. Are mothers guaranteed an equivalent position after maternity leave?	Yes	Yes
34. Does the government support or provide childcare services?	Yes	Yes
35. Are payments for childcare tax deductible?	No	Yes
36. Is primary education free and compulsory?	Yes	Yes
37. Are there tax deductions or credits specific to men?	No	No

GOING TO COURT

	Score: 50	Score: 100
38. Does a woman's testimony carry the same evidentiary weight in court as a man's?	Yes	Yes
39. Does the law establish an anti-discrimination commission?	No	Yes
40. Does the law mandate legal aid in civil/family matters?	Yes	Yes
41. Is there a small claims court/fast-track procedure?	No	Yes

BUILDING CREDIT

	Score: 0	Score: 25
42. Do retailers provide information to credit agencies?	N/A	No
43. Do utility companies provide information to credit agencies?	N/A	No
44. Is discrimination based on gender prohibited in access to credit?	No	Yes
45. Is discrimination based on marital status prohibited in access to credit?	No	No

PROTECTING WOMEN FROM VIOLENCE

	Score: 0	Score: 100
46. Is there legislation specifically addressing domestic violence? If not, are there aggravated penalties for crimes committed against a spouse or family member?	No	Yes
47. Is there legislation on sexual harassment in employment?	No	Yes
48. Is there legislation on sexual harassment in education?	No	Yes
49. Are there criminal penalties for sexual harassment in employment?	No	Yes
50. Are there civil remedies for sexual harassment in employment?	No	Yes

Note: See the data notes for more details on the scoring of each indicator.

	MARSHALL ISLANDS	MAURITANIA
REGION	East Asia & Pacific	Sub-Saharan Africa
INCOME GROUP	Upper middle income	Lower middle income
FEMALE POPULATION	..	2,136,387
FEMALE LABOR FORCE (% OF TOTAL LABOR FORCE)	..	31%

ACCESSING INSTITUTIONS

	Score: 100	Score: 73
1. Are wives required to obey their husbands?	No	Yes
Can a woman legally do the following in the same way as a man:		
2. Apply for a passport?	Yes	Yes
3. Apply for a national ID card?	Yes	Yes
4. Travel outside the country?	Yes	Yes
5. Travel outside her home?	Yes	Yes
6. Get a job?	Yes	No
7. Sign a contract?	Yes	Yes
8. Register a business?	Yes	Yes
9. Open a bank account?	Yes	Yes
10. Choose where to live?	Yes	Yes
11. Be *head of household*?	N/A	No

USING PROPERTY

	Score: 50	Score: 20
12. Who legally administers marital property?	Other	Other
13. Does the law provide for valuation of nonmonetary contributions?	No	No
14. Do men and women have equal ownership rights to immovable property?	..	No
15. Do sons and daughters have equal inheritance rights?	..	No
16. Do female and male surviving spouses have equal inheritance rights?	..	No

GETTING A JOB

	Score: 46	Score: 57
17. Is there paid leave available to women of at least 14 weeks?	No	Yes
18. Do women receive at least 2/3 of their wages for the first 14 weeks or the duration of the leave if it is shorter?	No	Yes
19. What is the percentage of maternity leave benefits paid by the government?	N/A	100%
20. What is the difference between leave reserved for women and men relative to leave reserved for women, as a function of who pays?	N/A	1
21. Is there paid parental leave?	No	No
22. Does the law mandate equal remuneration for work of equal value?	No	No
23. Does the law mandate nondiscrimination based on gender in employment?	No	Yes
24. Is dismissal of pregnant workers prohibited?	No	No
25. Can parents work flexibly?	No	No
26. Can women work the same night hours as men?	Yes	Yes
27. Can women work in jobs deemed hazardous, arduous or morally inappropriate in the same way as men?	Yes	No
28. Are women able to work in the same industries as men?	Yes	No
29. Are women able to perform the same tasks at work as men?	Yes	Yes
30. Are the ages at which men and women can retire with full pension benefits equal?	Yes	Yes
31. Are the ages at which men and women can retire with partial pension benefits equal?	Yes	N/A
32. Are the mandatory retirement ages for men and women equal?	N/A	N/A

PROVIDING INCENTIVES TO WORK

	Score: 40	Score: 60
33. Are mothers guaranteed an equivalent position after maternity leave?	No	Yes
34. Does the government support or provide childcare services?	No	No
35. Are payments for childcare tax deductible?	No	No
36. Is primary education free and compulsory?	Yes	Yes
37. Are there tax deductions or credits specific to men?	No	No

GOING TO COURT

	Score: 100	Score: 25
38. Does a woman's testimony carry the same evidentiary weight in court as a man's?	Yes	No
39. Does the law establish an anti-discrimination commission?	Yes	No
40. Does the law mandate legal aid in civil/family matters?	Yes	Yes
41. Is there a small claims court/fast-track procedure?	Yes	No

BUILDING CREDIT

	Score: 0	Score: 0
42. Do retailers provide information to credit agencies?	N/A	No
43. Do utility companies provide information to credit agencies?	N/A	No
44. Is discrimination based on gender prohibited in access to credit?	No	No
45. Is discrimination based on marital status prohibited in access to credit?	No	No

PROTECTING WOMEN FROM VIOLENCE

	Score: 20	Score: 0
46. Is there legislation specifically addressing domestic violence? If not, are there aggravated penalties for crimes committed against a spouse or family member?	Yes	No
47. Is there legislation on sexual harassment in employment?	No	No
48. Is there legislation on sexual harassment in education?	No	No
49. Are there criminal penalties for sexual harassment in employment?	No	No
50. Are there civil remedies for sexual harassment in employment?	No	No

Note: See the data notes for more details on the scoring of each indicator.

	MAURITIUS	MEXICO
REGION	Sub-Saharan Africa	Latin America & Caribbean
INCOME GROUP	Upper middle income	Upper middle income
FEMALE POPULATION	639,906	64,096,833
FEMALE LABOR FORCE (% OF TOTAL LABOR FORCE)	39%	36%

ACCESSING INSTITUTIONS

	Score: 91	Score: 100
1. Are wives required to obey their husbands?	No	No
Can a woman legally do the following in the same way as a man:		
2. Apply for a passport?	Yes	Yes
3. Apply for a national ID card?	No	N/A
4. Travel outside the country?	Yes	Yes
5. Travel outside her home?	Yes	Yes
6. Get a job?	Yes	Yes
7. Sign a contract?	Yes	Yes
8. Register a business?	Yes	Yes
9. Open a bank account?	Yes	Yes
10. Choose where to live?	Yes	Yes
11. Be "head of household"?	N/A	N/A

USING PROPERTY

	Score: 100	Score: 100
12. Who legally administers marital property?	Both must agree	Other
13. Does the law provide for valuation of nonmonetary contributions?	Yes	Yes
14. Do men and women have equal ownership rights to immovable property?	Yes	Yes
15. Do sons and daughters have equal inheritance rights?	Yes	Yes
16. Do female and male surviving spouses have equal inheritance rights?	Yes	Yes

GETTING A JOB

	Score: 75	Score: 78
17. Is there paid leave available to women of at least 14 weeks?	Yes	No
18. Do women receive at least 2/3 of their wages for the first 14 weeks or the duration of the leave if it is shorter?	Yes	Yes
19. What is the percentage of maternity leave benefits paid by the government?	0%	100%
20. What is the difference between leave reserved for women and men relative to leave reserved for women, as a function of who pays?	0.05	1
21. Is there paid parental leave?	No	No
22. Does the law mandate equal remuneration for work of equal value?	Yes	No
23. Does the law mandate nondiscrimination based on gender in employment?	Yes	Yes
24. Is dismissal of pregnant workers prohibited?	Yes	Yes
25. Can parents work flexibly?	No	No
26. Can women work the same night hours as men?	Yes	Yes
27. Can women work in jobs deemed hazardous, arduous or morally inappropriate in the same way as men?	Yes	Yes
28. Are women able to work in the same industries as men?	Yes	Yes
29. Are women able to perform the same tasks at work as men?	Yes	Yes
30. Are the ages at which men and women can retire with full pension benefits equal?	Yes	Yes
31. Are the ages at which men and women can retire with partial pension benefits equal?	Yes	N/A
32. Are the mandatory retirement ages for men and women equal?	Yes	N/A

PROVIDING INCENTIVES TO WORK

	Score: 40	Score: 100
33. Are mothers guaranteed an equivalent position after maternity leave?	No	Yes
34. Does the government support or provide childcare services?	No	Yes
35. Are payments for childcare tax deductible?	Yes	Yes
36. Is primary education free and compulsory?	No	Yes
37. Are there tax deductions or credits specific to men?	No	No

GOING TO COURT

	Score: 100	Score: 100
38. Does a woman's testimony carry the same evidentiary weight in court as a man's?	Yes	Yes
39. Does the law establish an anti-discrimination commission?	Yes	Yes
40. Does the law mandate legal aid in civil/family matters?	Yes	Yes
41. Is there a small claims court/fast-track procedure?	Yes	Yes

BUILDING CREDIT

	Score: 100	Score: 100
42. Do retailers provide information to credit agencies?	Yes	Yes
43. Do utility companies provide information to credit agencies?	Yes	Yes
44. Is discrimination based on gender prohibited in access to credit?	Yes	Yes
45. Is discrimination based on marital status prohibited in access to credit?	Yes	Yes

PROTECTING WOMEN FROM VIOLENCE

	Score: 100	Score: 80
46. Is there legislation specifically addressing domestic violence? If not, are there aggravated penalties for crimes committed against a spouse or family member?	Yes	Yes
47. Is there legislation on sexual harassment in employment?	Yes	Yes
48. Is there legislation on sexual harassment in education?	Yes	Yes
49. Are there criminal penalties for sexual harassment in employment?	Yes	Yes
50. Are there civil remedies for sexual harassment in employment?	Yes	No

Note: See the data notes for more details on the scoring of each indicator.

	MICRONESIA, FED. STS.	MOLDOVA
REGION	East Asia & Pacific	Europe & Central Asia
INCOME GROUP	Lower middle income	Lower middle income
FEMALE POPULATION	51,157	1,845,430
FEMALE LABOR FORCE (% OF TOTAL LABOR FORCE)	..	49%

ACCESSING INSTITUTIONS

	Score: 100	Score: 100
1. Are wives required to obey their husbands?	No	No
Can a woman legally do the following in the same way as a man:		
2. Apply for a passport?	Yes	Yes
3. Apply for a national ID card?	N/A	Yes
4. Travel outside the country?	Yes	Yes
5. Travel outside her home?	Yes	Yes
6. Get a job?	Yes	Yes
7. Sign a contract?	Yes	Yes
8. Register a business?	Yes	Yes
9. Open a bank account?	Yes	Yes
10. Choose where to live?	Yes	Yes
11. Be "head of household"?	N/A	N/A

USING PROPERTY

	Score: 75	Score: 100
12. Who legally administers marital property?	Other	Both must agree
13. Does the law provide for valuation of nonmonetary contributions?	No	Yes
14. Do men and women have equal ownership rights to immovable property?	..	Yes
15. Do sons and daughters have equal inheritance rights?	Yes	Yes
16. Do female and male surviving spouses have equal inheritance rights?	Yes	Yes

GETTING A JOB

	Score: 46	Score: 71
17. Is there paid leave available to women of at least 14 weeks?	No	Yes
18. Do women receive at least 2/3 of their wages for the first 14 weeks or the duration of the leave if it is shorter?	No	Yes
19. What is the percentage of maternity leave benefits paid by the government?	N/A	100%
20. What is the difference between leave reserved for women and men relative to leave reserved for women, as a function of who pays?	N/A	1
21. Is there paid parental leave?	No	Yes
22. Does the law mandate equal remuneration for work of equal value?	No	No
23. Does the law mandate nondiscrimination based on gender in employment?	No	Yes
24. Is dismissal of pregnant workers prohibited?	No	Yes
25. Can parents work flexibly?	No	Yes
26. Can women work the same night hours as men?	Yes	Yes
27. Can women work in jobs deemed hazardous, arduous or morally inappropriate in the same way as men?	Yes	No
28. Are women able to work in the same industries as men?	Yes	No
29. Are women able to perform the same tasks at work as men?	Yes	No
30. Are the ages at which men and women can retire with full pension benefits equal?	Yes	Yes
31. Are the ages at which men and women can retire with partial pension benefits equal?	Yes	N/A
32. Are the mandatory retirement ages for men and women equal?	N/A	N/A

PROVIDING INCENTIVES TO WORK

	Score: 40	Score: 80
33. Are mothers guaranteed an equivalent position after maternity leave?	No	Yes
34. Does the government support or provide childcare services?	No	Yes
35. Are payments for childcare tax deductible?	No	No
36. Is primary education free and compulsory?	Yes	Yes
37. Are there tax deductions or credits specific to men?	No	No

GOING TO COURT

	Score: 25	Score: 75
38. Does a woman's testimony carry the same evidentiary weight in court as a man's?	Yes	Yes
39. Does the law establish an anti-discrimination commission?	No	Yes
40. Does the law mandate legal aid in civil/family matters?	No	Yes
41. Is there a small claims court/fast-track procedure?	No	No

BUILDING CREDIT

	Score: 0	Score: 25
42. Do retailers provide information to credit agencies?	N/A	No
43. Do utility companies provide information to credit agencies?	N/A	No
44. Is discrimination based on gender prohibited in access to credit?	No	Yes
45. Is discrimination based on marital status prohibited in access to credit?	No	No

PROTECTING WOMEN FROM VIOLENCE

	Score: 0	Score: 40
46. Is there legislation specifically addressing domestic violence? If not, are there aggravated penalties for crimes committed against a spouse or family member?	No	Yes
47. Is there legislation on sexual harassment in employment?	No	Yes
48. Is there legislation on sexual harassment in education?	No	No
49. Are there criminal penalties for sexual harassment in employment?	No	No
50. Are there civil remedies for sexual harassment in employment?	No	No

Note: See the data notes for more details on the scoring of each indicator.

	MONGOLIA	MONTENEGRO
REGION	East Asia & Pacific	Europe & Central Asia
INCOME GROUP	Lower middle income	Upper middle income
FEMALE POPULATION	1,529,574	314,988
FEMALE LABOR FORCE (% OF TOTAL LABOR FORCE)	45%	45%

ACCESSING INSTITUTIONS

	Score: 100	Score: 100
1. Are wives required to obey their husbands?	No	No
Can a woman legally do the following in the same way as a man:		
2. Apply for a passport?	Yes	Yes
3. Apply for a national ID card?	Yes	Yes
4. Travel outside the country?	Yes	Yes
5. Travel outside her home?	Yes	Yes
6. Get a job?	Yes	Yes
7. Sign a contract?	Yes	Yes
8. Register a business?	Yes	Yes
9. Open a bank account?	Yes	Yes
10. Choose where to live?	Yes	Yes
11. Be "head of household"?	N/A	N/A

USING PROPERTY

	Score: 100	Score: 100
12. Who legally administers marital property?	Other	Both must agree
13. Does the law provide for valuation of nonmonetary contributions?	Yes	Yes
14. Do men and women have equal ownership rights to immovable property?	Yes	Yes
15. Do sons and daughters have equal inheritance rights?	Yes	Yes
16. Do female and male surviving spouses have equal inheritance rights?	Yes	Yes

GETTING A JOB

	Score: 73	Score: 73
17. Is there paid leave available to women of at least 14 weeks?	Yes	Yes
18. Do women receive at least 2/3 of their wages for the first 14 weeks or the duration of the leave if it is shorter?	Yes	Yes
19. What is the percentage of maternity leave benefits paid by the government?	100%	100%
20. What is the difference between leave reserved for women and men relative to leave reserved for women, as a function of who pays?	1	1
21. Is there paid parental leave?	No	Yes
22. Does the law mandate equal remuneration for work of equal value?	No	Yes
23. Does the law mandate nondiscrimination based on gender in employment?	Yes	Yes
24. Is dismissal of pregnant workers prohibited?	Yes	Yes
25. Can parents work flexibly?	No	Yes
26. Can women work the same night hours as men?	Yes	No
27. Can women work in jobs deemed hazardous, arduous or morally inappropriate in the same way as men?	Yes	No
28. Are women able to work in the same industries as men?	Yes	No
29. Are women able to perform the same tasks at work as men?	No	No
30. Are the ages at which men and women can retire with full pension benefits equal?	Yes	Yes
31. Are the ages at which men and women can retire with partial pension benefits equal?	N/A	N/A
32. Are the mandatory retirement ages for men and women equal?	Yes	Yes

PROVIDING INCENTIVES TO WORK

	Score: 80	Score: 80
33. Are mothers guaranteed an equivalent position after maternity leave?	Yes	Yes
34. Does the government support or provide childcare services?	Yes	Yes
35. Are payments for childcare tax deductible?	No	No
36. Is primary education free and compulsory?	Yes	Yes
37. Are there tax deductions or credits specific to men?	No	No

GOING TO COURT

	Score: 50	Score: 100
38. Does a woman's testimony carry the same evidentiary weight in court as a man's?	Yes	Yes
39. Does the law establish an anti-discrimination commission?	Yes	Yes
40. Does the law mandate legal aid in civil/family matters?	No	Yes
41. Is there a small claims court/fast-track procedure?	No	Yes

BUILDING CREDIT

	Score: 75	Score: 0
42. Do retailers provide information to credit agencies?	No	No
43. Do utility companies provide information to credit agencies?	Yes	No
44. Is discrimination based on gender prohibited in access to credit?	Yes	No
45. Is discrimination based on marital status prohibited in access to credit?	Yes	No

PROTECTING WOMEN FROM VIOLENCE

	Score: 60	Score: 60
46. Is there legislation specifically addressing domestic violence? If not, are there aggravated penalties for crimes committed against a spouse or family member?	Yes	Yes
47. Is there legislation on sexual harassment in employment?	Yes	Yes
48. Is there legislation on sexual harassment in education?	No	No
49. Are there criminal penalties for sexual harassment in employment?	No	No
50. Are there civil remedies for sexual harassment in employment?	Yes	Yes

Note: See the data notes for more details on the scoring of each indicator.

	MOROCCO	MOZAMBIQUE
REGION	Middle East & North Africa	Sub-Saharan Africa
INCOME GROUP	Lower middle income	Low income
FEMALE POPULATION	17,828,919	14,733,138
FEMALE LABOR FORCE (% OF TOTAL LABOR FORCE)	26%	55%

ACCESSING INSTITUTIONS
	Score: 91	Score: 100
1. Are wives required to obey their husbands?	No	No
Can a woman legally do the following in the same way as a man:		
2. Apply for a passport?	Yes	Yes
3. Apply for a national ID card?	Yes	Yes
4. Travel outside the country?	Yes	Yes
5. Travel outside her home?	Yes	Yes
6. Get a job?	Yes	Yes
7. Sign a contract?	Yes	Yes
8. Register a business?	Yes	Yes
9. Open a bank account?	Yes	Yes
10. Choose where to live?	Yes	Yes
11. Be "head of household"?	No	N/A

USING PROPERTY
	Score: 40	Score: 100
12. Who legally administers marital property?	Original owner	Both must agree
13. Does the law provide for valuation of nonmonetary contributions?	No	Yes
14. Do men and women have equal ownership rights to immovable property?	Yes	Yes
15. Do sons and daughters have equal inheritance rights?	No	Yes
16. Do female and male surviving spouses have equal inheritance rights?	No	Yes

GETTING A JOB
	Score: 67	Score: 62
17. Is there paid leave available to women of at least 14 weeks?	Yes	No
18. Do women receive at least 2/3 of their wages for the first 14 weeks or the duration of the leave if it is shorter?	Yes	Yes
19. What is the percentage of maternity leave benefits paid by the government?	100%	100%
20. What is the difference between leave reserved for women and men relative to leave reserved for women, as a function of who pays?	1	1
21. Is there paid parental leave?	No	No
22. Does the law mandate equal remuneration for work of equal value?	Yes	No
23. Does the law mandate nondiscrimination based on gender in employment?	Yes	Yes
24. Is dismissal of pregnant workers prohibited?	Yes	Yes
25. Can parents work flexibly?	No	No
26. Can women work the same night hours as men?	Yes	Yes
27. Can women work in jobs deemed hazardous, arduous or morally inappropriate in the same way as men?	No	No
28. Are women able to work in the same industries as men?	No	Yes
29. Are women able to perform the same tasks at work as men?	No	Yes
30. Are the ages at which men and women can retire with full pension benefits equal?	Yes	No
31. Are the ages at which men and women can retire with partial pension benefits equal?	N/A	N/A
32. Are the mandatory retirement ages for men and women equal?	Yes	No

PROVIDING INCENTIVES TO WORK
	Score: 60	Score: 60
33. Are mothers guaranteed an equivalent position after maternity leave?	Yes	No
34. Does the government support or provide childcare services?	Yes	Yes
35. Are payments for childcare tax deductible?	No	No
36. Is primary education free and compulsory?	Yes	Yes
37. Are there tax deductions or credits specific to men?	Yes	No

GOING TO COURT
	Score: 75	Score: 100
38. Does a woman's testimony carry the same evidentiary weight in court as a man's?	Yes	Yes
39. Does the law establish an anti-discrimination commission?	No	Yes
40. Does the law mandate legal aid in civil/family matters?	Yes	Yes
41. Is there a small claims court/fast-track procedure?	Yes	Yes

BUILDING CREDIT
	Score: 50	Score: 0
42. Do retailers provide information to credit agencies?	No	No
43. Do utility companies provide information to credit agencies?	No	No
44. Is discrimination based on gender prohibited in access to credit?	Yes	No
45. Is discrimination based on marital status prohibited in access to credit?	Yes	No

PROTECTING WOMEN FROM VIOLENCE
	Score: 70	Score: 100
46. Is there legislation specifically addressing domestic violence? If not, are there aggravated penalties for crimes committed against a spouse or family member?	No, but aggravated penalties exist	Yes
47. Is there legislation on sexual harassment in employment?	Yes	Yes
48. Is there legislation on sexual harassment in education?	No	Yes
49. Are there criminal penalties for sexual harassment in employment?	Yes	Yes
50. Are there civil remedies for sexual harassment in employment?	Yes	Yes

Note: See the data notes for more details on the scoring of each indicator.

	MYANMAR	NAMIBIA
REGION	East Asia & Pacific	Sub-Saharan Africa
INCOME GROUP	Lower middle income	Upper middle income
FEMALE POPULATION	27,040,191	1,271,887
FEMALE LABOR FORCE (% OF TOTAL LABOR FORCE)	41%	50%

ACCESSING INSTITUTIONS

	Score: 91	Score: 91
1. Are wives required to obey their husbands?	No	No
Can a woman legally do the following in the same way as a man:		
2. Apply for a passport?	No	Yes
3. Apply for a national ID card?	Yes	No
4. Travel outside the country?	Yes	Yes
5. Travel outside her home?	Yes	Yes
6. Get a job?	Yes	Yes
7. Sign a contract?	Yes	Yes
8. Register a business?	Yes	Yes
9. Open a bank account?	Yes	Yes
10. Choose where to live?	Yes	Yes
11. Be "head of household"?	N/A	N/A

USING PROPERTY

	Score: 80	Score: 100
12. Who legally administers marital property?	Other	Both must agree
13. Does the law provide for valuation of nonmonetary contributions?	No	Yes
14. Do men and women have equal ownership rights to immovable property?	Yes	Yes
15. Do sons and daughters have equal inheritance rights?	Yes	Yes
16. Do female and male surviving spouses have equal inheritance rights?	Yes	Yes

GETTING A JOB

	Score: 54	Score: 85
17. Is there paid leave available to women of at least 14 weeks?	Yes	No
18. Do women receive at least 2/3 of their wages for the first 14 weeks or the duration of the leave if it is shorter?	Yes	Yes
19. What is the percentage of maternity leave benefits paid by the government?	100%	100%
20. What is the difference between leave reserved for women and men relative to leave reserved for women, as a function of who pays?	1	1
21. Is there paid parental leave?	No	No
22. Does the law mandate equal remuneration for work of equal value?	No	Yes
23. Does the law mandate nondiscrimination based on gender in employment?	No	Yes
24. Is dismissal of pregnant workers prohibited?	No	Yes
25. Can parents work flexibly?	No	No
26. Can women work the same night hours as men?	Yes	Yes
27. Can women work in jobs deemed hazardous, arduous or morally inappropriate in the same way as men?	Yes	Yes
28. Are women able to work in the same industries as men?	No	Yes
29. Are women able to perform the same tasks at work as men?	Yes	Yes
30. Are the ages at which men and women can retire with full pension benefits equal?	N/A	Yes
31. Are the ages at which men and women can retire with partial pension benefits equal?	N/A	N/A
32. Are the mandatory retirement ages for men and women equal?	N/A	N/A

PROVIDING INCENTIVES TO WORK

	Score: 40	Score: 60
33. Are mothers guaranteed an equivalent position after maternity leave?	No	Yes
34. Does the government support or provide childcare services?	No	No
35. Are payments for childcare tax deductible?	No	No
36. Is primary education free and compulsory?	Yes	Yes
37. Are there tax deductions or credits specific to men?	No	No

GOING TO COURT

	Score: 50	Score: 75
38. Does a woman's testimony carry the same evidentiary weight in court as a man's?	Yes	Yes
39. Does the law establish an anti-discrimination commission?	Yes	Yes
40. Does the law mandate legal aid in civil/family matters?	No	Yes
41. Is there a small claims court/fast-track procedure?	No	No

BUILDING CREDIT

	Score: 0	Score: 50
42. Do retailers provide information to credit agencies?	N/A	Yes
43. Do utility companies provide information to credit agencies?	N/A	Yes
44. Is discrimination based on gender prohibited in access to credit?	No	No
45. Is discrimination based on marital status prohibited in access to credit?	No	No

PROTECTING WOMEN FROM VIOLENCE

	Score: 0	Score: 80
46. Is there legislation specifically addressing domestic violence? If not, are there aggravated penalties for crimes committed against a spouse or family member?	No	Yes
47. Is there legislation on sexual harassment in employment?	No	Yes
48. Is there legislation on sexual harassment in education?	No	Yes
49. Are there criminal penalties for sexual harassment in employment?	No	No
50. Are there civil remedies for sexual harassment in employment?	No	Yes

Note: See the data notes for more details on the scoring of each indicator.

	NEPAL	NETHERLANDS
REGION	South Asia	High income: OECD
INCOME GROUP	Low income	High income
FEMALE POPULATION	14,936,536	8,567,739
FEMALE LABOR FORCE (% OF TOTAL LABOR FORCE)	52%	46%

ACCESSING INSTITUTIONS

	Score: 100	Score: 100
1. Are wives required to obey their husbands?	No	No
Can a woman legally do the following in the same way as a man:		
2. Apply for a passport?	Yes	Yes
3. Apply for a national ID card?	N/A	Yes
4. Travel outside the country?	Yes	Yes
5. Travel outside her home?	Yes	Yes
6. Get a job?	Yes	Yes
7. Sign a contract?	Yes	Yes
8. Register a business?	Yes	Yes
9. Open a bank account?	Yes	Yes
10. Choose where to live?	Yes	Yes
11. Be "head of household"?	Yes	N/A

USING PROPERTY

	Score: 60	Score: 100
12. Who legally administers marital property?	Original owner	Both must agree
13. Does the law provide for valuation of nonmonetary contributions?	No	Yes
14. Do men and women have equal ownership rights to immovable property?	Yes	Yes
15. Do sons and daughters have equal inheritance rights?	No	Yes
16. Do female and male surviving spouses have equal inheritance rights?	Yes	Yes

GETTING A JOB

	Score: 32	Score: 93
17. Is there paid leave available to women of at least 14 weeks?	No	Yes
18. Do women receive at least 2/3 of their wages for the first 14 weeks or the duration of the leave if it is shorter?	Yes	Yes
19. What is the percentage of maternity leave benefits paid by the government?	0%	100%
20. What is the difference between leave reserved for women and men relative to leave reserved for women, as a function of who pays?	0	1
21. Is there paid parental leave?	No	No
22. Does the law mandate equal remuneration for work of equal value?	No	Yes
23. Does the law mandate nondiscrimination based on gender in employment?	No	Yes
24. Is dismissal of pregnant workers prohibited?	No	Yes
25. Can parents work flexibly?	No	Yes
26. Can women work the same night hours as men?	No	Yes
27. Can women work in jobs deemed hazardous, arduous or morally inappropriate in the same way as men?	Yes	Yes
28. Are women able to work in the same industries as men?	Yes	Yes
29. Are women able to perform the same tasks at work as men?	No	Yes
30. Are the ages at which men and women can retire with full pension benefits equal?	N/A	Yes
31. Are the ages at which men and women can retire with partial pension benefits equal?	N/A	N/A
32. Are the mandatory retirement ages for men and women equal?	Yes	N/A

PROVIDING INCENTIVES TO WORK

	Score: 20	Score: 80
33. Are mothers guaranteed an equivalent position after maternity leave?	No	Yes
34. Does the government support or provide childcare services?	No	Yes
35. Are payments for childcare tax deductible?	No	No
36. Is primary education free and compulsory?	No	Yes
37. Are there tax deductions or credits specific to men?	No	No

GOING TO COURT

	Score: 100	Score: 100
38. Does a woman's testimony carry the same evidentiary weight in court as a man's?	Yes	Yes
39. Does the law establish an anti-discrimination commission?	Yes	Yes
40. Does the law mandate legal aid in civil/family matters?	Yes	Yes
41. Is there a small claims court/fast-track procedure?	Yes	Yes

BUILDING CREDIT

	Score: 0	Score: 75
42. Do retailers provide information to credit agencies?	N/A	Yes
43. Do utility companies provide information to credit agencies?	N/A	No
44. Is discrimination based on gender prohibited in access to credit?	No	Yes
45. Is discrimination based on marital status prohibited in access to credit?	No	Yes

PROTECTING WOMEN FROM VIOLENCE

	Score: 80	Score: 80
46. Is there legislation specifically addressing domestic violence? If not, are there aggravated penalties for crimes committed against a spouse or family member?	Yes	Yes
47. Is there legislation on sexual harassment in employment?	Yes	Yes
48. Is there legislation on sexual harassment in education?	No	Yes
49. Are there criminal penalties for sexual harassment in employment?	Yes	Yes
50. Are there civil remedies for sexual harassment in employment?	Yes	No

Note: See the data notes for more details on the scoring of each indicator.

	NEW ZEALAND	NICARAGUA
REGION	High income: OECD	Latin America & Caribbean
INCOME GROUP	High income	Lower middle income
FEMALE POPULATION	2,400,044	3,118,126
FEMALE LABOR FORCE (% OF TOTAL LABOR FORCE)	47%	39%

ACCESSING INSTITUTIONS

	Score: 100	Score: 100
1. Are wives required to obey their husbands?	No	No
Can a woman legally do the following in the same way as a man:		
2. Apply for a passport?	Yes	Yes
3. Apply for a national ID card?	N/A	Yes
4. Travel outside the country?	Yes	Yes
5. Travel outside her home?	Yes	Yes
6. Get a job?	Yes	Yes
7. Sign a contract?	Yes	Yes
8. Register a business?	Yes	Yes
9. Open a bank account?	Yes	Yes
10. Choose where to live?	Yes	Yes
11. Be "head of household"?	N/A	N/A

USING PROPERTY

	Score: 100	Score: 100
12. Who legally administers marital property?	Both must agree	Original owner
13. Does the law provide for valuation of nonmonetary contributions?	Yes	Yes
14. Do men and women have equal ownership rights to immovable property?	Yes	Yes
15. Do sons and daughters have equal inheritance rights?	Yes	Yes
16. Do female and male surviving spouses have equal inheritance rights?	Yes	Yes

GETTING A JOB

	Score: 93	Score: 65
17. Is there paid leave available to women of at least 14 weeks?	Yes	No
18. Do women receive at least 2/3 of their wages for the first 14 weeks or the duration of the leave if it is shorter?	Yes	Yes
19. What is the percentage of maternity leave benefits paid by the government?	100%	60%
20. What is the difference between leave reserved for women and men relative to leave reserved for women, as a function of who pays?	1	0.62
21. Is there paid parental leave?	Yes	No
22. Does the law mandate equal remuneration for work of equal value?	No	No
23. Does the law mandate nondiscrimination based on gender in employment?	Yes	Yes
24. Is dismissal of pregnant workers prohibited?	Yes	Yes
25. Can parents work flexibly?	Yes	No
26. Can women work the same night hours as men?	Yes	Yes
27. Can women work in jobs deemed hazardous, arduous or morally inappropriate in the same way as men?	Yes	Yes
28. Are women able to work in the same industries as men?	Yes	Yes
29. Are women able to perform the same tasks at work as men?	Yes	No
30. Are the ages at which men and women can retire with full pension benefits equal?	Yes	Yes
31. Are the ages at which men and women can retire with partial pension benefits equal?	N/A	N/A
32. Are the mandatory retirement ages for men and women equal?	N/A	N/A

PROVIDING INCENTIVES TO WORK

	Score: 100	Score: 80
33. Are mothers guaranteed an equivalent position after maternity leave?	Yes	Yes
34. Does the government support or provide childcare services?	Yes	Yes
35. Are payments for childcare tax deductible?	Yes	No
36. Is primary education free and compulsory?	Yes	Yes
37. Are there tax deductions or credits specific to men?	No	No

GOING TO COURT

	Score: 100	Score: 50
38. Does a woman's testimony carry the same evidentiary weight in court as a man's?	Yes	Yes
39. Does the law establish an anti-discrimination commission?	Yes	No
40. Does the law mandate legal aid in civil/family matters?	Yes	No
41. Is there a small claims court/fast-track procedure?	Yes	Yes

BUILDING CREDIT

	Score: 100	Score: 100
42. Do retailers provide information to credit agencies?	Yes	Yes
43. Do utility companies provide information to credit agencies?	Yes	Yes
44. Is discrimination based on gender prohibited in access to credit?	Yes	Yes
45. Is discrimination based on marital status prohibited in access to credit?	Yes	Yes

PROTECTING WOMEN FROM VIOLENCE

	Score: 80	Score: 80
46. Is there legislation specifically addressing domestic violence? If not, are there aggravated penalties for crimes committed against a spouse or family member?	Yes	Yes
47. Is there legislation on sexual harassment in employment?	Yes	Yes
48. Is there legislation on sexual harassment in education?	Yes	Yes
49. Are there criminal penalties for sexual harassment in employment?	No	Yes
50. Are there civil remedies for sexual harassment in employment?	Yes	No

Note: See the data notes for more details on the scoring of each indicator.

	NIGER	NIGERIA
REGION	Sub-Saharan Africa	Sub-Saharan Africa
INCOME GROUP	Low income	Lower middle income
FEMALE POPULATION	10,251,649	91,244,915
FEMALE LABOR FORCE (% OF TOTAL LABOR FORCE)	43%	45%

ACCESSING INSTITUTIONS

	Score: 64	Score: 91
1. Are wives required to obey their husbands?	No	No
Can a woman legally do the following in the same way as a man:		
2. Apply for a passport?	Yes	No
3. Apply for a national ID card?	Yes	Yes
4. Travel outside the country?	Yes	Yes
5. Travel outside her home?	Yes	Yes
6. Get a job?	No	Yes
7. Sign a contract?	Yes	Yes
8. Register a business?	Yes	Yes
9. Open a bank account?	No	Yes
10. Choose where to live?	No	Yes
11. Be *head of household*?	No	N/A

USING PROPERTY

	Score: 50	Score: 80
12. Who legally administers marital property?	Other	Original owner
13. Does the law provide for valuation of nonmonetary contributions?	No	No
14. Do men and women have equal ownership rights to immovable property?	..	Yes
15. Do sons and daughters have equal inheritance rights?	..	Yes
16. Do female and male surviving spouses have equal inheritance rights?	..	Yes

GETTING A JOB

	Score: 57	Score: 40
17. Is there paid leave available to women of at least 14 weeks?	Yes	No
18. Do women receive at least 2/3 of their wages for the first 14 weeks or the duration of the leave if it is shorter?	Yes	No
19. What is the percentage of maternity leave benefits paid by the government?	50%	0%
20. What is the difference between leave reserved for women and men relative to leave reserved for women, as a function of who pays?	0.51	0
21. Is there paid parental leave?	No	No
22. Does the law mandate equal remuneration for work of equal value?	Yes	No
23. Does the law mandate nondiscrimination based on gender in employment?	Yes	No
24. Is dismissal of pregnant workers prohibited?	Yes	Yes
25. Can parents work flexibly?	No	No
26. Can women work the same night hours as men?	Yes	Yes
27. Can women work in jobs deemed hazardous, arduous or morally inappropriate in the same way as men?	No	Yes
28. Are women able to work in the same industries as men?	No	No
29. Are women able to perform the same tasks at work as men?	No	No
30. Are the ages at which men and women can retire with full pension benefits equal?	Yes	Yes
31. Are the ages at which men and women can retire with partial pension benefits equal?	N/A	N/A
32. Are the mandatory retirement ages for men and women equal?	N/A	N/A

PROVIDING INCENTIVES TO WORK

	Score: 60	Score: 60
33. Are mothers guaranteed an equivalent position after maternity leave?	Yes	No
34. Does the government support or provide childcare services?	Yes	Yes
35. Are payments for childcare tax deductible?	No	No
36. Is primary education free and compulsory?	No	Yes
37. Are there tax deductions or credits specific to men?	No	No

GOING TO COURT

	Score: 50	Score: 100
38. Does a woman's testimony carry the same evidentiary weight in court as a man's?	Yes	Yes
39. Does the law establish an anti-discrimination commission?	No	Yes
40. Does the law mandate legal aid in civil/family matters?	Yes	Yes
41. Is there a small claims court/fast-track procedure?	No	Yes

BUILDING CREDIT

	Score: 0	Score: 50
42. Do retailers provide information to credit agencies?	N/A	Yes
43. Do utility companies provide information to credit agencies?	N/A	Yes
44. Is discrimination based on gender prohibited in access to credit?	No	No
45. Is discrimination based on marital status prohibited in access to credit?	No	No

PROTECTING WOMEN FROM VIOLENCE

	Score: 40	Score: 80
46. Is there legislation specifically addressing domestic violence? If not, are there aggravated penalties for crimes committed against a spouse or family member?	No	Yes
47. Is there legislation on sexual harassment in employment?	Yes	Yes
48. Is there legislation on sexual harassment in education?	No	Yes
49. Are there criminal penalties for sexual harassment in employment?	Yes	Yes
50. Are there civil remedies for sexual harassment in employment?	No	No

Note: See the data notes for more details on the scoring of each indicator.

	NORWAY	OMAN
REGION	High income: OECD	Middle East & North Africa
INCOME GROUP	High income	High income
FEMALE POPULATION	2,595,280	1,484,086
FEMALE LABOR FORCE (% OF TOTAL LABOR FORCE)	47%	13%

ACCESSING INSTITUTIONS

	Score: 100	Score: 55
1. Are wives required to obey their husbands?	No	No

Can a woman legally do the following in the same way as a man:

2. Apply for a passport?	Yes	No
3. Apply for a national ID card?	N/A	No
4. Travel outside the country?	Yes	Yes
5. Travel outside her home?	Yes	No
6. Get a job?	Yes	Yes
7. Sign a contract?	Yes	Yes
8. Register a business?	Yes	Yes
9. Open a bank account?	Yes	Yes
10. Choose where to live?	Yes	No
11. Be "head of household"?	N/A	No

USING PROPERTY

	Score: 100	Score: 40
12. Who legally administers marital property?	Original owner	Original owner
13. Does the law provide for valuation of nonmonetary contributions?	Yes	No
14. Do men and women have equal ownership rights to immovable property?	Yes	Yes
15. Do sons and daughters have equal inheritance rights?	Yes	No
16. Do female and male surviving spouses have equal inheritance rights?	Yes	No

GETTING A JOB

	Score: 100	Score: 50
17. Is there paid leave available to women of at least 14 weeks?	Yes	No
18. Do women receive at least 2/3 of their wages for the first 14 weeks or the duration of the leave if it is shorter?	Yes	Yes
19. What is the percentage of maternity leave benefits paid by the government?	100%	0%
20. What is the difference between leave reserved for women and men relative to leave reserved for women, as a function of who pays?	1	0
21. Is there paid parental leave?	Yes	No
22. Does the law mandate equal remuneration for work of equal value?	Yes	No
23. Does the law mandate nondiscrimination based on gender in employment?	Yes	Yes
24. Is dismissal of pregnant workers prohibited?	Yes	Yes
25. Can parents work flexibly?	Yes	No
26. Can women work the same night hours as men?	Yes	No
27. Can women work in jobs deemed hazardous, arduous or morally inappropriate in the same way as men?	Yes	No
28. Are women able to work in the same industries as men?	Yes	Yes
29. Are women able to perform the same tasks at work as men?	Yes	Yes
30. Are the ages at which men and women can retire with full pension benefits equal?	Yes	No
31. Are the ages at which men and women can retire with partial pension benefits equal?	Yes	Yes
32. Are the mandatory retirement ages for men and women equal?	N/A	Yes

PROVIDING INCENTIVES TO WORK

	Score: 80	Score: 40
33. Are mothers guaranteed an equivalent position after maternity leave?	No	No
34. Does the government support or provide childcare services?	Yes	No
35. Are payments for childcare tax deductible?	Yes	No
36. Is primary education free and compulsory?	Yes	Yes
37. Are there tax deductions or credits specific to men?	No	No

GOING TO COURT

	Score: 100	Score: 25
38. Does a woman's testimony carry the same evidentiary weight in court as a man's?	Yes	No
39. Does the law establish an anti-discrimination commission?	Yes	No
40. Does the law mandate legal aid in civil/family matters?	Yes	No
41. Is there a small claims court/fast-track procedure?	Yes	Yes

BUILDING CREDIT

	Score: 0	Score: 0
42. Do retailers provide information to credit agencies?	No	No
43. Do utility companies provide information to credit agencies?	No	No
44. Is discrimination based on gender prohibited in access to credit?	No	No
45. Is discrimination based on marital status prohibited in access to credit?	No	No

PROTECTING WOMEN FROM VIOLENCE

	Score: 80	Score: 40
46. Is there legislation specifically addressing domestic violence? If not, are there aggravated penalties for crimes committed against a spouse or family member?	Yes	No
47. Is there legislation on sexual harassment in employment?	Yes	Yes
48. Is there legislation on sexual harassment in education?	Yes	No
49. Are there criminal penalties for sexual harassment in employment?	No	No
50. Are there civil remedies for sexual harassment in employment?	Yes	Yes

Note: See the data notes for more details on the scoring of each indicator.

	PAKISTAN	PALAU
REGION	South Asia	East Asia & Pacific
INCOME GROUP	Lower middle income	High income
FEMALE POPULATION	93,957,227	..
FEMALE LABOR FORCE (% OF TOTAL LABOR FORCE)	22%	..

ACCESSING INSTITUTIONS

	Score: 73	Score: 100
1. Are wives required to obey their husbands?	No	No
Can a woman legally do the following in the same way as a man:		
2. Apply for a passport?	No	Yes
3. Apply for a national ID card?	No	N/A
4. Travel outside the country?	Yes	Yes
5. Travel outside her home?	Yes	Yes
6. Get a job?	Yes	Yes
7. Sign a contract?	Yes	Yes
8. Register a business?	No	Yes
9. Open a bank account?	Yes	Yes
10. Choose where to live?	Yes	Yes
11. Be "head of household"?	N/A	N/A

USING PROPERTY

	Score: 40	Score: 50
12. Who legally administers marital property?	Original owner	Other
13. Does the law provide for valuation of nonmonetary contributions?	No	No
14. Do men and women have equal ownership rights to immovable property?	Yes	..
15. Do sons and daughters have equal inheritance rights?	No	..
16. Do female and male surviving spouses have equal inheritance rights?	No	..

GETTING A JOB

	Score: 26	Score: 46
17. Is there paid leave available to women of at least 14 weeks?	No	No
18. Do women receive at least 2/3 of their wages for the first 14 weeks or the duration of the leave if it is shorter?	Yes	No
19. What is the percentage of maternity leave benefits paid by the government?	0%	N/A
20. What is the difference between leave reserved for women and men relative to leave reserved for women, as a function of who pays?	0	N/A
21. Is there paid parental leave?	No	No
22. Does the law mandate equal remuneration for work of equal value?	No	No
23. Does the law mandate nondiscrimination based on gender in employment?	No	No
24. Is dismissal of pregnant workers prohibited?	Yes	No
25. Can parents work flexibly?	No	No
26. Can women work the same night hours as men?	No	Yes
27. Can women work in jobs deemed hazardous, arduous or morally inappropriate in the same way as men?	No	Yes
28. Are women able to work in the same industries as men?	No	Yes
29. Are women able to perform the same tasks at work as men?	No	Yes
30. Are the ages at which men and women can retire with full pension benefits equal?	No	Yes
31. Are the ages at which men and women can retire with partial pension benefits equal?	No	Yes
32. Are the mandatory retirement ages for men and women equal?	N/A	N/A

PROVIDING INCENTIVES TO WORK

	Score: 40	Score: 40
33. Are mothers guaranteed an equivalent position after maternity leave?	No	No
34. Does the government support or provide childcare services?	No	No
35. Are payments for childcare tax deductible?	No	No
36. Is primary education free and compulsory?	Yes	Yes
37. Are there tax deductions or credits specific to men?	No	No

GOING TO COURT

	Score: 50	Score: 50
38. Does a woman's testimony carry the same evidentiary weight in court as a man's?	No	Yes
39. Does the law establish an anti-discrimination commission?	No	No
40. Does the law mandate legal aid in civil/family matters?	Yes	No
41. Is there a small claims court/fast-track procedure?	Yes	Yes

BUILDING CREDIT

	Score: 0	Score: 0
42. Do retailers provide information to credit agencies?	No	N/A
43. Do utility companies provide information to credit agencies?	No	N/A
44. Is discrimination based on gender prohibited in access to credit?	No	No
45. Is discrimination based on marital status prohibited in access to credit?	No	No

PROTECTING WOMEN FROM VIOLENCE

	Score: 100	Score: 20
46. Is there legislation specifically addressing domestic violence? If not, are there aggravated penalties for crimes committed against a spouse or family member?	Yes	Yes
47. Is there legislation on sexual harassment in employment?	Yes	No
48. Is there legislation on sexual harassment in education?	Yes	No
49. Are there criminal penalties for sexual harassment in employment?	Yes	No
50. Are there civil remedies for sexual harassment in employment?	Yes	No

Note: See the data notes for more details on the scoring of each indicator.

	PANAMA	PAPUA NEW GUINEA
REGION	Latin America & Caribbean	East Asia & Pacific
INCOME GROUP	Upper middle income	Lower middle income
FEMALE POPULATION	2,012,452	3,960,661
FEMALE LABOR FORCE (% OF TOTAL LABOR FORCE)	40%	49%

ACCESSING INSTITUTIONS

	Score: 100	Score: 100
1. Are wives required to obey their husbands?	No	No
Can a woman legally do the following in the same way as a man:		
2. Apply for a passport?	Yes	Yes
3. Apply for a national ID card?	Yes	Yes
4. Travel outside the country?	Yes	Yes
5. Travel outside her home?	Yes	Yes
6. Get a job?	Yes	Yes
7. Sign a contract?	Yes	Yes
8. Register a business?	Yes	Yes
9. Open a bank account?	Yes	Yes
10. Choose where to live?	Yes	Yes
11. Be "head of household"?	N/A	N/A

USING PROPERTY

	Score: 100	Score: 80
12. Who legally administers marital property?	Original owner	Original owner
13. Does the law provide for valuation of nonmonetary contributions?	Yes	No
14. Do men and women have equal ownership rights to immovable property?	Yes	Yes
15. Do sons and daughters have equal inheritance rights?	Yes	Yes
16. Do female and male surviving spouses have equal inheritance rights?	Yes	Yes

GETTING A JOB

	Score: 67	Score: 42
17. Is there paid leave available to women of at least 14 weeks?	Yes	No
18. Do women receive at least 2/3 of their wages for the first 14 weeks or the duration of the leave if it is shorter?	Yes	No
19. What is the percentage of maternity leave benefits paid by the government?	100%	N/A
20. What is the difference between leave reserved for women and men relative to leave reserved for women, as a function of who pays?	1	N/A
21. Is there paid parental leave?	No	No
22. Does the law mandate equal remuneration for work of equal value?	No	No
23. Does the law mandate nondiscrimination based on gender in employment?	Yes	Yes
24. Is dismissal of pregnant workers prohibited?	Yes	Yes
25. Can parents work flexibly?	No	No
26. Can women work the same night hours as men?	Yes	Yes
27. Can women work in jobs deemed hazardous, arduous or morally inappropriate in the same way as men?	No	No
28. Are women able to work in the same industries as men?	Yes	No
29. Are women able to perform the same tasks at work as men?	Yes	Yes
30. Are the ages at which men and women can retire with full pension benefits equal?	No	Yes
31. Are the ages at which men and women can retire with partial pension benefits equal?	No	N/A
32. Are the mandatory retirement ages for men and women equal?	N/A	N/A

PROVIDING INCENTIVES TO WORK

	Score: 80	Score: 20
33. Are mothers guaranteed an equivalent position after maternity leave?	Yes	No
34. Does the government support or provide childcare services?	Yes	No
35. Are payments for childcare tax deductible?	No	No
36. Is primary education free and compulsory?	Yes	No
37. Are there tax deductions or credits specific to men?	No	No

GOING TO COURT

	Score: 75	Score: 75
38. Does a woman's testimony carry the same evidentiary weight in court as a man's?	Yes	Yes
39. Does the law establish an anti-discrimination commission?	Yes	No
40. Does the law mandate legal aid in civil/family matters?	No	Yes
41. Is there a small claims court/fast-track procedure?	Yes	Yes

BUILDING CREDIT

	Score: 50	Score: 25
42. Do retailers provide information to credit agencies?	Yes	Yes
43. Do utility companies provide information to credit agencies?	Yes	No
44. Is discrimination based on gender prohibited in access to credit?	No	No
45. Is discrimination based on marital status prohibited in access to credit?	No	No

PROTECTING WOMEN FROM VIOLENCE

	Score: 100	Score: 20
46. Is there legislation specifically addressing domestic violence? If not, are there aggravated penalties for crimes committed against a spouse or family member?	Yes	Yes
47. Is there legislation on sexual harassment in employment?	Yes	No
48. Is there legislation on sexual harassment in education?	Yes	No
49. Are there criminal penalties for sexual harassment in employment?	Yes	No
50. Are there civil remedies for sexual harassment in employment?	Yes	No

Note: See the data notes for more details on the scoring of each indicator.

	PARAGUAY	PERU
REGION	Latin America & Caribbean	Latin America & Caribbean
INCOME GROUP	Upper middle income	Upper middle income
FEMALE POPULATION	3,313,112	15,903,171
FEMALE LABOR FORCE (% OF TOTAL LABOR FORCE)	40%	45%

ACCESSING INSTITUTIONS

	Score: 100	Score: 100
1. Are wives required to obey their husbands?	No	No
Can a woman legally do the following in the same way as a man:		
2. Apply for a passport?	Yes	Yes
3. Apply for a national ID card?	Yes	Yes
4. Travel outside the country?	Yes	Yes
5. Travel outside her home?	Yes	Yes
6. Get a job?	Yes	Yes
7. Sign a contract?	Yes	Yes
8. Register a business?	Yes	Yes
9. Open a bank account?	Yes	Yes
10. Choose where to live?	Yes	Yes
11. Be "head of household"?	N/A	N/A

USING PROPERTY

	Score: 100	Score: 100
12. Who legally administers marital property?	Both must agree	Both must agree
13. Does the law provide for valuation of nonmonetary contributions?	Yes	Yes
14. Do men and women have equal ownership rights to immovable property?	Yes	Yes
15. Do sons and daughters have equal inheritance rights?	Yes	Yes
16. Do female and male surviving spouses have equal inheritance rights?	Yes	Yes

GETTING A JOB

	Score: 87	Score: 87
17. Is there paid leave available to women of at least 14 weeks?	Yes	Yes
18. Do women receive at least 2/3 of their wages for the first 14 weeks or the duration of the leave if it is shorter?	Yes	Yes
19. What is the percentage of maternity leave benefits paid by the government?	100%	100%
20. What is the difference between leave reserved for women and men relative to leave reserved for women, as a function of who pays?	1	1
21. Is there paid parental leave?	No	No
22. Does the law mandate equal remuneration for work of equal value?	Yes	Yes
23. Does the law mandate nondiscrimination based on gender in employment?	Yes	Yes
24. Is dismissal of pregnant workers prohibited?	Yes	Yes
25. Can parents work flexibly?	No	No
26. Can women work the same night hours as men?	Yes	Yes
27. Can women work in jobs deemed hazardous, arduous or morally inappropriate in the same way as men?	Yes	Yes
28. Are women able to work in the same industries as men?	Yes	Yes
29. Are women able to perform the same tasks at work as men?	Yes	Yes
30. Are the ages at which men and women can retire with full pension benefits equal?	Yes	Yes
31. Are the ages at which men and women can retire with partial pension benefits equal?	Yes	N/A
32. Are the mandatory retirement ages for men and women equal?	N/A	Yes

PROVIDING INCENTIVES TO WORK

	Score: 100	Score: 80
33. Are mothers guaranteed an equivalent position after maternity leave?	Yes	Yes
34. Does the government support or provide childcare services?	Yes	Yes
35. Are payments for childcare tax deductible?	Yes	No
36. Is primary education free and compulsory?	Yes	Yes
37. Are there tax deductions or credits specific to men?	No	No

GOING TO COURT

	Score: 75	Score: 75
38. Does a woman's testimony carry the same evidentiary weight in court as a man's?	Yes	Yes
39. Does the law establish an anti-discrimination commission?	No	Yes
40. Does the law mandate legal aid in civil/family matters?	Yes	Yes
41. Is there a small claims court/fast-track procedure?	Yes	No

BUILDING CREDIT

	Score: 75	Score: 50
42. Do retailers provide information to credit agencies?	Yes	No
43. Do utility companies provide information to credit agencies?	Yes	Yes
44. Is discrimination based on gender prohibited in access to credit?	Yes	Yes
45. Is discrimination based on marital status prohibited in access to credit?	No	No

PROTECTING WOMEN FROM VIOLENCE

	Score: 60	Score: 80
46. Is there legislation specifically addressing domestic violence? If not, are there aggravated penalties for crimes committed against a spouse or family member?	Yes	Yes
47. Is there legislation on sexual harassment in employment?	Yes	Yes
48. Is there legislation on sexual harassment in education?	No	Yes
49. Are there criminal penalties for sexual harassment in employment?	Yes	No
50. Are there civil remedies for sexual harassment in employment?	No	Yes

Note: See the data notes for more details on the scoring of each indicator.

	PHILIPPINES	POLAND
REGION	East Asia & Pacific	High income: OECD
INCOME GROUP	Lower middle income	High income
FEMALE POPULATION	51,215,335	19,598,040
FEMALE LABOR FORCE (% OF TOTAL LABOR FORCE)	40%	45%

ACCESSING INSTITUTIONS

	Score: 90	Score: 100
1. Are wives required to obey their husbands?	No	No
Can a woman legally do the following in the same way as a man:		
2. Apply for a passport?	No	Yes
3. Apply for a national ID card?	N/A	Yes
4. Travel outside the country?	Yes	Yes
5. Travel outside her home?	Yes	Yes
6. Get a job?	Yes	Yes
7. Sign a contract?	Yes	Yes
8. Register a business?	Yes	Yes
9. Open a bank account?	Yes	Yes
10. Choose where to live?	Yes	Yes
11. Be "head of household"?	Yes	N/A

USING PROPERTY

	Score: 80	Score: 100
12. Who legally administers marital property?	Other	Both must agree
13. Does the law provide for valuation of nonmonetary contributions?	Yes	Yes
14. Do men and women have equal ownership rights to immovable property?	No	Yes
15. Do sons and daughters have equal inheritance rights?	Yes	Yes
16. Do female and male surviving spouses have equal inheritance rights?	Yes	Yes

GETTING A JOB

	Score: 84	Score: 82
17. Is there paid leave available to women of at least 14 weeks?	No	Yes
18. Do women receive at least 2/3 of their wages for the first 14 weeks or the duration of the leave if it is shorter?	Yes	Yes
19. What is the percentage of maternity leave benefits paid by the government?	100%	100%
20. What is the difference between leave reserved for women and men relative to leave reserved for women, as a function of who pays?	1	1
21. Is there paid parental leave?	No	Yes
22. Does the law mandate equal remuneration for work of equal value?	Yes	No
23. Does the law mandate nondiscrimination based on gender in employment?	Yes	Yes
24. Is dismissal of pregnant workers prohibited?	Yes	Yes
25. Can parents work flexibly?	No	No
26. Can women work the same night hours as men?	Yes	Yes
27. Can women work in jobs deemed hazardous, arduous or morally inappropriate in the same way as men?	Yes	Yes
28. Are women able to work in the same industries as men?	Yes	Yes
29. Are women able to perform the same tasks at work as men?	Yes	Yes
30. Are the ages at which men and women can retire with full pension benefits equal?	Yes	No
31. Are the ages at which men and women can retire with partial pension benefits equal?	N/A	N/A
32. Are the mandatory retirement ages for men and women equal?	Yes	N/A

PROVIDING INCENTIVES TO WORK

	Score: 40	Score: 80
33. Are mothers guaranteed an equivalent position after maternity leave?	No	Yes
34. Does the government support or provide childcare services?	Yes	Yes
35. Are payments for childcare tax deductible?	No	No
36. Is primary education free and compulsory?	Yes	Yes
37. Are there tax deductions or credits specific to men?	Yes	No

GOING TO COURT

	Score: 100	Score: 50
38. Does a woman's testimony carry the same evidentiary weight in court as a man's?	Yes	Yes
39. Does the law establish an anti-discrimination commission?	Yes	No
40. Does the law mandate legal aid in civil/family matters?	Yes	No
41. Is there a small claims court/fast-track procedure?	Yes	Yes

BUILDING CREDIT

	Score: 50	Score: 50
42. Do retailers provide information to credit agencies?	No	No
43. Do utility companies provide information to credit agencies?	No	Yes
44. Is discrimination based on gender prohibited in access to credit?	Yes	Yes
45. Is discrimination based on marital status prohibited in access to credit?	Yes	No

PROTECTING WOMEN FROM VIOLENCE

	Score: 100	Score: 80
46. Is there legislation specifically addressing domestic violence? If not, are there aggravated penalties for crimes committed against a spouse or family member?	Yes	Yes
47. Is there legislation on sexual harassment in employment?	Yes	Yes
48. Is there legislation on sexual harassment in education?	Yes	Yes
49. Are there criminal penalties for sexual harassment in employment?	Yes	No
50. Are there civil remedies for sexual harassment in employment?	Yes	Yes

Note: See the data notes for more details on the scoring of each indicator.

	PORTUGAL	PUERTO RICO (U.S.)
REGION	High income: OECD	Latin America & Caribbean
INCOME GROUP	High income	High income
FEMALE POPULATION	5,441,042	1,771,259
FEMALE LABOR FORCE (% OF TOTAL LABOR FORCE)	49%	42%

ACCESSING INSTITUTIONS

	Score: 100	Score: 100
1. Are wives required to obey their husbands?	No	No
Can a woman legally do the following in the same way as a man:		
2. Apply for a passport?	Yes	Yes
3. Apply for a national ID card?	Yes	N/A
4. Travel outside the country?	Yes	Yes
5. Travel outside her home?	Yes	Yes
6. Get a job?	Yes	Yes
7. Sign a contract?	Yes	Yes
8. Register a business?	Yes	Yes
9. Open a bank account?	Yes	Yes
10. Choose where to live?	Yes	Yes
11. Be "head of household"?	N/A	N/A

USING PROPERTY

	Score: 100	Score: 100
12. Who legally administers marital property?	Both must agree	Both must agree
13. Does the law provide for valuation of nonmonetary contributions?	Yes	Yes
14. Do men and women have equal ownership rights to immovable property?	Yes	Yes
15. Do sons and daughters have equal inheritance rights?	Yes	Yes
16. Do female and male surviving spouses have equal inheritance rights?	Yes	Yes

GETTING A JOB

	Score: 100	Score: 64
17. Is there paid leave available to women of at least 14 weeks?	Yes	No
18. Do women receive at least 2/3 of their wages for the first 14 weeks or the duration of the leave if it is shorter?	Yes	Yes
19. What is the percentage of maternity leave benefits paid by the government?	100%	0%
20. What is the difference between leave reserved for women and men relative to leave reserved for women, as a function of who pays?	1	0
21. Is there paid parental leave?	Yes	No
22. Does the law mandate equal remuneration for work of equal value?	Yes	No
23. Does the law mandate nondiscrimination based on gender in employment?	Yes	Yes
24. Is dismissal of pregnant workers prohibited?	Yes	Yes
25. Can parents work flexibly?	Yes	No
26. Can women work the same night hours as men?	Yes	Yes
27. Can women work in jobs deemed hazardous, arduous or morally inappropriate in the same way as men?	Yes	Yes
28. Are women able to work in the same industries as men?	Yes	Yes
29. Are women able to perform the same tasks at work as men?	Yes	Yes
30. Are the ages at which men and women can retire with full pension benefits equal?	Yes	Yes
31. Are the ages at which men and women can retire with partial pension benefits equal?	Yes	Yes
32. Are the mandatory retirement ages for men and women equal?	N/A	N/A

PROVIDING INCENTIVES TO WORK

	Score: 100	Score: 100
33. Are mothers guaranteed an equivalent position after maternity leave?	Yes	Yes
34. Does the government support or provide childcare services?	Yes	Yes
35. Are payments for childcare tax deductible?	Yes	Yes
36. Is primary education free and compulsory?	Yes	Yes
37. Are there tax deductions or credits specific to men?	No	No

GOING TO COURT

	Score: 100	Score: 50
38. Does a woman's testimony carry the same evidentiary weight in court as a man's?	Yes	Yes
39. Does the law establish an anti-discrimination commission?	Yes	No
40. Does the law mandate legal aid in civil/family matters?	Yes	No
41. Is there a small claims court/fast-track procedure?	Yes	Yes

BUILDING CREDIT

	Score: 25	Score: 100
42. Do retailers provide information to credit agencies?	No	Yes
43. Do utility companies provide information to credit agencies?	No	Yes
44. Is discrimination based on gender prohibited in access to credit?	Yes	Yes
45. Is discrimination based on marital status prohibited in access to credit?	No	Yes

PROTECTING WOMEN FROM VIOLENCE

	Score: 60	Score: 100
46. Is there legislation specifically addressing domestic violence? If not, are there aggravated penalties for crimes committed against a spouse or family member?	Yes	Yes
47. Is there legislation on sexual harassment in employment?	Yes	Yes
48. Is there legislation on sexual harassment in education?	No	Yes
49. Are there criminal penalties for sexual harassment in employment?	No	Yes
50. Are there civil remedies for sexual harassment in employment?	Yes	Yes

Note: See the data notes for more details on the scoring of each indicator.

	QATAR	ROMANIA
REGION	Middle East & North Africa	Europe & Central Asia
INCOME GROUP	High income	Upper middle income
FEMALE POPULATION	714,493	10,164,461
FEMALE LABOR FORCE (% OF TOTAL LABOR FORCE)	14%	43%

ACCESSING INSTITUTIONS

	Score: 55	Score: 100
1. Are wives required to obey their husbands?	Yes	No
Can a woman legally do the following in the same way as a man:		
2. Apply for a passport?	Yes	Yes
3. Apply for a national ID card?	Yes	Yes
4. Travel outside the country?	No	Yes
5. Travel outside her home?	No	Yes
6. Get a job?	No	Yes
7. Sign a contract?	Yes	Yes
8. Register a business?	Yes	Yes
9. Open a bank account?	Yes	Yes
10. Choose where to live?	No	Yes
11. Be "head of household"?	N/A	N/A

USING PROPERTY

	Score: 40	Score: 100
12. Who legally administers marital property?	Original owner	Both must agree
13. Does the law provide for valuation of nonmonetary contributions?	No	Yes
14. Do men and women have equal ownership rights to immovable property?	Yes	Yes
15. Do sons and daughters have equal inheritance rights?	No	Yes
16. Do female and male surviving spouses have equal inheritance rights?	No	Yes

GETTING A JOB

	Score: 40	Score: 90
17. Is there paid leave available to women of at least 14 weeks?	No	Yes
18. Do women receive at least 2/3 of their wages for the first 14 weeks or the duration of the leave if it is shorter?	Yes	Yes
19. What is the percentage of maternity leave benefits paid by the government?	0%	100%
20. What is the difference between leave reserved for women and men relative to leave reserved for women, as a function of who pays?	0	1
21. Is there paid parental leave?	No	Yes
22. Does the law mandate equal remuneration for work of equal value?	No	Yes
23. Does the law mandate nondiscrimination based on gender in employment?	No	Yes
24. Is dismissal of pregnant workers prohibited?	No	Yes
25. Can parents work flexibly?	No	No
26. Can women work the same night hours as men?	Yes	Yes
27. Can women work in jobs deemed hazardous, arduous or morally inappropriate in the same way as men?	No	Yes
28. Are women able to work in the same industries as men?	Yes	Yes
29. Are women able to perform the same tasks at work as men?	Yes	Yes
30. Are the ages at which men and women can retire with full pension benefits equal?	No	No
31. Are the ages at which men and women can retire with partial pension benefits equal?	Yes	Yes
32. Are the mandatory retirement ages for men and women equal?	N/A	No

PROVIDING INCENTIVES TO WORK

	Score: 60	Score: 80
33. Are mothers guaranteed an equivalent position after maternity leave?	No	Yes
34. Does the government support or provide childcare services?	Yes	Yes
35. Are payments for childcare tax deductible?	No	No
36. Is primary education free and compulsory?	Yes	Yes
37. Are there tax deductions or credits specific to men?	No	No

GOING TO COURT

	Score: 25	Score: 100
38. Does a woman's testimony carry the same evidentiary weight in court as a man's?	No	Yes
39. Does the law establish an anti-discrimination commission?	No	Yes
40. Does the law mandate legal aid in civil/family matters?	No	Yes
41. Is there a small claims court/fast-track procedure?	Yes	Yes

BUILDING CREDIT

	Score: 0	Score: 25
42. Do retailers provide information to credit agencies?	No	No
43. Do utility companies provide information to credit agencies?	No	No
44. Is discrimination based on gender prohibited in access to credit?	No	Yes
45. Is discrimination based on marital status prohibited in access to credit?	No	No

PROTECTING WOMEN FROM VIOLENCE

	Score: 0	Score: 100
46. Is there legislation specifically addressing domestic violence? If not, are there aggravated penalties for crimes committed against a spouse or family member?	No	Yes
47. Is there legislation on sexual harassment in employment?	No	Yes
48. Is there legislation on sexual harassment in education?	No	Yes
49. Are there criminal penalties for sexual harassment in employment?	No	Yes
50. Are there civil remedies for sexual harassment in employment?	No	Yes

Note: See the data notes for more details on the scoring of each indicator.

	RUSSIAN FEDERATION	RWANDA
REGION	Europe & Central Asia	Sub-Saharan Africa
INCOME GROUP	Upper middle income	Low income
FEMALE POPULATION	77,274,683	6,206,417
FEMALE LABOR FORCE (% OF TOTAL LABOR FORCE)	49%	52%

ACCESSING INSTITUTIONS

	Score: 100	Score: 100
1. Are wives required to obey their husbands?	No	No
Can a woman legally do the following in the same way as a man:		
2. Apply for a passport?	Yes	Yes
3. Apply for a national ID card?	Yes	Yes
4. Travel outside the country?	Yes	Yes
5. Travel outside her home?	Yes	Yes
6. Get a job?	Yes	Yes
7. Sign a contract?	Yes	Yes
8. Register a business?	Yes	Yes
9. Open a bank account?	Yes	Yes
10. Choose where to live?	Yes	Yes
11. Be "head of household"?	N/A	Yes

USING PROPERTY

	Score: 100	Score: 100
12. Who legally administers marital property?	Both must agree	Both must agree
13. Does the law provide for valuation of nonmonetary contributions?	Yes	Yes
14. Do men and women have equal ownership rights to immovable property?	Yes	Yes
15. Do sons and daughters have equal inheritance rights?	Yes	Yes
16. Do female and male surviving spouses have equal inheritance rights?	Yes	Yes

GETTING A JOB

	Score: 68	Score: 63
17. Is there paid leave available to women of at least 14 weeks?	Yes	No
18. Do women receive at least 2/3 of their wages for the first 14 weeks or the duration of the leave if it is shorter?	Yes	Yes
19. What is the percentage of maternity leave benefits paid by the government?	100%	50%
20. What is the difference between leave reserved for women and men relative to leave reserved for women, as a function of who pays?	1	0.52
21. Is there paid parental leave?	Yes	No
22. Does the law mandate equal remuneration for work of equal value?	No	No
23. Does the law mandate nondiscrimination based on gender in employment?	Yes	Yes
24. Is dismissal of pregnant workers prohibited?	Yes	No
25. Can parents work flexibly?	Yes	No
26. Can women work the same night hours as men?	Yes	Yes
27. Can women work in jobs deemed hazardous, arduous or morally inappropriate in the same way as men?	No	Yes
28. Are women able to work in the same industries as men?	No	Yes
29. Are women able to perform the same tasks at work as men?	No	Yes
30. Are the ages at which men and women can retire with full pension benefits equal?	No	Yes
31. Are the ages at which men and women can retire with partial pension benefits equal?	N/A	N/A
32. Are the mandatory retirement ages for men and women equal?	N/A	N/A

PROVIDING INCENTIVES TO WORK

	Score: 100	Score: 60
33. Are mothers guaranteed an equivalent position after maternity leave?	Yes	Yes
34. Does the government support or provide childcare services?	Yes	No
35. Are payments for childcare tax deductible?	Yes	No
36. Is primary education free and compulsory?	Yes	Yes
37. Are there tax deductions or credits specific to men?	No	No

GOING TO COURT

	Score: 50	Score: 75
38. Does a woman's testimony carry the same evidentiary weight in court as a man's?	Yes	Yes
39. Does the law establish an anti-discrimination commission?	No	Yes
40. Does the law mandate legal aid in civil/family matters?	Yes	Yes
41. Is there a small claims court/fast-track procedure?	No	No

BUILDING CREDIT

	Score: 0	Score: 25
42. Do retailers provide information to credit agencies?	No	No
43. Do utility companies provide information to credit agencies?	No	Yes
44. Is discrimination based on gender prohibited in access to credit?	No	No
45. Is discrimination based on marital status prohibited in access to credit?	No	No

PROTECTING WOMEN FROM VIOLENCE

	Score: 0	Score: 60
46. Is there legislation specifically addressing domestic violence? If not, are there aggravated penalties for crimes committed against a spouse or family member?	No	Yes
47. Is there legislation on sexual harassment in employment?	No	Yes
48. Is there legislation on sexual harassment in education?	No	No
49. Are there criminal penalties for sexual harassment in employment?	No	Yes
50. Are there civil remedies for sexual harassment in employment?	No	No

Note: See the data notes for more details on the scoring of each indicator.

	SAMOA	SAN MARINO
REGION	East Asia & Pacific	Europe & Central Asia
INCOME GROUP	Upper middle income	High income
FEMALE POPULATION	94,498	..
FEMALE LABOR FORCE (% OF TOTAL LABOR FORCE)	36%	..

ACCESSING INSTITUTIONS

	Score: 90	Score: 91
1. Are wives required to obey their husbands?	No	No
Can a woman legally do the following in the same way as a man:		
2. Apply for a passport?	No	Yes
3. Apply for a national ID card?	N/A	Yes
4. Travel outside the country?	Yes	Yes
5. Travel outside her home?	Yes	Yes
6. Get a job?	Yes	Yes
7. Sign a contract?	Yes	Yes
8. Register a business?	Yes	Yes
9. Open a bank account?	Yes	Yes
10. Choose where to live?	Yes	Yes
11. Be "head of household"?	N/A	No

USING PROPERTY

	Score: 100	Score: 100
12. Who legally administers marital property?	Other	Both must agree
13. Does the law provide for valuation of nonmonetary contributions?	Yes	Yes
14. Do men and women have equal ownership rights to immovable property?	Yes	Yes
15. Do sons and daughters have equal inheritance rights?	Yes	Yes
16. Do female and male surviving spouses have equal inheritance rights?	Yes	Yes

GETTING A JOB

	Score: 68	Score: 87
17. Is there paid leave available to women of at least 14 weeks?	No	Yes
18. Do women receive at least 2/3 of their wages for the first 14 weeks or the duration of the leave if it is shorter?	Yes	Yes
19. What is the percentage of maternity leave benefits paid by the government?	0%	100%
20. What is the difference between leave reserved for women and men relative to leave reserved for women, as a function of who pays?	0.18	1
21. Is there paid parental leave?	No	No
22. Does the law mandate equal remuneration for work of equal value?	Yes	No
23. Does the law mandate nondiscrimination based on gender in employment?	Yes	Yes
24. Is dismissal of pregnant workers prohibited?	Yes	Yes
25. Can parents work flexibly?	No	Yes
26. Can women work the same night hours as men?	Yes	Yes
27. Can women work in jobs deemed hazardous, arduous or morally inappropriate in the same way as men?	Yes	Yes
28. Are women able to work in the same industries as men?	Yes	Yes
29. Are women able to perform the same tasks at work as men?	Yes	Yes
30. Are the ages at which men and women can retire with full pension benefits equal?	Yes	Yes
31. Are the ages at which men and women can retire with partial pension benefits equal?	N/A	Yes
32. Are the mandatory retirement ages for men and women equal?	N/A	N/A

PROVIDING INCENTIVES TO WORK

	Score: 40	Score: 100
33. Are mothers guaranteed an equivalent position after maternity leave?	Yes	Yes
34. Does the government support or provide childcare services?	No	Yes
35. Are payments for childcare tax deductible?	No	Yes
36. Is primary education free and compulsory?	No	Yes
37. Are there tax deductions or credits specific to men?	No	No

GOING TO COURT

	Score: 75	Score: 25
38. Does a woman's testimony carry the same evidentiary weight in court as a man's?	Yes	Yes
39. Does the law establish an anti-discrimination commission?	Yes	No
40. Does the law mandate legal aid in civil/family matters?	No	No
41. Is there a small claims court/fast-track procedure?	Yes	No

BUILDING CREDIT

	Score: 0	Score: 0
42. Do retailers provide information to credit agencies?	N/A	N/A
43. Do utility companies provide information to credit agencies?	N/A	N/A
44. Is discrimination based on gender prohibited in access to credit?	No	No
45. Is discrimination based on marital status prohibited in access to credit?	No	No

PROTECTING WOMEN FROM VIOLENCE

	Score: 20	Score: 40
46. Is there legislation specifically addressing domestic violence? If not, are there aggravated penalties for crimes committed against a spouse or family member?	Yes	Yes
47. Is there legislation on sexual harassment in employment?	No	No
48. Is there legislation on sexual harassment in education?	No	Yes
49. Are there criminal penalties for sexual harassment in employment?	No	No
50. Are there civil remedies for sexual harassment in employment?	No	No

Note: See the data notes for more details on the scoring of each indicator.

	SÃO TOMÉ AND PRÍNCIPE	SAUDI ARABIA
REGION	Sub-Saharan Africa	Middle East & North Africa
INCOME GROUP	Lower middle income	High income
FEMALE POPULATION	100,377	14,037,495
FEMALE LABOR FORCE (% OF TOTAL LABOR FORCE)	36%	16%

ACCESSING INSTITUTIONS

	Score: 100	Score: 36
1. Are wives required to obey their husbands?	No	Yes
Can a woman legally do the following in the same way as a man:		
2. Apply for a passport?	Yes	No
3. Apply for a national ID card?	Yes	No
4. Travel outside the country?	Yes	No
5. Travel outside her home?	Yes	No
6. Get a job?	Yes	Yes
7. Sign a contract?	Yes	Yes
8. Register a business?	Yes	Yes
9. Open a bank account?	Yes	Yes
10. Choose where to live?	Yes	No
11. Be "head of household"?	N/A	No

USING PROPERTY

	Score: 100	Score: 40
12. Who legally administers marital property?	Both must agree	Original owner
13. Does the law provide for valuation of nonmonetary contributions?	Yes	No
14. Do men and women have equal ownership rights to immovable property?	Yes	Yes
15. Do sons and daughters have equal inheritance rights?	Yes	No
16. Do female and male surviving spouses have equal inheritance rights?	Yes	No

GETTING A JOB

	Score: 50	Score: 16
17. Is there paid leave available to women of at least 14 weeks?	Yes	No
18. Do women receive at least 2/3 of their wages for the first 14 weeks or the duration of the leave if it is shorter?	Yes	Yes
19. What is the percentage of maternity leave benefits paid by the government?	100%	0%
20. What is the difference between leave reserved for women and men relative to leave reserved for women, as a function of who pays?	1	0.04
21. Is there paid parental leave?	No	No
22. Does the law mandate equal remuneration for work of equal value?	No	No
23. Does the law mandate nondiscrimination based on gender in employment?	Yes	No
24. Is dismissal of pregnant workers prohibited?	No	No
25. Can parents work flexibly?	No	No
26. Can women work the same night hours as men?	No	No
27. Can women work in jobs deemed hazardous, arduous or morally inappropriate in the same way as men?	No	No
28. Are women able to work in the same industries as men?	No	No
29. Are women able to perform the same tasks at work as men?	Yes	No
30. Are the ages at which men and women can retire with full pension benefits equal?	Yes	No
31. Are the ages at which men and women can retire with partial pension benefits equal?	N/A	N/A
32. Are the mandatory retirement ages for men and women equal?	N/A	No

PROVIDING INCENTIVES TO WORK

	Score: 40	Score: 40
33. Are mothers guaranteed an equivalent position after maternity leave?	No	No
34. Does the government support or provide childcare services?	No	No
35. Are payments for childcare tax deductible?	No	No
36. Is primary education free and compulsory?	Yes	Yes
37. Are there tax deductions or credits specific to men?	No	No

GOING TO COURT

	Score: 25	Score: 25
38. Does a woman's testimony carry the same evidentiary weight in court as a man's?	Yes	No
39. Does the law establish an anti-discrimination commission?	No	No
40. Does the law mandate legal aid in civil/family matters?	No	No
41. Is there a small claims court/fast-track procedure?	No	Yes

BUILDING CREDIT

	Score: 0	Score: 50
42. Do retailers provide information to credit agencies?	No	Yes
43. Do utility companies provide information to credit agencies?	No	Yes
44. Is discrimination based on gender prohibited in access to credit?	No	No
45. Is discrimination based on marital status prohibited in access to credit?	No	No

PROTECTING WOMEN FROM VIOLENCE

	Score: 60	Score: 20
46. Is there legislation specifically addressing domestic violence? If not, are there aggravated penalties for crimes committed against a spouse or family member?	Yes	Yes
47. Is there legislation on sexual harassment in employment?	Yes	No
48. Is there legislation on sexual harassment in education?	No	No
49. Are there criminal penalties for sexual harassment in employment?	Yes	No
50. Are there civil remedies for sexual harassment in employment?	No	No

Note: See the data notes for more details on the scoring of each indicator.

	SENEGAL	SERBIA
REGION	Sub-Saharan Africa	Europe & Central Asia
INCOME GROUP	Low income	Upper middle income
FEMALE POPULATION	7,839,987	3,613,798
FEMALE LABOR FORCE (% OF TOTAL LABOR FORCE)	41%	44%

ACCESSING INSTITUTIONS

	Score: 82	Score: 100
1. Are wives required to obey their husbands?	No	No
Can a woman legally do the following in the same way as a man:		
2. Apply for a passport?	Yes	Yes
3. Apply for a national ID card?	Yes	Yes
4. Travel outside the country?	Yes	Yes
5. Travel outside her home?	Yes	Yes
6. Get a job?	Yes	Yes
7. Sign a contract?	Yes	Yes
8. Register a business?	Yes	Yes
9. Open a bank account?	Yes	Yes
10. Choose where to live?	No	Yes
11. Be "head of household"?	No	N/A

USING PROPERTY

	Score: 40	Score: 100
12. Who legally administers marital property?	Original owner	Both must agree
13. Does the law provide for valuation of nonmonetary contributions?	No	Yes
14. Do men and women have equal ownership rights to immovable property?	Yes	Yes
15. Do sons and daughters have equal inheritance rights?	No	Yes
16. Do female and male surviving spouses have equal inheritance rights?	No	Yes

GETTING A JOB

	Score: 50	Score: 93
17. Is there paid leave available to women of at least 14 weeks?	Yes	Yes
18. Do women receive at least 2/3 of their wages for the first 14 weeks or the duration of the leave if it is shorter?	Yes	Yes
19. What is the percentage of maternity leave benefits paid by the government?	100%	100%
20. What is the difference between leave reserved for women and men relative to leave reserved for women, as a function of who pays?	1	1
21. Is there paid parental leave?	No	Yes
22. Does the law mandate equal remuneration for work of equal value?	No	Yes
23. Does the law mandate nondiscrimination based on gender in employment?	No	Yes
24. Is dismissal of pregnant workers prohibited?	No	Yes
25. Can parents work flexibly?	No	No
26. Can women work the same night hours as men?	Yes	Yes
27. Can women work in jobs deemed hazardous, arduous or morally inappropriate in the same way as men?	No	Yes
28. Are women able to work in the same industries as men?	No	Yes
29. Are women able to perform the same tasks at work as men?	No	Yes
30. Are the ages at which men and women can retire with full pension benefits equal?	Yes	Yes
31. Are the ages at which men and women can retire with partial pension benefits equal?	Yes	N/A
32. Are the mandatory retirement ages for men and women equal?	Yes	Yes

PROVIDING INCENTIVES TO WORK

	Score: 80	Score: 60
33. Are mothers guaranteed an equivalent position after maternity leave?	Yes	No
34. Does the government support or provide childcare services?	Yes	Yes
35. Are payments for childcare tax deductible?	No	No
36. Is primary education free and compulsory?	Yes	Yes
37. Are there tax deductions or credits specific to men?	No	No

GOING TO COURT

	Score: 50	Score: 75
38. Does a woman's testimony carry the same evidentiary weight in court as a man's?	Yes	Yes
39. Does the law establish an anti-discrimination commission?	No	Yes
40. Does the law mandate legal aid in civil/family matters?	Yes	No
41. Is there a small claims court/fast-track procedure?	No	Yes

BUILDING CREDIT

	Score: 0	Score: 50
42. Do retailers provide information to credit agencies?	N/A	No
43. Do utility companies provide information to credit agencies?	N/A	No
44. Is discrimination based on gender prohibited in access to credit?	No	Yes
45. Is discrimination based on marital status prohibited in access to credit?	No	Yes

PROTECTING WOMEN FROM VIOLENCE

	Score: 60	Score: 60
46. Is there legislation specifically addressing domestic violence? If not, are there aggravated penalties for crimes committed against a spouse or family member?	Yes	Yes
47. Is there legislation on sexual harassment in employment?	Yes	Yes
48. Is there legislation on sexual harassment in education?	No	No
49. Are there criminal penalties for sexual harassment in employment?	Yes	No
50. Are there civil remedies for sexual harassment in employment?	No	Yes

Note: See the data notes for more details on the scoring of each indicator.

	SEYCHELLES	SIERRA LEONE
REGION	Sub-Saharan Africa	Sub-Saharan Africa
INCOME GROUP	High income	Low income
FEMALE POPULATION	46,807	3,734,967
FEMALE LABOR FORCE (% OF TOTAL LABOR FORCE)	..	50%

ACCESSING INSTITUTIONS

	Score: 91	Score: 100
1. Are wives required to obey their husbands?	No	No
Can a woman legally do the following in the same way as a man:		
2. Apply for a passport?	No	Yes
3. Apply for a national ID card?	Yes	Yes
4. Travel outside the country?	Yes	Yes
5. Travel outside her home?	Yes	Yes
6. Get a job?	Yes	Yes
7. Sign a contract?	Yes	Yes
8. Register a business?	Yes	Yes
9. Open a bank account?	Yes	Yes
10. Choose where to live?	Yes	Yes
11. Be "head of household"?	N/A	N/A

USING PROPERTY

	Score: 80	Score: 80
12. Who legally administers marital property?	Original owner	Original owner
13. Does the law provide for valuation of nonmonetary contributions?	No	No
14. Do men and women have equal ownership rights to immovable property?	Yes	Yes
15. Do sons and daughters have equal inheritance rights?	Yes	Yes
16. Do female and male surviving spouses have equal inheritance rights?	Yes	Yes

GETTING A JOB

	Score: 77	Score: 46
17. Is there paid leave available to women of at least 14 weeks?	Yes	No
18. Do women receive at least 2/3 of their wages for the first 14 weeks or the duration of the leave if it is shorter?	No	Yes
19. What is the percentage of maternity leave benefits paid by the government?	100%	0%
20. What is the difference between leave reserved for women and men relative to leave reserved for women, as a function of who pays?	1	0
21. Is there paid parental leave?	No	No
22. Does the law mandate equal remuneration for work of equal value?	No	No
23. Does the law mandate nondiscrimination based on gender in employment?	Yes	No
24. Is dismissal of pregnant workers prohibited?	Yes	No
25. Can parents work flexibly?	No	No
26. Can women work the same night hours as men?	Yes	Yes
27. Can women work in jobs deemed hazardous, arduous or morally inappropriate in the same way as men?	Yes	Yes
28. Are women able to work in the same industries as men?	Yes	No
29. Are women able to perform the same tasks at work as men?	Yes	Yes
30. Are the ages at which men and women can retire with full pension benefits equal?	Yes	Yes
31. Are the ages at which men and women can retire with partial pension benefits equal?	N/A	Yes
32. Are the mandatory retirement ages for men and women equal?	Yes	N/A

PROVIDING INCENTIVES TO WORK

	Score: 60	Score: 60
33. Are mothers guaranteed an equivalent position after maternity leave?	No	No
34. Does the government support or provide childcare services?	Yes	Yes
35. Are payments for childcare tax deductible?	No	No
36. Is primary education free and compulsory?	Yes	Yes
37. Are there tax deductions or credits specific to men?	No	No

GOING TO COURT

	Score: 50	Score: 100
38. Does a woman's testimony carry the same evidentiary weight in court as a man's?	Yes	Yes
39. Does the law establish an anti-discrimination commission?	No	Yes
40. Does the law mandate legal aid in civil/family matters?	Yes	Yes
41. Is there a small claims court/fast-track procedure?	No	Yes

BUILDING CREDIT

	Score: 0	Score: 0
42. Do retailers provide information to credit agencies?	No	N/A
43. Do utility companies provide information to credit agencies?	No	N/A
44. Is discrimination based on gender prohibited in access to credit?	No	No
45. Is discrimination based on marital status prohibited in access to credit?	No	No

PROTECTING WOMEN FROM VIOLENCE

	Score: 20	Score: 20
46. Is there legislation specifically addressing domestic violence? If not, are there aggravated penalties for crimes committed against a spouse or family member?	Yes	Yes
47. Is there legislation on sexual harassment in employment?	No	No
48. Is there legislation on sexual harassment in education?	No	No
49. Are there criminal penalties for sexual harassment in employment?	No	No
50. Are there civil remedies for sexual harassment in employment?	No	No

Note: See the data notes for more details on the scoring of each indicator.

	SINGAPORE	SLOVAK REPUBLIC
REGION	East Asia & Pacific	High income: OECD
INCOME GROUP	High income	High income
FEMALE POPULATION	2,840,579	2,797,436
FEMALE LABOR FORCE (% OF TOTAL LABOR FORCE)	45%	45%

ACCESSING INSTITUTIONS

	Score: 100	Score: 100
1. Are wives required to obey their husbands?	No	No
Can a woman legally do the following in the same way as a man:		
2. Apply for a passport?	Yes	Yes
3. Apply for a national ID card?	Yes	Yes
4. Travel outside the country?	Yes	Yes
5. Travel outside her home?	Yes	Yes
6. Get a job?	Yes	Yes
7. Sign a contract?	Yes	Yes
8. Register a business?	Yes	Yes
9. Open a bank account?	Yes	Yes
10. Choose where to live?	Yes	Yes
11. Be "head of household"?	N/A	N/A

USING PROPERTY

	Score: 100	Score: 100
12. Who legally administers marital property?	Original owner	Both must agree
13. Does the law provide for valuation of nonmonetary contributions?	Yes	Yes
14. Do men and women have equal ownership rights to immovable property?	Yes	Yes
15. Do sons and daughters have equal inheritance rights?	Yes	Yes
16. Do female and male surviving spouses have equal inheritance rights?	Yes	Yes

GETTING A JOB

	Score: 67	Score: 100
17. Is there paid leave available to women of at least 14 weeks?	Yes	Yes
18. Do women receive at least 2/3 of their wages for the first 14 weeks or the duration of the leave if it is shorter?	Yes	Yes
19. What is the percentage of maternity leave benefits paid by the government?	50%	100%
20. What is the difference between leave reserved for women and men relative to leave reserved for women, as a function of who pays?	0.55	1
21. Is there paid parental leave?	Yes	Yes
22. Does the law mandate equal remuneration for work of equal value?	No	Yes
23. Does the law mandate nondiscrimination based on gender in employment?	No	Yes
24. Is dismissal of pregnant workers prohibited?	No	Yes
25. Can parents work flexibly?	No	Yes
26. Can women work the same night hours as men?	Yes	Yes
27. Can women work in jobs deemed hazardous, arduous or morally inappropriate in the same way as men?	Yes	Yes
28. Are women able to work in the same industries as men?	Yes	Yes
29. Are women able to perform the same tasks at work as men?	Yes	Yes
30. Are the ages at which men and women can retire with full pension benefits equal?	Yes	Yes
31. Are the ages at which men and women can retire with partial pension benefits equal?	N/A	Yes
32. Are the mandatory retirement ages for men and women equal?	Yes	N/A

PROVIDING INCENTIVES TO WORK

	Score: 60	Score: 80
33. Are mothers guaranteed an equivalent position after maternity leave?	No	Yes
34. Does the government support or provide childcare services?	Yes	Yes
35. Are payments for childcare tax deductible?	No	No
36. Is primary education free and compulsory?	Yes	Yes
37. Are there tax deductions or credits specific to men?	No	No

GOING TO COURT

	Score: 75	Score: 75
38. Does a woman's testimony carry the same evidentiary weight in court as a man's?	Yes	Yes
39. Does the law establish an anti-discrimination commission?	No	No
40. Does the law mandate legal aid in civil/family matters?	Yes	Yes
41. Is there a small claims court/fast-track procedure?	Yes	Yes

BUILDING CREDIT

	Score: 0	Score: 50
42. Do retailers provide information to credit agencies?	No	No
43. Do utility companies provide information to credit agencies?	No	No
44. Is discrimination based on gender prohibited in access to credit?	No	Yes
45. Is discrimination based on marital status prohibited in access to credit?	No	Yes

PROTECTING WOMEN FROM VIOLENCE

	Score: 60	Score: 80
46. Is there legislation specifically addressing domestic violence? If not, are there aggravated penalties for crimes committed against a spouse or family member?	Yes	Yes
47. Is there legislation on sexual harassment in employment?	Yes	Yes
48. Is there legislation on sexual harassment in education?	No	Yes
49. Are there criminal penalties for sexual harassment in employment?	No	No
50. Are there civil remedies for sexual harassment in employment?	Yes	Yes

Note: See the data notes for more details on the scoring of each indicator.

	SLOVENIA	SOLOMON ISLANDS
REGION	High income: OECD	East Asia & Pacific
INCOME GROUP	High income	Lower middle income
FEMALE POPULATION	1,041,173	295,031
FEMALE LABOR FORCE (% OF TOTAL LABOR FORCE)	47%	44%

ACCESSING INSTITUTIONS

	Score: 100	Score: 90
1. Are wives required to obey their husbands?	No	No
Can a woman legally do the following in the same way as a man:		
2. Apply for a passport?	Yes	No
3. Apply for a national ID card?	Yes	N/A
4. Travel outside the country?	Yes	Yes
5. Travel outside her home?	Yes	Yes
6. Get a job?	Yes	Yes
7. Sign a contract?	Yes	Yes
8. Register a business?	Yes	Yes
9. Open a bank account?	Yes	Yes
10. Choose where to live?	Yes	Yes
11. Be "head of household"?	N/A	N/A

USING PROPERTY

	Score: 100	Score: 100
12. Who legally administers marital property?	Both must agree	Original owner
13. Does the law provide for valuation of nonmonetary contributions?	Yes	Yes
14. Do men and women have equal ownership rights to immovable property?	Yes	Yes
15. Do sons and daughters have equal inheritance rights?	Yes	Yes
16. Do female and male surviving spouses have equal inheritance rights?	Yes	Yes

GETTING A JOB

	Score: 93	Score: 30
17. Is there paid leave available to women of at least 14 weeks?	Yes	No
18. Do women receive at least 2/3 of their wages for the first 14 weeks or the duration of the leave if it is shorter?	Yes	No
19. What is the percentage of maternity leave benefits paid by the government?	100%	0%
20. What is the difference between leave reserved for women and men relative to leave reserved for women, as a function of who pays?	1	0
21. Is there paid parental leave?	Yes	No
22. Does the law mandate equal remuneration for work of equal value?	Yes	No
23. Does the law mandate nondiscrimination based on gender in employment?	Yes	No
24. Is dismissal of pregnant workers prohibited?	Yes	No
25. Can parents work flexibly?	Yes	No
26. Can women work the same night hours as men?	Yes	No
27. Can women work in jobs deemed hazardous, arduous or morally inappropriate in the same way as men?	Yes	Yes
28. Are women able to work in the same industries as men?	No	No
29. Are women able to perform the same tasks at work as men?	Yes	Yes
30. Are the ages at which men and women can retire with full pension benefits equal?	Yes	Yes
31. Are the ages at which men and women can retire with partial pension benefits equal?	Yes	N/A
32. Are the mandatory retirement ages for men and women equal?	N/A	N/A

PROVIDING INCENTIVES TO WORK

	Score: 60	Score: 20
33. Are mothers guaranteed an equivalent position after maternity leave?	No	No
34. Does the government support or provide childcare services?	Yes	No
35. Are payments for childcare tax deductible?	No	No
36. Is primary education free and compulsory?	Yes	No
37. Are there tax deductions or credits specific to men?	No	No

GOING TO COURT

	Score: 100	Score: 50
38. Does a woman's testimony carry the same evidentiary weight in court as a man's?	Yes	Yes
39. Does the law establish an anti-discrimination commission?	Yes	No
40. Does the law mandate legal aid in civil/family matters?	Yes	No
41. Is there a small claims court/fast-track procedure?	Yes	Yes

BUILDING CREDIT

	Score: 25	Score: 0
42. Do retailers provide information to credit agencies?	No	N/A
43. Do utility companies provide information to credit agencies?	No	N/A
44. Is discrimination based on gender prohibited in access to credit?	Yes	No
45. Is discrimination based on marital status prohibited in access to credit?	No	No

PROTECTING WOMEN FROM VIOLENCE

	Score: 100	Score: 20
46. Is there legislation specifically addressing domestic violence? If not, are there aggravated penalties for crimes committed against a spouse or family member?	Yes	Yes
47. Is there legislation on sexual harassment in employment?	Yes	No
48. Is there legislation on sexual harassment in education?	Yes	No
49. Are there criminal penalties for sexual harassment in employment?	Yes	No
50. Are there civil remedies for sexual harassment in employment?	Yes	No

Note: See the data notes for more details on the scoring of each indicator.

	SOUTH AFRICA	SOUTH SUDAN
REGION	Sub-Saharan Africa	Sub-Saharan Africa
INCOME GROUP	Upper middle income	Low income
FEMALE POPULATION	28,396,315	6,104,255
FEMALE LABOR FORCE (% OF TOTAL LABOR FORCE)	45%	49%

ACCESSING INSTITUTIONS

	Score: 100	Score: 100
1. Are wives required to obey their husbands?	No	No
Can a woman legally do the following in the same way as a man:		
2. Apply for a passport?	Yes	Yes
3. Apply for a national ID card?	Yes	Yes
4. Travel outside the country?	Yes	Yes
5. Travel outside her home?	Yes	Yes
6. Get a job?	Yes	Yes
7. Sign a contract?	Yes	Yes
8. Register a business?	Yes	Yes
9. Open a bank account?	Yes	Yes
10. Choose where to live?	Yes	Yes
11. Be "head of household"?	N/A	N/A

USING PROPERTY

	Score: 100	Score: 67
12. Who legally administers marital property?	Both must agree	Other
13. Does the law provide for valuation of nonmonetary contributions?	Yes	No
14. Do men and women have equal ownership rights to immovable property?	Yes	..
15. Do sons and daughters have equal inheritance rights?	Yes	Yes
16. Do female and male surviving spouses have equal inheritance rights?	Yes	..

GETTING A JOB

	Score: 85	Score: 20
17. Is there paid leave available to women of at least 14 weeks?	Yes	No
18. Do women receive at least 2/3 of their wages for the first 14 weeks or the duration of the leave if it is shorter?	No	Yes
19. What is the percentage of maternity leave benefits paid by the government?	100%	0%
20. What is the difference between leave reserved for women and men relative to leave reserved for women, as a function of who pays?	1	0
21. Is there paid parental leave?	No	No
22. Does the law mandate equal remuneration for work of equal value?	Yes	No
23. Does the law mandate nondiscrimination based on gender in employment?	Yes	No
24. Is dismissal of pregnant workers prohibited?	Yes	Yes
25. Can parents work flexibly?	No	No
26. Can women work the same night hours as men?	Yes	No
27. Can women work in jobs deemed hazardous, arduous or morally inappropriate in the same way as men?	Yes	No
28. Are women able to work in the same industries as men?	Yes	No
29. Are women able to perform the same tasks at work as men?	Yes	No
30. Are the ages at which men and women can retire with full pension benefits equal?	N/A	N/A
31. Are the ages at which men and women can retire with partial pension benefits equal?	N/A	N/A
32. Are the mandatory retirement ages for men and women equal?	N/A	N/A

PROVIDING INCENTIVES TO WORK

	Score: 40	Score: 40
33. Are mothers guaranteed an equivalent position after maternity leave?	No	No
34. Does the government support or provide childcare services?	Yes	No
35. Are payments for childcare tax deductible?	No	No
36. Is primary education free and compulsory?	No	Yes
37. Are there tax deductions or credits specific to men?	No	No

GOING TO COURT

	Score: 100	Score: 25
38. Does a woman's testimony carry the same evidentiary weight in court as a man's?	Yes	Yes
39. Does the law establish an anti-discrimination commission?	Yes	No
40. Does the law mandate legal aid in civil/family matters?	Yes	No
41. Is there a small claims court/fast-track procedure?	Yes	No

BUILDING CREDIT

	Score: 100	Score: 0
42. Do retailers provide information to credit agencies?	Yes	N/A
43. Do utility companies provide information to credit agencies?	Yes	N/A
44. Is discrimination based on gender prohibited in access to credit?	Yes	No
45. Is discrimination based on marital status prohibited in access to credit?	Yes	No

PROTECTING WOMEN FROM VIOLENCE

	Score: 40	Score: 0
46. Is there legislation specifically addressing domestic violence? If not, are there aggravated penalties for crimes committed against a spouse or family member?	Yes	No
47. Is there legislation on sexual harassment in employment?	Yes	No
48. Is there legislation on sexual harassment in education?	No	No
49. Are there criminal penalties for sexual harassment in employment?	No	No
50. Are there civil remedies for sexual harassment in employment?	No	No

Note: See the data notes for more details on the scoring of each indicator.

	SPAIN	SRI LANKA
REGION	High income: OECD	South Asia
INCOME GROUP	High income	Lower middle income
FEMALE POPULATION	23,675,226	11,000,805
FEMALE LABOR FORCE (% OF TOTAL LABOR FORCE)	46%	34%

ACCESSING INSTITUTIONS

	Score: 100	Score: 100
1. Are wives required to obey their husbands?	No	No

Can a woman legally do the following in the same way as a man:

2. Apply for a passport?	Yes	Yes
3. Apply for a national ID card?	Yes	Yes
4. Travel outside the country?	Yes	Yes
5. Travel outside her home?	Yes	Yes
6. Get a job?	Yes	Yes
7. Sign a contract?	Yes	Yes
8. Register a business?	Yes	Yes
9. Open a bank account?	Yes	Yes
10. Choose where to live?	Yes	Yes
11. Be "head of household"?	N/A	N/A

USING PROPERTY

	Score: 100	Score: 80
12. Who legally administers marital property?	Both must agree	Original owner
13. Does the law provide for valuation of nonmonetary contributions?	Yes	No
14. Do men and women have equal ownership rights to immovable property?	Yes	Yes
15. Do sons and daughters have equal inheritance rights?	Yes	Yes
16. Do female and male surviving spouses have equal inheritance rights?	Yes	Yes

GETTING A JOB

	Score: 93	Score: 38
17. Is there paid leave available to women of at least 14 weeks?	Yes	No
18. Do women receive at least 2/3 of their wages for the first 14 weeks or the duration of the leave if it is shorter?	Yes	Yes
19. What is the percentage of maternity leave benefits paid by the government?	100%	0%
20. What is the difference between leave reserved for women and men relative to leave reserved for women, as a function of who pays?	1	0
21. Is there paid parental leave?	No	No
22. Does the law mandate equal remuneration for work of equal value?	Yes	No
23. Does the law mandate nondiscrimination based on gender in employment?	Yes	No
24. Is dismissal of pregnant workers prohibited?	Yes	Yes
25. Can parents work flexibly?	Yes	No
26. Can women work the same night hours as men?	Yes	No
27. Can women work in jobs deemed hazardous, arduous or morally inappropriate in the same way as men?	Yes	Yes
28. Are women able to work in the same industries as men?	Yes	No
29. Are women able to perform the same tasks at work as men?	Yes	Yes
30. Are the ages at which men and women can retire with full pension benefits equal?	Yes	No
31. Are the ages at which men and women can retire with partial pension benefits equal?	Yes	N/A
32. Are the mandatory retirement ages for men and women equal?	N/A	N/A

PROVIDING INCENTIVES TO WORK

	Score: 100	Score: 40
33. Are mothers guaranteed an equivalent position after maternity leave?	Yes	No
34. Does the government support or provide childcare services?	Yes	No
35. Are payments for childcare tax deductible?	Yes	No
36. Is primary education free and compulsory?	Yes	Yes
37. Are there tax deductions or credits specific to men?	No	No

GOING TO COURT

	Score: 100	Score: 100
38. Does a woman's testimony carry the same evidentiary weight in court as a man's?	Yes	Yes
39. Does the law establish an anti-discrimination commission?	Yes	Yes
40. Does the law mandate legal aid in civil/family matters?	Yes	Yes
41. Is there a small claims court/fast-track procedure?	Yes	Yes

BUILDING CREDIT

	Score: 75	Score: 0
42. Do retailers provide information to credit agencies?	Yes	No
43. Do utility companies provide information to credit agencies?	Yes	No
44. Is discrimination based on gender prohibited in access to credit?	Yes	No
45. Is discrimination based on marital status prohibited in access to credit?	No	No

PROTECTING WOMEN FROM VIOLENCE

	Score: 100	Score: 100
46. Is there legislation specifically addressing domestic violence? If not, are there aggravated penalties for crimes committed against a spouse or family member?	Yes	Yes
47. Is there legislation on sexual harassment in employment?	Yes	Yes
48. Is there legislation on sexual harassment in education?	Yes	Yes
49. Are there criminal penalties for sexual harassment in employment?	Yes	Yes
50. Are there civil remedies for sexual harassment in employment?	Yes	Yes

Note: See the data notes for more details on the scoring of each indicator.

	ST. KITTS AND NEVIS	ST. LUCIA
REGION	Latin America & Caribbean	Latin America & Caribbean
INCOME GROUP	High income	Upper middle income
FEMALE POPULATION	..	90,706
FEMALE LABOR FORCE (% OF TOTAL LABOR FORCE)	..	46%

ACCESSING INSTITUTIONS

	Score: 100	Score: 100
1. Are wives required to obey their husbands?	No	No
Can a woman legally do the following in the same way as a man:		
2. Apply for a passport?	Yes	Yes
3. Apply for a national ID card?	Yes	Yes
4. Travel outside the country?	Yes	Yes
5. Travel outside her home?	Yes	Yes
6. Get a job?	Yes	Yes
7. Sign a contract?	Yes	Yes
8. Register a business?	Yes	Yes
9. Open a bank account?	Yes	Yes
10. Choose where to live?	Yes	Yes
11. Be "head of household"?	N/A	N/A

USING PROPERTY

	Score: 80	Score: 100
12. Who legally administers marital property?	Original owner	Both must agree
13. Does the law provide for valuation of nonmonetary contributions?	No	Yes
14. Do men and women have equal ownership rights to immovable property?	Yes	Yes
15. Do sons and daughters have equal inheritance rights?	Yes	Yes
16. Do female and male surviving spouses have equal inheritance rights?	Yes	Yes

GETTING A JOB

	Score: 71	Score: 86
17. Is there paid leave available to women of at least 14 weeks?	No	No
18. Do women receive at least 2/3 of their wages for the first 14 weeks or the duration of the leave if it is shorter?	No	No
19. What is the percentage of maternity leave benefits paid by the government?	100%	100%
20. What is the difference between leave reserved for women and men relative to leave reserved for women, as a function of who pays?	1	1
21. Is there paid parental leave?	No	No
22. Does the law mandate equal remuneration for work of equal value?	No	Yes
23. Does the law mandate nondiscrimination based on gender in employment?	No	Yes
24. Is dismissal of pregnant workers prohibited?	Yes	Yes
25. Can parents work flexibly?	No	No
26. Can women work the same night hours as men?	Yes	Yes
27. Can women work in jobs deemed hazardous, arduous or morally inappropriate in the same way as men?	Yes	Yes
28. Are women able to work in the same industries as men?	Yes	Yes
29. Are women able to perform the same tasks at work as men?	Yes	Yes
30. Are the ages at which men and women can retire with full pension benefits equal?	Yes	Yes
31. Are the ages at which men and women can retire with partial pension benefits equal?	N/A	Yes
32. Are the mandatory retirement ages for men and women equal?	N/A	N/A

PROVIDING INCENTIVES TO WORK

	Score: 60	Score: 60
33. Are mothers guaranteed an equivalent position after maternity leave?	No	Yes
34. Does the government support or provide childcare services?	Yes	No
35. Are payments for childcare tax deductible?	No	No
36. Is primary education free and compulsory?	Yes	Yes
37. Are there tax deductions or credits specific to men?	No	No

GOING TO COURT

	Score: 50	Score: 75
38. Does a woman's testimony carry the same evidentiary weight in court as a man's?	Yes	Yes
39. Does the law establish an anti-discrimination commission?	No	No
40. Does the law mandate legal aid in civil/family matters?	No	Yes
41. Is there a small claims court/fast-track procedure?	Yes	Yes

BUILDING CREDIT

	Score: 0	Score: 0
42. Do retailers provide information to credit agencies?	N/A	N/A
43. Do utility companies provide information to credit agencies?	N/A	N/A
44. Is discrimination based on gender prohibited in access to credit?	No	No
45. Is discrimination based on marital status prohibited in access to credit?	No	No

PROTECTING WOMEN FROM VIOLENCE

	Score: 20	Score: 80
46. Is there legislation specifically addressing domestic violence? If not, are there aggravated penalties for crimes committed against a spouse or family member?	Yes	Yes
47. Is there legislation on sexual harassment in employment?	No	Yes
48. Is there legislation on sexual harassment in education?	No	No
49. Are there criminal penalties for sexual harassment in employment?	No	Yes
50. Are there civil remedies for sexual harassment in employment?	No	Yes

Note: See the data notes for more details on the scoring of each indicator.

	ST. VINCENT AND THE GRENADINES	SUDAN
REGION	Latin America & Caribbean	Sub-Saharan Africa
INCOME GROUP	Upper middle income	Lower middle income
FEMALE POPULATION	54,334	19,709,905
FEMALE LABOR FORCE (% OF TOTAL LABOR FORCE)	42%	26%

ACCESSING INSTITUTIONS

	Score: 91	Score: 36
1. Are wives required to obey their husbands?	No	Yes
Can a woman legally do the following in the same way as a man:		
2. Apply for a passport?	No	No
3. Apply for a national ID card?	Yes	Yes
4. Travel outside the country?	Yes	No
5. Travel outside her home?	Yes	No
6. Get a job?	Yes	No
7. Sign a contract?	Yes	Yes
8. Register a business?	Yes	Yes
9. Open a bank account?	Yes	Yes
10. Choose where to live?	Yes	No
11. Be "head of household"?	N/A	No

USING PROPERTY

	Score: 100	Score: 40
12. Who legally administers marital property?	Original owner	Original owner
13. Does the law provide for valuation of nonmonetary contributions?	Yes	No
14. Do men and women have equal ownership rights to immovable property?	Yes	Yes
15. Do sons and daughters have equal inheritance rights?	Yes	No
16. Do female and male surviving spouses have equal inheritance rights?	Yes	No

GETTING A JOB

	Score: 63	Score: 35
17. Is there paid leave available to women of at least 14 weeks?	No	No
18. Do women receive at least 2/3 of their wages for the first 14 weeks or the duration of the leave if it is shorter?	Yes	Yes
19. What is the percentage of maternity leave benefits paid by the government?	75%	0%
20. What is the difference between leave reserved for women and men relative to leave reserved for women, as a function of who pays?	0.75	0
21. Is there paid parental leave?	No	No
22. Does the law mandate equal remuneration for work of equal value?	No	No
23. Does the law mandate nondiscrimination based on gender in employment?	No	No
24. Is dismissal of pregnant workers prohibited?	Yes	Yes
25. Can parents work flexibly?	No	No
26. Can women work the same night hours as men?	Yes	No
27. Can women work in jobs deemed hazardous, arduous or morally inappropriate in the same way as men?	Yes	No
28. Are women able to work in the same industries as men?	No	No
29. Are women able to perform the same tasks at work as men?	Yes	No
30. Are the ages at which men and women can retire with full pension benefits equal?	Yes	Yes
31. Are the ages at which men and women can retire with partial pension benefits equal?	Yes	Yes
32. Are the mandatory retirement ages for men and women equal?	N/A	Yes

PROVIDING INCENTIVES TO WORK

	Score: 60	Score: 60
33. Are mothers guaranteed an equivalent position after maternity leave?	No	No
34. Does the government support or provide childcare services?	Yes	Yes
35. Are payments for childcare tax deductible?	No	No
36. Is primary education free and compulsory?	Yes	Yes
37. Are there tax deductions or credits specific to men?	No	No

GOING TO COURT

	Score: 50	Score: 50
38. Does a woman's testimony carry the same evidentiary weight in court as a man's?	Yes	No
39. Does the law establish an anti-discrimination commission?	No	Yes
40. Does the law mandate legal aid in civil/family matters?	No	Yes
41. Is there a small claims court/fast-track procedure?	Yes	No

BUILDING CREDIT

	Score: 0	Score: 0
42. Do retailers provide information to credit agencies?	N/A	N/A
43. Do utility companies provide information to credit agencies?	N/A	N/A
44. Is discrimination based on gender prohibited in access to credit?	No	No
45. Is discrimination based on marital status prohibited in access to credit?	No	No

PROTECTING WOMEN FROM VIOLENCE

	Score: 20	Score: 0
46. Is there legislation specifically addressing domestic violence? If not, are there aggravated penalties for crimes committed against a spouse or family member?	Yes	No
47. Is there legislation on sexual harassment in employment?	No	No
48. Is there legislation on sexual harassment in education?	No	No
49. Are there criminal penalties for sexual harassment in employment?	No	No
50. Are there civil remedies for sexual harassment in employment?	No	No

Note: See the data notes for more details on the scoring of each indicator.

	SURINAME	SWAZILAND
REGION	Latin America & Caribbean	Sub-Saharan Africa
INCOME GROUP	Upper middle income	Lower middle income
FEMALE POPULATION	278,688	678,197
FEMALE LABOR FORCE (% OF TOTAL LABOR FORCE)	39%	41%

ACCESSING INSTITUTIONS

	Score: 91	Score: 100
1. Are wives required to obey their husbands?	No	No
Can a woman legally do the following in the same way as a man:		
2. Apply for a passport?	Yes	Yes
3. Apply for a national ID card?	Yes	Yes
4. Travel outside the country?	Yes	Yes
5. Travel outside her home?	Yes	Yes
6. Get a job?	Yes	Yes
7. Sign a contract?	Yes	Yes
8. Register a business?	No	Yes
9. Open a bank account?	Yes	Yes
10. Choose where to live?	Yes	Yes
11. Be "head of household"?	N/A	N/A

USING PROPERTY

	Score: 100	Score: 75
12. Who legally administers marital property?	Both must agree	Both must agree
13. Does the law provide for valuation of nonmonetary contributions?	Yes	Yes
14. Do men and women have equal ownership rights to immovable property?	Yes	Yes
15. Do sons and daughters have equal inheritance rights?	Yes	No
16. Do female and male surviving spouses have equal inheritance rights?	Yes	..

GETTING A JOB

	Score: 42	Score: 51
17. Is there paid leave available to women of at least 14 weeks?	No	No
18. Do women receive at least 2/3 of their wages for the first 14 weeks or the duration of the leave if it is shorter?	No	Yes
19. What is the percentage of maternity leave benefits paid by the government?	N/A	0%
20. What is the difference between leave reserved for women and men relative to leave reserved for women, as a function of who pays?	N/A	0
21. Is there paid parental leave?	No	No
22. Does the law mandate equal remuneration for work of equal value?	No	No
23. Does the law mandate nondiscrimination based on gender in employment?	No	Yes
24. Is dismissal of pregnant workers prohibited?	No	Yes
25. Can parents work flexibly?	No	No
26. Can women work the same night hours as men?	Yes	Yes
27. Can women work in jobs deemed hazardous, arduous or morally inappropriate in the same way as men?	Yes	Yes
28. Are women able to work in the same industries as men?	Yes	No
29. Are women able to perform the same tasks at work as men?	Yes	Yes
30. Are the ages at which men and women can retire with full pension benefits equal?	Yes	Yes
31. Are the ages at which men and women can retire with partial pension benefits equal?	N/A	N/A
32. Are the mandatory retirement ages for men and women equal?	N/A	N/A

PROVIDING INCENTIVES TO WORK

	Score: 60	Score: 40
33. Are mothers guaranteed an equivalent position after maternity leave?	No	Yes
34. Does the government support or provide childcare services?	Yes	No
35. Are payments for childcare tax deductible?	No	No
36. Is primary education free and compulsory?	Yes	No
37. Are there tax deductions or credits specific to men?	No	No

GOING TO COURT

	Score: 50	Score: 75
38. Does a woman's testimony carry the same evidentiary weight in court as a man's?	Yes	Yes
39. Does the law establish an anti-discrimination commission?	No	Yes
40. Does the law mandate legal aid in civil/family matters?	Yes	No
41. Is there a small claims court/fast-track procedure?	No	Yes

BUILDING CREDIT

	Score: 0	Score: 50
42. Do retailers provide information to credit agencies?	N/A	Yes
43. Do utility companies provide information to credit agencies?	N/A	Yes
44. Is discrimination based on gender prohibited in access to credit?	No	No
45. Is discrimination based on marital status prohibited in access to credit?	No	No

PROTECTING WOMEN FROM VIOLENCE

	Score: 20	Score: 0
46. Is there legislation specifically addressing domestic violence? If not, are there aggravated penalties for crimes committed against a spouse or family member?	Yes	No
47. Is there legislation on sexual harassment in employment?	No	No
48. Is there legislation on sexual harassment in education?	No	No
49. Are there criminal penalties for sexual harassment in employment?	No	No
50. Are there civil remedies for sexual harassment in employment?	No	No

Note: See the data notes for more details on the scoring of each indicator.

	SWEDEN	SWITZERLAND
REGION	High income: OECD	High income: OECD
INCOME GROUP	High income	High income
FEMALE POPULATION	4,952,147	4,223,477
FEMALE LABOR FORCE (% OF TOTAL LABOR FORCE)	48%	47%

ACCESSING INSTITUTIONS

	Score: 100	Score: 100
1. Are wives required to obey their husbands?	No	No
Can a woman legally do the following in the same way as a man:		
2. Apply for a passport?	Yes	Yes
3. Apply for a national ID card?	Yes	Yes
4. Travel outside the country?	Yes	Yes
5. Travel outside her home?	Yes	Yes
6. Get a job?	Yes	Yes
7. Sign a contract?	Yes	Yes
8. Register a business?	Yes	Yes
9. Open a bank account?	Yes	Yes
10. Choose where to live?	Yes	Yes
11. Be "head of household"?	N/A	N/A

USING PROPERTY

	Score: 100	Score: 100
12. Who legally administers marital property?	Original owner	Original owner
13. Does the law provide for valuation of nonmonetary contributions?	Yes	Yes
14. Do men and women have equal ownership rights to immovable property?	Yes	Yes
15. Do sons and daughters have equal inheritance rights?	Yes	Yes
16. Do female and male surviving spouses have equal inheritance rights?	Yes	Yes

GETTING A JOB

	Score: 100	Score: 85
17. Is there paid leave available to women of at least 14 weeks?	Yes	Yes
18. Do women receive at least 2/3 of their wages for the first 14 weeks or the duration of the leave if it is shorter?	Yes	Yes
19. What is the percentage of maternity leave benefits paid by the government?	100%	100%
20. What is the difference between leave reserved for women and men relative to leave reserved for women, as a function of who pays?	1	1
21. Is there paid parental leave?	Yes	No
22. Does the law mandate equal remuneration for work of equal value?	Yes	Yes
23. Does the law mandate nondiscrimination based on gender in employment?	Yes	Yes
24. Is dismissal of pregnant workers prohibited?	Yes	Yes
25. Can parents work flexibly?	Yes	No
26. Can women work the same night hours as men?	Yes	Yes
27. Can women work in jobs deemed hazardous, arduous or morally inappropriate in the same way as men?	Yes	Yes
28. Are women able to work in the same industries as men?	Yes	Yes
29. Are women able to perform the same tasks at work as men?	Yes	Yes
30. Are the ages at which men and women can retire with full pension benefits equal?	Yes	No
31. Are the ages at which men and women can retire with partial pension benefits equal?	Yes	No
32. Are the mandatory retirement ages for men and women equal?	Yes	No

PROVIDING INCENTIVES TO WORK

	Score: 80	Score: 80
33. Are mothers guaranteed an equivalent position after maternity leave?	Yes	No
34. Does the government support or provide childcare services?	Yes	Yes
35. Are payments for childcare tax deductible?	No	Yes
36. Is primary education free and compulsory?	Yes	Yes
37. Are there tax deductions or credits specific to men?	No	No

GOING TO COURT

	Score: 100	Score: 75
38. Does a woman's testimony carry the same evidentiary weight in court as a man's?	Yes	Yes
39. Does the law establish an anti-discrimination commission?	Yes	No
40. Does the law mandate legal aid in civil/family matters?	Yes	Yes
41. Is there a small claims court/fast-track procedure?	Yes	Yes

BUILDING CREDIT

	Score: 25	Score: 25
42. Do retailers provide information to credit agencies?	No	Yes
43. Do utility companies provide information to credit agencies?	No	No
44. Is discrimination based on gender prohibited in access to credit?	Yes	No
45. Is discrimination based on marital status prohibited in access to credit?	No	No

PROTECTING WOMEN FROM VIOLENCE

	Score: 80	Score: 60
46. Is there legislation specifically addressing domestic violence? If not, are there aggravated penalties for crimes committed against a spouse or family member?	Yes	Yes
47. Is there legislation on sexual harassment in employment?	Yes	Yes
48. Is there legislation on sexual harassment in education?	Yes	No
49. Are there criminal penalties for sexual harassment in employment?	No	No
50. Are there civil remedies for sexual harassment in employment?	Yes	Yes

Note: See the data notes for more details on the scoring of each indicator.

	SYRIAN ARAB REPUBLIC	TAIWAN, CHINA
REGION	Middle East & North Africa	East Asia & Pacific
INCOME GROUP	Lower middle income	High income
FEMALE POPULATION	9,110,598	11,820,546
FEMALE LABOR FORCE (% OF TOTAL LABOR FORCE)	14%	..

ACCESSING INSTITUTIONS

	Score: 64	Score: 100
1. Are wives required to obey their husbands?	No	No
Can a woman legally do the following in the same way as a man:		
2. Apply for a passport?	Yes	Yes
3. Apply for a national ID card?	Yes	Yes
4. Travel outside the country?	No	Yes
5. Travel outside her home?	No	Yes
6. Get a job?	No	Yes
7. Sign a contract?	Yes	Yes
8. Register a business?	Yes	Yes
9. Open a bank account?	Yes	Yes
10. Choose where to live?	No	Yes
11. Be "head of household"?	Yes	N/A

USING PROPERTY

	Score: 40	Score: 100
12. Who legally administers marital property?	Original owner	Original owner
13. Does the law provide for valuation of nonmonetary contributions?	No	Yes
14. Do men and women have equal ownership rights to immovable property?	Yes	Yes
15. Do sons and daughters have equal inheritance rights?	No	Yes
16. Do female and male surviving spouses have equal inheritance rights?	No	Yes

GETTING A JOB

	Score: 33	Score: 88
17. Is there paid leave available to women of at least 14 weeks?	Yes	Yes
18. Do women receive at least 2/3 of their wages for the first 14 weeks or the duration of the leave if it is shorter?	Yes	Yes
19. What is the percentage of maternity leave benefits paid by the government?	0%	0%
20. What is the difference between leave reserved for women and men relative to leave reserved for women, as a function of who pays?	0	0.09
21. Is there paid parental leave?	No	Yes
22. Does the law mandate equal remuneration for work of equal value?	No	Yes
23. Does the law mandate nondiscrimination based on gender in employment?	Yes	Yes
24. Is dismissal of pregnant workers prohibited?	No	Yes
25. Can parents work flexibly?	No	Yes
26. Can women work the same night hours as men?	No	Yes
27. Can women work in jobs deemed hazardous, arduous or morally inappropriate in the same way as men?	No	Yes
28. Are women able to work in the same industries as men?	No	Yes
29. Are women able to perform the same tasks at work as men?	No	Yes
30. Are the ages at which men and women can retire with full pension benefits equal?	Yes	Yes
31. Are the ages at which men and women can retire with partial pension benefits equal?	N/A	Yes
32. Are the mandatory retirement ages for men and women equal?	Yes	Yes

PROVIDING INCENTIVES TO WORK

	Score: 40	Score: 60
33. Are mothers guaranteed an equivalent position after maternity leave?	No	No
34. Does the government support or provide childcare services?	No	Yes
35. Are payments for childcare tax deductible?	No	No
36. Is primary education free and compulsory?	Yes	Yes
37. Are there tax deductions or credits specific to men?	No	No

GOING TO COURT

	Score: 25	Score: 75
38. Does a woman's testimony carry the same evidentiary weight in court as a man's?	No	Yes
39. Does the law establish an anti-discrimination commission?	No	No
40. Does the law mandate legal aid in civil/family matters?	No	Yes
41. Is there a small claims court/fast-track procedure?	Yes	Yes

BUILDING CREDIT

	Score: 0	Score: 50
42. Do retailers provide information to credit agencies?	No	Yes
43. Do utility companies provide information to credit agencies?	No	Yes
44. Is discrimination based on gender prohibited in access to credit?	No	No
45. Is discrimination based on marital status prohibited in access to credit?	No	No

PROTECTING WOMEN FROM VIOLENCE

	Score: 0	Score: 100
46. Is there legislation specifically addressing domestic violence? If not, are there aggravated penalties for crimes committed against a spouse or family member?	No	Yes
47. Is there legislation on sexual harassment in employment?	No	Yes
48. Is there legislation on sexual harassment in education?	No	Yes
49. Are there criminal penalties for sexual harassment in employment?	No	Yes
50. Are there civil remedies for sexual harassment in employment?	No	Yes

Note: See the data notes for more details on the scoring of each indicator.

	TAJIKISTAN	TANZANIA
REGION	Europe & Central Asia	Sub-Saharan Africa
INCOME GROUP	Lower middle income	Low income
FEMALE POPULATION	4,311,855	27,945,843
FEMALE LABOR FORCE (% OF TOTAL LABOR FORCE)	39%	49%

ACCESSING INSTITUTIONS

	Score: 100	Score: 100
1. Are wives required to obey their husbands?	No	No
Can a woman legally do the following in the same way as a man:		
2. Apply for a passport?	Yes	Yes
3. Apply for a national ID card?	Yes	Yes
4. Travel outside the country?	Yes	Yes
5. Travel outside her home?	Yes	Yes
6. Get a job?	Yes	Yes
7. Sign a contract?	Yes	Yes
8. Register a business?	Yes	Yes
9. Open a bank account?	Yes	Yes
10. Choose where to live?	Yes	Yes
11. Be *head of household*?	N/A	Yes

USING PROPERTY

	Score: 100	Score: 60
12. Who legally administers marital property?	Both must agree	Original owner
13. Does the law provide for valuation of nonmonetary contributions?	Yes	Yes
14. Do men and women have equal ownership rights to immovable property?	Yes	Yes
15. Do sons and daughters have equal inheritance rights?	Yes	No
16. Do female and male surviving spouses have equal inheritance rights?	Yes	No

GETTING A JOB

	Score: 75	Score: 86
17. Is there paid leave available to women of at least 14 weeks?	Yes	No
18. Do women receive at least 2/3 of their wages for the first 14 weeks or the duration of the leave if it is shorter?	Yes	Yes
19. What is the percentage of maternity leave benefits paid by the government?	100%	100%
20. What is the difference between leave reserved for women and men relative to leave reserved for women, as a function of who pays?	1	1
21. Is there paid parental leave?	Yes	No
22. Does the law mandate equal remuneration for work of equal value?	Yes	Yes
23. Does the law mandate nondiscrimination based on gender in employment?	Yes	Yes
24. Is dismissal of pregnant workers prohibited?	Yes	Yes
25. Can parents work flexibly?	Yes	No
26. Can women work the same night hours as men?	Yes	Yes
27. Can women work in jobs deemed hazardous, arduous or morally inappropriate in the same way as men?	No	Yes
28. Are women able to work in the same industries as men?	No	Yes
29. Are women able to perform the same tasks at work as men?	No	Yes
30. Are the ages at which men and women can retire with full pension benefits equal?	No	Yes
31. Are the ages at which men and women can retire with partial pension benefits equal?	N/A	Yes
32. Are the mandatory retirement ages for men and women equal?	N/A	N/A

PROVIDING INCENTIVES TO WORK

	Score: 80	Score: 80
33. Are mothers guaranteed an equivalent position after maternity leave?	Yes	Yes
34. Does the government support or provide childcare services?	Yes	Yes
35. Are payments for childcare tax deductible?	No	No
36. Is primary education free and compulsory?	Yes	Yes
37. Are there tax deductions or credits specific to men?	No	No

GOING TO COURT

	Score: 25	Score: 50
38. Does a woman's testimony carry the same evidentiary weight in court as a man's?	Yes	Yes
39. Does the law establish an anti-discrimination commission?	No	No
40. Does the law mandate legal aid in civil/family matters?	No	Yes
41. Is there a small claims court/fast-track procedure?	No	No

BUILDING CREDIT

	Score: 25	Score: 25
42. Do retailers provide information to credit agencies?	No	Yes
43. Do utility companies provide information to credit agencies?	No	No
44. Is discrimination based on gender prohibited in access to credit?	Yes	No
45. Is discrimination based on marital status prohibited in access to credit?	No	No

PROTECTING WOMEN FROM VIOLENCE

	Score: 20	Score: 60
46. Is there legislation specifically addressing domestic violence? If not, are there aggravated penalties for crimes committed against a spouse or family member?	Yes	No
47. Is there legislation on sexual harassment in employment?	No	Yes
48. Is there legislation on sexual harassment in education?	No	No
49. Are there criminal penalties for sexual harassment in employment?	No	Yes
50. Are there civil remedies for sexual harassment in employment?	No	Yes

Note: See the data notes for more details on the scoring of each indicator.

	THAILAND	TIMOR-LESTE
REGION	East Asia & Pacific	East Asia & Pacific
INCOME GROUP	Upper middle income	Lower middle income
FEMALE POPULATION	34,938,030	624,533
FEMALE LABOR FORCE (% OF TOTAL LABOR FORCE)	46%	32%

ACCESSING INSTITUTIONS

	Score: 100	Score: 100
1. Are wives required to obey their husbands?	No	No
Can a woman legally do the following in the same way as a man:		
2. Apply for a passport?	Yes	Yes
3. Apply for a national ID card?	Yes	Yes
4. Travel outside the country?	Yes	Yes
5. Travel outside her home?	Yes	Yes
6. Get a job?	Yes	Yes
7. Sign a contract?	Yes	Yes
8. Register a business?	Yes	Yes
9. Open a bank account?	Yes	Yes
10. Choose where to live?	Yes	Yes
11. Be "head of household"?	N/A	Yes

USING PROPERTY

	Score: 100	Score: 100
12. Who legally administers marital property?	Both must agree	Both must agree
13. Does the law provide for valuation of nonmonetary contributions?	Yes	Yes
14. Do men and women have equal ownership rights to immovable property?	Yes	Yes
15. Do sons and daughters have equal inheritance rights?	Yes	Yes
16. Do female and male surviving spouses have equal inheritance rights?	Yes	Yes

GETTING A JOB

	Score: 57	Score: 76
17. Is there paid leave available to women of at least 14 weeks?	No	No
18. Do women receive at least 2/3 of their wages for the first 14 weeks or the duration of the leave if it is shorter?	Yes	Yes
19. What is the percentage of maternity leave benefits paid by the government?	50%	100%
20. What is the difference between leave reserved for women and men relative to leave reserved for women, as a function of who pays?	0.5	1
21. Is there paid parental leave?	No	No
22. Does the law mandate equal remuneration for work of equal value?	No	No
23. Does the law mandate nondiscrimination based on gender in employment?	Yes	Yes
24. Is dismissal of pregnant workers prohibited?	Yes	Yes
25. Can parents work flexibly?	No	No
26. Can women work the same night hours as men?	Yes	Yes
27. Can women work in jobs deemed hazardous, arduous or morally inappropriate in the same way as men?	Yes	Yes
28. Are women able to work in the same industries as men?	No	Yes
29. Are women able to perform the same tasks at work as men?	No	Yes
30. Are the ages at which men and women can retire with full pension benefits equal?	Yes	N/A
31. Are the ages at which men and women can retire with partial pension benefits equal?	N/A	N/A
32. Are the mandatory retirement ages for men and women equal?	N/A	N/A

PROVIDING INCENTIVES TO WORK

	Score: 80	Score: 80
33. Are mothers guaranteed an equivalent position after maternity leave?	No	Yes
34. Does the government support or provide childcare services?	Yes	Yes
35. Are payments for childcare tax deductible?	Yes	No
36. Is primary education free and compulsory?	Yes	Yes
37. Are there tax deductions or credits specific to men?	No	No

GOING TO COURT

	Score: 75	Score: 75
38. Does a woman's testimony carry the same evidentiary weight in court as a man's?	Yes	Yes
39. Does the law establish an anti-discrimination commission?	Yes	Yes
40. Does the law mandate legal aid in civil/family matters?	No	Yes
41. Is there a small claims court/fast-track procedure?	Yes	No

BUILDING CREDIT

	Score: 0	Score: 0
42. Do retailers provide information to credit agencies?	No	No
43. Do utility companies provide information to credit agencies?	No	No
44. Is discrimination based on gender prohibited in access to credit?	No	No
45. Is discrimination based on marital status prohibited in access to credit?	No	No

PROTECTING WOMEN FROM VIOLENCE

	Score: 60	Score: 40
46. Is there legislation specifically addressing domestic violence? If not, are there aggravated penalties for crimes committed against a spouse or family member?	Yes	Yes
47. Is there legislation on sexual harassment in employment?	Yes	Yes
48. Is there legislation on sexual harassment in education?	No	No
49. Are there criminal penalties for sexual harassment in employment?	Yes	No
50. Are there civil remedies for sexual harassment in employment?	No	No

Note: See the data notes for more details on the scoring of each indicator.

	TOGO	TONGA
REGION	Sub-Saharan Africa	East Asia & Pacific
INCOME GROUP	Low income	Upper middle income
FEMALE POPULATION	3,845,982	53,391
FEMALE LABOR FORCE (% OF TOTAL LABOR FORCE)	49%	38%

ACCESSING INSTITUTIONS

	Score: 100	Score: 100
1. Are wives required to obey their husbands?	No	No
Can a woman legally do the following in the same way as a man:		
2. Apply for a passport?	Yes	Yes
3. Apply for a national ID card?	Yes	Yes
4. Travel outside the country?	Yes	Yes
5. Travel outside her home?	Yes	Yes
6. Get a job?	Yes	Yes
7. Sign a contract?	Yes	Yes
8. Register a business?	Yes	Yes
9. Open a bank account?	Yes	Yes
10. Choose where to live?	Yes	Yes
11. Be *head of household*?	N/A	N/A

USING PROPERTY

	Score: 80	Score: 20
12. Who legally administers marital property?	Original owner	Original owner
13. Does the law provide for valuation of nonmonetary contributions?	No	No
14. Do men and women have equal ownership rights to immovable property?	Yes	No
15. Do sons and daughters have equal inheritance rights?	Yes	No
16. Do female and male surviving spouses have equal inheritance rights?	Yes	No

GETTING A JOB

	Score: 80	Score: 42
17. Is there paid leave available to women of at least 14 weeks?	Yes	No
18. Do women receive at least 2/3 of their wages for the first 14 weeks or the duration of the leave if it is shorter?	Yes	No
19. What is the percentage of maternity leave benefits paid by the government?	50%	N/A
20. What is the difference between leave reserved for women and men relative to leave reserved for women, as a function of who pays?	0.51	N/A
21. Is there paid parental leave?	No	No
22. Does the law mandate equal remuneration for work of equal value?	Yes	No
23. Does the law mandate nondiscrimination based on gender in employment?	Yes	No
24. Is dismissal of pregnant workers prohibited?	Yes	No
25. Can parents work flexibly?	No	No
26. Can women work the same night hours as men?	Yes	Yes
27. Can women work in jobs deemed hazardous, arduous or morally inappropriate in the same way as men?	Yes	Yes
28. Are women able to work in the same industries as men?	Yes	Yes
29. Are women able to perform the same tasks at work as men?	Yes	Yes
30. Are the ages at which men and women can retire with full pension benefits equal?	Yes	Yes
31. Are the ages at which men and women can retire with partial pension benefits equal?	Yes	N/A
32. Are the mandatory retirement ages for men and women equal?	N/A	N/A

PROVIDING INCENTIVES TO WORK

	Score: 40	Score: 40
33. Are mothers guaranteed an equivalent position after maternity leave?	Yes	N/A
34. Does the government support or provide childcare services?	No	Yes
35. Are payments for childcare tax deductible?	No	No
36. Is primary education free and compulsory?	Yes	No
37. Are there tax deductions or credits specific to men?	Yes	No

GOING TO COURT

	Score: 50	Score: 50
38. Does a woman's testimony carry the same evidentiary weight in court as a man's?	Yes	Yes
39. Does the law establish an anti-discrimination commission?	No	No
40. Does the law mandate legal aid in civil/family matters?	Yes	No
41. Is there a small claims court/fast-track procedure?	No	Yes

BUILDING CREDIT

	Score: 0	Score: 0
42. Do retailers provide information to credit agencies?	N/A	No
43. Do utility companies provide information to credit agencies?	N/A	No
44. Is discrimination based on gender prohibited in access to credit?	No	No
45. Is discrimination based on marital status prohibited in access to credit?	No	No

PROTECTING WOMEN FROM VIOLENCE

	Score: 60	Score: 20
46. Is there legislation specifically addressing domestic violence? If not, are there aggravated penalties for crimes committed against a spouse or family member?	No	Yes
47. Is there legislation on sexual harassment in employment?	Yes	No
48. Is there legislation on sexual harassment in education?	No	No
49. Are there criminal penalties for sexual harassment in employment?	Yes	No
50. Are there civil remedies for sexual harassment in employment?	Yes	No

Note: See the data notes for more details on the scoring of each indicator.

	TRINIDAD AND TOBAGO	TUNISIA
REGION	Latin America & Caribbean	Middle East & North Africa
INCOME GROUP	High income	Lower middle income
FEMALE POPULATION	691,993	5,769,754
FEMALE LABOR FORCE (% OF TOTAL LABOR FORCE)	42%	26%

ACCESSING INSTITUTIONS

	Score: 91	Score: 91
1. Are wives required to obey their husbands?	No	No
Can a woman legally do the following in the same way as a man:		
2. Apply for a passport?	No	Yes
3. Apply for a national ID card?	Yes	Yes
4. Travel outside the country?	Yes	Yes
5. Travel outside her home?	Yes	Yes
6. Get a job?	Yes	Yes
7. Sign a contract?	Yes	Yes
8. Register a business?	Yes	Yes
9. Open a bank account?	Yes	Yes
10. Choose where to live?	Yes	Yes
11. Be "head of household"?	N/A	No

USING PROPERTY

	Score: 100	Score: 40
12. Who legally administers marital property?	Original owner	Original owner
13. Does the law provide for valuation of nonmonetary contributions?	Yes	No
14. Do men and women have equal ownership rights to immovable property?	Yes	Yes
15. Do sons and daughters have equal inheritance rights?	Yes	No
16. Do female and male surviving spouses have equal inheritance rights?	Yes	No

GETTING A JOB

	Score: 64	Score: 52
17. Is there paid leave available to women of at least 14 weeks?	Yes	No
18. Do women receive at least 2/3 of their wages for the first 14 weeks or the duration of the leave if it is shorter?	Yes	Yes
19. What is the percentage of maternity leave benefits paid by the government?	33%	100%
20. What is the difference between leave reserved for women and men relative to leave reserved for women, as a function of who pays?	0.33	1
21. Is there paid parental leave?	No	No
22. Does the law mandate equal remuneration for work of equal value?	No	No
23. Does the law mandate nondiscrimination based on gender in employment?	Yes	Yes
24. Is dismissal of pregnant workers prohibited?	No	Yes
25. Can parents work flexibly?	No	No
26. Can women work the same night hours as men?	Yes	No
27. Can women work in jobs deemed hazardous, arduous or morally inappropriate in the same way as men?	Yes	Yes
28. Are women able to work in the same industries as men?	Yes	No
29. Are women able to perform the same tasks at work as men?	Yes	No
30. Are the ages at which men and women can retire with full pension benefits equal?	Yes	Yes
31. Are the ages at which men and women can retire with partial pension benefits equal?	Yes	N/A
32. Are the mandatory retirement ages for men and women equal?	N/A	N/A

PROVIDING INCENTIVES TO WORK

	Score: 80	Score: 40
33. Are mothers guaranteed an equivalent position after maternity leave?	Yes	No
34. Does the government support or provide childcare services?	Yes	Yes
35. Are payments for childcare tax deductible?	No	No
36. Is primary education free and compulsory?	Yes	Yes
37. Are there tax deductions or credits specific to men?	No	Yes

GOING TO COURT

	Score: 100	Score: 75
38. Does a woman's testimony carry the same evidentiary weight in court as a man's?	Yes	Yes
39. Does the law establish an anti-discrimination commission?	Yes	No
40. Does the law mandate legal aid in civil/family matters?	Yes	Yes
41. Is there a small claims court/fast-track procedure?	Yes	Yes

BUILDING CREDIT

	Score: 75	Score: 25
42. Do retailers provide information to credit agencies?	No	No
43. Do utility companies provide information to credit agencies?	Yes	Yes
44. Is discrimination based on gender prohibited in access to credit?	Yes	No
45. Is discrimination based on marital status prohibited in access to credit?	Yes	No

PROTECTING WOMEN FROM VIOLENCE

	Score: 20	Score: 10
46. Is there legislation specifically addressing domestic violence? If not, are there aggravated penalties for crimes committed against a spouse or family member?	Yes	No, but aggravated penalties exist
47. Is there legislation on sexual harassment in employment?	No	No
48. Is there legislation on sexual harassment in education?	No	No
49. Are there criminal penalties for sexual harassment in employment?	No	No
50. Are there civil remedies for sexual harassment in employment?	No	No

Note: See the data notes for more details on the scoring of each indicator.

	TURKEY	UGANDA
REGION	Europe & Central Asia	Sub-Saharan Africa
INCOME GROUP	Upper middle income	Low income
FEMALE POPULATION	40,420,720	20,752,889
FEMALE LABOR FORCE (% OF TOTAL LABOR FORCE)	32%	48%

ACCESSING INSTITUTIONS

	Score: 100	Score: 91
1. Are wives required to obey their husbands?	No	No
Can a woman legally do the following in the same way as a man:		
2. Apply for a passport?	Yes	No
3. Apply for a national ID card?	Yes	Yes
4. Travel outside the country?	Yes	Yes
5. Travel outside her home?	Yes	Yes
6. Get a job?	Yes	Yes
7. Sign a contract?	Yes	Yes
8. Register a business?	Yes	Yes
9. Open a bank account?	Yes	Yes
10. Choose where to live?	Yes	Yes
11. Be *head of household*?	N/A	N/A

USING PROPERTY

	Score: 100	Score: 40
12. Who legally administers marital property?	Both must agree	Original owner
13. Does the law provide for valuation of nonmonetary contributions?	Yes	No
14. Do men and women have equal ownership rights to immovable property?	Yes	Yes
15. Do sons and daughters have equal inheritance rights?	Yes	No
16. Do female and male surviving spouses have equal inheritance rights?	Yes	No

GETTING A JOB

	Score: 70	Score: 73
17. Is there paid leave available to women of at least 14 weeks?	Yes	No
18. Do women receive at least 2/3 of their wages for the first 14 weeks or the duration of the leave if it is shorter?	Yes	Yes
19. What is the percentage of maternity leave benefits paid by the government?	100%	0%
20. What is the difference between leave reserved for women and men relative to leave reserved for women, as a function of who pays?	1	0.05
21. Is there paid parental leave?	No	No
22. Does the law mandate equal remuneration for work of equal value?	Yes	Yes
23. Does the law mandate nondiscrimination based on gender in employment?	Yes	Yes
24. Is dismissal of pregnant workers prohibited?	Yes	Yes
25. Can parents work flexibly?	Yes	No
26. Can women work the same night hours as men?	No	Yes
27. Can women work in jobs deemed hazardous, arduous or morally inappropriate in the same way as men?	Yes	Yes
28. Are women able to work in the same industries as men?	No	Yes
29. Are women able to perform the same tasks at work as men?	No	Yes
30. Are the ages at which men and women can retire with full pension benefits equal?	No	Yes
31. Are the ages at which men and women can retire with partial pension benefits equal?	N/A	Yes
32. Are the mandatory retirement ages for men and women equal?	N/A	N/A

PROVIDING INCENTIVES TO WORK

	Score: 60	Score: 60
33. Are mothers guaranteed an equivalent position after maternity leave?	No	Yes
34. Does the government support or provide childcare services?	Yes	No
35. Are payments for childcare tax deductible?	No	No
36. Is primary education free and compulsory?	Yes	Yes
37. Are there tax deductions or credits specific to men?	No	No

GOING TO COURT

	Score: 75	Score: 100
38. Does a woman's testimony carry the same evidentiary weight in court as a man's?	Yes	Yes
39. Does the law establish an anti-discrimination commission?	Yes	Yes
40. Does the law mandate legal aid in civil/family matters?	Yes	Yes
41. Is there a small claims court/fast-track procedure?	No	Yes

BUILDING CREDIT

	Score: 0	Score: 0
42. Do retailers provide information to credit agencies?	No	No
43. Do utility companies provide information to credit agencies?	No	No
44. Is discrimination based on gender prohibited in access to credit?	No	No
45. Is discrimination based on marital status prohibited in access to credit?	No	No

PROTECTING WOMEN FROM VIOLENCE

	Score: 100	Score: 80
46. Is there legislation specifically addressing domestic violence? If not, are there aggravated penalties for crimes committed against a spouse or family member?	Yes	Yes
47. Is there legislation on sexual harassment in employment?	Yes	Yes
48. Is there legislation on sexual harassment in education?	Yes	No
49. Are there criminal penalties for sexual harassment in employment?	Yes	Yes
50. Are there civil remedies for sexual harassment in employment?	Yes	Yes

Note: See the data notes for more details on the scoring of each indicator.

	UKRAINE	UNITED ARAB EMIRATES
REGION	Europe & Central Asia	Middle East & North Africa
INCOME GROUP	Lower middle income	High income
FEMALE POPULATION	24,153,211	2,513,544
FEMALE LABOR FORCE (% OF TOTAL LABOR FORCE)	47%	12%

ACCESSING INSTITUTIONS

	Score: 100	Score: 45
1. Are wives required to obey their husbands?	No	Yes
Can a woman legally do the following in the same way as a man:		
2. Apply for a passport?	Yes	No
3. Apply for a national ID card?	Yes	Yes
4. Travel outside the country?	Yes	Yes
5. Travel outside her home?	Yes	No
6. Get a job?	Yes	No
7. Sign a contract?	Yes	Yes
8. Register a business?	Yes	Yes
9. Open a bank account?	Yes	Yes
10. Choose where to live?	Yes	No
11. Be "head of household"?	N/A	No

USING PROPERTY

	Score: 100	Score: 40
12. Who legally administers marital property?	Both must agree	Original owner
13. Does the law provide for valuation of nonmonetary contributions?	Yes	No
14. Do men and women have equal ownership rights to immovable property?	Yes	Yes
15. Do sons and daughters have equal inheritance rights?	Yes	No
16. Do female and male surviving spouses have equal inheritance rights?	Yes	No

GETTING A JOB

	Score: 60	Score: 20
17. Is there paid leave available to women of at least 14 weeks?	Yes	No
18. Do women receive at least 2/3 of their wages for the first 14 weeks or the duration of the leave if it is shorter?	Yes	Yes
19. What is the percentage of maternity leave benefits paid by the government?	100%	0%
20. What is the difference between leave reserved for women and men relative to leave reserved for women, as a function of who pays?	1	0
21. Is there paid parental leave?	Yes	No
22. Does the law mandate equal remuneration for work of equal value?	No	No
23. Does the law mandate nondiscrimination based on gender in employment?	Yes	No
24. Is dismissal of pregnant workers prohibited?	Yes	No
25. Can parents work flexibly?	No	No
26. Can women work the same night hours as men?	No	No
27. Can women work in jobs deemed hazardous, arduous or morally inappropriate in the same way as men?	No	No
28. Are women able to work in the same industries as men?	No	No
29. Are women able to perform the same tasks at work as men?	No	No
30. Are the ages at which men and women can retire with full pension benefits equal?	Yes	Yes
31. Are the ages at which men and women can retire with partial pension benefits equal?	Yes	No
32. Are the mandatory retirement ages for men and women equal?	N/A	N/A

PROVIDING INCENTIVES TO WORK

	Score: 80	Score: 60
33. Are mothers guaranteed an equivalent position after maternity leave?	Yes	No
34. Does the government support or provide childcare services?	Yes	Yes
35. Are payments for childcare tax deductible?	No	No
36. Is primary education free and compulsory?	Yes	Yes
37. Are there tax deductions or credits specific to men?	No	No

GOING TO COURT

	Score: 75	Score: 50
38. Does a woman's testimony carry the same evidentiary weight in court as a man's?	Yes	Yes
39. Does the law establish an anti-discrimination commission?	Yes	No
40. Does the law mandate legal aid in civil/family matters?	Yes	No
41. Is there a small claims court/fast-track procedure?	No	Yes

BUILDING CREDIT

	Score: 25	Score: 50
42. Do retailers provide information to credit agencies?	No	Yes
43. Do utility companies provide information to credit agencies?	No	Yes
44. Is discrimination based on gender prohibited in access to credit?	Yes	No
45. Is discrimination based on marital status prohibited in access to credit?	No	No

PROTECTING WOMEN FROM VIOLENCE

	Score: 60	Score: 0
46. Is there legislation specifically addressing domestic violence? If not, are there aggravated penalties for crimes committed against a spouse or family member?	Yes	No
47. Is there legislation on sexual harassment in employment?	Yes	No
48. Is there legislation on sexual harassment in education?	No	No
49. Are there criminal penalties for sexual harassment in employment?	No	No
50. Are there civil remedies for sexual harassment in employment?	Yes	No

Note: See the data notes for more details on the scoring of each indicator.

	UNITED KINGDOM	UNITED STATES
REGION	High income: OECD	High income: OECD
INCOME GROUP	High income	High income
FEMALE POPULATION	33,266,827	162,932,617
FEMALE LABOR FORCE (% OF TOTAL LABOR FORCE)	47%	46%

ACCESSING INSTITUTIONS

	Score: 100	Score: 100
1. Are wives required to obey their husbands?	No	No
Can a woman legally do the following in the same way as a man:		
2. Apply for a passport?	Yes	Yes
3. Apply for a national ID card?	N/A	N/A
4. Travel outside the country?	Yes	Yes
5. Travel outside her home?	Yes	Yes
6. Get a job?	Yes	Yes
7. Sign a contract?	Yes	Yes
8. Register a business?	Yes	Yes
9. Open a bank account?	Yes	Yes
10. Choose where to live?	Yes	Yes
11. Be "head of household"?	N/A	N/A

USING PROPERTY

	Score: 100	Score: 100
12. Who legally administers marital property?	Original owner	Original owner
13. Does the law provide for valuation of nonmonetary contributions?	Yes	Yes
14. Do men and women have equal ownership rights to immovable property?	Yes	Yes
15. Do sons and daughters have equal inheritance rights?	Yes	Yes
16. Do female and male surviving spouses have equal inheritance rights?	Yes	Yes

GETTING A JOB

	Score: 99	Score: 62
17. Is there paid leave available to women of at least 14 weeks?	Yes	No
18. Do women receive at least 2/3 of their wages for the first 14 weeks or the duration of the leave if it is shorter?	Yes	No
19. What is the percentage of maternity leave benefits paid by the government?	92%	N/A
20. What is the difference between leave reserved for women and men relative to leave reserved for women, as a function of who pays?	0.94	N/A
21. Is there paid parental leave?	Yes	No
22. Does the law mandate equal remuneration for work of equal value?	Yes	No
23. Does the law mandate nondiscrimination based on gender in employment?	Yes	Yes
24. Is dismissal of pregnant workers prohibited?	Yes	Yes
25. Can parents work flexibly?	Yes	No
26. Can women work the same night hours as men?	Yes	Yes
27. Can women work in jobs deemed hazardous, arduous or morally inappropriate in the same way as men?	Yes	Yes
28. Are women able to work in the same industries as men?	Yes	Yes
29. Are women able to perform the same tasks at work as men?	Yes	Yes
30. Are the ages at which men and women can retire with full pension benefits equal?	Yes	Yes
31. Are the ages at which men and women can retire with partial pension benefits equal?	N/A	Yes
32. Are the mandatory retirement ages for men and women equal?	N/A	N/A

PROVIDING INCENTIVES TO WORK

	Score: 100	Score: 100
33. Are mothers guaranteed an equivalent position after maternity leave?	Yes	Yes
34. Does the government support or provide childcare services?	Yes	Yes
35. Are payments for childcare tax deductible?	Yes	Yes
36. Is primary education free and compulsory?	Yes	Yes
37. Are there tax deductions or credits specific to men?	No	No

GOING TO COURT

	Score: 75	Score: 75
38. Does a woman's testimony carry the same evidentiary weight in court as a man's?	Yes	Yes
39. Does the law establish an anti-discrimination commission?	No	No
40. Does the law mandate legal aid in civil/family matters?	Yes	Yes
41. Is there a small claims court/fast-track procedure?	Yes	Yes

BUILDING CREDIT

	Score: 100	Score: 100
42. Do retailers provide information to credit agencies?	Yes	Yes
43. Do utility companies provide information to credit agencies?	Yes	Yes
44. Is discrimination based on gender prohibited in access to credit?	Yes	Yes
45. Is discrimination based on marital status prohibited in access to credit?	Yes	Yes

PROTECTING WOMEN FROM VIOLENCE

	Score: 100	Score: 80
46. Is there legislation specifically addressing domestic violence? If not, are there aggravated penalties for crimes committed against a spouse or family member?	Yes	Yes
47. Is there legislation on sexual harassment in employment?	Yes	Yes
48. Is there legislation on sexual harassment in education?	Yes	Yes
49. Are there criminal penalties for sexual harassment in employment?	Yes	No
50. Are there civil remedies for sexual harassment in employment?	Yes	Yes

Note: See the data notes for more details on the scoring of each indicator.

	URUGUAY	UZBEKISTAN
REGION	Latin America & Caribbean	Europe & Central Asia
INCOME GROUP	High income	Lower middle income
FEMALE POPULATION	1,780,968	16,185,637
FEMALE LABOR FORCE (% OF TOTAL LABOR FORCE)	45%	42%

ACCESSING INSTITUTIONS

	Score: 100	Score: 100
1. Are wives required to obey their husbands?	No	No
Can a woman legally do the following in the same way as a man:		
2. Apply for a passport?	Yes	Yes
3. Apply for a national ID card?	Yes	N/A
4. Travel outside the country?	Yes	Yes
5. Travel outside her home?	Yes	Yes
6. Get a job?	Yes	Yes
7. Sign a contract?	Yes	Yes
8. Register a business?	Yes	Yes
9. Open a bank account?	Yes	Yes
10. Choose where to live?	Yes	Yes
11. Be "head of household"?	N/A	N/A

USING PROPERTY

	Score: 100	Score: 100
12. Who legally administers marital property?	Both must agree	Both must agree
13. Does the law provide for valuation of nonmonetary contributions?	Yes	Yes
14. Do men and women have equal ownership rights to immovable property?	Yes	Yes
15. Do sons and daughters have equal inheritance rights?	Yes	Yes
16. Do female and male surviving spouses have equal inheritance rights?	Yes	Yes

GETTING A JOB

	Score: 73	Score: 51
17. Is there paid leave available to women of at least 14 weeks?	Yes	Yes
18. Do women receive at least 2/3 of their wages for the first 14 weeks or the duration of the leave if it is shorter?	Yes	Yes
19. What is the percentage of maternity leave benefits paid by the government?	100%	0%
20. What is the difference between leave reserved for women and men relative to leave reserved for women, as a function of who pays?	1	0
21. Is there paid parental leave?	No	Yes
22. Does the law mandate equal remuneration for work of equal value?	No	No
23. Does the law mandate nondiscrimination based on gender in employment?	Yes	Yes
24. Is dismissal of pregnant workers prohibited?	Yes	Yes
25. Can parents work flexibly?	No	No
26. Can women work the same night hours as men?	Yes	Yes
27. Can women work in jobs deemed hazardous, arduous or morally inappropriate in the same way as men?	Yes	Yes
28. Are women able to work in the same industries as men?	Yes	No
29. Are women able to perform the same tasks at work as men?	No	No
30. Are the ages at which men and women can retire with full pension benefits equal?	Yes	No
31. Are the ages at which men and women can retire with partial pension benefits equal?	Yes	N/A
32. Are the mandatory retirement ages for men and women equal?	N/A	No

PROVIDING INCENTIVES TO WORK

	Score: 80	Score: 80
33. Are mothers guaranteed an equivalent position after maternity leave?	No	Yes
34. Does the government support or provide childcare services?	Yes	Yes
35. Are payments for childcare tax deductible?	Yes	No
36. Is primary education free and compulsory?	Yes	Yes
37. Are there tax deductions or credits specific to men?	No	No

GOING TO COURT

	Score: 50	Score: 25
38. Does a woman's testimony carry the same evidentiary weight in court as a man's?	Yes	Yes
39. Does the law establish an anti-discrimination commission?	No	No
40. Does the law mandate legal aid in civil/family matters?	No	No
41. Is there a small claims court/fast-track procedure?	Yes	No

BUILDING CREDIT

	Score: 50	Score: 0
42. Do retailers provide information to credit agencies?	Yes	No
43. Do utility companies provide information to credit agencies?	Yes	No
44. Is discrimination based on gender prohibited in access to credit?	No	No
45. Is discrimination based on marital status prohibited in access to credit?	No	No

PROTECTING WOMEN FROM VIOLENCE

	Score: 80	Score: 0
46. Is there legislation specifically addressing domestic violence? If not, are there aggravated penalties for crimes committed against a spouse or family member?	Yes	No
47. Is there legislation on sexual harassment in employment?	Yes	No
48. Is there legislation on sexual harassment in education?	Yes	No
49. Are there criminal penalties for sexual harassment in employment?	No	No
50. Are there civil remedies for sexual harassment in employment?	Yes	No

Note: See the data notes for more details on the scoring of each indicator.

	VANUATU	VENEZUELA, RB
REGION	East Asia & Pacific	Latin America & Caribbean
INCOME GROUP	Lower middle income	Upper middle income
FEMALE POPULATION	133,488	15,859,592
FEMALE LABOR FORCE (% OF TOTAL LABOR FORCE)	44%	40%

ACCESSING INSTITUTIONS

	Score: 100	Score: 100
1. Are wives required to obey their husbands?	No	No
Can a woman legally do the following in the same way as a man:		
2. Apply for a passport?	Yes	Yes
3. Apply for a national ID card?	N/A	Yes
4. Travel outside the country?	Yes	Yes
5. Travel outside her home?	Yes	Yes
6. Get a job?	Yes	Yes
7. Sign a contract?	Yes	Yes
8. Register a business?	Yes	Yes
9. Open a bank account?	Yes	Yes
10. Choose where to live?	Yes	Yes
11. Be "head of household"?	N/A	N/A

USING PROPERTY

	Score: 75	Score: 100
12. Who legally administers marital property?	Other	Separate with spousal consent
13. Does the law provide for valuation of nonmonetary contributions?	Yes	Yes
14. Do men and women have equal ownership rights to immovable property?	..	Yes
15. Do sons and daughters have equal inheritance rights?	No	Yes
16. Do female and male surviving spouses have equal inheritance rights?	Yes	Yes

GETTING A JOB

	Score: 52	Score: 70
17. Is there paid leave available to women of at least 14 weeks?	No	Yes
18. Do women receive at least 2/3 of their wages for the first 14 weeks or the duration of the leave if it is shorter?	No	Yes
19. What is the percentage of maternity leave benefits paid by the government?	0%	67%
20. What is the difference between leave reserved for women and men relative to leave reserved for women, as a function of who pays?	0	0.69
21. Is there paid parental leave?	No	No
22. Does the law mandate equal remuneration for work of equal value?	No	No
23. Does the law mandate nondiscrimination based on gender in employment?	No	Yes
24. Is dismissal of pregnant workers prohibited?	Yes	Yes
25. Can parents work flexibly?	No	No
26. Can women work the same night hours as men?	No	Yes
27. Can women work in jobs deemed hazardous, arduous or morally inappropriate in the same way as men?	Yes	Yes
28. Are women able to work in the same industries as men?	Yes	Yes
29. Are women able to perform the same tasks at work as men?	Yes	Yes
30. Are the ages at which men and women can retire with full pension benefits equal?	Yes	No
31. Are the ages at which men and women can retire with partial pension benefits equal?	Yes	N/A
32. Are the mandatory retirement ages for men and women equal?	N/A	N/A

PROVIDING INCENTIVES TO WORK

	Score: 40	Score: 80
33. Are mothers guaranteed an equivalent position after maternity leave?	Yes	Yes
34. Does the government support or provide childcare services?	No	Yes
35. Are payments for childcare tax deductible?	No	No
36. Is primary education free and compulsory?	No	Yes
37. Are there tax deductions or credits specific to men?	No	No

GOING TO COURT

	Score: 50	Score: 75
38. Does a woman's testimony carry the same evidentiary weight in court as a man's?	Yes	Yes
39. Does the law establish an anti-discrimination commission?	No	Yes
40. Does the law mandate legal aid in civil/family matters?	No	No
41. Is there a small claims court/fast-track procedure?	Yes	Yes

BUILDING CREDIT

	Score: 25	Score: 0
42. Do retailers provide information to credit agencies?	No	No
43. Do utility companies provide information to credit agencies?	No	No
44. Is discrimination based on gender prohibited in access to credit?	Yes	No
45. Is discrimination based on marital status prohibited in access to credit?	No	No

PROTECTING WOMEN FROM VIOLENCE

	Score: 20	Score: 100
46. Is there legislation specifically addressing domestic violence? If not, are there aggravated penalties for crimes committed against a spouse or family member?	Yes	Yes
47. Is there legislation on sexual harassment in employment?	No	Yes
48. Is there legislation on sexual harassment in education?	No	Yes
49. Are there criminal penalties for sexual harassment in employment?	No	Yes
50. Are there civil remedies for sexual harassment in employment?	No	Yes

Note: See the data notes for more details on the scoring of each indicator.

	VIETNAM	WEST BANK AND GAZA
REGION	East Asia & Pacific	Middle East & North Africa
INCOME GROUP	Lower middle income	Lower middle income
FEMALE POPULATION	46,834,625	2,244,170
FEMALE LABOR FORCE (% OF TOTAL LABOR FORCE)	48%	21%

ACCESSING INSTITUTIONS

	Score: 100	Score: 64
1. Are wives required to obey their husbands?	No	Yes
Can a woman legally do the following in the same way as a man:		
2. Apply for a passport?	Yes	Yes
3. Apply for a national ID card?	Yes	Yes
4. Travel outside the country?	Yes	Yes
5. Travel outside her home?	Yes	No
6. Get a job?	Yes	No
7. Sign a contract?	Yes	Yes
8. Register a business?	Yes	Yes
9. Open a bank account?	Yes	Yes
10. Choose where to live?	Yes	No
11. Be "head of household"?	Yes	N/A

USING PROPERTY

	Score: 100	Score: 40
12. Who legally administers marital property?	Both must agree	Original owner
13. Does the law provide for valuation of nonmonetary contributions?	Yes	No
14. Do men and women have equal ownership rights to immovable property?	Yes	Yes
15. Do sons and daughters have equal inheritance rights?	Yes	No
16. Do female and male surviving spouses have equal inheritance rights?	Yes	No

GETTING A JOB

	Score: 64	Score: 49
17. Is there paid leave available to women of at least 14 weeks?	Yes	No
18. Do women receive at least 2/3 of their wages for the first 14 weeks or the duration of the leave if it is shorter?	Yes	Yes
19. What is the percentage of maternity leave benefits paid by the government?	100%	100%
20. What is the difference between leave reserved for women and men relative to leave reserved for women, as a function of who pays?	1	1
21. Is there paid parental leave?	No	No
22. Does the law mandate equal remuneration for work of equal value?	Yes	No
23. Does the law mandate nondiscrimination based on gender in employment?	Yes	Yes
24. Is dismissal of pregnant workers prohibited?	Yes	No
25. Can parents work flexibly?	No	No
26. Can women work the same night hours as men?	Yes	No
27. Can women work in jobs deemed hazardous, arduous or morally inappropriate in the same way as men?	Yes	Yes
28. Are women able to work in the same industries as men?	No	No
29. Are women able to perform the same tasks at work as men?	No	No
30. Are the ages at which men and women can retire with full pension benefits equal?	No	Yes
31. Are the ages at which men and women can retire with partial pension benefits equal?	N/A	N/A
32. Are the mandatory retirement ages for men and women equal?	No	N/A

PROVIDING INCENTIVES TO WORK

	Score: 80	Score: 60
33. Are mothers guaranteed an equivalent position after maternity leave?	Yes	No
34. Does the government support or provide childcare services?	Yes	Yes
35. Are payments for childcare tax deductible?	No	No
36. Is primary education free and compulsory?	Yes	Yes
37. Are there tax deductions or credits specific to men?	No	No

GOING TO COURT

	Score: 50	Score: 25
38. Does a woman's testimony carry the same evidentiary weight in court as a man's?	Yes	No
39. Does the law establish an anti-discrimination commission?	No	No
40. Does the law mandate legal aid in civil/family matters?	Yes	No
41. Is there a small claims court/fast-track procedure?	No	Yes

BUILDING CREDIT

	Score: 25	Score: 50
42. Do retailers provide information to credit agencies?	No	Yes
43. Do utility companies provide information to credit agencies?	No	Yes
44. Is discrimination based on gender prohibited in access to credit?	Yes	No
45. Is discrimination based on marital status prohibited in access to credit?	No	No

PROTECTING WOMEN FROM VIOLENCE

	Score: 60	Score: 0
46. Is there legislation specifically addressing domestic violence? If not, are there aggravated penalties for crimes committed against a spouse or family member?	Yes	No
47. Is there legislation on sexual harassment in employment?	Yes	No
48. Is there legislation on sexual harassment in education?	No	No
49. Are there criminal penalties for sexual harassment in employment?	No	No
50. Are there civil remedies for sexual harassment in employment?	Yes	No

Note: See the data notes for more details on the scoring of each indicator.

	YEMEN, REP.	ZAMBIA
REGION	Middle East & North Africa	Sub-Saharan Africa
INCOME GROUP	Lower middle income	Lower middle income
FEMALE POPULATION	13,653,577	8,308,472
FEMALE LABOR FORCE (% OF TOTAL LABOR FORCE)	8%	48%

ACCESSING INSTITUTIONS

	Score: 45	Score: 91
1. Are wives required to obey their husbands?	Yes	No
Can a woman legally do the following in the same way as a man:		
2. Apply for a passport?	No	No
3. Apply for a national ID card?	Yes	Yes
4. Travel outside the country?	Yes	Yes
5. Travel outside her home?	No	Yes
6. Get a job?	No	Yes
7. Sign a contract?	Yes	Yes
8. Register a business?	Yes	Yes
9. Open a bank account?	Yes	Yes
10. Choose where to live?	No	Yes
11. Be "head of household"?	No	N/A

USING PROPERTY

	Score: 40	Score: 80
12. Who legally administers marital property?	Original owner	Original owner
13. Does the law provide for valuation of nonmonetary contributions?	No	No
14. Do men and women have equal ownership rights to immovable property?	Yes	Yes
15. Do sons and daughters have equal inheritance rights?	No	Yes
16. Do female and male surviving spouses have equal inheritance rights?	No	Yes

GETTING A JOB

	Score: 43	Score: 72
17. Is there paid leave available to women of at least 14 weeks?	No	No
18. Do women receive at least 2/3 of their wages for the first 14 weeks or the duration of the leave if it is shorter?	Yes	Yes
19. What is the percentage of maternity leave benefits paid by the government?	0%	0%
20. What is the difference between leave reserved for women and men relative to leave reserved for women, as a function of who pays?	0	0
21. Is there paid parental leave?	No	No
22. Does the law mandate equal remuneration for work of equal value?	No	Yes
23. Does the law mandate nondiscrimination based on gender in employment?	Yes	Yes
24. Is dismissal of pregnant workers prohibited?	No	Yes
25. Can parents work flexibly?	No	No
26. Can women work the same night hours as men?	No	Yes
27. Can women work in jobs deemed hazardous, arduous or morally inappropriate in the same way as men?	No	Yes
28. Are women able to work in the same industries as men?	Yes	Yes
29. Are women able to perform the same tasks at work as men?	Yes	Yes
30. Are the ages at which men and women can retire with full pension benefits equal?	No	Yes
31. Are the ages at which men and women can retire with partial pension benefits equal?	No	Yes
32. Are the mandatory retirement ages for men and women equal?	Yes	N/A

PROVIDING INCENTIVES TO WORK

	Score: 40	Score: 60
33. Are mothers guaranteed an equivalent position after maternity leave?	No	No
34. Does the government support or provide childcare services?	No	Yes
35. Are payments for childcare tax deductible?	No	No
36. Is primary education free and compulsory?	Yes	Yes
37. Are there tax deductions or credits specific to men?	No	No

GOING TO COURT

	Score: 0	Score: 100
38. Does a woman's testimony carry the same evidentiary weight in court as a man's?	No	Yes
39. Does the law establish an anti-discrimination commission?	No	Yes
40. Does the law mandate legal aid in civil/family matters?	No	Yes
41. Is there a small claims court/fast-track procedure?	No	Yes

BUILDING CREDIT

	Score: 0	Score: 100
42. Do retailers provide information to credit agencies?	N/A	Yes
43. Do utility companies provide information to credit agencies?	N/A	Yes
44. Is discrimination based on gender prohibited in access to credit?	No	Yes
45. Is discrimination based on marital status prohibited in access to credit?	No	Yes

PROTECTING WOMEN FROM VIOLENCE

	Score: 0	Score: 100
46. Is there legislation specifically addressing domestic violence? If not, are there aggravated penalties for crimes committed against a spouse or family member?	No	Yes
47. Is there legislation on sexual harassment in employment?	No	Yes
48. Is there legislation on sexual harassment in education?	No	Yes
49. Are there criminal penalties for sexual harassment in employment?	No	Yes
50. Are there civil remedies for sexual harassment in employment?	No	Yes

Note: See the data notes for more details on the scoring of each indicator.

	ZIMBABWE
REGION	Sub-Saharan Africa
INCOME GROUP	Low income
FEMALE POPULATION	8,194,300
FEMALE LABOR FORCE (% OF TOTAL LABOR FORCE)	49%

ACCESSING INSTITUTIONS

Score: 100

1. Are wives required to obey their husbands?	No
Can a woman legally do the following in the same way as a man:	
2. Apply for a passport?	Yes
3. Apply for a national ID card?	Yes
4. Travel outside the country?	Yes
5. Travel outside her home?	Yes
6. Get a job?	Yes
7. Sign a contract?	Yes
8. Register a business?	Yes
9. Open a bank account?	Yes
10. Choose where to live?	Yes
11. Be "head of household"?	N/A

USING PROPERTY

Score: 100

12. Who legally administers marital property?	Original owner
13. Does the law provide for valuation of nonmonetary contributions?	Yes
14. Do men and women have equal ownership rights to immovable property?	Yes
15. Do sons and daughters have equal inheritance rights?	Yes
16. Do female and male surviving spouses have equal inheritance rights?	Yes

GETTING A JOB

Score: 64

17. Is there paid leave available to women of at least 14 weeks?	Yes
18. Do women receive at least 2/3 of their wages for the first 14 weeks or the duration of the leave if it is shorter?	Yes
19. What is the percentage of maternity leave benefits paid by the government?	0%
20. What is the difference between leave reserved for women and men relative to leave reserved for women, as a function of who pays?	0
21. Is there paid parental leave?	No
22. Does the law mandate equal remuneration for work of equal value?	No
23. Does the law mandate nondiscrimination based on gender in employment?	Yes
24. Is dismissal of pregnant workers prohibited?	Yes
25. Can parents work flexibly?	No
26. Can women work the same night hours as men?	Yes
27. Can women work in jobs deemed hazardous, arduous or morally inappropriate in the same way as men?	Yes
28. Are women able to work in the same industries as men?	Yes
29. Are women able to perform the same tasks at work as men?	Yes
30. Are the ages at which men and women can retire with full pension benefits equal?	Yes
31. Are the ages at which men and women can retire with partial pension benefits equal?	N/A
32. Are the mandatory retirement ages for men and women equal?	N/A

PROVIDING INCENTIVES TO WORK

Score: 40

33. Are mothers guaranteed an equivalent position after maternity leave?	Yes
34. Does the government support or provide childcare services?	No
35. Are payments for childcare tax deductible?	No
36. Is primary education free and compulsory?	No
37. Are there tax deductions or credits specific to men?	No

GOING TO COURT

Score: 100

38. Does a woman's testimony carry the same evidentiary weight in court as a man's?	Yes
39. Does the law establish an anti-discrimination commission?	Yes
40. Does the law mandate legal aid in civil/family matters?	Yes
41. Is there a small claims court/fast-track procedure?	Yes

BUILDING CREDIT

Score: 75

42. Do retailers provide information to credit agencies?	Yes
43. Do utility companies provide information to credit agencies?	Yes
44. Is discrimination based on gender prohibited in access to credit?	Yes
45. Is discrimination based on marital status prohibited in access to credit?	No

PROTECTING WOMEN FROM VIOLENCE

Score: 60

46. Is there legislation specifically addressing domestic violence? If not, are there aggravated penalties for crimes committed against a spouse or family member?	Yes
47. Is there legislation on sexual harassment in employment?	Yes
48. Is there legislation on sexual harassment in education?	No
49. Are there criminal penalties for sexual harassment in employment?	No
50. Are there civil remedies for sexual harassment in employment?	Yes

Note: See the data notes for more details on the scoring of each indicator.

ACKNOWLEDGMENTS

Data collection and analysis for *Women, Business and the Law 2018* was conducted by a team led by Sarah Iqbal (Program Manager, Indicator Development), under the general direction of Rita Ramalho (Senior Manager, Global Indicators Group, Development Economics) since March 2017, and prior to that under Augusto López-Claros (Director, Global Indicators Group, Development Economics) and Melissa Johns (Adviser, Global Indicators Group, Development Economics). Overall guidance for the preparation of the report was provided by Shantayanan Devarajan (Senior Director, Development Economics, and Acting Chief Economist). The project was managed with the support of Tazeen Hasan and Tanya Primiani.

Members of the core research team included Souad Adnane, Maereg Tewoldebirhan Alemayehu, Gharam Alkastalani Dexter, Nayda Almodóvar-Reteguis, Nisha Arekapudi, Shirin Batshon, Julia Constanze Braunmiller, Diana Eugenia Chacon, Claudia Lenny Corminales, Maia D'Anna, Marina Elefante, Philippine de Maere, Dimitra Christina Heliotis, Juliette Herault, Asif Islam, Kavell Gianina Joseph, Anna Kalashyan, Viktoria Khaitina, Gloria Daniele Kuoh, Elizabeth Makumbi, Marie Nezam, Alena Sakhonchik, Isabel Santagostino Recavarren, Warner G. Santiago Acevedo, Camilla Schloss, Katrin Schulz, Aarushi Sinha, Paula Tavares and Aliaksandra Tyhrytskaya. The core research team was assisted by Paulina Maribel Flewitt. John Arzinos, Vanessa Maria Cervello Ferrando, Joseph Antoine Lemoine, Mirabelle Sirri Chi Epse Okezie, Etienne Mbala and Gergana Tsvetanova Tsvetanova assisted in the months before publication. Deborah Eskinazi, Cynthia Joyce Marie Raphael Kabore, Julieth Santamaria and Veronica Trujillo provided assistance on the case study on Women's Financial Inclusion and the Law.

The team is grateful for valuable comments provided by colleagues in the World Bank Group. The team would especially like to acknowledge the comments and support of Simeon Djankov and Caren Grown. Comments were also received from: Amatalalim Ali Mohamed Al-Soswa, Rabah Arezki, Mark Austin, Ciro Avitabile, Yasmin Bin-Humam, Helle Buchhave, Tamoya Christie, Maria Davalos, Bénédicte de la Brière, Francesca de Nicola, Gabriel Demombynes, Marianne Fay, Achim Fock, Markus Goldstein, Thu Ha Le, Faris Hadad-Zervos, Birgit Hansl, Bingjie Hu, Keiko Inoue, Marijana Jasarevic, Daniel Kirkwood, Andy Kotikula, Gladys Lopez-Acevedo, Catherine Martin, Andrew Mason, Shabih Mohib, Lili Mottaghi, Rinku Murgai, Stephen N. Ndegwa, Giang Tam Nguyen, Ngan Hong Nguyen, Aristeidis Panou, Elizaveta Perova, Carla Pittalis, Paul Prettitore, Martin Rama, Eliana Rubiano, Mariam Sherman, Sudhir Shetty, Rucheta Singh, Cia Sjetnan, Victoria Stanley, Emcet Tas, Anne Tully, Anuja Utz, Patricia Van de Velde, Georgia Wallen, Degi Young, Albert G. Zeufack and Wenqing Zhang.

The report was edited by Chris Cavanaugh and Sandra Gain, with design and graphics by Corporate Visions. The online *Women, Business and the Law* database (http://wbl.worldbank.org) is supported by Manas Ranjan Behera, Varun V. Doiphode, Fengsheng Huang, Manoj Mathew, Flora Rezaei Mood, Arun Chakravarthi Nageswaran, Kunal H. Patel, Akash Pradhan, Ana Cristina Santos Felix, Rajesh Sargunan, Kamalesh Sengaonkar, Geoffrey Shott, Bishal Raj Thakuri, Vinod Vasudevan Thottikkatu and Hashim Zia.

The *Women, Business and the Law* outreach strategy is managed by Indira Chand working with Mikael Reventar, Christopher M. Walsh and Ruihua (Rayna) Zhang. The events strategy is supported by Sushmitha Narsiah Pidatala.

Support for *Women, Business and the Law* is provided by: The Bill & Melinda Gates Foundation; The William and Flora Hewlett Foundation; the United Kingdom Department for International Development (DFID); the United States Agency for International Development (USAID); and the Swedish Ministry of Foreign Affairs.

This report was made possible by the generous contributions of close to 2,000 lawyers, judges, academics, civil society representatives and public officials in 189 economies. Contact details for local partners are available on the *Women, Business and the Law* website at: http://wbl.worldbank.org.

The names of local partners wishing to be acknowledged individually are listed. The global and regional contributors listed are firms or organizations that have completed multiple questionnaires in their various offices around the world.

GLOBAL CONTRIBUTORS

Advocates for International Development (A4ID)

African Bar Association

Allen & Overy LLP

American Bar Association

CARE International

Dechert LLP

Duane Morris LLP

Equality Now

Freshfields Bruckhaus Deringer

Global Alliance for Justice Education (GAJE)

Global Campaign for Equal Nationality Rights

Global Partnership for Education

Hogan Lovells

International Association of Women Judges

International Bar Association

International Development Law Organization (IDLO)

International Property Registries Association (IPRA-CINDER)

Linklaters LLP

Organization of American States

Plan International

Qatar University College of Law Legal Clinic

Save the Children

The Law Society of England & Wales

Thomson Reuters Foundation

UNDP

UNICEF

UN Women

Vital Strategies

World Organisation for Early Childhood Education and Care (OMEP)

AFGHANISTAN

Ahmad Shekib Gran
ACCI

Hadley Rose

Sayed Asil Sadiqi

Abdul Basir Sarwari
Abdul Basir Sarwari Advocacy Company

Negina Sultani
Legal Oracles

Durani Waziri
Lawyer

ALBANIA

Iris Aliaj
Centre for Legal Civic Initiatives

Mirela Arqimandriti
Gender Alliance for Development Center

Blerta Balilaj Brovina
Women's Democracy Network Albania (WDN-Albania)

Sokol Elmazaj
Boga & Associates

Miranda Harizaj
Albanian Financial Supervisory Authority

Adriatik Lapaj
Lawyer

Ines Leskaj
AWEN-Albanian Women Empowerment Network

Aida Lico
LLF Legal & Tax

Enkeleda Olldashi
Faculty of Law, University of Tirana

Suela Qoqja

Elona Saliaj
Notary

Suela Shundi

Elona Xhepa
Boga & Associates

ALGERIA

Radia Abdous
Ghellal & Mekerba

Kada Afia
Université de la Formation Continue

Sonia Benbouzid
Cabinet Tabet Avocats & Conseils

Yamina Kebir
Cabinet Kebir

Larbaoui Malika
Bouchaib Law Firm

Lamine Tabet
Cabinet Tabet Avocats & Conseils

ANGOLA

Inês Albuquerque e Castro
FCB Sociedade de Advogados

Sofia Chaves

Arão Chimbinja
Lourdes Caposso Fernandes & Associados (LCF)

Daniela Cristovão
Lourdes Caposso Fernandes & Associados (LCF)

Bruno Xavier de Pina

Lourdes Caposso Fernandes
Lourdes Caposso Fernandes & Associados (LCF)

Catarina Neto Fernandes
Abreu Advogados

Carmen Monclús i Gironès
UNICEF

Ana Leão
Consultant

Yuma Munana
Lourdes Caposso Fernandes & Associados (LCF)

Christopher Ngwerume
UNICEF

Gildo Reis
Lourdes Caposso Fernandes & Associados (LCF)

Edila Maria Melo Ribeiro
Lawyer

ANTIGUA AND BARBUDA

Sherrie-Ann Bradshaw
S. Bradshaw & Associates

Alethea Byers
Family and Social Services

Kalisia Marks
Richards & Company

Kari-Anne Reynolds
Hill & Hill

Kamilah Roberts
Roberts & Co.

Alexandrina Wong
Women Against Rape Inc.

ARGENTINA

Ana Alicia Ariet Guevara
Poder Judicial Pcia. de Mendoza

Úrsula Basset
Universidad Austral and Pontificia Universidad Católica Argentina

Pablo Belaich
EY - Pistrelli, Henry Martin y Asociados SRL

Carlos Casanovas
EY - Pistrelli, Henry Martin y Asociados SRL

Carina Marcela Castrillón
Bulló Abogados

Esteban de Dobrzynski
Lawyer

Graciela De Oto
Etudio Grispo & Asociados

Osvaldo Flores
EY - Pistrelli, Henry Martin y Asociados SRL

Consuelo García
Consuelo García Law Firm

Jorge Daniel Grispo
Estudio Grispo & Asociados

Leticia Andrea Kabusacki
Harari & Kabusacki Abogados

Diego Sebastián Kelly
Marval, O'Farrell & Mairal, Lex Mundi Association of Law Firms

Ezequiel Alcides Landry
Estudio Grispo & Asociados

Sofia Gabriela Nuñez
Marval, O'Farrell & Mairal, Lex Mundi Association of Law Firms

Paola Pecora
EY - Pistrelli, Henry Martin y
Asociados SRL

Beatriz Ramos
Universidad Católica del
Uruguay

Romina Rodríguez
Registro de las Personas de la
Provincia de Buenos Aires

Enrique Mariano Stile
Marval, O'Farrell & Mairal, Lex
Mundi Association of Law Firms

Gustavo Torassa
Bulló Abogados

ARMENIA

Hayk Abrahamyan
Open Society Foundations

Tsovinar Ananyan
Brave Law Firm

Aida Baghdasaryan
Ucom LLC

Anahit Chilingaryan

Mariam Ghulyan
Ghulyan and Partners Law Firm

Ara Khzmalyan
Adwise Business & Legal
Consulting

Isabella Merabova

Larisa Minasyan
Open Society Foundations

Mariam Mkrtichyan
Hovhannisyan & Partners LLC

Tiruhi Nazaretyan
Tempus NGO

Hasmik Ohnikyan
Ilex Law Firm

Davit Srapionyan
Lawyer

Argam Stepanyan
Ministry of Justice

Gayane Virabyan
K & P Law Firm

Arpine Yeghikyan
Marseral LLC

Karen Zadoyan
Armenian Lawyers' Association

AUSTRALIA

Libby Abraham
Department of Finance,
Services & Innovation, Office of
the Registrar General

Bryony Binns
PwC

Stephen Page
Harrington Family Lawyers

Susan Pearson
Pearson Emerson Meyer

Jane Wright
Work Dynamic Australia

AUSTRIA

Victoria Bazil
Freshfields Bruckhaus Deringer

Petra Cernochova
Attorney-at-Law

Julia Eichinger
Wirtschaftsuniversität Wien

Sandra Maria Eichner
Freshfields Bruckhaus Deringer

Marlene Grois
Freshfields Bruckhaus Deringer

Birgitt Haller
Institute of Conflict Research
(IKF)

Valerie Kramer
DLA Piper

Wieland Anastasios Leopold
Freshfields Bruckhaus Deringer

Gert-Peter Reissner
University of Innsbruck

Patrick W. Tauber
Freshfields Bruckhaus Deringer

AZERBAIJAN

Gulnaz Alasgarova
Baku State University

Ramil Atayev

Khayala Hamzaliyea

Ramil Iskandarli
Legal Analysis and Research
Public Union

Gunel Ismayilbeyli

Ummi Jalilova
GRATA International

Akif Kazimli

Shabnam Sadigova
GRATA International

Shahla Samedova
Baku State University

Khalisa Shahverdiyeva
UNFPA

Konul Soltanova

Taleh Zarbali

Mehriban Zeynalova
Clean World Social Union

BAHAMAS, THE

Tecoyo Bridgewater
Bridgewater Legal Advocates

Vann P. Gaitor
Higgs & Johnson

Katie Jervis

D'Andra Johnson
Lennox Paton

Knijah Knowles
Court of Appeal of The
Bahamas

Shantelle Munroe
Graham Thompson & Co.

Chad D. Roberts
Callenders & Co.

BAHRAIN

Rana Al Alawi
Zu'bi & Partners Attorneys &
Legal Consultants

Faten Al Haddad
Al Haddad Law Firm

Zeenat Al Mansoori
Zeenat Al Mansoori &
Associates

Reem Al Rayes
Zeenat Al Mansoori &
Associates

Noor Al Taraif
Zu'bi & Partners Attorneys &
Legal Consultants

Ismaeel Elnasri
Inovest

Nitya Kumar
King Hamad University Hospital

Eman Omar
Zu'bi & Partners Attorneys &
Legal Consultants

Amr Omran
Freshfields Bruckhaus Deringer

Rohit Srivastava
Royal Bahrain Hospital

Sami Tannous
Freshfields Bruckhaus Deringer

BANGLADESH

Kazi M.U. Ahamed
Imperidus Law Associates

Nasim Akhter

Shajib Mahmood Alam
Counsels Law Partners

Monirul Azam
University of Chittagong,
Department of Law

Junayed Chowdhury
Vertex Chambers

Md. Khademul Islam Choyon
Bangladesh Lawyers' and Law
Students' Association

Rafiqul Islam
Obiter Dictum

Wahid Sadiq Khan
Obiter Dictum

Sifat Jahan Nikita
Vertex Chambers

Shahana Rahman Shumii

Christabel Randolph
Supreme Court of Bangladesh

Muhammad Rashel Siddiqui
Obiter Dictum

Tasnima Tabassum

Md. Moyeen Uddin
Vital Strategies

BARBADOS

Christopher Birch
Government of Barbados

Winston Coppin
Land Registry Department

Olivia dos Santos
Elliott D. Mottley & Co.

Ryan Omari Drakes
Clarke Gittens Farmer
Attorneys-at-Law

Cadian Drummond
Harridyal-Sodha & Associates
(LizaLaw)

Joy Green
Land Adjudication Unit

Theo Jones
Emeth Chambers

Leandre Murrell-Forde
Lands and Surveys Department

Leisa Perch
Consultant

Shakieda Sealy
Leslie F. Haynes Q.C. Chambers

Jill St. George
University of the West Indies

Gerald Trotman

Sade Williams

BELARUS

Irina Alkhovka
International Public Association
"Gender Perspectives"

Ahniya Asanovich

Alexander Karankevich
UNICEF

Sergei Makarchuk
CHSH Cerha Hempel Spiegelfeld
Hlawati

Andrei Neviadouski
Cierech, Neviadouski and
Partners Advocates Bureau

Anna Pinayeva
UNICEF

Natallia Raisanen
Cierech, Neviadouski and
Partners Advocates Bureau

Katsiaryna Shmatsina
American Bar Association
Section of International Law

Dzmitryj Shylau
Cierech, Neviadouski and
Partners Advocates Bureau

Juri Slepitch
Arzinger & Partners

Nikita Tolkanitsa
CHSH Cerha Hempel Spiegelfeld
Hlawati

Alena Zhdanovich
Law Practice and Family
Mediation

BELGIUM

Mayer Brown International LLP

Ibrahim Akrouh
Legisquadra

Eleanor Jenifer Coets
Hôpital Erasme

Amélie d'Aspremont
Dechert LLP

Marjolein De Backer
Dechert LLP

Marie de Fauconval
Université de Namur

Roxane de Giey
White & Case LLP

Pierre-Yves Materne
Legisquadra

Pauline Tart
White & Case LLP

Aurélie Terlinden
White & Case LLP

Ysabelle Vuillard
Dechert LLP

Karla Vuyts
Dechert LLP

BELIZE

Melissa Balderamos Mahler
Balderamos Arthurs LLP

Robertha Magnus-Usher
Robertha Magnus-Usher and
Associates

Andrea McSweaney McKoy
McKoyTorres LLP

Leslie Mendez
Marine Parade Chambers

Deshawn Arzu Torres
McKoyTorres LLP

Ann-Marie Williams
The National Women's
Commission

BENIN

Serge Egnon Akpaka
UNICEF

André Akpinfa
Consultant

Agnila Rafikou Alabi
Cabinet Rafikou A. Alabi

Albert Djidohokpin
SOS Children's Villages Benin

Joseph Foundohou
Direction Générale des Impôts
et des Domaines

Christel Akofa Gomez
Kepha Consultants

Lionel Camus Lokossou

Yacoubou Moutairou
Réseau Pour l'Intégration des
Femmes des Organisations
Non Gouvernementales
et Associations Africaines
(RIFONGA)

Alexandrine Saïzonou-Bedie
Cabinet Saizonou

Guy-Lambert Yêkpê
Cabinet G.L. Yêkpê

BHUTAN

Karma Chhoden
Renew

Nima Dorji
Jigme Singye Wangchuck
School of Law

Kesang Wangmo
Jigme Singye Wangchuck
School of Law

BELIZE

BOLIVIA

Claudia Acosta Echavarría
Claudia Acosta Law Firm

Andrea Bollmann Duarte
Salazar, Salazar & Asociados
Soc. Civ.

Polina Chtchelok
ESPCS Multidisciplinary
Consulting

Syntia Villma Cuentas Zeballos
Salazar, Salazar & Asociados
Soc. Civ.

Claudia López Monterrey
ESPCS Multidisciplinary
Consulting

Julieta Montaño
Oficina Jurídica Para la Mujer

Sandra Salinas
C.R. & F. Rojas Abogados

BOSNIA AND
HERZEGOVINA

Gerc Sumejja Mostar Sjever
Potoci

Jasmin Cengic
Erc Zipo DOO Sarajevo

Selma Demirović-Hamzić
Marić & Co. Law Firm

Feđa Dupovac
Advokatska Kancelarija Spaho

Vedran Hadžimustafić
Wolf Theiss

Samra Hadžović
Wolf Theiss

Mervan Miraščija

Adnan Sarajlić
Wolf Theiss

Emir Spaho
Advokatska Kancelarija Spaho

Mehmed Spaho
Advokatska Kancelarija Spaho

Selma Spaho
Advokatska Kancelarija Spaho

Maja Vezmar

BOTSWANA

Kealeboga Kelly Dambuza

Tatenda Dumba
Armstrongs Attorneys Notaries
& Conveyancers

Lesego Gaetwesepe

Gaofenngwe Kabubi

Mpho Leteane
Lawyer

Refilwe Mogwe

Julia Dineo Poloko
Civil & National Registration
Botswana

BRAZIL

Barbosa Müssnich Aragão
(BMA)

Josycler Arana
Universidade Federal
Fluminense

José Baltazar
3rd Land Registry of Campo
Grande

Letícia Calderaro Batista
Calderaro Advocacia

Pedro Pimenta Bossi
Federal Regional Court of 4th
Region

Luiz Calixto
Bichara Advogados

Karen Cárdenas
Foreign Ministry

Carla Appollinário Castro
Universidade Federal
Fluminense

Ligia Maura Costa
Ligia Maura Costa, Advocacia

Carolina Candida da Cunha
Vital Strategies

Tamara de Farias
Order of Attorneys of Brazil

Christiana Fontenelle
Bichara Advogados

Ashley Frederes
Vital Strategies

Karina de Fatima Bonalume
Freire

Espaço Singular Berçario e
Educação Infantil

Murilo Caldeira Germiniani
Machado, Meyer, Sendacz e
Opice Advogados

Renata Braga Klevenhusen
Universidade Federal
Fluminense

Natalia Lorena Loscocco
Universidad de Buenos Aires,
Facultad de Derecho

Thais Machado
Federal Regional Court of 4th
Region

Jorge Gonzaga Matsumoto
Bichara Advogados

João Pedro Eyler Póvoa
Bichara Advogados

Nickolas Valentin Risovas
Machado, Meyer, Sendacz e
Opice Advogados

Andrea Giamondo Massei Rossi
Machado, Meyer, Sendacz e
Opice Advogados

Mauricio Quadros Soares
Quadros e Quadros Sociedade
de Advogados

Naomy Christiani Takara

Iane Pontes Vieira
Pontes Vieira Advogados

Iure Pontes Vieira
Pontes Vieira Advogados

BRUNEI DARUSSALAM

Syarifah Safinatul Najah Bte
Malai Haji Abdul Hamid
Abas Serudin & Partners

Hajah Norajimah Haji Aji
Ministry of Home Affairs,
Department of Labor

Aziimah Hambali
Zico Law

Norizzah Hazirah Hussin
Ministry of Home Affairs,
Department of Labor

Nava Palaniandy
Ahmad Isa & Partners

Rokiah Swed
Abas Serudin & Partners

BULGARIA

Registry Agency

Roza Dimova
Center of Women's Studies and
Policies

Kate Dinovska
Nova Jus

Boris Georgiev
Nova Jus

Dessislava Illieva

Milena Kadieva
Gender Alternatives Foundation

Tatyana Kmetova
Center of Women's Studies and
Policies

Tsvetelina Marinova
Dontchev, Zamfirova, Marinova
Law Firm

Diliana Markova
Animus Association Foundation

Katerina Partenova
Dimov & Tashev Law Firm

Tereza Shishkova
Lawyer

BURKINA FASO

Samirah Dera

Lucien Hien
Ministère de l'Education
Nationale et de
l'Alphabétisation

Safièta Nawalagumba Koanda
Dera

Mariam Lamizana
Voix de Femmes (VdF)

Honorine Medah
GOLD

Julie Rose Ouedraogo
Judge

Karim Ouedraogo
DGI

Noraogo Henri Ouedraogo
Direction Générale des Impôts

Victoria Ouedraogo
Judge

Emma Ouedraogo Zoma
Projet de Renforcement de
Gouvernance Locale

Charles Ribgoalinga
Judge

Souleymane Sawadogo
Judge

Abdoulaye Sedogo
Agence du Partenariat pour le
Développement

Abdoulaye Soma
Centre d'Études et de
Recherches sur le Droit
International et les droits de
l'Homme (CERDIH)

Aimé Gérard Yameogo
GOLD

BURUNDI

Célestin Bahati
Centre for Development and
Enterprise

Pascasie Barampama
Association Réseau Femmes
et Paix

Protais Bugabo
Press Ikiriho

Jean Marie Hahombuwungutse
Ballon des Avocats du Burundi

Jean Paul Kagoye
Centre for Development and
Enterprise

Aimable Manirkiza
Centre for Development and
Enterprise

Diomede Miburo
Ballon des Avocats du Burundi

Salvator Minani
Alpha Justice Chambers

Paul Muhirwa
Association de Lutte Contre
l'Impunité et l'Injustice au
Burundi

Christian Nduwayo
Maître Placide Gatoto, Cabinet
d'Avocats

Arcade Nivyintizo
Ntizo SA

Fabien Segatwa
Cabinet Segatwa Fabien &
Associés

Jean Berchmans Siboniyo
AMEBE/Mentorship Club

CABO VERDE

Teresa Teixeira B. Amado
Lawyer

Jessica Andre

Ilídio Cruz
Ilídio Cruz & Associados,
Sociedade de Advogados RL

Amanda Fernandes
Ilídio Cruz & Associados,
Sociedade de Advogados RL

Arianna Lopes
Neville de Rougemont &
Associados

Nedson Pimenta Maurício
Lawyer

João Medina
Neville de Rougemont &
Associados

Clóvis Santos
Ilídio Cruz & Associados,
Sociedade de Advogados RL

Arnaldo Silva
Arnaldo Silva & Associados,
Sociedade de Advogados RL

Bartolomeu Lopes Varela
Researcher and Consultant

CAMBODIA

The Cambodian Center for
Human Rights

Chankoulika Bo
BNG Legal

Anne Breillat

Sophal Chea
Better Factories Cambodia

Channeang Chim
The Cambodian NGO
Committee on CEDAW

Darwin (Naryth) Hem
BNG Legal

Bunthea Keo
Cambodian Human Rights Task
Force

Sok Hun Ngov
BNG Legal

Ratana Pen

Heng Sophat
Department of Civil Registration

Dana Wallack
The Cambodian NGO
Committee on CEDAW

CAMEROON

Adidja Amani
Ministère de la Santé Publique
du Cameroun

Abel Epse Piskopani Armelle
Silvana
Monde Juridique et Fiscal
(MOJUFISC)

Angelina Atabong

Dieudonné Behlong
World Organisation for Early
Childhood Education and Care
(OMEP)

Jean-Marie Vianney Bendégué
IG/MINDCAF

Alain Philippe Binyet Bi Mbog
World Organisation for Early
Childhood Education and Care
(OMEP)

Chunga Collins Che
Voice of Grace Foundation

Hyacinthe Fansi
Ngassam, Fansi & Mouafo
Avocats Associés

Samuel Kelodjoue
Demographer

Cynthia Ndukong
Voice of Grace Foundations

Suzanne Ngo Ntamack
World Organisation for Early
Childhood Education and Care
(OMEP)

Bolleri Pym
Université de Douala

Dieudonné Takam
Cabinet Takam & Associés

Oben Besong Takow
Voice of Grace Foundation

Bergerele Reine Tsafack
Dongmo
Monde Juridique et Fiscal
(MOJUFISC)

Ndonwi Wilfred
Voice of Grace Foundation

CANADA

Brian Ballantyne
Surveyor General Branch
Natural Resources Canada

Jennifer Bernardo
Baker & McKenzie

Stefanie Di Francesco
McMillan LLP Toronto

Cheryl Elliott
Baker & McKenzie

Caroline Kim
Miller Thomson LLP

Anne Levesque
University of Ottawa

Deepa Mattoo
Barbra Schlifer Commemorative
Clinic

Petra Molnar
Barbra Schlifer Commemorative
Clinic

Erin Tompkins
Surveyor General Branch
Natural Resources Canada

CENTRAL AFRICAN
REPUBLIC

Edgard Stephane Balegbaya
Sutter & Pearce RCA

Aurolle Euphrasie Donon
Bizon Ingénierie Juridique

Gabin Gracchus Guele
Primature

Brice Kevin Kakpayen
Cabinet Morouba

Dorothée Malenzapa
RESOLEP-FC

Raymond Ndakala
Barreau de Centrafrique

Adrien Nifasha
Avocats Sans Frontières

Kainda Zoungoula
Lawyer

CHAD

Victoire Alnoudji
Cabinet Thomas

Frédéric Dainonet Jouhinet
Dainonet Consulting & Partner

Masra Djimas
Société Civile d'Avocats

Lucas Madji Laoro
Cabinet Abdoulaye Adam Bahar

Tar Marie-France

Guy Emmanuel Ngankam
PwC

Bakari Thomas Ronelingaye

Foba Toukpleye

CHILE

Jorge Álvarez Vásquez
Servicio de Registro Civil e
Identificación Chile

Constanza Busquets Escuer
Energía Llaima SpA

Lidia Casas
Human Rights Center at
Universidad Diego Portales

Rosita Gaete
Superintendencia de Educación,
Región del Maule

Beatriz Garfias

Juan Ignacio Ipinza Mayor
Lawyer

Daniela Juica

Myriam Oyaneder
Mineduc

Lucía Planet Sepúlveda
Defesoría Laboral

Roberto Rodríguez

Selma Simonstein
World Organisation for Early
Childhood Education and Care
(OMEP)

Ligia Toro Araya
Servicio de Registro Civil e
Identificación Chile

Luis Andrés Ulloa Martínez
Energía Llaima SpA

CHINA

Dechert LLP

Xiaoying Huang
Yingke Law Firm

Gloria Li
China Top Credit Financial
Information Service

Xiaofei Li
Yingke Law Firm

Yawen Liu
Legal Assistant

Yilin Lu
Linklaters LLP

Meixin Ou
Yingke Law Firm

Xuekai Vincent Qian
Dentons

Jeffrey Wilson
Jun He LLP

Jianlei Xu
Dentons

Anderson Zhang
Dacheng Law Offices

Michael Hongtao Zhang
Dentons

Zhiwei Zhao
Sidley Austin

Yijia Zhu

COLOMBIA

Superintendencia de Notariado
y Registro

Paola Andrea Álvarez Murillo
Secretaría de Paz y Cultura
Ciudadana, Alcaldía de Santiago
de Cali

María Margarita Bucheli Eraso

Marianna Caballero
Dentons

Shadia Dager
Cavelier Abogados

Diana Sofia Gomez Giraldo
Secretaría de Paz y Cultura
Ciudadana, Alcaldía de Santiago
de Cali

Juan Camilo Guevara Ortíz
Secretaría de Paz y Cultura
Ciudadana, Alcaldía de Santiago
de Cali

Patricia Hernández
Cavelier Abogados

Adriana Martínez Piedrahita
DG&A Abogados

Dora Sofia Morales-Soto
Arrieta, Mantilla y Asociados

Catalina Ortiz-Suarez
Arrieta, Mantilla y Asociados

Mónica Rodríguez
Dentons

María Tafur
Registraduría Nacional del
Estado Civil

COMOROS

Djamal El-Dine Bacar
Barreau de Moroni

Azad Mze
Cabinet d'Avocats Mze

Ibrahim A. Mzimba
Cabinet Mzimba Avocats

Faïzat Said Bacar
CSI Avocats

CONGO, DEM. REP.

Justine Masika Bihamba
Synergie des Femmes pour les
Victimes de Violence Sexuelle
(SFVS)

Serge Faray Salumu

Eve Ingwa

Fabien Kadima

Upio Kakura Wapol
Emery Mukendi Wafwana &
Associates

Romaric Kavayita Talyamwayna
Fonds pour les Femmes
Congolaises

Noel Luenda
Office of Civil Registration and
Population

Rigobert Nzundu Mawunga
Emery Mukendi Wafwana &
Associates

Roger Mulamba
RMK & Associés

Vanessa Wirth
UNICEF

Dunia Zongwe
University of Namibia

CONGO, REP.

Patrice Bazolo
PwC

Kevin Kodia
Cabinet Quenum

Laetitia Nadine Loko

Issan Giska Ntsila
Cabinet d'Avocat Ntsila

COSTA RICA

Rocío Amador Hasbun
Bufete Amador

Larissa Arroyo Navarrete
Asociación Ciudadana ACCEDER

Carlos Luis Brenes Molina
Tribunal Supremo de Elecciones

Carolina Flores Bedoya
Arias

Vanessa Gómez
Kinder Sueños y Sonrisas

Cristina Guerrini
Arias

Angie Gumustas Carvajal
Centro Infantil Manitas
Creativas

Anna Karina Jiménez
Arias

Ana Priscilla Ortíz Saborío
Batalla Salto Luna

Laura Oviedo
Arias

Marianne Pál-Hegedüs Ortega
Gómez & Galindo LatamLex
Abogados

Daniel Rodríguez
Arias

Oscar Rodríguez Sánchez
Registro Nacional

CÔTE D'IVOIRE

Zirignon Constant Delbe
Ministère de l'Agriculture et du
Développement Rural

Claude-Andrée Groga
Cabinet Jean-François
Chauveau

Moumouni Konaté
Konfirm-Advies

Koffi Messou Kouassi
UNICEF

Xavier Edouard N'Cho
Ministère de l'Agriculture et du
Développement Rural

Eric-Didier N'dri
ONG AVIDE (Africa's Volunteers
for International Development)

Simon-Pierre N'dri-Kouakou
ONG AVIDE (Africa's Volunteers
for International Development)

Edwige N'Gouan
Cabinet Jean-François
Chauveau

Patricia N'Guessan
Cabinet Jean-François
Chauveau

Aimee Zebeyoux
Association des Femmes
Juristes de Côte d'Ivoire

CROATIA

Ministry of Public Administration

Marko Borsky
Marko Borsky Law Office

Saša Divjak
Divjak, Topić & Bahtijarević Law Firm

Sandra Kozić
Posavec, Rašica & Liszt Law Firm

Marko Lovrić
Divjak, Topić & Bahtijarević Law Firm

Ema Marušić
Marko Borsky Law Office

Dominik Musulin
Divjak, Topić & Bahtijarević Law Firm

Karlo Novosel
Law Office Karlo Novosel

Zdravka Sadžakov
B.a.B.e. - Be active, Be emancipated

Adrijana Visnjic Jevtic
University of Zagreb, Faculty of Teacher Education

Miroslav Zadro

CYPRUS

Marios Agrotes
Researcher

Panayiota Chrysochou

Demetris Georgiades
Harneys Aristodemou Loizides Yiolitis LLC

Martha Kalana
Association for the Prevention and Handling of Violence in the Family (SPAVO)

Nadia Kornioti
Cyprus Red Cross Society

Mary Koutselini

Nicholas Ktenas
Andreas Neocleous & Co. Legal Consultants

Olga Lambrou-Ioannou
Mouaimis & Mouaimis LLC

Marina Massoura

Michalis Mouaimis
Mouaimis & Mouaimis LLC

Panayotis Mouaimis
Mouaimis & Mouaimis LLC

Demetris Nicolaou
Harneys Aristodemou Loizides Yiolitis LLC

Susana Pavlou
Mediterranean Institute of Gender Studies

CZECH REPUBLIC

Marek Dvorak
Advokát JUDr. Marek Dvořák

Milanda Kurtosiova
Kocián Šolc Balaštík

Radek Matouš
Dvořák Hager & Partners

Lenka B. Olejnikova

Zuzana Ondrůjová
Office of the Public Defender of Rights

Katerina Ronovska
Masaryk University

Sasha Stepanova
Kocián Šolc Balaštík

DENMARK

Elsebeth Aaes-Jørgensen
Norrbom Vinding

Hanne Hartoft
Aalborg University

Majken Johansen
Advokat Majken Johansen

Stig G. Lund
BUPL

Márcia Télya Mesquita Viana Madsen

Laust Hvas Mortensen
Statistics Denmark

Tina Reissmann
Plesner

Mathilde Worch Jensen
The Danish Institute for Human Rights

DJIBOUTI

Mohammed Abayazid
Cabinet Avocats Associés Djibouti Abayazid & Abdourahman

Ali Dini
Cabinet d'Avocat Ali Dini

Abdoulkader Hassan Mouhoumed
Université de Djibouti

Zahra Youssouf Kayad

DOMINICA

Kimala Alfred
Dominica Legal Aid Clinic

Jo-Anne Cuffy

Danielle Edwards
Attorney-at-Law

Noelize Knight Didier
Harris, Harris & Didier

Tara Leevy
Attorney-at-Law

Eric Mendes
Ministry of Justice, Immigration and National Security

Melissa Morgan
Bureau of Gender Affairs

Pearl Williams
Supreme Court Registry

DOMINICAN REPUBLIC

Junta Central Electoral

José Manuel Alburquerque Prieto
Albuquerque & Albuquerque

Merielin Almonte
Merielin Almonte Estudio Legal

Isabel Andrickson
Pellerano & Herrera

Joan Carolina Arbaje Bergés
Distrito Legal

Pamela Benzán Arbaje
Guzmán Ariza & Asociados, Santo Domingo

Diógenes Bergés N.
Gilbert Tapia Legal SRL

Norvia Fernandez
Distrito Legal

Aura Celeste Fernández Rodríguez
Guzmán Ariza & Asociados, Santo Domingo

Melissa Gilbert
Gilbert Tapia Legal SRL

Laura Rosario Liberato
Guzmán Ariza & Asociados, Santo Domingo

Andreina Pérez
Gilbert Tapia Legal SRL

Laura Patricia Serrata Asmar
Albuquerque & Albuquerque

ECUADOR

María Fernanda Aguirre Salamea
Consejo de la Judicatura, Corte de Justicia de la Ciudad de Cuenca

Maria Laura Barrera
Barrera, Andrade-Cevallos & Abogados

María Angélica Campoverde
Lawyer

Dalila Cárdenas Ordóñez
Consejo de la Judicatura, Corte de Justicia de la Ciudad de Cuenca

Stefania Castro
Barrera, Andrade-Cevallos & Abogados

Elba Domaccin
World Organisation for Early Childhood Education and Care (OMEP)

Sarah Espinosa-MoraBowen
Universidad de las Américas Quito

Pablo Javier Falconí Castillo
Registro de la Propiedad del Distrito Metropolitano de Quito

Ashley Frederes
Vital Strategies

Cinthya Game
Universidad Catòlica de Santiago de Guayaquil

Monica García
Hospital Abel Gilbert Pontón

Ana Lucía Iñiguez
Universidad de Cuenca

María Dolores Mino
Universidad de las Américas Quito

Beatriz Orellana Serrano
Corporación Mujer a Mujer

Viviana Lissette Puyol Moscoso
Empresa Publica Municipal Registro de la Propiedad de Guataquil

Lorena Quintana
World Organisation for Early Childhood Education and Care (OMEP)

Michael Suquilanda
World Organisation for Early Childhood Education and Care (OMEP)

Verónica Tobar Molina
Registro de la Propiedad del Distrito Metropolitano de Quito

Cristina Valencia Araujo

Veronica Vargas
Vital Strategies

Germania del Pilar Zapata Vega
Empresa Publica Municipal
Registro de la Propiedad de
Guataquil

Ivole Segundo Zurita Zambrano
Empresa Publica Municipal
Registro de la Propiedad de
Guataquil

EGYPT, ARAB REP.

Dalia Abdel Ghany
Sharkawy & Sarhan

Nagla Abou-Yousef
Rise & Shine Kinder-Care

Sahar Emam
Menoufia University

Rabha Fathy
Association of Egyptian Female
Lawyers

Mohamed Hashish
Soliman, Hashish & Partners

Saif Allah Kadry
Soliman, Hashish & Partners

Alyaa Rabea
Soliman, Hashish & Partners

EL SALVADOR

Lilian Arias
Arias

Christian Bará Cousin
Bara Legal Corporation

María José Benítez

Daniela Bravo

Helga Cuéllar-Marchelli
FUSADES

Xenia Díaz
UNDP

Marcela López
FUSADES

Angel Pineda
FUSADES

Aida Carolina Quinteros
FUSADES

Enrique Toruella
Arias

Ana María Umaña de Jovel
Centro Nacional de Registros
(CNR)

Julio César Vargas Solano
García & Bodán

Margarita Velado
Registro Nacional de las
Personas Naturales

Roberto Vidales
FUSADES

Morena Zavaleta
Arias

Ileana Zepeda Lopez
García & Bodán

EQUATORIAL GUINEA

Irene Balaguer Delgado
L&S Abogados

Javier Iñiguez

Estela Mercedes Nse Mansogo
Centurion Law Group

Pablo Obama
Centurion Law Group

Miguel Santos Osa Nkara
Lawyer

ERITREA

Senai Andemariam

Biniam F. Ghebremichael
Lawyer

Haben Fecadu

Natnael Fitsum
Ministry of Justice

Henok Gebregzabiher

Aman Habtezghi
Public Prosecution Office

Senay Kuflu

Merhawi W Semere
Public Prosecution Office

Adam Teklehaymanot
Lawyer

Isaias Teklia
Asmara University

Wegahta Zere

ESTONIA

Merle Albrant
Estonian Human Rights Centre

Triin Antsov
Law Office Arvisto & Partners

Kelli Eilart
Law Firm Sorainen

Indrek Ergma
PwC

Merle Erikson
University of Tartu

Triinu Hiob
Njord Law Firm

Karin Madisson
Law Firm Sorainen

Rando Maisvee
Advokaadibüroo Eversheds Ots
& Co.

Anne Värvimann
Law Office Leppik & Partners

ETHIOPIA

Fikadu Asfaw
Fikadu Asfaw and Associates
Law Office

Selam Gebretsion Beyene

Bayeh Dessie
Land Registration Expert

Ousman Esleman Esmale
Ministry of Health

Lemlem Fiseha Minale
Ministry of Foreign Affairs

Yodit Gurji
Fikadu Asfaw and Associates
Law Office

Abhilasha Joshi Kataria

Anchinesh Mulu
Addis Ababa University

Dunia Tegegn
Lawyer

Behailu Weldeyohannes
Researcher

FIJI

Shamima Ali
Fiji Women's Crisis Center

Madonna Fong
Jamnadas and Associates

Sargam Goundar
UNICEF

Radhika Naidu
Sherani & Co.

Armish Pal
AP Legal

FINLAND

Rita Aalto-Saari
Castrén & Snellman Attorneys
Ltd.

Duin Ghazi

Lisa Grans
Åbo Akademi University

Pia Holm
Law Office Pia Holm Ltd.

Johanna Jacobsson
IE University

Päivi Kovalainen
UNICEF

Tuulikki Mikkola
University of Turku

Janne Murtoniemi
The National Land Survey of
Finland

Raija-Leena Ojanen
Dittmar & Indrenius

Mika Pahlsten
PwC

Johanna Pakkanen
NYTKIS - The Coalition of
Finnish Women's Associations

FRANCE

Jérémie Blond
Cabinet Jérémie Blond

Julie Boitard
ABC Puériculture

Noëlle Buton
ABC Puériculture

Béatrice Collette

Alexia Delahousse
Dechert LLP

Aude Chloé Froment
FLA Avocats

Paul Gallix
Gallix Avocats

Leyla Hamilton
ABC Puériculture

Vincent Latournerie
Dechert LLP

Marc Payant
TNDA Cabinet D'Avocats

Virginie J.M. Tassin
BHM Penlaw

Véronique Tuffal-Nerson
TNDA Cabinet D'Avocats

Maria Varela
TNDA Cabinet D'Avocats

Emilie Xio Chi Hu
Dechert LLP

GABON

Delphine Lemboumba

Casimira Oliveira
Cabinet d'Avocats A. Bikalou

Catherine Teya
F.E.A.G. Conseil

Bernie Yala-Tchimbakala
Cabinet d'Avocats A. Bikalou

GAMBIA, THE

Simeon Ateh Abi
Judiciary of The Gambia

Musu Bakoto Sawo
Think Young Women

Haddy Mboge Barrow
Network Against Gender Based
Violence (NGBV)

Abdul Aziz Bensouda
Amie Bensouda & Co.

Buba Darboe

Elizabeth J.C. Dunn
Judiciary of The Gambia

Mohamad Edirissa Faal
Lawyer

Malick Fafa M'Bai
Fajara Chambers

Oludayo Fagbemi
Institute for Human Rights and
Development in Africa

Lamin Fatty

Sheikh Tijan Hydara
Lex Fori Law Chamber

Cherno Marenah
Ministry of Justice

Satang Nabaneh
Think Young Women

Ya Amie Touray
University of The Gambia and
The Public Utilities Regulatory
Authority

Sanjally Trawally

GEORGIA

Sopio Akhaladze
GL Consulting LLC

Nino Bakakuri
Supreme Court of Georgia

Tamar Jikia
Dechert Georgia LLC

Ana Kochiashvili
Dechert Georgia LLC

Ana Kostava
Dechert Georgia LLC

Natia Lapiashvili
Dechert Georgia LLC

Ekaterine Lobadze
Sakhli (Union) - Advice Center
for Women

Nicola Mariani
Dechert Georgia LLC

Ketevan Shubashvili
Public Defender of Georgia

Victoria Wincott
Lawyer

GERMANY

Diclehan Demir
Ashurst LLP

Nancy M. Gage-Lindner
Hessisches Ministerium für
Soziales und Integration

Silvia Knittl

Greg Lourie
WilmerHale

Heinrich Nemeczek
Lawyer

Heiko Recktenwald

Nicole Schlatter
Kirkland & Ellis International
LLP

Bärbel Schmidt
Independent Consultant

Alexander Schumacher
Ashurst LLP

Jürgen Streng
Mayer Brown International LLP

Juditha von der Heydt
Ashurst LLP

Martin Wiesner
Ashurst LLP

GHANA

Births and Deaths Registry

Rahama Abdul-Rahman
Empowering and Transforming
Communities (ETC)

Lom Ahlijah

Valery Atuwo
Kimathi & Partners

Hilary Gbedemah
The Law Institute

Mubarik Ibrahim
Northern Girl Initiative

Nicole-Marie Poku
Sory @ Law

Senu Pomevor
Office of the Administrator of
Stool Lands

Grace Sackey

Judith Naa Ode Stephens

GREECE

Ministry of Interior, Directorate
of Civil Affairs

Moraitis School

Korina Batzikosta
A. Koudrouglou-Ioannidou and
Associates Law Firm

Emmanuel Kosmas
Lawyer

Kostis Krimizis
Krimlaw Law Offices

Evangelia Makri
Lawyer

Effie Mitsopoulou
Kyriakides Georgopoulos Law
Firm

Markella Papadouli

Kalliopi Paschalidou

Paraskevi-Vivianna Paschou
Panagiotis Paschos Law Office

Alexandra Pentaraki
Brain Matters Institute

Panagiota Tsinouli
Kyriakides Georgopoulos Law
Firm

Ioanna Tzinieri

Viktoria Zioga
Data Protection Office,
European Commission

GRENADA

Rosana John
Wilkinson, Wilkinson &
Wilkinson

Tanya K. Lambert
Wilkinson, Wilkinson &
Wilkinson

Jacqueline Lorice Pascal
Grenada National Organisation
of Women (GNOW)

Lisa Taylor
Lisa Taylor & Co.

Rae Thomas

Herricia Willis
H.L. Willis & Associates

GUATEMALA

Pedro Aragón
Aragón & Aragón

Geovani Javier Avendaño
Maldonado

María Elena Barrientos
Arias

María Caballeros
Roquita Fuerte Day Care

María Mercedes Castro
García & Bodán

Ana Gabriela Contreras García
Lawyer

Liz Gordillo Anleu
Arias

Rita María Grajeda Díaz

Brenda Amarilis Gramajo
González
Registro Nacional de las
Personas (RENAP)

Iris Hécica Hernández Galicia
Registro Nacional de las
Personas (RENAP)

Gabriela Rivera

GUINEA

Amadou Babahein Camara
Cabinet Soumah & Camara
(SouCa)

Ibrahima Diallo
P.C.U.D.

Mohamed Lamine Fofana
Sylla & Partners

Frederic Loua Foromo

Aimé Raphael Haba
Université pour Développement
Communautaire de Guinée

Alpha Toubab Millimono
Ask Me Plus

Sadou Savané
Sylla & Partners

GUINEA-BISSAU

Humiliano Alves Cardoso
Gabinete Advocacia

Adelaida Mesa D'Almeida
Jurisconta SRL

João Pedro C. Alves de Campos
Ministry of Justice

Ismael Mendes de Medina
GB Legal - Miranda Alliance

Monica Indami
Bissau First Instance Court,
Commercial Division

Ana Leão
Consultant

Emílio Ano Mendes
GB Legal - Miranda Alliance

GUYANA

Shaunella Glen
Temple Chambers, Ramjattan &
Associates

Rocky Hanoman

Sherrie Hewitt
Guyana Sugar Corporation Inc.

Ayana McCalman
Lawyer

Nirvana Singh

Judy Stuart-Adonis
Ministry of Legal Affairs and
Attorney General Chambers

HAITI

Mimose Andre Royal
Ministère à la Condition
Féminine et aux Droits des
Femmes

Francoise Bouzi Bonhomme
Cabinet Dantès P. Colimon

Elisabeth Colimon Woolley
Cabinet Dantès P. Colimon

Marie F. Missly Gilles
Lawyer

Daniel Jean
Themis Cabinet d'Avocats

Patrice Laventure
International Labour
Organization

Martine Romain Mégie
Cabinet Dantès P. Colimon

Charlotte Marie Tessy Romulus
Ministère à la Condition
Féminine et aux Droits des
Femmes (MCFDF)

HONDURAS

Alma Coello
INAM

Alejandra Paola Cruz Navas
Bufete Casco-Fortín-Cruz &
Asociados

Shadia García
Grupo Terra

Oscar Anibal Puerto Gómez
OFALAM

Roberto Williams Cruz
Bufete Casco-Fortín-Cruz &
Asociados

HONG KONG SAR, CHINA

Citrine Ho
Kirkland & Ellis

Camille Leung
Squire Patton Boggs

Anna Li
Dechert LLP

Nga Kit Christy Tang

Yang Wang
Dechert LLP

Sandy Yeung
Kirkland & Ellis

David Yun
Kirkland & Ellis

HUNGARY

Patent Association Hungary

Schalkház Eva Edit
Schalkház Law Office

Szilvi Gyurko
Hintalovon Foundation

Mariann Miskovics

Petra Ruzsvánszky
Schmidt Law Office

Réka Török
Law Office of Marianna Toth

Marianna Toth
Law Office of Marianna Toth

Márton Leó Zaccaria
University of Debrecen, Faculty
of Law

Piroska Zalaba
Ministry of Agriculture

Csató Zoltán
Csató Law Office

ICELAND

Guðrún Bergsteinsdóttir
Local Attorneys

Helga Bogadóttir

Ólafur Eiríksson
Logos Legal Services

Steinunn Holm Gudbjarsdottir
Law Firm of Holm & Partners

Hjördís Guðbrandsdóttir

Aron Freyr Jóhannsson
Logos Legal Services

Davíd Sveinbjörnsson
Advel Attorneys-at-Law

INDIA

Saravanan A
Rajiv Gandhi School of
Intellectual Property Law, IIT
Kharagpur

Saurav Agarwal
India Law LLP

Meghna Bal
Hammurabi & Solomon

Shweta Bharti
Hammurabi & Solomon

Benarji Chakka
School of Law, Symbiosis
International University

Sneha Dubey
India Law LLP

Aanchal Kapoor

Rajas Kasbekar
Little & Co. Advocates &
Solicitors

Soumyashree Kulkarni
Lawyer

Manoj Kumar
Hammurabi & Solomon

J. Mandakini
India Law LLP

Shiju P.V.
India Law LLP

Suryakanta Sahoo
Legum Amicuss

Vrajlal Sapovadia

Mandavi Singh

Kanisshka Tyagi
Kesar Dass B. & Associates

Eklavya Vasudev
Delhi High Court

INDONESIA

Virgo Eresta Jaya
Ministry of Agrarian and Spatial
Planning

Lany Harijanti

Nursyahbani Katjasungkana
Indonesian Legal Aid
Association for Women

Andreas Kodrat
Andreas FK & Katjasungkana

Rusmaini Lenggogeni
Soewito Suhardiman
Eddymurthy Kardono

Ijechi Nwaozuzu

Niken Prawesti
Griya Group

Dhanu Prayogo
Prayogo Advocaten Law Office

Tanita Dhiyaan Rahmani
Soewito Suhardiman
Eddymurthy Kardono

Achmad Rifai

Kiki Setiawan
Kiki Setiawan and Partners

Bhredipta Socarana

IRAN, ISLAMIC REP.

Camelia Abdolsamad
International Law Office of Dr.
Behrooz Akhlaghi & Associates

Behrooz Akhlaghi
International Law Office of Dr.
Behrooz Akhlaghi & Associates

Fatemeh Azizi
Azizi Law Firm

Roza Einifar
International Law Office of Dr.
Behrooz Akhlaghi & Associates

Shahin Fadakar
International Law Office of Dr.
Behrooz Akhlaghi & Associates

Nasim Gheidi
Gheidi & Associates Law Office

Razieh Heidary
Gheidi & Associates Law Office

Mahsa Kayyal

Parya Maleknia
Attorney-at-Law

Negin Saberi
International Law Office of Dr.
Behrooz Akhlaghi & Associates

Armis Sadri
Student, American University
Washington College of Law

Khatereh Shahbazi
International Law Office of Dr.
Behrooz Akhlaghi & Associates

Sahar Sotoodehnia
International Law Office of Dr.
Behrooz Akhlaghi & Associates

Sara Tajdini
Gheidi & Associates Law Office

IRAQ

Bushra Al-Aubadi
University of Baghdad

Ahmed Al Janabi
Mena Associates in Association
with Amereller

Fadhel Alqaseer
Yes For Human Rights
Organization

Adnan Alsakban
Accountant and Auditor Bar

Maha Alsakban
Women's Human Rights Center

Muhanad Altubee
Together For Human Rights
Organization

Dana Asa'ad

Muhammed Yassin Hamami

Fatin Nabil

Zeyad Saeed
Iraqi Law Firm

IRELAND

Women's Aid

Anna C. Brennan

Ellen Campbell

Marilyn Cooney
Dechert LLP

Roisin Aine Costello
Lambert FitzGerald Consulting

Barbara Cronin
Dechert LLP

Louise O'Byrne
Arthur Cox

Colman O'Loghlen
Dechert LLP

ISRAEL

Gali Atzion

Pnina Broder Manor
Naschitz, Brandes, Amir & Co.

Tali Eisenberg
Lawyer

Roxanne E. Formey

Irit Gazit

Moien Odeh
Odeh and Partners

ITALY

Enrichetta Sandra Bellini
Fornera
Business and Professional
Women International (BPWI)

Gianluigi Borghero
Lawyer

Luca Calabrese
Studio Legale Calabrese & A.

Marco Calabrese
Studio Legale Calabrese & A.

Federica Di Mario
Salonia Associati Studio Legale

Andrea Gangemi
Portolano Cavallo

Giliola Langher
Business and Professional
Women International (BPWI)

Miriam Mangieri
Lawyer

Irene Piccolo
A Me Importa Soltanto di
Sapere

Federica Re Depaolini
Lawyer

Paola Regina

Serena Spadavecchia

Valentina Turco
Portolano Cavallo

JAMAICA

Kamille Adair Morgan

Deborah Dowding
Nunes, Scholefield, DeLeon
& Co.

Brittney Elliott-Williams
University of the West Indies

Gabrielle Elliott-Williams
University of the West Indies

Kellye-Rae Fisher Campbell
Book Fusion Limited

Stephanie Forte
Attorney-at-Law

Carla-Anne Harris-Roper

Jennifer Jones
Independent Consultant

Monique Lyn Quee
Registrar General's Department

Affette McCaw-Binns
University of the West Indies

Sharon Neil Smith
Patterson Mair Hamilton

Natasha Parkins
Caribbean Accreditation
Authority

JAPAN

Tokyo District Public
Prosecutors Office

Kentaro Christophe Furusawa
Kanagawa International Law
Offices

Yasushi Higashizawa
Meiji Gakuin University

Kenichi Kojima
Ushijima & Partners

Tetsuya Kondo
Kanagawa International Law
Offices

Yuka Nakayama
Linklaters LLP

Fumie Saito
Interpraxis

Shin Ushijima
Ushijima & Partners

Makiko Yageta
Ushijima & Partners

JORDAN

Amer Mohamed Abu-Hassan
Abu-Hassan & Associates,
Lawyers & Consultants

Reem Abu-Ragheb
Book n Brush

Randa Adel
Civil Status Department

Osama Al Husamie
Osama Sukkari & Associates,
Attorneys-at-Law

Emad Al Khattab

Omar Aljazy
Aljazy & Co. (Advocates & Legal
Consultants)

Khaleel Al-Naimat
Al-Naimat Real Estate

Rana Atwan
Atwan & Partners Attorneys
and Legal

George Kara'a
USAID

Talar Karakashian
USAID

Mahmoud Ktitat
Department of Lands and
Survey

Suad Nabhan
UNFPA

Mohammad Sawafeen
Department of Lands and
Survey

Mouen Sayegh
Department of Lands and
Survey

J. David Thompson

KAZAKHSTAN

Tatiana Aderikhina
UNICEF

Yulia Chumachenko
Aequitas Law Firm

Dmitriy Chumakov
Sayat Zholshy & Partners Law
Firm

Yekaterina Khamidullina
Aequitas Law Firm

Marina Kolesnikova
GRATA International

Abylkhair Nakipov
Signum Law Firm

Aliya Sabitova
GRATA International

Maya Sattarova
Crisis Center for Women and
Children

Aida Shadirova
Dechert LLP

Artem Timoshenko
Unicase Law Firm

Guldan Tlegenova
Crisis Center for Women and
Children

Yerzhan Toktarov
Sayat Zholshy & Partners

Ulzhan Uzimirova
Happy Baby

Sergei Vataev
Dechert LLP

Larisa Yemelyanova
Aequitas Law Firm

Kaysar Zaira
GRATA International

KENYA

Ben Akech
New Market Lab Inc.

Lilian Atieno Oloo
World Organisation for Early
Childhood Education and Care
(OMEP)

Peter Gachuhi
Kaplan & Stratton Advocates

Asiimwe Fred Johnson
Tumusiime, Kabega & Co.
Advocates

Jane Kariuki
Civil Registration Services
Kenya

Catherine Kiama
TripleOK Law Advocates LLP

Mercy Machocho

Valentine Njogu
Njogu & Ngugi Advocates

Angela Waweru
Kaplan & Stratton Advocates

KIRIBATI

Ministry of Health & Medical
Services

Ministry of Health & Medical
Services, Gender-Based
Violence Program

Tabotabo Auatabu
Ministry of Women, Youth and
Social Affairs

Sister Bernadette Eberi
Kiribati Law Society

Tomitiana Eritama
Ministry of Labour & Human
Resource Development

Anne Kautu
Ministry of Women, Youth and
Social Affairs

George Ueantabo Mackenzie
Maneaba Ni Maungatabu,
Kiribati Parliament

Anieli Fuatino Noa
Office of the People's Lawyer

Mireta Taaiteiti
Kiribati Police and Prison
Services (KPPS)

Sister Rosarin Tataua
OLSH Crisis Center

Kaitiro Tebano Tiroam
Ministry of Commerce, Industry
and Cooperation (MCIC)

Birimaka Tekanene
Office of the Attorney General

Batilea Tekanito
Batilea Tekanito Law Firm

Moia Tetoa
AMAK (National Council of
Women)

Teetua Tewera
Office of the People's Lawyer

Reei Tioti
Land Information Department

KOREA, REP.

Sun-Hee Cha
Kim & Chang

Eun-Jung Chin
Kim & Chang

Bongsoo Jung
Kang Nam Labor Law Firm

Weon-Jung Kim
Kim & Chang

Hyeji Lee
Kang Nam Labor Law Firm

Yong Min Lee
YM Law Office

Kumsung Yu
Kang Nam Labor Law Firm

KOSOVO

Adelina Berisha
Kosovo Women's Network

Sokol Elmazaj
Boga & Associates

Zana Govori

Drenushë Januzi
Kosovo Cadastral Agency

Besarta Kllokoqi
Boga & Associates

Vjollca Krasniqi
University of Pristina

Murat Meha
Kosovo Cadastral Agency

Vjosa Pllana
FOL Movement

Ariana Qosaj
Kosovo Women's Network

Fisnik Salihu
Fisnik Salihu & Partners LLC

Valbona Salihu
Lawyers Association Norma

Klit Shala
Fisnik Salihu & Partners LLC

Xhevdet Shala
Kosovo Cadastral Agency

Amantina Tolaj
Boga & Associates

KUWAIT

Ahmad Abo Al Majd
Al-Hamad Legal Group

Esra Alamiri
Wracati

Rana Al-Hamad
Al-Hamad Legal Group

Ali Matar Taher Alwawan
Ali Alwawan Lawyer Office

Amr Omran
Freshfields Bruckhaus Deringer

Ahmad Saleh
Lawyer

Mai Sartawi
Al-Hamad Legal Group

Sami Tannous
Freshfields Bruckhaus Deringer

KYRGYZ REPUBLIC

Elena Bit-Avragim
Veritas Law Agency

Saltanat Imanova
Veritas Law Agency

Lenara Mambetalieva
Promotion of Foreign
Investment to Kyrgyzstan

Elvira Maratova
GRATA International

Natalia Molodanova
Veritas Law Agency

Aalamgul Osmonalieva

Jyldyz Tagaeva
Kalikova & Associates Law Firm

Meerim Talantbek Kyzy
Kalikova & Associates Law Firm

LAO PDR

Steve Goddard
Arion Legal

Nancy Kim
The Asia Foundation

Florence Lo
Arion Legal

Vadsana Sinthavong
The Asia Foundation

Danyel Thomson
DFDL

LATVIA

Juris Dilba
Marta Resource Centre for
Women

Agnija Granger
Granger Law

Valerijs Ickevics
V. Ickevics, Sworn
Attorneys-at-Law

Jelena Kvjatkovska
ZAB Rode & Partneri

Ivo Maskalāns
Cobalt Legal

LEBANON

Leila Alem Hammoud
Alem & Associates Law Firm

Guida Anani

Aurore Deeb
Deeb & Co. for Legal Services

Lamia El Hachem Aassaf

Melkar El Khoury
International Federation of
Red Cross and Red Crescent
Societies

Fatima Hojeij

Sandra Khairallah

Ziad Maadarani
Ministry of Finance, Directorate
General of Land Registry and
Cadastre

Georges Maarrawi
Ministry of Finance, Directorate
General of Land Registry and
Cadastre

Nicole Maassab
Claire Maassab Nursery

Chafic Majdalani
Roula Abdallah Law Firm

Ghassan Moghabghab
Moghabghab & Associates Law
Firm

Tarek Moghabghab
Moghabghab & Associates Law
Firm

Mohammad Saleh

LESOTHO

Thuto Hlalele
Centre for Human Rights

Matsiu Lephaka
Land Administration Authority

Rethabile Mathealira-Molapo

Mamohale Matsoso
Ministry of Labour and
Employment

Mpho Matoka Molupe
Land Administration Authority

Mankuebe Moshoeshoe
Land Administration Authority

Mats'eliso Mota
Land Administration Authority

Itumeleng Mots'oene
Mofilikoane
Judiciary of Lesotho

Lipotso Musi
UNICEF

Nthoateng Russel
Ministry of Energy, Meteorology
and Water Affairs

Itumeleng Shale
National University of Lesotho

LIBERIA

Lucia D.S. Gbala
Heritage Partners and
Associates Inc.

Selma S. Gibson

James N. Jensen
The International Group
of Legal Advocates and
Counsultants

Al King
Primus Law Group

Milton D. Taylor
Law Offices of Taylor &
Associates Inc.

Etty Weah
Christian Women Peace
Initiative

LIBYA

Majdi Abdou
Tumi Law Firm

Aimen Almaloul

Nisreen Eisse
Lawyer

Mostafa Emsek

Bahloul Kelbash
Mukhtar, Kelbash & Elgharabli

Najla Mangoush
Lawyer

LITHUANIA

Lina Balkevičienė
State Enterprise Centre of
Registers

Manvydas Borusas
Eversheds Saladžius

Gerda Diniūtė
Eversheds Saladžius

Aušra Juknaitė
Law Firm Foresta

Juliana Pavilovska
Law Firm Sorainen

Algirdas Pekšys
Law Firm Sorainen

Vilana Pilinkaitė Sotirovič
Lithuanian Social Research
Center

Evelina Žurauskaitė
Vytautas Magnus University

LUXEMBOURG

Louis Berns
Arendt & Medernach SA

Raphaëlle Carpentier
Linklaters LLP

Katia Fettes
Linklaters LLP

Harry Ghillemyn
Linklaters LLP

Melinda Perera
Linklaters LLP

MACEDONIA, FYR

Ljupco Cvetkovski
Debarliev, Dameski & Kelesoska
Attorneys-at-Law

Vesna Donceva
Notary

Jasminka Frishchikj
Association for Emancipation,
Solidarity and Equality of
Women

Marija Gelevska
Association for Emancipation,
Solidarity and Equality of
Women

Ana Kashirska
Karanović & Nikolić

Emilija Kelesoska Sholjakovska
Debarliev, Dameski & Kelesoska
Attorneys-at-Law

Lidija Krstevska
Agency for Real Estate
Cadastre

Stojan Mishev
Association for Emancipation,
Solidarity and Equality of
Women

Martin Monevski
Monevski Law Firm

Valerjan Monevski
Monevski Law Firm

Vojdan Monevski
Monevski Law Firm

Veton Qoku
Karanović & Nikolić

Mirjana Stankovic
Law Office Stankovic and
Stankovic

MADAGASCAR

Johanne Andria-Manantena
Lawyer

Raphaël Jakoba
Madagascar Conseil
International

Nathalie Rajaonarivelo
JWF Legal

Olivia Alberte Rajerison
Cabinet Rajerison

Hoby Rakotoniary
JWF Legal

Veroniaina Ramananjohany
Catholic Relief Services

Hanitra Rasendrasoa

Hasimpirenena
Rasolomampionona

MALAWI

Masauko Chamkakala

Hendrina Givah
FAWEMA

Emma Kaliya
Malawi Human Rights Resource
Centre

Carol Tendai Makoko
KD Freeman & Associates

Burton Mhango
Mbendera & Nkhono Associates

Alinikisa Mphongolo
Plan International

Wongani Mvula
Malawi Law Commission

Zione Ntaba
Judge

Atusaye Nyondo
Community Development
Practitioner

MALAYSIA

National Council of Women's
Organisations, Malaysia

UNICEF

Suryna Ali

Amy Bala
Malaysian Association of Social
Workers

Heng Keng Chiam
Early Childhood Care &
Education Council

Natasha Dandavati
Women's Aid Organisation
(WAO)

Jamie Goh
Shearn Delamore & Co.

Irene Leow
Seri Mawar Child Care &
Development Centre

Norsuraya Pinjaman
National Registration
Department

Muhendaran Suppiah
Muhendaran Sri

Dominic Gan Teck Long
Dominic Gan & Co.

MALDIVES

Hope for Women

Suha Hussain
Shah, Hussain & Co.

Hisaan Hussein
Hisaan, Riffath & Co

Hamza Khaleel
Wisham & Co. LLP

Shafa Maseeh

Shuaib Shah
Shah, Hussein and Co.

Fathmath Yasmeen Shamaal
Suood & Anwar LLP

Maryam Manal Shihab
Suood & Anwar LLP

Mariyam Zulfa

MALI

Daouda Ba
Vaughan Avocats

Moussa Sinayoko
Jurifis Consult, Cabinet
d'Avocats

Cheick Oumar Tounkara
Hera Conseils

MALTA

Romina Bartolo
Iuris Malta Advocates

Karl Briffa
GVZH Advocates

Angela Bruno
GVZH Advocates

Christine Calleja
Mamo TCV Advocates

Ariana Falzon
GVZH Advocates

Annabel Hili
GVZH Advocates

Isotta Rossoni
University of Malta

Andrew J. Zammit
GVZH Advocates

MARSHALL ISLANDS

Micronesian Legal Services
Corporation

Alison Birchall
Weto in Mour: Violence Against
Women and Girls Support
Service, Women United
Together Marshall Islands
(WUTMI)

Eric Iban
Office of the Attorney General

Susanne Kayser-Schillegger

Marilyn Lakabung
Ministry of Internal Affairs

Kathryn Relang
Women United Together
Marshall Islands

Divine Waiti
Marsol Lawyers & Consultants

MAURITANIA

Mounina Abdellah

Sidi Ould Sid'Ahmed El Bkaye

Diego Gaspar de Valenzuela
Cueto
HADES Consulting

Oum Kalthoum Hamdinou

MAURITIUS

Daya Auckloo
Banymandhub Boolell
Chambers

Urmila Banymandhub Boolell
Banymandhub Boolell
Chambers

Sheren Govinden
Bibi Chambers

Sanjana Gujadhur
Etude Guy Rivalland

Pooja Luchmun
Chambers of A.R.M.A. Peeroo
SC Gosk

Darshani Devi Parsuramen

Navina Parsuramen

Bhomitrajeet Ramlochund
Mardemootoo Solicitors

Rajroop Roshan
Rajroop Chambers

Bhoyroo Shahila Deena
Aberystwyth University

Karyn Teck Yong

MEXICO

Fernando Carrasco
Hogan Lovells

María Fernanda Castellanos
Balcázar
Sánchez Devanny Eseverri SC

María de la Paloma Ferrer
Guerra
Consultores Integrales

Irma Garcia
Universidad Nacional Autónoma
de México (UNAM)

Lila Alejandra Gasca Enríquez
Hogan Lovells

Blanca Esther Jimenez Franco
Comisión de los Derechos
Humanos del Estado de
Coahuila de Zaragoza

Carlos López
Goodrich, Riquelme y
Asociados

Ricardo Mendoza
Comisión Nacional de los
Derechos Humanos

Lourdes Rincón Maltos
Lawyer

María José Ríos Hurtado
Secretaria Técnica, Comisión
de los Derechos Humanos del
Estado de Coahuila de Zaragoza

Jimena Robles García
Sánchez Devanny Eseverri SC

Mónica Schiaffino
Littler Mexico

Jorge Francisco Valdés King
Hogan Lovells

MICRONESIA, FED. STS.

David C. Angyal
Ramp & Mida Law Firm

Erick Divinagracia
Ramp & Mida Law Firm

Maria Donre
Pohnpei Women's Council

Jane Iwo
Micronesian Legal Services
Corporation

Marstella Jack
Law Office of Marstella Jack

Lorrie Johnson-Asher
Office of the Public Defender

Lululeen Santos
Pohnpei State Social Affairs
Office

Alona Tate
Pohnpei State Supreme Court

MOLDOVA

Promo-LEX Association

University of European
Economic and Political Studies
"Constantin Stere"

Andriana Cebotari
Moldova State University,
Faculty of Law

Eduard Digore
Lawyer

Iulia Furtuna
Turcan Cazac

Ecaterina Madan
The National Bureau of Motor
Insurers of Moldova

Vladimir Palamarciuc
Turcan Cazac

Alexander Tuceac
Turcan Cazac

MONGOLIA

O&T Law Firm

Otgon Altankhuyag
ELB Partners Attorneys-at-Law

Oyunzul Amartsengel
National Center for Public
Health

Delgermaa Anbat
Mongolian Legal Experts LLP

Erdenechimeg Badrakh
Mongolian Women's Fund
(MONES)

Solongo Batsuren
AZS & Associates LLP

Galmandakh Boldbaatar
Administration of Land
Management, Geodesy and
Cartography

Enkhjargal Davaasuren
National Center Against
Violence

Dulguun Erdenebulgan
Penn State Law

Enkhzul Jargal
Bayanzurkh District Health
Center

Ariungoo Khurelbaatar
Hogan Lovells

Ichinnorov Manjaa
Women's Leadership
Foundation

Dorjkhand Maravdorj
Lawyer

Chris Melville
Hogan Lovells

Arvintaria Nordogjav
National Center Against
Violence

Gerelmaa Surenjav
National Center for Public
Health

Anthony Woolley
Hogan Lovells

MONTENEGRO

Bisera Andrijašević
BDK Advokati

Jelena Bogetić
BDK Advokati

Jelena Danilović
Karanović & Nikolić

Aleksandra Gligorovic
Lawyer

Milan Novakov
Karanović & Nikolić

MOROCCO

Association Démocratique des
Femmes du Maroc

Mohammed Bentalha
Faculté de Droit de Marrakech

Samirah Bouachraoui

Samira Bouzid
Ministry of Interior

Kira Bromwich
CDC Foundation

Hicham Darfouf
CDC Foundation

Moulay El Amine El Hammoumi
Idrissi
Hajji & Associés

Abdelilah El Marnissi
CDC Foundation

Mourad Faouzi
Association Droit et Justice

Reda Gzouli
Gzouli Law Firm

Ali Lachgar Essahili
Ali Lachgar Essahili Law Firm

Adil Morsad
Cabinet d'Avocats Morsad

Amal Oummih
Oummih Law Firm

Sofia Rais
Association Droit et Justice

Elhabib Stati
Lycée Ibn Rochd

MOZAMBIQUE

Amina Abdala
TTA Sociedade de Advogados

Ancha Abdala

Anselmo Bila
ABA - Anselmo Bila &
Associados Advogados

Eduardo Calú
Sal & Caldeira Advogados LDA

Edina Culolo-Kozma
UNICEF

Baltazar Domingos Egidio
Lawyer

Catherine Flagothier

Ana Leão
Consultant

Sofia Vitória Magaia
Sal & Caldeira Advogados LDA

Gimina Mahumana
Sal & Caldeira Advogados LDA

Eunice Sepúlveda Matete
CM&A, Mozambique

Eugénia Nkutumula
Lawyer

Diana Ramalho
Sal & Caldeira Advogados LDA

Cesar Vamos Ver
Sal & Caldeira Advogados LDA

MYANMAR

NweNwe Aung
Yinthway Foundation

Ommar Kyaw
Central Statistical Organization
Myanmar

U San Lwin
JLPW Legal Services

Natalie Matranga
UNDP

Cho Myint
Interactive Co. Ltd.

Khin Zar Naing
UNFPA

Sanda Thant
Socio Economic and Gender
Resource Institute (SEGRI)

Aye Lei Tun
Enlightened Myanmar Research
Foundation (EMReF)

Thant Zin
United Nations Industrial
Development Organization

NAMIBIA

Anette Bayer Forsingdal
Ministry of Home Affairs and
Immigration

Christiaan Cronjé
Cronjé & Co.

Willem Eiseb
Ministry of Land Reform

Petrine Hango
Office of the
Prosecutor-General

Kennedy Haraseb
Metcalfe Attorneys Windhoek

Dianne Hubbard
Legal Assistance Centre

Razikua Kaviua

Jennilee Kohima
Du Toit Town Planning
Consultants

Gabriel Francios Kopplinger
Kopplinger Boltman Legal
Practitioners

Zandre la Cock
Cronjé & Co.

Alice Makemba
Metcalfe Attorneys Windhoek

Hilleni Tangi Shikongo
Office of the Attorney-General

Murray Shikongo
Office of the Judiciary

Salatiel Shinedima
Women's Action for
Development (WAD)

Rauha Shipindo
Kopplinger Boltman Legal
Practitioners

Cobus Visser
Koep & Partners

NEPAL

Archana Aryal
UNDP

Bishnu Bashyal
Women Lawyers of Nepal

Rishi Bhattarai
Milestone Law Firm

Shirsak Ghimire
Dhakal and Ghimire Law Offices
Pvt. Ltd.

Janak Raj Joshi
Ministry of Land Reform
and Management, Far West
Development Commission

Prakash Kafle
Save the Children

Gourish Krishna Kharel
KTO Inc.

Prakat Khati
Kathmandu School of Law

Joshi Krishna Datt

Jyoti Lamsal Poudel
Jyoti Poudel & Associates

Binda Magar
UNDP

Lachhindra Maharjan
Save the Children

Kumari Kaushalya Ojha
Law and Lawyer's Company

Surendra Pokharel

Kalyan Pokhrel
F-Dimensional Legal Services
and Research Centre Pvt. Ltd.

Manisha Poudel
Legal Aid and Consultancy
Center Nepal

Bishwa Ratna Pun
Save the Children

Tek Tamata
UNDP

Kirti Thapa
Save the Children

NETHERLANDS

Phinney Disseldorp
Stibbe

Galatée Fouquet
The Hague University of
Applied Sciences

Catherine Garcia van
Hoogstraten
The Hague University of
Applied Sciences

Wendy Guns
Open Universiteit

Alexander Kostin
The Hague University of
Applied Sciences

Alva Lindahl
The Hague University of
Applied Sciences

Eugenie Nunes
Dentons Boekel

Marije Ozinga
Dentons Boekel

Jaap van Slooten
Stibbe

Thessa van Zoeren

Jacques Vos
Cadastre, Land Registry and
Mapping Agency (Kadaster)

NEW ZEALAND

Tim Bain

Ruth Ballantyne
University of Otago

Josie Beverwijk

Simon Davies-Colley
WRMK Lawyers

Oliver Hailes
Court of Appeal of New Zealand

Lucy Harris
Simpson Grierson

Mark Henaghan
University of Otago

Tim Marshall
Tauawhi Men's Centre

Phillipa Muir
Simpson Grierson

Mary O'Dwyer

Nicola Peart
University of Otago

Josie Te Rata

Rachel Webster
Lawyer

NICARAGUA

Bertha Arguello
Arias

María Alejandra Aubert
Cárcamo
García & Bodán

Minerva Adriana Bellorín
Rodríguez
Pacheco Coto

Blanca Paola Buitrago Molina
García & Bodán

María Elena Dominguez
Centro de Mujeres ISNIN

Miriam del Socorro Espinosa
Pacheco Coto

Claraliz Oviedo Maglione
Alvarado y Asociados

Sofía de Carmen Rivas
Arias

Hansel Guillermo Saborío
González
García & Bodán

Carlos Eduardo Téllez Páramo
García & Bodán

NIGER

Issouf Baadhio
Cabinet d'Avocats Baadhio

Balkissa Ibrahim Aladou

Nassirou Lawali
Cabinet d'Avocats Baadhio

P. Kafui Elome Rachel Molley
Organisation Nationale d'Appui
au Développement (ONAD)

Haoua Moussa Dan Malam
African Network of Youth Policy
Experts Niger (AFRINYPE)

Moutari Moussa Oumarou
Cabinet d'Avocats Baadhio

Mai Moussa Moustapha
Souleymane
Cabinet d'Avocats Baadhio

Bachir Talfi
Faculté des Sciences
Economiques et Juridiques de
l'Université Abdou Moumouni
de Niamey

Idrissa Tchernaka
Société Civile Professionnelle
d'Avocats LBTI & Partners

NIGERIA

Surajudeen Abolade
National Bureau of Statistics

Adedolapo Adesina
Udo Udoma & Belo-Osagie

Agbolade Adeyemi
Udo Udoma & Belo-Osagie

Edidiong Ajayi
Udo Udoma & Belo-Osagie

Adebola Amao
Udo Udoma & Belo-Osagie

Folasayo Bakare
Udo Udoma & Belo-Osagie

Ogochukwu Ebubechukwu

Joseph Eimunjeze
Udo Udoma & Belo-Osagie

Mary Ekemezie
Udo Udoma & Belo-Osagie

Folake Elias Adebowale
Udo Udoma & Belo-Osagie

Sylvia Iwejuo
Lawyer

Mojisola Jawando
Udo Udoma & Belo-Osagie

Fe Obinali
Lawyer

Ozofu Ogiemudia
Udo Udoma & Belo-Osagie

Anthonia Okolie
Lawyer

Kelechi Ugbeva
KCU Legal

Hannibal Uwaifo
African Bar Association

NORWAY

Advokatfirmaet Næss, Lærum,
Lier & Stende AS

Eivind Arntsen
Dalan Advokatfirma DA

Marte Bauge

Maja Berthelsen Lindgren

Maria Cabrera Stråtveit
Dalan Advokatfirma DA

Tron Dalheim
Arntzen de Besche
Advokatfirma AS

Lill Egeland
Advokatfirmaet Simonsen Vogt
Wiig

Eirin Kogstad
Arntzen de Besche
Advokatfirma AS

Erik A. Øyen
Advokat Erik A. Øyen MNA

Jan-Erik Sverre
Kvale Advokatfirma DA

Thomas Talen
Deloitte Advokatfirma AS

OMAN

Sumaiya Al Balushi
Mohammed Al Ruqaishi Law
Firm

Amel Kamel Abdallah
Sultan Qaboos University
College of Law

George Kassimos
Curtis, Mallet-Prevost, Colt &
Mosle LLP

Tariq Abdulaziz Mohamed Sadiq
Oman Environmental Services
Holding Company SAOC

Alessandra Zingales
Curtis, Mallet-Prevost, Colt &
Mosle LLP

PAKISTAN

Hanif Afridi

Zulfiqar Ali Shah
Sindh Revenue Board

Muhammad Asif
Ministry of Planning,
Development and Reform

Erfaan Hussein Babak
The Awakening

Ahmed Bashir
Ahmed Bashir & Associates

Awais Choudhry

Hina Hafeezullah Ishaq

Jalal Hussain
SZH Law

Syed Akbar Hussain
SZH Law

Sana Iftikhar
Pfizer Pakistan Limited

Shakeel Imtiaz

Asif Karim
Sindh Revenue Board

Maria Karim
SZH Law

Ali Kirmani
SZH Law

Nazar Muhammad Leghari

Ghulam Abbas Naich
Abbas

Zermina Naveed
Usmani & Iqbal

Farah Nawaz

Adnan Qureshi
Qureshi Law Associates

Neelam Rahim
Shirkat Gah, Women's Resource
Centre

Syed Sameer Shah
SZH Law

Ameena Sohail
Qureshi Law Associates

Aamir Sultan
Ahmed Bashir & Associates

Shaiq Usmani
Usmani & Iqbal

Haya Eman Zahid
Lawyer

PALAU

Micronesian Legal Services
Corporation

Kenneth Barden
Attorney-at-Law

Danail Mizinov
Palau Office of the Public
Defender

PANAMA

Programa de Asistencia Legal
Comunitaria de Fundamorgan

Yeremi Marina Barria Arenas
Dirección Nacional de Registro
Civil del Tribunal Electoral

Milagros Caballero
Morgan & Morgan

Sophia Castillero
Suarez, Castillero, Holmes y
Richa

Nelly Cedeño de Paredes
Organo Judicial

Rocío Abril de Vidal
Registro Público de Panamá
(Sede Central)

Jennifer Delgado Urueta
Defensoría del Pueblo de la
República de Panamá

Karyne Mora
Cedeño & Méndez

Jose Antonio Perez
PGS Abogados

Elvia María Rengifo Rodríguez
Dirección Nacional de Registro
Civil del Tribunal Electoral

Sharon Michelle Sinclaire Roa
Dirección Nacional de Registro
Civil del Tribunal Electoral

Odalys Troudart
Arias

PAPUA NEW GUINEA

Deborah Edo
Ashurst LLP

Ethel Heagi
Ashurst LLP

Wavie Kendino
Dentons

Desmond Kipa
Twivey Lawyers

Lisa Kudada
Dentons

Gregory Lay
Judge

Eunice Parua
Leahy Lewin Lowing Sullivan
Lawyers

Michelle Pint
Leahy Lewin Lowing Sullivan
Lawyers

Anthony William Roden-Paru

Lucy Sabo-Kelis
Kumul Consolidated Holdings

Simeon Waia
Yalapan & Associates

Sherrie Williams
Ashurst LLP

PARAGUAY

María José Ayala
Centro de Estudios Ambientales
y Sociales (CEAMSO)

Patricia Doldán
Secretaría Nacional de
la Vivienda y el Hábitat
(SENAVITAT)

Marysol Estigarribia
Ferrere Abogados

Liliana Giménez
Dirección General de los
Registros Públicos

Lourdes Elizabeth González
Pereira
Dirección General de los
Registros Públicos

Sonia Elizabeth Von Lepel
Acosta
Colegio de Abogados del
Paraguay

María del Rocío Penayo Zarza
Moreno Ruffinelli & Asociados

PERU

María Fe Álvarez Calderón
Campos
Universidad del Pacífico

Javier Fernando Quiñones
Quiñones & Cia.

Diego Angel Florez Cama
Instituto de Estudios Politicos
Andinos

Nelson García
Morey & Morey Rotalde
Abogados SAC

Clea Yenipher Guerra Romero
Centro de la Mujer Peruana
Flora Tristan

Alonso Gurmendi Dunkelberg
Universidad del Pacífico

Francisco Ibazeta

Fiorella Patricia Morey Rotalde
Morey & Morey Rotalde
Abogados SAC

María José Paredes Vereau
Estudio Miranda & Amado

Diego Alonso Salazar Morales
Instituto de Estudios Políticos
Andinos

Carla Santillan
Morey & Morey Rotalde
Abogados SAC

Lorenza Beatriz Sarria García
Registro Nacional de
Identificación y Estado Civil
(RENIEC)

Sandra Melita Tagle García
Instituto de Estudios Políticos
Andinos

PHILIPPINES

Tomas Africa
Vital Event Records Certified
Inc.

Amy Avellano

Janeth Baclao
Philippines Statistics Authority

Kenneth Chua
Quisumbing Torres, Member
Firm of Baker & McKenzie

Sara Francesca De Guzman
O.B. Montessori Center

Leslie Dy
SyCip Salazar Hernandez &
Gatmaitan

Marizza Grande
Philippines Statistics Authority

Maria Cecilia Kristina Africa
Vital Event Records Certified
Inc.

Marie Hazel Lavitoria
SALIGAN

Amelia Lourdes Mendoza

Carmelita Nuqui
Development Action for
Women Network

Editha Orcilla
Philippines Statistics Authority

Henry Pacis
Land Management Bureau,
DENR

Vivien Leigh Rodulfo
Quisumbing Torres, Member
Firm of Baker & McKenzie

Karen Mae Sarinas-Baydo
Senate of the Philippines

Marjorie Villaver
Philippines Statistics Authority

POLAND

Dominika Dörre-Kolasa
Sobczyk & Współpracownicy

Rafał Góralczyk
BNT Neupert Zamorska &
Partnerzy

Elena Kachanovich-Shlyk
The Other Space Foundation
(Fundacja Inna Przestrzeń)

Monika Kamińska
University of Warsaw, Faculty
of Law and Administration

Kamil Kucharski
BNT Neupert Zamorska &
Partnerzy

Anna Masiota
Masiota - Adwokaci i Radcowie
Prawni

Adrian Szutkiewicz
Sobczyk & Współpracownicy

Dominika Wagrodzka
BNT Neupert Zamorska &
Partnerzy

Monika Wołłk-Łaniewska
Warsaw Bar Association

Anna Wysocka-Bar
Jagiellonian University

PORTUGAL

José Manuel Pinto Alves

Telma Carvalho
Cuatrecasas, Gonçalves Pereira

Daniel Cotrim
Portuguese Association for
Victim Support (APAV)

Catarina de Oliveira Carvalho
Universidade Catolica
Portuguesa, Faculdade de
Direito, Porto

Ana Helena Farinha
Cuatrecasas, Gonçalves Pereira

Elisabete Ferreira
Universidade Catolica
Portuguesa, Faculdade de
Direito, Porto

Inês Cabral Ferreira
Cuatrecasas, Gonçalves Pereira

Sandra Jesus
Caiado Guerreiro - Sociedade
de Advogados, SP, RL

Maria da Glória Leitão
Cuatrecasas, Gonçalves Pereira

Ricardo Lopes
Caiado Guerreiro - Sociedade
de Advogados, SP, RL

Paula Luz
Cartório Notarial de Lisboa

Tânia Pinheiro
Caiado Guerreiro - Sociedade
de Advogados, SP, RL

Graça Quintas
Cuatrecasas, Gonçalves Pereira

Margarida Telo Rasquilha
Caiado Guerreiro - Sociedade
de Advogados, SP, RL

Mariana Mendonça Saraiva
Cuatrecasas, Gonçalves Pereira

Catarina Vaz
Caiado Guerreiro - Sociedade
de Advogados, SP, RL

Rita Lobo Xavier

PUERTO RICO (U.S.)

Billy Carrasquillo
Policía de Puerto Rico

Carolene Fontanet Smith

Manuel Martinez-Torres
Oficina del Gobernador

Jaymarie A. Miranda Mendoza

Janice del Rosario
Rodriguez-Zayas
Lawyer

Giselle Santana Aquino

Linette Vega
Aon Risk Solutions

QATAR

The Law Clinic at Qatar
University College of Law

Lama Bakroun
Sultan Al-Abdulla & Partners

Buthaina Elgahani
Sultan Al-Abdulla & Partners

Sarra Eljaili
Sultan Al-Abdulla & Partners

Mohammed Fouad
Sultan Al-Abdulla & Partners

Moonira Mamoon
Sultan Al-Abdulla & Partners

Mohamed Y. Mattar
Professor of Law

Michael Palmer
Squire Patton Boggs LLP

Shahab Siddiqui
Sultan Al-Abdulla & Partners

ROMANIA

Silvia Burcea

Alexandra Columban
Equality and Human Rights
Action Centre (ACTEDO)

Ioana-Maria Dumitru
Popovici Nițu Stoica & Asociații

Elena Ghitescu
Englishkinder

Ileana Glodeanu
Wolf Theiss

Adelina Iftime-Blagean
Wolf Theiss

Smaranda Mihaela Mandrescu
Pop & Partners SCA
Attorneys-at-Law

Mircea Milos
Covasna County Police
Inspectorate

Mirela Nathanzon
Gilescu Valeanu Nathanzon &
Partenerii

Vlad Neacsu
Popovici Nițu Stoica & Asociații

Diana Şteţiu
Wolf Theiss

RUSSIAN FEDERATION

Maryana Batalova
Dechert LLP

Svetlana Biryukova
National Research University
Higher School of Economics

Nikita Boenko
Dechert LLP

Yulia Erme
Lawyer

Evgenia Korotkova
Dechert LLP

Elena Kukushkina
Baker & McKenzie

Nina Mogutova
Baker & McKenzie

Aliya Prenova
UC Berkeley School of Law

Nadezhda Smakhtina
American University, School of
International Service

Nadezhda Zamotaeva
Regional NGO and Independent
Charity "Sisters"

RWANDA

Pamela Abbott
University of Aberdeen

Valentin Akayezu Muhumuza
Institute of Legal Practice and
Development

Rucamumihigo Gregoire
Adepe Organization

Pie Habimana
Amicus Jurists

Anne Iragena

Antoine Kabandana

Désiré Kamanzi
ENSafrica Rwanda

Penelope Kwarikunda
Lawyer

Pothin Muvara
Rwanda Land Management and
Use Authority

Grace Nishimwe
Rwanda Land Management and
Use Authority

Patrick Nshimiyimana

Jean Claude Rwibasira
Inara Legal Aid Service (INALAS)

Yves Sangano
Rwanda Development Board

SAMOA

Treena F. Atoa
Atoa Law Firm Lawyers &
Notary Public

Lina Chang
Samoa Victim Support Group
(SVSG)

Ruby Drake
Drake & Co. Barristers &
Solicitors, Notary Public

Tuautu Kalepo
Samoa Bureau of Statistics

Tima Leavai
Leavai Law

Suisala Mele Maualaivao
UN Women

Tomasi Peni
International Labour Organization

Afamasaga Michael Soonalole
Police of Samoa

SAN MARINO

Gianna Burgagni
Studio Legale e Notarile

Marialaura Marinozzi
Studio Legale Marinozzi

Emanuela Montanari

Alessia Scarano
Studio Scarano

Alida Tosi
Studio Legale Notarile Avv.
Alida Tosi

SÃO TOMÉ AND PRÍNCIPE

Weiko Bastos
SoLima & Associados

Sofia Chaves

Bruno Xavier de Pina

Edinha Soares Lima
SoLima & Associados

Euclerio Neto
INPG

Ernestina Menezes Neves
INPG

Joel Teixeira
Vilhete Teixeira Advogado

Mondlane Tome
Ministry of Justice and Human
Rights

Neany Wilfref
INPG

SAUDI ARABIA

Aljoharah Albasri
Law Office of Looaye M.
Al-Akkas in Association with
Vinson & Elkins LLP

Karim Fawaz
Cisco Capital

Amr Omran
Freshfields Bruckhaus Deringer

Muhammad El Haggan
Freshfields Bruckhaus Deringer

Sami Tannous
Freshfields Bruckhaus Deringer

Amena Yahya
Law Office of Looaye M.
Al-Akkas in Association with
Vinson & Elkins LLP

SENEGAL

Laetitia Bazzi Veil
UNICEF

Boubacar Diakité
Géni & Kébé SCP d'Avocats

Soukeyna Ndao Diallo
The Girl Generation

Mactar Diassi
Etude Maître Mactar Dassi

Ibrahima Dieng
ALPHADEV

Alioune Dione
Ministère de la Femme de
l'Enfance et de l'Entreprenariat
Féminin

Massamba Diouf
UNICEF

Sokhna Mbaye Thiaw
Cabinet Me Cheikh FALL

Diakhaté Mor
ALPHADEV

Alioune Badara Ndiaye
Cabinet Me Cheikh FALL

Mame Coumba Ngom

Adia Aïssatou Niang
Direction Générale des Impôts
et Domaines

Sokhna Mbaye Thiaw
Cabinet Me Cheikh FALL

SERBIA

Mirjana Antic
Lawyer

Kosana Beker
Lawyer

Ivana Bulatović
Lawyer

Aleksandar Djordjevic
Aleksandar N. Djordjevic
Attorney at Law

Borko Draškovic
Republic Geodetic Authority

Jovan Grubić
Save the Children

Aleksandra Ivankovic
Tamamovic
Mental Disability Advocacy
Centre

Marija Jovanovic
The Guardianship Authority
Belgrade

Olga Jovic-Prlainovic

Jelena Kuveljic Dmitric
Law Offices Zecevic & Lukic

Vasilije Ljubinkovic

Sena Maric

Jovana Tomić
Živković Samardžić Law Office

SEYCHELLES

Jessica Kerr
Judiciary of Seychelles

Alexander Kukuev

Angelique Pouponneau
Lawyer

Divino Sabino
Pardiwalla Twomey Lablache

Monica Servina
Citizens Engagement Platform
Seychelles

SIERRA LEONE

Francis Kaifala
Kaifala, Conteh & Co.

Abdul Karim Koroma
Yada Williams & Associates,
Barristers and Solicitors

Simitie Lavaly
AdvocAid

Oredola Valerie Martyn
G.K. Tholley & Co. Solicitors

Victor Massaquoi

Victor Moinina
Forum for the Development of
Young People

Mark Ngegba
Human Rights Commission of
Sierra Leone

SINGAPORE

Amelia Chew

Limin Chuan

Nithya Devi

Belle Lim
Association of Women for
Action & Research (AWARE)

Corinna Lim
Association of Women for
Action & Research (AWARE)

Ijechi Nwaozuzu

Francis Xavier
Rajah & Tann Asia LLP

Vinna Yip
Rajah & Tann Asia LLP

SLOVAK REPUBLIC

Allen & Overy Bratislava SRO

Iveta Abelovská
Abelovsky & Sulva Legal SRO

Michaela Chladekova
Slovak Bar Association

Stanislav Durica
Squire Patton Boggs

Matej Jankovic
Squire Patton Boggs

Daniela Ježová
Lawyer

Zuzana Ocenasova
Coordination and Methodological
Centre for Prevention of Violence
against Women

Maroš Terkanič
Abelovsky & Sulva Legal SRO

SLOVENIA

Fatur Law Firm

Ministry of Interior

Odvetniki Šelih & Partnerji

Waldorfska Šola Ljubljana

Živa Dragonja
Law Firm Miro Senica and
Attorneys DOO

Andrej Ekart

Damijan Gregorc
Law Firm Miro Senica and
Attorneys DOO

Suzana Kraljić
University of Maribor, Faculty
of Law

Luka Mišič
University of Ljubljana, Faculty
of Law

Petra Plevnik
Law Firm Miro Senica and
Attorneys DOO

Primož Rataj
University of Ljubljana, Faculty
of Law

Darja Senčur Peček
University of Maribor

Grega Strban
University of Ljubljana, Faculty
of Law

Spela Veselic
Association SOS Help-line for
Women and Children Victims of
Violence

SOLOMON ISLANDS

Kim Abbey
Seif Ples

Casper Joseph Fa'asala
National Council on Women

Doreen Fernando
Oxfam

Bitibule Kaehuna
Rano & Company

Philip Kanairara
Law Reform Commission

Anika Kingmele
UNICEF

Rodney Kingmele
Sol-Law

Kathleen Kohata
Public Solicitor's Office

Gemma Pinol Puig

Olga Rabade
UNDP

Koisau Sade
World Vision

Makario Tagini

John Taupongi
Michael Pitakaka Law Chamber

Josephine Teakeni
Vois Blo Mere

Julieanne Wickham

Lynffer Wini-Maltungtung
Family Support Centre

Katalaini Ziru
Solomon Islands Bar
Association

SOUTH AFRICA

Department of Justice and
Constitutional Development

Chantelle de Sousa
The SADC Lawyers' Association

Richard Hastie
Nowitz Attorneys

Lupwana Kandala
University of Johannesburg

Chantal Kur
The Mediation Clinic and
Divorce Mediations

Nkosi Lolah
University of Johannesburg

Makaziwe Ntuli
Deeds Registry Johannesburg

Aaron Ramodumo
Department of Home Affairs

Lusanda Raphulu
Bowmans

Sheena Swemmer
University of the Witwatersrand

SOUTH SUDAN

Rowland Cole
UNDP

Kwany Dau Dan
Nurture South Sudan

Lejukole Gori
Noel and Associates

Sarah Kindu
Jubek State Women Association

Peter Kwaje
World Food Programme

Mambo Leonard
Nurture South Sudan

Zahra Lillian Mokgosi
World Food Programme

Suzan Loro
Jubek State Women Union

Victor Lowilla
South Sudan Law Society

Rukaya Mohammed
UN Women

Vicent Museke
UNDP

Judy Wakahiu
UNDP

SPAIN

Blanca Ballester Casanella
Universitat Oberta de Catalunya

Ramón Barjabad
Universitat Oberta de Catalunya

Mario Barros García
Uría Menéndez

Enrichetta Sandra Bellini
Fornera
Business and Professional
Women International (BPWI)

Ignasi Beltran de Heredia Ruiz
Universitat Oberta de Catalunya

Ana María Delgado García
Universitat Oberta de Catalunya

Maria Susana Fernandez
Iglesias
Susana Fdez Abogados

Marta García Mandaloniz
Universidad Carlos III de Madrid

Maria Josefa García Tamargo
Norte Abogados

Cristina García-Gil
Lawyer

Mireia Llobera
Universitat de València

Maria Mercedes Lomo Carasa
Ministerio de Justicia de
España, Registro Civil Central

Nicolás Nogueroles
Colegio de Registradores de
la Propiedad y Mercantiles de
España

Francisco Javier Pérez Blesa

Eugenia Revilla Esteve
Federació de Municipis de
Catalunya

Bettina Steible
Autonomous University of
Barcelona

Aura Esther Vilalta Nicuesa
Universitat Oberta de Catalunya

SRI LANKA

Wasanthi Adikari
Colombo Municipal Council

Menaca Calyaneratne

Ruwani Dantanarayana
John Wilson Partners,
Attorneys-at-Law & Notaries
Public

Thuwaraka Ganeshan
Tiruchelvam Associates

Saranee Gunathilaka

Anushka Gunawardena
Lawyer

Samurdhi Jayamaha

Ramani Jayasundere
The Asian Foundation

Shashini Kulanayaka

Menaka Lecamwasam

Anura Meddegoda
Varners

Ramani Muttettuwegama
Tiruchelvam Associates

Andrea Ranasinghe
Varners

Naganathan Selvakkumaran
University of Colombo

Shashini Vidanapathirana

John Wilson
John Wilson Partners,
Attorneys-at-Law & Notaries
Public

ST. KITTS AND NEVIS

Dane Elliott-Hamilton
Elliott MacClure

Keinya Blake Gordon
Blake Ferguson Law Office

Jennifer Harding-Marlin

Angelina Sookoo

Rohan Walters
Government of St. Kitts and
Nevis

ST. LUCIA

Francis Belle
The High Court of Saint Lucia

Veronica S. P. Cenac
Veronica Cenac Law Offices

Daniel E. J. Francis
Peirre Mondesir & Associates

Leandra Gabrielle Verneuil
Jennifer Remy & Associates

ST. VINCENT AND THE
GRENADINES

Heidi Badenock
Joseph Delves Chambers

Marcia Shirlan Barnwell

Moureeze Franklyn
Baptiste & Co. Law Firm Inc.

Nerissa Gittens
Department of Labour

Jeannie Ollivierre

SUDAN

Fatima Abass
AIH Law Firm

Mohamed Abdeen
Law Office of Mohamed
Abdeen

Mawada Ahmed
AIH Law Firm

Yassir Ali
AIH Law Firm

Mohamed Elmutaz

Aziza Ismat Hassanien
AIH Law Firm

Amel Sayed
Lawyer

Kesho Scott
Grinnell College

Sue Tatten
Lawyer

SURINAME

Yvonne Baal
Anton de Kom University of
Suriname

Arielle Delprado
Arielle's Consultancy

Seema Doelam
Lim A Po Law Firm

Justina Eduards
Lawyer

Serena Essed
Schurman Advocaten

Antoon Karg
Lim A Po Law Firm

Michelle Lau-Kerssenberg
Legal Aid Advocaten

SWAZILAND

University of Swaziland

Marleigh Austin
Family Life Association of
Swaziland

Phumzile Dlamini
UNFPA

Olivia Lwabukuna
Konrad Adenauer Stiftung

Simangele Mavundla
Women and Law in Southern
Africa (WLSA) and University
of Venda

Nozipho Msibi
Federation of Swaziland
Employers and Chamber of
Commerce

SWEDEN

National Centre for Knowledge
on Men's Violence Against
Women (NCK)

Eva Ärlemalm-Hagsér
Mälardalens University

Per Bergling

Geraldine R. Bjallerstedt
Independent Gender Specialist

Pia Björstrand
Advokatbyrån Omnia AB

Mia Edwall Insulander
Insulander Lindh Advokatbyrå

Ingrid Engdahl
Stockholm University

Josefin Gjälby
Insulander Lindh Advokatbyrå

Anna Hellron
Insulander Lindh Advokatbyrå

Viktoria Hybbinette
Wistrand Law Firm

Jenny Jilmstad
Advokatfirman Cederquist K.B.

Maria Kosteska Fägerquist
Wistrand Law Firm

Dennis Linden
Lantmäteriet

Eva Löndahl Thurang

Alexandra Lyckman
Insulander Lindh Advokatbyrå

Llorene Grace Razo-Ompod

Rolf Ring
Raoul Wallenberg Institute
of Human Rights and
Humanitarian Law

SWITZERLAND

Marion Binder
LALIVE

Michael Burkart

Franziska Geiser-Bedon
Frauenberatung Sexuelle Gewalt

Werner Jahnel
LALIVE

Valentin Jentsch

Nils Kapferer
Bureau de l'Egalité

Emilie Praz

Elisabeth Prügl
Graduate Institute of
International and Development
Studies

Christelle Rigual
Graduate Institute of
International and Development
Studies

Gaëlle Sauthier
Etat de Vaud

Daima Vuilleumier
LALIVE

TAIWAN, CHINA

Jasmine Bai
Taipei Women's Rescue
Foundation

Shu-Chien Chen
Heffels Spiegeler Advocaten

Yu-Shiou (Clarence) Chou
Li & Cai International Law Firm

Hsin-Yun Han
Sanrio Taiwan Co. Ltd.

Hung Hsieh
Pontis Law

Sophia Hsieh
Tsar & Tsai Law Firm

Yen-Jong Lee
Themis Attorneys-at-Law

Jo-Tzu Ma
Formosa Laboratories Inc.

Yen-Fun Shih
Via Justice Law Offices

Scarlett Tang
Tsar & Tsai Law Firm, Member
of Lex Mundi

Po-Chen Tsao
Innolux Corporation

TAJIKISTAN

Mubarakhon Abdulakhitova
Sprout

Khujanazar Aslamshoev
Infrastructure Consulting LLC

Zouhal Avzalchoeva

Anthony Cameron
UNDP

Obid Islomov

Alisher Khoshimov
Centil Law Firm

Mumin Kurbonaliev

Lola Latypova
UNDP

Kamoliddin Mukhamedov
GRATA International

Gulbahor Nematova
UNDP

Kanat Seidaliev
GRATA International

Jaffarbek Uldashev
Law and Prosperity

TANZANIA

Ben Akech
New Market Lab Inc.

Angela Anatory
Registration Insolvency and
Trusteeship Agency

Emilian Karugendo
National Bureau of Statistics

Jackline Mlay
Oxfam

Anthony Mseke
Arbogast Mseke Advocates

Eve Hawa Sinare

Simeon Sungi
United States International
University - Africa

THAILAND

Gender and Development
Research Institute (GDRI)

UNHCR

John Lewis
Anglo-Thai Legal

Premkamon Nakhwan
Pisut and Partners Co. Ltd.

Tunyatorn Nettakul

Natcha Prakaranont
Pisut and Partners Co. Ltd.

Pisut Rakwong
Pisut and Partners Co. Ltd.

Krittichai Sumranbumrung

Sita Sumrit
Thailand Institute of Justice

Chayanich (Mint)
Thamparipattra

Nalanta Tonghom
Pisut and Partners Co. Ltd.

TIMOR-LESTE

Lourenço Alvares
Abreu Advogados and C&C
Advogados

Mariana Baptista Borges

Eusebio Guterres
UNIDO Business Regulatory
Consultant

Gonçalo Neves Lestro

Liliana Coutinho Magalhães
CRA Law Firm Timor-Leste

Elisa Pereira
Abreu Advogados and C&C
Advogados

Eliana Silva Pereira

Pedro Venâncio

Anna Yang
The Asia Foundation, Ending
Violence Against Women
Program (EVAW)

TOGO

Toyi A.M. Abbi
Direction des Affaires
Domaniales et Cadastrales
(DADC)

Claude Folly Adama
Aquereburu & Partners

Djifa Emefa Adjalé Suku

Kékéli Edo Agboli
Tribunal de Première Instance
de Première Classe de Lomé

Aissah Akanti Ouro-Akondo
Santé de la Famille en Milieu
Rural et Semi-Urbain

Sophie Mawussé Akpama
Centre de Recherche
d'Information et de Formation
pour la Femme (GF2D/CRIFF)

Têko Seyram Amenyinu
Cabinet d'Avocats Toble Yawo
Gagnon

Alexis Coffi Aquereburu
SCP Aquereburu & Partners

Souradji Fankeba
Préfecture du Golfe

Ehonam Yvette Gamisso
Yévénou
SCP Aquereburu & Partners

Mayi Gnofam
Programme d'Appui à
la Femme et à l'Enfance
Déshéritée (PAFED)

Hansa Kapi
Aquereburu & Partners

Rouky Kloutse-Kegbero
Tribunal de Lomé

Baltché Lare
Préfecture du Golfe

Komlavi Malanbo M'Boma
Direction de L'Administration
Territoriale et des Frontières

Hada Tchingué
Plan International

Komla Yovo
Avocats Yovo Sika

TONGA

´Akanesi E. Katoa
Attorney General's Office of
Tonga

Aminiasi Kefu
Attorney General's Office of
Tonga

Lute Takau

Milika Tuita
United Nations

TRINIDAD AND TOBAGO

Chanelle Aching
Wills Mohamed R & CO

Karinna Alexander

Petal Alexander
Lawyer

Sherna Alexander Benjamin
Organization for Abused and
Battered Individuals (OABI)

Johnathan Bhagan
Organization for Abused and
Battered Individuals (OABI)

Charisse Griffith-Charles
University of the West Indies

Akhail Khan

Chantal La Roche

Debrah Lewis
Mamatoto Resource & Birth
Centre

Delrene Liverpool-Young
Organization for Abused and
Battered Individuals (OABI)

Geeta Maharaj
Lawyer

Gina Maharaj
Organization for Abused and
Battered Individuals (OABI)

Duane Murray
Lawyer

Umesh Nandalal
Deloitte & Touche

Esther Shade

Antoinette Sydney
Linton Chambers

Lisa Theodore

Simone Yallery
Lawyer

TUNISIA

Adel Dhahri
Impact Foundation for Research
and Development

Amel El Mejri
Faculté des Sciences Juridiques,
Politiques et Sociales de Tunis

Béchir Ghachem
GLA

Wael Haffar
Lawyer

Nada Riahi
International Development
Organization (IDLO)

Aziz Sammoud
CAG Law Firm

TURKEY

Elif Akyüz
Serap Zuvin Law Offices

Duygu Alkan
Mavioglu & Alkan Law Office
(ADMD)

Ayca Bayburan
Mavioglu & Alkan Law Office
(ADMD)

Duygu Beyazo
Özyıldırım Law Office

Serap Erdoğan
Association for the
Development of Early Childhood
Education in Turkey (Türkiye
Okul Öncesi Eğitimini Geliştirme
Derneği)

Roberto Frifrini
Human Rights Agenda
Association

Ayse Gonullu Atakan

Aybala Kurtuldu
Serap Zuvin Law Offices

Afife Nazlıgül Özkan
Mavioglu & Alkan Law Office
(ADMD)

Tuba Özyıldırım
Özyıldırım Law Office

Nurbanu Parpucu
Association for the
Development of Early Childhood
Education in Turkey (Türkiye
Okul Öncesi Eğitimini Geliştirme
Derneği)

Batuhan Sahmay
Bener Law Firm

Elif Selin Cila
Yeditepe University, Faculty
of Law

Irmak Seymen
Mavioglu & Alkan Law Office
(ADMD)

Dilara Tamtürk
Mavioglu & Alkan Law Office
(ADMD)

Serap Zuvin
Serap Zuvin Law Offices

UGANDA

Ben Akech
New Market Lab Inc.

Brenda Peace Amito
Tulane International (TILLC)

Charles Kalumiya
Kampala Associated Advocates

Nusula Kizito Nassuna
African Development Bank

Rachel Musoke
Masembe, Makubuya, Adriko,
Karugaba & Ssekatawa
Advocates

Patrick Mwesigye
Uganda Youth and Adolescents
Health Forum

Doreen Nawaali
Masembe, Makubuya, Adriko,
Karugaba & Ssekatawa
Advocates

Emma Ssali Namuli
Uganda Christian University

Lauben Tushemereirwe
Child Aid Uganda (CHAU)

UKRAINE

Anastasiya Bolkhovitinova
DLA Piper

Kateryna Borozdina
International Women's Rights
Center "La Strada-Ukraine"

Oleg Gromovyi
Pro Bono

Artem Hrytsak
DLA Piper

Kateryna Ilikchiieva
Kyiv National Economics
University

Oksana Klymovych
Emory University

Olena Koptieva
International Development Law
Organization (IDLO)

Olena Kuchynska
Kinstellar Ukraine

Roman Mohyla
Law Offices of Roman Mohyla

Olga Prosyanyuk
AVER LEX

Andriy Tsvyetkov
Attorneys' Association Gestors

Serhiy Yaroshenko
Kinstellar Ukraine

Galyna Zagorodniuk
DLA Piper

UNITED ARAB EMIRATES

Amr Abdel Rehim
Lawyer

Raya Abu Gulal
Manaar Legal Consultancy

Ikram Adnani
Ibn Zohr University (Agadir,
Morocco)

Amal Afifi
Afifi Law Office

Taiba Alsafar
Al Tamimi & Company

Fathima Al Sakkaf
STA Law Firm

Deborah Broyles
Reed Smith LLP

Muhammad El Haggan
Freshfields Bruckhaus Deringer

Sarah Florer
Axiom Telecom

Stefania Franchini
Hamdan Al Kaabi Advocates
and Legal Consultants

Diana Hamade
International Advocate Legal
Services

Alyazia Khalifa Al Marri
AK Accounting & Auditing

Sara Khoja
Clyde & Co.

Donald Moore
Reed Smith LLP

Ahmed Zaher Moussa
Abu Dhabi Judicial Department

Amr Omran
Freshfields Bruckhaus Deringer

Sai Pidatala
Reed Smith LLP

Zisha Rizvi
STA Law Firm

Sheena Shibu
Axiom Telecom

George SK
STA Law Firm

Sami Tannous
Freshfields Bruckhaus Deringer

UNITED KINGDOM

Chloe-Jane Belton
Dechert LLP

Melissa Conway
Freshfields Bruckhaus Deringer

Stephanie Creese
Linklaters LLP

Irene Ding
Linklaters LLP

Chelsea Fish

Jasmine Fisher
Freshfields Bruckhaus Deringer

Daniel Hawthorne

James Kemp

Nicolas Kokkinos

Pascal Lalande
Her Majesty's Land Registry

Jamie Murray-Jones
Freshfields Bruckhaus Deringer

Markella Papadouli

Kalliopi Paschalidou

Evgeniya Rubinina
Freshfields Bruckhaus Deringer

Nivedita S

Elizabeth Street-Thompson
Ashurst LLP

Jeremy Townend
JLWT Consultancy

UNITED STATES

Sanctuary for Families

Marta Baffy
Georgetown University Law
Center

Jessica Childress
The Childress Firm PLLC

Areej Faiz
Lawyer

Elizabeth Hague
Freshfields Bruckhaus Deringer

Jerry Hoffman
Dechert LLP

Katerina Housos

Olga Helena Joos
CDC Foundation

Joshi Krishna Datt

Soumyashree Kulkarni
Lawyer

Gregory Reith
Dechert LLP

Steve Schwartz
New York City Department of
Health and Mental Hygiene

Gillian Teo
Dechert LLP

URUGUAY

Leticia Barrios
Bergstein Abogados

Adriana Boggio
Dirección General de Registro
del Estado Civil

Noemi Caballero
Estudio Bado, Kuster, Zerbino
& Rachetti

Alvaro Carrau
Estudio Bado, Kuster, Zerbino
& Rachetti

Guillermo Duarte
Bergstein Abogados

Geanella Pígola
Pígola-Zeballos & Asociados

Verónica Raffo
Ferrere Abogados

Agustin Texo
Estudio Bado, Kuster, Zerbino
& Rachetti

Pablo Varela

Daniel Wildbaum
Dirección General de Registro
del Estado Civil

Carla Zeballos
Pígola-Zeballos & Asociados

UZBEKISTAN

UNICEF

Nafisa Abdullaeva
Lawyer

Kimiya Abdurakhmanova
National Centre of Geodesy and
Cartography

Azamat Fayzullaev
Leges Advokat

Ulughbek Mamadjanov
Prosecutor General's Office of
Uzbekistan

Bobomurod Muminov

Alexander Samborsky
National Centre of Geodesy and
Cartography

Nargiza Turgunova
GRATA International

VANUATU

Stephen Barlow
Public Solicitor's Office

Elizabeth Fano Bebe
VANWODS Microfinance, Inc.

Astrid Boulekone
Vanuatu Chamber of Commerce
and Industry

Geoffrey Gee
Geoffrey Gee & Partners

Anita Jowitt
University of the South Pacific

Bertha Pakoasongi
Vanuatu Law Reform
Commission

Gemma Pinol Puig

Sofia Shah
University of the South Pacific

Merilyn Tahi
Vanuatu Women's Center

Christopher Tavoa
State Law Office

Jin Wen
Geoffrey Gee & Partners

VENEZUELA, RB

Gabriela Longo V.
Palacios, Ortega y Asociados

Maria Corina Muskus

Liliana Ortega Mendoza
COFAVIC

José Manuel Ortega Pérez
Palacios, Ortega y Asociados

Luis Esteban Palacios
Palacios, Ortega y Asociados

Barbara Puglisi
Presidencia de la Asamblea
Nacional de Venezuela

Pedro Vicente Ramos
Rodríguez & Mendoza

Ricardo Rojas Gaona
Rojas Gaona & Bandres

Inés Sosa

Karla A. Subero P.
Lawyer

VIETNAM

Freshfields Bruckhaus Deringer

Do Duc Doi

Loc Le Thi
YKVN

Anh Phuong Nguyen
Researcher

Tien Lap Nguyen
NHQuang & Associates

Tieu My Nguyen
Honor Partnership Law
Company Limited (HPLaw)

Van Anh Nguyen
Center for Studies and Applied
Sciences in Gender, Family,
Women and Adolescents
(CSAGA)

Thuy Nguyen Thu
Center for Studies and Applied
Sciences in Gender, Family,
Women and Adolescents
(CSAGA)

Anh Phuong Pham
Honor Partnership Law
Company Limited (HPLaw)

Pham Thi Huong
YKVN

Kim Cuong Phung
Honor Partnership Law
Company Limited (HPLaw)

Dang Thi Tuong Vi
RHTLaw Taylor Wessing
Vietnam

Thu Trang Vo Thi
Le Nguyen Law Office

Dieu Thao Vu
NHQuang & Associates

Thu Hang Vu
Honor Partnership Law
Company Limited (HPLaw)

Benjamin Yap
RHTLaw Taylor Wessing
Vietnam

WEST BANK AND GAZA

Ashraf Abu Hayyeh
Al-Haq

Basem Bushnaq

Mohammed El Nahhal
Islamic University of Gaza

Hanna N. Hanania
Hanna Hanania Law Office

Mohannad Kababji
Al-Kababji Law Office and
Associate

Ahmed Mustafa Toutah
Islamic University of Gaza

YEMEN, REP.

Aromaimh Mostafa Abdulgalil
Office of Agents Law Firm,
Consulting and Legal

Ameen Abdulraqeb
Office of Agents Law Firm,
Consulting and Legal

Alshrihy Mohammed
Abdulrazaq
Office of Agents Law Firm,
Consulting and Legal

Khaled Al-Buraihi
Khaled Al-Buraihi for Advocacy
& Legal Services

Emad Algarash
Yemen Organization for
Defending Rights and
Democratic Freedoms

Nabil Alshami
The Counselor for Legal
Services

Ahmed Arman
Lawyer

Fairouz Jaradi
Lawyer

ZAMBIA

Isaac and Partners

Chanda Chungu
Mulenga Mundashi Kasonde
Legal Practitioners

Soi Kaingu
Chibesakunda & Co., Member
of DLA Piper

Makalo Mwaanza

Gilbert Mwanza
Zambia Law Development
Commission

Mabvuto Sakala
Corpus Legal Practioners

Natasha Shamutete
Corpus Legal Practioners

Wantemwa Simutenda
Messrs GDC Chambers

Kenneth Tembo
Legal Aid Board

ZIMBABWE

Precious Chakasikwa
Kantor and Immerman

Aulline Chapisa

Slyvia Chirawu-Mugomba
Women and Law In Southern
Africa (WLSA)

Trust Maanda
Maungamaanda & Associates

Charles Maunga
Maungamaanda & Associates

Roselyn Mhlanga
Kanokanga & Partners

Sara Nyaradzo Moyo
Honey & Blanckenberg

Tatenda Mushanguri
Kantor and Immerman